W9-ADU-561

Redeeming the Communist Past

This major study examines one of the most surprising developments in East Central European politics after the democratic transitions of 1989: the completely unexpected regeneration of the former communist parties. After the collapse of the communist regimes in 1989, these ruling communist parties seemed consigned to oblivion. However, confounding scholarly and popular expectations, all of them survived, and some have even returned to power.

This in-depth, comparative study systematically analyzes the trajectories of four cases: the Czech Republic, Slovakia, Poland, and Hungary (with additional examination of other authoritarian party successors). Relying on extensive and unprecedented primary research, this analysis employs a consistent analytical framework that combines the peculiarities of the postsocialist cases with broad theoretical concerns of institutional analysis, party politics, and democratic transitions and consolidation.

ANNA M. GRZYMAŁA-BUSSE is assistant professor of political science at Yale University. Her doctoral dissertation was awarded the Gabriel Almond Award for Best Dissertation in Comparative Politics by the American Political Science Association.

Cambridge Studies in Comparative Politics

General Editor

Margaret Levi   *University of Washington, Seattle*

Associate Editors

Robert H. Bates   *Harvard University*
Peter Hall   *Harvard University*
Stephen Hanson   *University of Washington, Seattle*
Helen Milner   *Columbia University*
Frances Rosenbluth   *Yale University*
Susan Stokes   *University of Chicago*
Sidney Tarrow   *Cornell University*

Other Books in the Series

Stefano Bartolini, *The Political Mobilization of the European Left, 1860–1980: The Class Cleavage*

Carles Boix, *Political Parties, Growth and Equality: Conservative and Social Democratic Economic Strategies in the World Economy*

Catherine Boone, *Merchant Capital and the Roots of State Power in Senegal, 1930–1985*

Michael Bratton and Nicolas van de Walle, *Democratic Experiments in Africa: Regime Transitions in Comparative Perspective*

Valerie Bunce, *Leaving Socialism and Leaving the State: The End of Yugoslavia, the Soviet Union, and Czechoslovakia*

Ruth Berins Collier, *Paths Toward Democracy: The Working Class and Elites in Western Europe and South America*

Donatella della Porta, *Social Movements, Political Violence, and the State*

Gerald Easter, *Reconstructing the State: Personal Networks and Elite Identity*

Roberto Franzosi, *The Puzzle of Strikes: Class and State Strategies in Postwar Italy*

Geoffrey Garrett, *Partisan Politics in the Global Economy*

Miriam Golden, *Heroic Defeats: The Politics of Job Loss*

Merilee Serrill Grindle, *Changing the State*

Frances Hagopian, *Traditional Politics and Regime Change in Brazil*

J. Rogers Hollingsworth and Robert Boyer, eds., *Contemporary Capitalism: The Embeddedness of Institutions*

Ellen Immergut, *Health Politics: Interests and Institutions in Western Europe*

Torben Iversen, *Contested Economic Institutions*

Continued on page following the Index

JN
76
A079
E79
2002

OSCAR RENNEBOHM LIBRARY
EDGEWOOD COLLEGE
1000 EDGEWOOD COLLEGE DR
MADISON WI 53711

Redeeming the Communist Past

THE REGENERATION OF COMMUNIST PARTIES IN EAST CENTRAL EUROPE

ANNA M. GRZYMAŁA-BUSSE

Yale University

CAMBRIDGE
UNIVERSITY PRESS

PUBLISHED BY THE PRESS SYNDICATE OF THE UNIVERSITY OF CAMBRIDGE
The Pitt Building, Trumpington Street, Cambridge, United Kingdom

CAMBRIDGE UNIVERSITY PRESS
The Edinburgh Building, Cambridge CB2 2RU, UK
40 West 20th Street, New York, NY 10011-4211, USA
477 Williamstown Road, Port Melbourne, VIC 3207, Australia
Ruiz de Alarcón 13, 28014 Madrid, Spain
Dock House, The Waterfront, Cape Town 8001, South Africa

http://www.cambridge.org

© Anna M. Grzymała-Busse 2002

This book is in copyright. Subject to statutory exception
and to the provisions of relevant collective licensing agreements,
no reproduction of any part may take place without
the written permission of Cambridge University Press.

First published 2002

Printed in the United Kingdom at the University Press, Cambridge

Typeface Janson Text 10/13 pt.   *System* QuarkXPress [BTS]

A catalog record for this book is available from the British Library.

Library of Congress Cataloging in Publication Data

Grzymała-Busse, Anna Maria, 1970–
    Redeeming the communist past: the regeneration of communist parties in East
    Central Europe / Anna Maria Grzymała-Busse.
        p. cm. – (Cambridge studies in comparative politics)
    Includes bibliographical references and index.
    ISBN 0-521-80669-0 – ISBN 0-521-00146-3 (pbk.)
        1. Communist parties – Europe, Eastern. 2. Europe, Eastern – Politics and
    government – 1989– . 3. Communist parties – Former Soviet republics. 4. Former
    Soviet republics – Politics and government. I. Title. II. Series.
    JN96.A979 G79   2001
    324.2′175′0943–dc21   2001025947

ISBN   0 521 80669 0   hardback
ISBN   0 521 00146 3   paperback

For my Parents,
Dobrosława and Jerzy

Contents

List of Tables		*page* x
List of Acronyms		xii
Acknowledgments		xvii
	INTRODUCTION: SURVIVING DEMOCRACY	1
1	THE ROOTS OF REGENERATION: COMMUNIST PRACTICES AND ELITE RESOURCES	19
2	BREAKING WITH THE PAST, REORGANIZING FOR THE FUTURE	69
3	DEVELOPING PROGRAMMATIC RESPONSIVENESS	123
4	CONVINCING THE VOTERS: CAMPAIGNS AND ELECTIONS	175
5	PARLIAMENTARY EFFECTIVENESS AND COALITIONS	227
	CONCLUSION: SUCCEEDING IN DEMOCRACY	265
	APPENDIX A: THE CONTENT ANALYSIS OF PROGRAMS	285
	APPENDIX B: THE QUANTITATIVE ANALYSIS OF ELECTORATES	294
	APPENDIX C: THE STRUCTURES OF COMPETITION	303
Bibliography		305
Index		333

List of Tables

1.1	Czech communist party membership	*page* 32
1.2	Slovak communist party membership	36
1.3	Changes in the Czechoslovak politburo	39
1.4	Polish communist party membership	43
1.5	Changes in the Polish politburo	47
1.6	Hungarian communist party membership	52
1.7	Changes in the Hungarian politburo	55
2.1	Communist party organizations by 1988	70
2.2	Bureaucratic attrition and elite turnover during the transition	72
2.3	Party memberships and local organizations, 1992–9	78
2.4	Summary of organizational transformation	82
3.1	Summary of variation in party programs, 1990–8	128
3.2	Voter orientations and policy trade-offs	133
3.3	Mean economic stances of party programs, 1990–8	135
3.4	Mean secular stances of party programs, 1990–8	136
3.5	Average gap in political priorities between the KSČM supporters and the rest of the electorate, 1992–6	142
3.6	Dominant themes in KSČM party programs in percentages	146
3.7	Economic stances of the KSČM, 1989–98	147
3.8	Average gap in political priorities between SDĽ supporters and the rest of the electorate, 1992–6	154
3.9	Dominant themes in SDĽ party programs in percentages, 1990–6	156
3.10	Economic stances of the SDĽ, 1990–6	158
3.11	Average gap in political priorities between SdRP supporters and the rest of the electorate, 1992–6	163

3.12	Dominant themes in SdRP party programs in percentages, 1990–7	165
3.13	Economic stances of the SdRP, 1990–7	166
3.14	Average gap in political priorities between MSzP supporters and the rest of the electorate, 1992–5	172
4.1	Electoral campaigns and outcomes as of 2001	181
4.2	Union support for the communist successor parties, 1992–6	185
4.3	Popular perceptions of KČSM	192
4.4	Determinants of KSČM support	193
4.5	Elections in the Czech Republic	196
4.6	Popular perceptions of SDĽ	201
4.7	Determinants of SDĽ support	202
4.8	Elections in Slovakia	203
4.9	Popular perceptions of SdRP	209
4.10	Determinants of SdRP support	212
4.11	Elections in Poland	213
4.12	Popular perceptions of MSzP	220
4.13	Determinants of MSzP support	222
4.14	Elections in Hungary	223
5.1	Summary of the communist successor parliamentary effectiveness	229
5.2	Turnover in parliamentary clubs	236
5.3	Leadership overlap between the parliamentary and central leaderships	237
5.4	KČSM representation in parliament	241
5.5	SDĽ representation in parliament	246
5.6	SdRP representation in parliament	252
5.7	MSzP representation in parliament	260
C.1	Party fragmentation and electoral institutions	304

List of Acronyms

Acronym	Organization	Translation
AWS	Akcja Wyborcza Solidarność	Electoral Action Solidarity (Poland)
BSP	Balgarska Socialisticheska Partija	Bulgarian Socialist Party
ČSSD	Česká Strana Sociálne Demokratická	Czech Social Democratic Party
DL	Demokratická Levice	Democratic Left (Czech)
DS	Demokratická Strana	Democratic Party (Slovakia)
DSP	Demokratická Strana Prace	Democratic Party of Labor (Czech)
DU	Demokratická Únia	Democratic Union (Slovakia)
Fidesz	Fiatal Demokraták Szövetsége	Alliance of Young Democrats (Hungary)
FKGP	Független Kisgazdapárt	Independent Smallholders' Party (Hungary)
FSN	Frontul Salvarii Nationale	National Salvation Front (Romania)
HSD-SMS	Hnutí za samosprávnou demokracii-Společnost pro Moravu a Slezsko	Movement for Self-Governing Democracy-Association for Moravia and Silesia
HZDS	Hnutie za Demokratické Slovensko	Movement for a Democratic Slovakia
KDH	Krest'ansko-demokratické Hnutie	Christian Democratic Movement (Czech)

List of Acronyms

KDNP	Kereszténydemokrata Néppárt	Christian Democratic Party (Hungary)
KDU-ČSL	Krest'ansko-demokratická Unie-Česka Strana Lidová	Christian Democratic Union-Czech People's Party
KLD	Kongres Liberalno-Demokratyczny	Liberal-Democratic Congress (Poland)
KPN	Konfederacja Polski Niepodległej	Confederation for an Independent Poland
KPRF	Komunisticheskaya Partia Rossiskoy Federatsii	Communist Party of the Russian Federation
KSČ	Komunistická Strana Československa	Communist Party of Czechoslovakia
KSČM	Komunistická Strana Čech a Moravy	Communist Party of Bohemia and Moravia (Czech Republic)
LPR	Liga Polskich Rodzin	League of Polish Families
MDF	Magyar Demokrata Fórum	Hungarian Democratic Forum
MIEP	Magyar Igazság és Élet Pártja	Hungarian Life and Justice Party
MKP	Magyar Komuniszta Párt	Hungarian Communist Party
MP	Munkáspárt	Workers' Party (Hungary)
MSzMP	Magyar Szocialista Munkás Párt	Hungarian Socialist Workers' Party
MSzOSz	Magyar Szakszervezetek Országos Szövetsége	Confederation of Hungarian Trade Unions
MSzP	Magyar Szocialista Párt	Hungary Socialist Party
ODA	Občanská Demokratická Aliance	Civic Democratic Alliance (Czech)
ODS	Občanská Demokratická Strana	Civic Democratic Party (Czech)
OPZZ	Ogólnopolskie Porozumienie Związków Zawodowych	All-Polish Alliance of Trade Unions
PC	Porozumienie Centrum	Center Alliance (Poland)
PDS	Partei des Demokratischen Sozialismus	Party of Democratic Socialism (Germany)

PDSR	Partidul Democraţiei Sociale din România	Party of Social Democracy in Romania
PiS	Prawo i Sprawiedliwość	Law and Justice (Poland)
PO	Platforma Obywatelska	Civic Platform (Poland)
PPP	Polska Partia Przyjaciół Piwa	Polish Beer Lovers' Party
PPS	Polska Partia Socjalistyczna	Polish Socialist Party
PSL	Polskie Stronnictwo Ludowe	Polish Peasants' Party
PSSH	Partia Socialiste ë Shqipërisë	Socialist Party of Albania
PUS	Polska Unia Socjaldemokratyczna	Polish Social Democratic Union
PZPR	Polska Zjednoczona Partia Robotnicza	Polish United Workers' Party
RLP	Ruch Ludzi Pracy	Movement of People of Labor (Poland)
SDK	Slovenská Demokratická Koalícia	Slovak Democratic Coalition
SDL	Strana Demokratické Levice	Party of the Democratic Left (Czech)
SDĽ	Strana Demokratickej Ľavici	Slovak Party of the Democratic Left
SdRP	Socjaldemokracja Rzeczpospolitej Polskiej	Social Democracy of the Republic of Poland
SDSS	Sociálnodemokratická Strana Slovenska	Social Democratic Party (Slovakia)
SED	Sozialistische Einheitspartei Deutschlands	Socialist Unity Party of Germany
SLB	Strana Levý Blok	Left Bloc Party (Czech Republic)
SNS	Slovenska Narodná Strana	Slovak National Party
SLD	Sojusz Lewicy Demokratycznej	Democratic Left Alliance (Poland)
SOP	Strana Občianského Porozumienia	Party for Civic Understanding (Slovak)
SPR-RSČ	Sdruženi Pro Republiku-Republikanská Strana Česka	Association for the Republic-Republican Party of the Czech Republic

List of Acronyms

SzDSz	Szabad Demokraták Szövetsége	Alliance of Free Democrats (Hungary)
SZS	Strana Zelených na Slovensku	Green Party of Slovakia
SZSP	Socjalistyczny Związek Studentów Polskich	Socialist Union of Polish Students
UD	Unia Demokratyczna	Democratic Union (Poland)
UP	Unia Pracy	Labor Union (Poland)
US	Unie Svobody	Freedom Union (Czech)
UW	Unia Wolności	Freedom Union (Poland)
ZChN	Zjednoczenie Chrześcijańsko-Narodowe	Christian-National Alliance (Poland)
ZKP	Związek Komunistów Polskich "Proletariat"	Union of Polish Communists "Proletariat"
ZRS	Združenie Robotníkov Slovenska	Association of Slovak Workers
ZSL	Zjednoczone Stronnictwo Ludowe	United Peasants' Party (Poland)

Acknowledgments

Most of the research for this book was done in the Czech Republic, Slovakia, Hungary, Poland, and Germany, throughout 1996–8. Much of it would have been impossible without the kindness of many colleagues and friends in the region. I greatly benefited from the assistance and advice of, among others, Attila Ágh, Zora Bútorová, Michał Federowicz, György Földes, Peter Havas, Michal Illner, Wojciech Kaźmierczak, László Keri, János Kornai, Darina Malová, Grigorij Mesežnikov, Gero Neugebauer, Andrzej Rychard, Dieter Segert, Dana Šivaková, Andrej Školkaj, Jindriška Syllová, Jonathan Stein, Gábor Tóka, Peter Talas, Pal Tamás, Zbysław Thomas, Jiří Večernik, Rafał Wiśniewski, and Vera Žežulková. The East-West Institute in Prague, the Institute of Sociology at the Czech Academy of Sciences, the Political Faculty of Comenius University, Central European University and the Open Society Archives in Budapest, and the Institute of Politics and Sociology of the Polish Academy of Sciences all graciously hosted me at various points.

In the United States, I am grateful to many friends and colleagues, whose comments, criticisms, and advice have greatly improved this book. Several have read different parts of the manuscript, including Peter Andreas, Grzegorz Ekiert, Peter Hall, and Gary King. I am especially grateful to those who read the manuscript in its entirety: Joshua Berke, Kanchan Chandra, Ellen Comisso, Stephen Hanson, Pauline Jones Luong, Herbert Kitschelt, and Andrew Schwartz. Tassos Kalandrakis, Gary King, and Ken Shepsle patiently answered various technical questions, while Gary Bass, Marc Busch, and Tim Snyder provided a great deal of advice. Ben Frommer, Abby Innes, Kevin Krause, and Diana Morlang shared war stories, data, and sources alike. Above all, I am indebted to Timothy Colton, Grzegorz Ekiert, and Peter Hall, each of whom brought a wealth

xvii

of wisdom and advice to this project in all its stages. They remain a source of inspiration, trenchant criticism, and high standards. I am also grateful to the anonymous reviewers, who offered helpful comments, suggestions, and critiques. Lew Bateman at Cambridge University Press and Margaret Levi were wonderful editors, and their advice was as expert as it was helpful. Megan Dean diligently checked the bibliography, and Nate Jensen compiled the index. Any shortcomings, needless to say, remain my own.

My peripatetic research and writing was supported by several institutions: the American Council of Learned Societies, the Brookings Institution, the German-American Center for Visiting Scholars, the Harvard Academy for Area and International Studies, the Krupp Foundation, the Mellon Foundation, the Davis Center for Russian Studies, the Program for the Study of Germany and Europe, Yale University, and above all, the Center for European Studies at Harvard University, source of both material and intellectual sustenance.

This book is dedicated to my parents – their fierce love, unconditional support, and penchant for dinnertime debates have been my encouragement and my strength. The final thanks goes to Joshua Berke, whose love, clarity of thought, and wit have made this project, and so many others, a delight.

Introduction: Surviving Democracy

Men make their own history, but they do not make it just as they please; they do not make it under circumstances chosen by themselves, but under circumstances directly encountered, given, and transmitted from the past.[1]

We cannot continue as we have. A radical transformation of the party is not a tactical concession, but a question of political survival.[2]

This book addresses a fundamental question in the study of democratic politics and institutional change: How can the discredited political actors of an *ancien régime* not only survive the collapse of the old order, but succeed in the new one? Among the most spectacular cases of such persistence and adaptation are the survival and regeneration of the communist successor parties in East Central Europe, the focus of this book.

As communist regimes collapsed across East Central Europe in 1989, the defeat of the communist parties seemed complete. After all, these were the same regimes that had shown no regard for basic civic rights, had "strategically planned" the economies into negative growth rates, and had displayed a remarkable propensity for corruption and self-enrichment. Over forty years of oppression had left the people with memories that were as bitter as they were vivid, and the popular uprisings of 1989 fought to remove the parties from power. The first demand voiced by the masses of demonstrators in the streets, and by their representatives negotiating with party officials, was that the communist stranglehold on the economy and

---

[1] Marx, Karl. *The Eighteenth Brumaire of Louis Bonaparte*. New York: International Publishers, 1963, p. 15.
[2] Jacek Zdrojewski, member of the Polish Warsaw Region Committee of the Polish United Workers' Party. *Trybuna Ludu*, 16 January 1989.

the polity finally end. The democratic breakthroughs of 1989 thus bade farewell to regimes widely despised by their own citizens.

Few predicted that the successors to these parties would survive in the democratic political system, much less thrive. As the new regimes took over, the communist parties were forced to exit from power and governance. They were no longer allowed to organize in the workplace (their mainstay), their assets were expropriated, and they were forced to relinquish their auxiliary organizations. It seemed simply a matter of time before these parties would be swept away into the "dustbin of history."

Yet all communist parties "survived democracy" and the regime transition that began in 1988–9, and all remained politically active afterwards. Several of the successor parties have even won free elections, returning to govern. These parties regenerated – they have gained long-term access to governmental power, by transforming their appeals, garnering broad support, and enforcing discipline and professionalism in their parliamentary behavior.

For the parties examined in this book, the outcomes varied from attempts to retain as much communist ideology and organization as possible to dramatic metamorphoses into broadly accepted, moderate, democratic competitors. Thus, the Czech successor party, the Communist Party of Bohemia and Moravia (Komunistická Strana Čech a Moravy, KSČM), pursued a strategy of continuity: It retained many of its organizational structures, much of its communist name and ideology, and many of its symbols. As a result, its electorate was relatively narrow and disgruntled, and the party continued to be excluded a priori from electoral or governmental coalitions. Rather than transforming itself to pursue voters and anticipate competition, the party relied chiefly on the protest vote, and expected its support to expand as a result of worsening economic and political conditions.

The Slovak Party of the Democratic Left (Strana Demokratickej Ľavici, SDĽ) followed a different path after 1989. The SDĽ denounced communist ideology and appeals, and became widely accepted as committed to upholding democracy in Slovakia. It gained almost 15% of the vote in 1992 and in 1998. The party had a relatively easy time joining coalitions, and was courted by both the government and opposition parties throughout the post-1989 era. On the other hand, its support remained highly unstable, and the party was accused of "fishtailing," of political inconsistency and programmatic ambiguity, as the party pursued shifting constituencies, often with radically different appeals.

Introduction

The more spectacular transformations lie to the north and to the south of the former Czechoslovakia. The Polish successor party, the Social Democracy of Poland (Socjaldemokracja Rzeczpospolitej Polskiej, SdRP), became the electoral darling of East Central Europe. Its turnaround was stunning – the party lost every seat it could in the semifree elections in 1989, but then went on to win elections only four years later, with 20% of the vote in 1993. Nor was the party's popularity hurt by its stay in office – in the next elections, in 1997, the SdRP actually *gained* voters, unlike any other incumbent in the region. In 2001, the party again won the elections, this time with an astounding 41% of the vote. However, in parliament, the SdRP suffered continued exclusion by parliamentary parties with roots in the former anticommunist opposition. In 1993, it could form a coalition only with the heir to a pre-1989 communist satellite organization, the Peasants' Party (PSL).

The Hungarian Socialist Party (Magyar Szocialista Párt, MSzP) enjoyed the greatest public success, especially in its parliamentary performance. The party's managerial competence and administrative effectiveness appealed to broad, cross-cutting constituencies, and the party won the April 1994 elections with 33% of the vote. Unlike its Polish counterpart, the MSzP could form a coalition with a party that arose from the pre-1989 anticommunist opposition (the Alliance of Free Democrats – Szabad Demokraták Szövetsége, SzDSz). After four years of coalition rule, it continued to be seen as committed to democracy and effective in governance, even if it lost the 1998 election with 32.3% of the vote.

This surprising survival and resurgence astonished and dismayed many observers. It was as if the Duvaliers in Haiti, or Franco's protégés in Spain, were voted back into power within five years of the collapse of their regimes on the promise that they would promote competitive democracy and an efficient market economy. Given the popular hatred of the communist regimes, how could their successors possibly return to power?

In both popular and scholarly circles, the favored explanations emphasized the enormous stress of the transition to capitalism begun in 1989. Despite the initial euphoria surrounding the promise of efficiency and prosperity, this transition quickly proved as burdensome and brutal as it had in Western Europe centuries earlier. It generated an entire class of the "losers of the transition" – those unable to exploit the new system, whose hopes for economic improvement quickly soured. As their circumstances worsened, scholars reasoned, these voters would naturally turn away from political parties representing the new order, and instead return to parties

3

representing the relative stability and security of the old regime. In short, the parties' success was simply a popular reaction to the privations of the transition to capitalism.

Yet, as this book argues, a closer examination of the parties' appeals and the electoral data shows that the parties have achieved their greatest successes where they could appeal to numerous, wide-ranging constituencies. Their electorates ranged from elderly pensioners to the intellectuals to successful, brash young entrepreneurs, and hence did not consist simply (or even mostly) of the "losers of the transition." Moreover, all the successor parties remained committed to democracy – and few questioned the necessity of market reforms. Instead, in their programs, electoral campaigns, and parliamentary performances, they argued how best to implement these reforms. The electoral winners were those who convinced the voters that they could best administer the new economic and political system – the very "bourgeois capitalist democracy" their communist predecessors had railed against for over four decades. The regeneration of the communist successor parties is thus not the retrograde reaction that many had supposed.

How, then, did the parties regenerate? This book argues that the parties' regeneration depends less on the vicissitudes of the transition and its economic consequences, or even on the democratic party competition faced by the communist successors, than it does on the parties' own actions. The overwhelming pressures of the democratic transition that began in 1989 provided both an impetus and an opportunity to change within the parties. The regime collapse opened up the political opportunity structure – formal structures of the political system opened up, elite alignments became unstable, and popular cleavages were made manifest (Tarrow 1994, McAdam, McCarthy, and Zald 1996). The parties could take advantage of these openings – remaking their appeals, behavior, and personnel.

The parties' very capacity to transform themselves is puzzling, however – how could authoritarian parties spawn successful democratic competitors? After all, communist parties have long been portrayed as moribund, stagnant backwaters where Kafkaesque party apparatchiks endlessly shuffled paper and paid obeisance to ideological orthodoxies. Their popular nicknames were telling; for example, party hacks in Poland were known as "concrete." Bureaucrats, not politicians, ran these parties, as the long tradition of communist studies suggests. It would seem highly implausible that such organizations and actors could give rise to effective campaign machines, successful democratic appeals, and professional politicians – in short, responsive and responsible political representatives.

Fundamentally, the answer lies in reexamining the structures and practices of the individual communist parties. Some did resemble the stereotypical fossilized bureaucracy with little interest in genuine representation or engagement. Their elite selection favored ideological loyalty over practical skills, and these elites neither reformed policy nor engaged society. Such parties were unable subsequently to transform themselves into broadly supported democratic competitors. Instead, they were more likely to retain their communist-era appeals and constituencies. Others, however, were far more flexible in their goals and practices, geared toward advancing pragmatic elites, willing to negotiate with the societies they ostensibly governed and to implement economic and political liberalization. These parties could more readily and credibly change their appeals and orientation.

These predemocratic organizational practices fostered a powerful set of elite political resources with which the new party leaders in 1989 could envision and implement strategies of political metamorphosis. These resources consisted both of the elites' "portable skills" (the expertise and administrative experiences gained in the previous regime) and their "usable pasts" (the historical record of party accomplishments to which the elites can point, and the public perceptions of this record – the repertoire of shared political references). Many of these political resources could arise only in the communist parties, since the anticommunist opposition could formulate policy alternatives, but not implement them.[3]

These political resources did not emerge during the transition, or in the months preceding it, but in decades-long practices of the communist parties. Policies of recruitment and advancement within the communist parties could select relatively pragmatic elite cohorts. Predemocratic policy reforms, however half-hearted, both emphasized the importance of cohesive leadership and required overcoming internal barriers and building coalitions. Engaging the anticommunist societal opposition forced the future successor elites to negotiate and to compete for the public's favor, emphasizing the need for popular, responsive appeals and effective persuasion of the public. These policies gave rise to a cohort of skilled and experienced politicians, with little attachment to communist

[3] Modzelewski, Karol. "Where Did Solidarity Go?" *Uncaptive Minds*, Winter–Spring 1994, 63–72.

ideology or its goals, but with the ability to reinvent the communist parties when the regime collapsed. Ironically, therefore, containing democracy in the communist era required many of the same skills and policies that would later make the parties such effective democratic competitors. The resulting configurations of elites and historical records prior to 1989 ranged from the ossified ideologues of the stagnating Czech party to the pragmatic technocratic experts of its relatively liberal Hungarian counterpart.

Even parties blessed with skilled new elites and a record of reform, however, faced the enormous task of becoming effective democratic competitors after 1989. Having been discredited and forced to exit from power, these parties now had to convince both the voters and other parties of their democratic intentions and capabilities. If they were to gain broad electoral support and a chance to enter government coalitions, they had to formulate responsive political programs, field attractive new candidates and campaigns, and maintain parliamentary effectiveness.

To that end, the elites had to first transform the party organizations, streamlining and vertically integrating the party structures, and symbolically breaking with the past. The break with the past signaled change, while organizational centralization then allowed the parties to be flexible, united, and disciplined. These strategies allowed the parties to adapt successfully to the postcommunist political contexts.

First, the general consensus on the need for economic and political reform in the countries under consideration called for responsive and flexible appeals that would both exploit the competitors' weaknesses and maintain commitment to the new democratic system. Centralization allowed the party elites to respond more readily to voter preferences. It minimized the trade-off between appealing to party members and to the broader electorate, so that the parties could broaden their voter base without sacrificing existing support. Elite skills also made it possible to create new grounds for competition that allowed the parties to compete successfully with the new democratic parties without questioning democracy or the free market itself. Otherwise, the parties would rely on narrow or "nonstandard" appeals, such as nostalgia for the old system. These pleased old party members, but did little to attract new voters. Moreover, as we will see in Chapters 2 and 4, responsive (if vague) and flexible appeals allowed the parties to pursue postcommunist voters more readily than the strategies of voter integration that earlier had served parties so well in Western

Europe, such as grass-roots mobilization, extensive structures, and auxiliary interest organizations.

Second, centralization allowed the elites to respond to the robust competition and to the fluid postcommunist electorates. Centralized parties could more readily orchestrate electoral campaigns that effectively disseminated the party's message, and hand-pick party candidates, by enforcing cohesion and privileging top leaders in decision making within the party. Those elites with earlier political experience of negotiating and bargaining with the opposition could then run effective campaigns that responded to the electorate's needs. Professional, moderate candidates, meanwhile, increased the party's appeal, and reinforced the message that the new successor had little in common with the stereotypical communist party hacks in bad suits.

Third, the successor parties faced considerable parliamentary isolation. Centralization promoted party discipline in parliament – and such unity and cohesion made for formidable parliamentary players. Even where the division between the successor parties and those from the pre-1989 anticommunist opposition persisted, parliamentary cohesion gave credence to claims of transformation and professionalism. As we will see, the more skilled and experienced the elites, the more likely they were to pursue these transformative strategies successfully.

Why would the electorate, or other parties, trust these efforts? In developed democracies, party reputations serve as a shortcut for both voters and potential parliamentary partners, establishing both the credibility of party claims and their attractiveness as coalition partners. Yet the communist successors did not have an established democratic record, and so had to rebuild their reputations. In the meantime, their communist past largely determined the parties' image and their credibility.

As a result, the communist successor parties were both handicapped and helped by their past; on the one hand, they were discredited as monopoly rulers, and faced a skeptical audience in any attempts to redeem themselves. This aspect of their past could confound coalition efforts and preclude wider acceptance by voters and other parties. On the other hand, the parties' usable past as reformers, negotiators, and policy innovators could reinforce their claims of democratic commitment and competence, allowing the communist successors to redeem their past authoritarian efforts into democratic credibility. As the parties developed their public behavior and declarations after 1989, their democratic record would eventually supplant the parties' usable communist past as a source of their reputation, and hence of their credibility. Consistency in parliamentary discipline and in attractive new electoral campaigns and candidates could further reinforce the parties' hard-earned new image.

Given the importance of organizational transformation and (re)building reputations, party elites had to implement their strategies early, quickly, and in a specific sequence that favored organizational streamlining and vertical integration prior to the transformation of programs, electoral methods, or parliamentary strategies. With enough time, sheer familiarity with the new face of the party could foster public acceptance. But to gain political effectiveness readily, parties needed to implement organizational centralization swiftly and decisively.

The chaotic nature of 1989 meant that there was little internal resistance to party transformation at that time. However, once the new democratic system began to consolidate, and the internal party tumult died down, barriers to further transformation could reemerge and begin to subvert party transformation from within. Since these barriers primarily took the form of vested interests within the party, such as orthodox regional leaders or the party bureaucracy, effective organizational transformations occurred *before* the parties attempted to change their appeals or their parliamentary strategies.

Therefore, while enormous differences could arise between the communist parties of 1989 and of 1991, efforts after this period had far less impact. Party programs and organizations continued to evolve, but there was no possibility of a dramatic turnaround of the sort that was feasible in 1989–91. Efforts by reformists-come-lately, such as the struggle that took place in the Czech party during 1993, had far less chance of success. Even if rapid party change could not guarantee its own credibility, slow or delayed transformation would be taken less seriously by both the electorate and other parties. In short, gradualism meant failure.

Paradoxically, then, despite the fact that the communist successor parties were the most despised political actors in 1989 to early 1990, and the unequivocal antagonists of the struggle for democracy, they had the greatest opportunity during this time to remake themselves and eventually gain the votes of the very people who had been calling for their exit from the political arena. This period of change and flux in the parties was also the time during which the political inheritances of the communist era exerted their greatest influence. Given the uncertainty regarding strategies and future outcomes, the tactics and values suggested by the communist era became the templates for future action. Once organizational change and reputations began to consolidate, the policies of the key reform era of 1989–90 began to exert their own influence.

Model Summary

The elite-driven explanation offered in this book focuses on the leaders' decisions to transform the party, and the political resources with which these leaders implemented the decisions. The logic of the model can be encapsulated as follows:

Communist Practice → Elite Resources → Transformation Strategies → Regeneration

• Recruitment	• Portable Skills	• Centralization	• Responsive Appeals
• Negotiation	• Usable Past	• Break with Party Past	• Electoral Support
• Policy Reform		• Rapid Implementation	• Coalition Potential

If this explanation is correct, the following general propositions should hold:

1. For parties that have been discredited and forced out of power, organizational transformation and a break with the past are the prerequisites for pursuing further party regeneration. Parties that do not manage to break with the past and to centralize early on have greater difficulty in consolidating elite power or pursuing strategies of regeneration – transforming their public appeals, conducting effective electoral campaigns, and maintaining parliamentary discipline. Without these, disgraced and disempowered parties are unlikely to regain power.
2. These transformations must occur early, rapidly, and decisively. Discredited political parties and organizations otherwise face increasing difficulties in their attempts to regenerate. The parties also must first transform their organization before transforming party appeals, electoral strategies, or parliamentary behavior.
3. Elite resources determine the degree of transformation and its credibility. Specifically, a usable past promotes cooperation in parliament and popular credibility for the new programs and appeals. Conversely, a deep *regime divide* (the history of conflict between society and the party) would preclude such parliamentary cooperation or public acceptance. For their part, elite skills allow the parties

9

to centralize and to respond to electoral concerns via programs and campaigns.

4. If the sources of these elite resources lie in previous authoritarian practices, these skills and usable pasts should reflect the variation in the organizational practices of the *ancien regime*. In the case of the communist successor parties, predemocratic organizational practices – internal policies of recruitment and advancement, policy reform, and negotiation with the opposition – influenced the elites' degree of pragmatic orientation, their ability and will to centralize the parties, and their skill in responding to and communicating effectively with the public, respectively.

As a corollary, these legacies will influence party strategies so long as they provide information or a template for action that is less costly to obtain than other alternatives, such as seeking international models or other historical templates. As the political situation stabilizes, and uncertainty regarding actions and outcomes decreases, other sources of elite decision making could eventually influence party strategies.

The Broader Setting

In explaining how these transformations took place and why the parties embarked on such distinct trajectories, this book contributes to three fields of scholarship in comparative politics: organizational transformation, the consolidation of new democracies, and political party development.

First, for all the attention paid to political organizations and institutions, both recent organizational theory in sociology and historical institutionalist analyses in political science have emphasized resistance to change. Transformation is said to occur either at the margins (North 1990) or in dramatic "critical junctures" (Collier and Collier 1991), while population ecology models argued that the environment will simply reward certain forms of organization and winnow out others (Aldrich 1979, Scott 1992). There are few examinations of how established organizations survive and adapt successfully to environmental changes that often undermine the very grounds for their existence.

Yet this sort of adaptation is especially crucial, and difficult, in revolutionary situations where the *ancien regime* is disgraced and its institutions face enormous obstacles to survival. Thus, after the revolutions of 1989, the communist parties appeared completely discredited, prompting scholars to predict that the parties were either doomed to disintegrate and eventually vanish, swept away with other features of communist life (Zubek 1990), or to persist as profoundly antidemocratic forces, unable to alter either their appeals or their organizations (Przeworski 1992). Therefore, the ways in which these parties reinvented themselves and regained support have much to tell us about the conditions under which other disgraced organizations can (re)build their reputations and credibility. Specifically, this study argues that the crucial factor that fosters successful organizational transformation is a set of new leaders with the individual and organizational resources to implement a rapid and decisive organizational centralization.

Moreover, scholars have noted that many historical institutionalist works neglect the mechanisms of reproduction of the institutional arrangements that emerge from such crises or critical junctures (Thelen 1999). That is, how do these initial outcomes translate into stable institutions or trajectories? This book identifies one such mechanism: the active replication by party elites of historical legacies, both in their symbolic dimension and as a strategic template. Specifically, when responding to political crises, elites are likely to rely on the political skills and experiences they had earlier gained, such as bargaining with the opposition, innovating and implementing policy, or emphasizing pragmatic solutions over achieving ideological goals.

The second distinct contribution is to the study of the consolidation of new democracies. Many scholars debating the relative influence of new institutions or the legacies of the past have emphasized that international pressures and the building of new democratic institutions overwhelm the influence of authoritarian legacies (Crawford and Lijphart 1995, 1997, Geddes 1995). Accordingly, scholars have mostly focused on the new structures of representation: the new political parties, nationalist appeals, trade unions, parliaments, and social movements (Bielasiak 1997, DiPalma 1991, Jasiewicz 1993b, Kopecký 1995). Insofar as the authoritarian past influenced democratic consolidation, its effects were said to be largely destabilizing and menacing to democracy. In other cases of democratic transitions, such as those in Latin America, the institutions of the former regime have often acted as a direct or implicit threat to democracy. Thus, students of "communist legacies," following Ken Jowitt (1992), have noted the negative influence of the social attitudes and political expectations developed during preceding five decades of authoritarianism (Hanson 1995, Baranyi and Volgyes 1995, Millar and Wolchik 1994). Other scholars have noted the degree of bureaucratization, entrenchment, and stagnation in the communist parties. These hinder transformation, by multiplying the organizational layers and sectors that need to be changed (Huntington 1968, Kitschelt 1994, Panebianco 1988).

However, this study demonstrates that the legacies of the past can also exert a positive influence. Some legacies of the past persist through the regime collapse to affect the new democratic order, and to foster adaptation to democracy, successful democratic competition, and stable governance. In particular, the forces behind the comeback of the successor parties lie, paradoxically, in their communist heritage. Communist organizational practices of elite recruitment and advancement, policy reform, and negotiation with the opposition all profoundly shaped the party elites' ability to act rapidly and to change credibly the party organizations, appeals, and so on. Thus, democratic transitions are not tabulae rasae, blank slates on which any given institutional arrangement can be imposed. Nor is the influence of the legacies of the previous regime exclusively negative. Rather, past organizational practices and networks persist, and can influence democratic development in surprisingly constructive ways.

A third potential contribution of this analysis is to the study of party development and transformation. Many of these studies of political parties and their behavior tend to emphasize environmental factors in explaining why some parties succeed and others do not. Following Lipset and Rokkan (1967), scholars have noted that parties must respond to changes in party competition and in underlying social cleavages, lest they be eliminated in electoral contests and in government coalitions (Kitschelt 1994, Sartori 1976, Sjöblom 1983, Strom 1990, Waller 1995). Similarly, electoral institutions often favor some parties over others (Rae 1971, Lijphart 1984). Finally, a protracted transition may also give the parties the time to adapt to their changing environment, while the nascent organizations of parties with opposition roots are only beginning to consolidate and mobilize (Cotta 1994, Geddes 1995).

The conditions under which parties respond to these incentives and pressures, and the mechanisms of this response, however, have often been simply assumed rather than examined. In the new democracies that follow a regime collapse, there may not be opportunity to respond to these signals. Party and electoral cleavages are often hard to identify. The influence of electoral institutions is often predicated on the development and consolidation of parties themselves (Moser 1999). The type and pace of the transitions themselves are actually endogenous to past party practices – the more the party had stonewalled and refused to address society's grievances, the more likely it was to collapse (as in East Germany, Romania, or in Czechoslovakia). In contrast, the more a party had earlier engaged in negotiation and policy reform, the more likely it was to negotiate its way out of power (as in Poland or in Hungary). Moreover, elections and the development of electoral rules and cleavages tended to *follow* the period when party regeneration began. Hence, retrospection and adjustment of strategy to reflect environmental feedback became far more problematic. Even as the *prospect* of democratic competition offered a major motive for the parties to transform in order to better compete, not all parties could respond to this incentive rapidly or effectively. Instead, the parties' responses to these powerful environmental factors were mediated by internal organizational factors, and specifically, the elites' ability to devise and implement strategies of regeneration.

Where scholars have emphasized internal factors in the transformation of political parties, they have tended to focus on elite configurations, actions, and conflicts (Harmel and Janda 1994, Panebianco 1988). In an influential study, John Ishiyama argued that the ideological distribution of elites (specifically the relative dominance of liberal and democratic reformers over conservative "standpatters") played a major role in the transformation of communist successor parties (Ishiyama 1995, following Huntington 1968). Other scholars also emphasized the political skills of the parties as their assets (Waller 1995, Lewis 1994). Less attention has been paid, however, to the *sources* of these constellations, strategies, and skills. As this book will argue, past patterns of organizational practices bear directly on the new elite configurations. Ideological stances per se matter less than the practical skills and experiences of the elites. In turn, the political resources of these new leaders heavily influence both the set of strategic options available to the parties, and the alternatives that the parties are more likely to choose.

Resolving the puzzle of communist party regeneration, therefore, holds considerable significance for studies of institutional transformation, democratic consolidation, and comparative party politics. In many ways, the study of politics in the former Soviet satellites in East Central Europe provides the perfect setting for exploring these issues. The dramatic nature of the break with the forty-year-old communist political and economic system in 1989 and the simultaneous rise of democratic pluralism and free market structures have created unprecedented opportunities for the study of rapid political development and transformation.

Definitions

Throughout this study, *successor parties* are defined as the formal descendants of the communist parties – that is, the main political parties that arose from the ruling communist parties in 1989 and that explicitly claim their successor status. *Regeneration* refers to gaining long-term access to governmental power – the capacity to compete successfully for and enter democratic government. This capacity consists of *programmatic responsiveness* (as measured by a focus on public issues rather than on internal party concerns, and the adaptability of party programs over time, rather than a simple match with public concerns at any given point), *popular support of the party* (as measured by both the share of the vote and the public opinion poll responses regarding the party's acceptability), and *parliamentary acceptance* (as measured by coalition membership, committee membership, and representation in the parliamentary leadership). A party needed to fulfill all three criteria of regeneration in order to gain long-term access to power in a parliamentary, proportional-representation system.

The mid-level elites of the communist party are defined by their positions (Mosca 1980, Putnam 1976): regional communist party bosses, government ministers and deputy ministers, and junior candidate members of the Central Committee. Once they became the party leaders in 1989–90, they were the driving forces behind the transformation of the parties. Theoretically, any number of party layers, such as the members or party functionaries, may influence party policy. However, the membership faces the collective action dilemma. Unless it is particularly homogeneous or given extraordinary powers, is simply too geographically and organizationally diffuse to have the final say in party policy. Party bureaucrats and activists face the problems of "middle management" – they are too dependent on both the party elites and the membership for their position within the party. Party elites, on the other hand, both place items on the party agenda and choose among proposed alternatives (Elster 1989, Harmel and Janda 1994). They can then implement these decisions, both through their executive authority and by placing like-minded individuals into key positions, thus further cementing their initial efforts (Suleiman 1978).

14

Rather than focusing on legacies as longstanding historical trajectories (Janos 1994), this analysis concentrates on the more immediate legacies of the postwar era, following Jowitt (1992). The "legacies" of the communist regime are the patterns of behavior, cognition, and organization that have clearly identifiable roots in the communist regime, and that persist despite a change in the conditions that initially gave rise to them. They range from individual education and skills, to reputations acquired with the historical record, to personal networks, to the physical infrastructure and state-led development projects. As we will see in Chapter 2, the authoritarian practices have to be consistent, clearly transmitted, and persistent to give rise to the legacies of elite political resources.

Case Selection and Source Materials

This book focuses on the Czech, Slovak, Polish, and Hungarian successor parties. This case selection has both theoretical and methodological bases. First, most analyses of postcommunist developments have focused on either extensions of one-country studies or on global comparisons of the entire postcommunist universe of cases. The first strategy, for all its empirical richness and sensitivity to multiple causes, is often unable to draw firmer comparative theoretical conclusions. The latter strategy, on the other hand, can more readily eliminate entire sets of potential explanatory variables, but has considerable difficulty assessing causal complexities or the importance of sequencing or timing.

Thus, a mid-level comparison of several cases accomplishes two goals: First, it enables discussion between the limited-case and the global-universe analyses, by providing both a comparative perspective and a new focus on causal mechanisms, sequencing, and timing, respectively. Second, mid-level comparative projects let us construct disciplined explanatory models, by allowing the use of multiple strategies of appraisal: nominal comparison (where the correlation of given categories eliminates certain causal variables), ordinal variables (where the rank ordering of the degree to which a phenomenon is present allows us to analyze partial causations), and narrative analysis (which focuses on the unique, sequentially unfolding, path-dependent developments within cases) (Mahoney 1999). As a result, this analysis can pursue the "chains of causation" that link both the recent and remote causes for party regeneration: organizational transformation and elite political resources gained in decades of communist party practices, respectively. It thus can avoid the pitfalls of either tautological triviality (due to excessive causal proximity in temporally "shallow" accounts) or obscuring transmission mechanisms (the result of unduly distant causal antecedents) (Kitschelt 1999).

The cases were also selected to maximize the variation on the dependent variable, illustrating the continuum of party trajectories in the decade after 1989: from complete regeneration (Hungarian MSzP, and more ambiguously, the Polish SdRP), via regeneration on some dimensions but not on others (the Slovak SDĽ), to more limited regeneration as a protest party (the Czech KSČM). The Hungarian and Czech parties are thus the most "different" in outcome, and the Hungarian and Polish parties are the most "similar." The Slovak and Czech parties are the most "similar" in background conditions: Since the Slovak party functioned under the auspices of the Czechoslovak communist party, sharing its economic and political policies, we would expect it to fail to regenerate. That this party has largely succeeded makes it an excellent test case for the model.

The environmental factors that could have affected the outcomes vary – their paths of transition range from lengthy negotiations (Poland and Hungary) to rapid collapses (the Czech Republic, Slovakia, and East Germany). The party system fragmentation ranged from the extreme (Poland pre-1993) to the minimal (the Czech Republic and Hungary). Their electorates varied from a disgruntled minority (the Czech Republic) to broad pluralities (Poland and Hungary). Hence, we can consider alternative explanations that give greater explanatory weight to more purely environmental forces.

At the same time, these parties share three crucial similarities, thus holding constant several potential explanatory factors. First, all were forced to exit from power in 1989, so neither inertia nor a conversion of one type of political authority for another allowed them to retain access to power, as in Albania and in several former Soviet republics. Second, the parties under consideration faced a strong and capable opposition, which contested the elections and further discredited the communist parties. Finally, these cases share a similar social and economic history: All were under the tight grip of the Soviet Union (unlike Yugoslavia, Albania, or arguably Romania) throughout the communist era, all faced economic difficulties prior to 1989,[4] and all had a history of democratic experience prior to World War II.

[4] The Czech economy did perform relatively well until the mid-1970s. However, by the 1980s, productivity, consumption, and real wages declined. Soviet oil subsidies no longer cushioned the economy, and economic growth continued to decline. Czechoslovakia's

These factors should have made party regeneration especially difficult for the Czech, Slovak, Polish, and Hungarian parties; they were discredited as Soviet agents, faced both economic problems and a forced exit from power, and the voters could rely on both the prewar democratic record and the post-1989 opposition to provide political alternatives. For all these reasons, these parties were completely rejected by their societies.

In contrast, where the parties did not exit from power or were not discredited, they could minimize the need to change. In such cases of limited or "managed" transitions – such as those in Romania, Bulgaria, or Albania – parties could rely on continuing patronage, nostalgia, or populist appeals. Many such parties also functioned in countries that have had greater difficulties achieving either a stable market economy or a consolidated democratic polity, and where the old communist formulas were not as discredited as a result. Where the competition was weak and unable to offer viable alternatives, even poor governmental or economic performance by the communist successor allowed it to retain power and popular support, as in the cases of Russia or Albania.

By the same token, parties maximizing existing supporter loyalty had little reason to centralize and break with the past. In fact, to do so would be to call into question the legitimacy of the very bases for this loyalty. Hence, parties pursuing narrow or protest electorates, or maximizing membership, have less need to centralize or to break with the past. They are more likely to succeed in their goals by retaining their existing organization and appeals as much as possible. The Conclusion will examine this larger universe of outcomes, compare the trajectories of other parties, and analyze how these differences affect the generalizability of the model.

To succeed against the odds faced by the parties examined here, however, required elites with the skills to formulate radical strategies of transformation. A wide variety of sources buttress this argument, including: 1) archival records, from national, party, and private collections, of party statistics, organizational practices, and the reasoning behind these policies during 1945–98; 2) interviews with party officials and leaders, participants in the first congresses and Round Table negotiations, contemporary observers, and party activists from both the main successor parties and the numerous splinters that arose; 3) transcripts and stenograms of Round

economic growth over the last five years of the communist regime was actually lower than Poland's. See Rothschild, Joseph. *Return to Diversity.* New York: Oxford University Press, 1989, p. 208. Haggard, Stephan, and Kauffman, Robert. *The Political Economy of Democratic Transitions.* Princeton, NJ: Princeton University Press, 1995, p. 34.

Table negotiations, party congresses, and coalition negotiations; 4) party programs, electoral platforms, and official party declarations after 1989 (their themes, emphases, and changes over time isolated by content analysis techniques); 5) public opinion surveys regarding the issues that were of main concern to the party supporters and the rest of the electorate, the image of the parties, and the bases for their support (analyzed using multinomial logit regressions and machine-learning algorithms); and 6) the parliamentary record – voting, committee assignments, the process of coalition formation, and coalitional stability.

Organization

The chapters follow the structure of the argument. The prerequisites of party transformation are examined in the first two chapters. Chapter 1 surveys the communist era in East Central Europe, showing how the organizational practices of the communist past produced elite political resources. Chapter 2 examines the strategies of organizational transformation, and how these began during the parties' Extraordinary Congresses that took place after the regime collapses. The analysis demonstrates the importance of sequencing and timing in the party elites' efforts to break with the past and decisively centralize party organizations. Chapter 3 analyzes the parties' programs and the degree to which the parties could respond effectively to both the electorates and the exigencies of new democracies. Chapter 4 explores how the parties attempted to gain a broader electorate and popular acceptance through their transformation, while Chapter 5 examines the conditions under which the parties gained parliamentary cohesion and acceptance. Finally, the Conclusion extends the argument both to other cases of *ancien regime* party survival and to theories of institutional transformation, democratic consolidation, and political party development.

1

The Roots of Regeneration: Communist Practices and Elite Resources

Communist parties seem a highly improbable source of democratic skills and effective political leadership. After all, during the four decades of their political and economic monopoly in East Central Europe, they had few incentives to devise responsive or responsible public policies and were far more adept at repression than at representation. They became the stereotype of unchanging behemoths, the progenitors of the stolid *homo sovieticus* and political organizations unable to change their bureaucratic and plodding ways.

Yet, as this chapter will show, elite resources held the key to the regeneration of ruling parties of the discredited regime. Since the successor party elites spent their careers in the communist parties and their auxiliaries, these resources were very likely to have their origin in the parties. Paradoxically, specific organizational practices of the communist parties – the privileging of young party activists, the constant tinkering with policy, and the "cat and mouse" game of negotiation with society and the opposition – could both sustain the parties' rule prior to 1989 and foster their democratic success afterwards.

After the communist governments fell in 1989, the opportunities presented by this regime collapse prompted scholars to ask what it took to "get the parties right."[1] The regime break was radical, and the communist

---

[1] Schmitter, Philippe C. "Intermediaries in the Consolidation of Neo-Democracies: The Role of Parties, Associations and Movements," working paper No. 130, Barcelona: Institut de Ciencies Politiques y Sociales, 1997. See also Evans, Geoffrey, and Whitefield, Stephen. "Identifying the Bases of Party Competition in Eastern Europe," *British Journal of Political Science*, October 1993: 521–48. Jasiewicz, Krzysztof. "Structures of Representation," in White, Stephen, Batt, Judy, and Lewis, Paul, eds. *Developments in East European Politics*. London: McMillan, 1993b: 124–46.

past was discredited as a source of political norms. Therefore, the dominant approach initially argued that institutional crafting and the immediate context of a democratic transition, "comprised of norms, institutions, and international pressures, matter[ed] most to the future of liberal capitalist democracy."[2]

Yet certain structures and patterns of the communist era persisted to shape political and economic developments after 1989, biasing decision making in favor of the familiar and the extant. Thus, the collapse of the communist regime may have removed the obvious structures of communist life, such as the monopoly of the party or economic planning. However, less visible institutions of the past – such as popular norms, patterns of political behavior, and organizational networks – continued to influence politics and political strategies (Barany and Volgyes 1995, Crawford 1995, Hanson 1995, Pridham and Lewis 1996).

If the regeneration of the communist successor parties "clearly demonstrat[es] the continuing effect of the Leninist legacy on post-communist politics,"[3] then it prompts an investigation of which legacies influence political development, how they are transmitted, and when they cease to be relevant. Such an examination can demonstrate the ways in which the legacies of the old regime often determined which institutional choices were made, and which economic and political imperatives become relevant to the political actors during a democratic transition. Moreover, it can generate generalizable propositions for further comparative research of the role of old regime practices in the regeneration of discredited political actors. Finally, the legacies of communism, as this chapter will show, were not merely the "tools of discourse and mobilization,"[4] but determined the available resources and strategies of party regeneration.

---

[2] Crawford, Beverly, and Lijphart, Arend. "Explaining Political and Economic Post-Communist Eastern Europe," *Comparative Political Studies*, Vol. 28: July 1995: 171–99, p. 176. Geddes, Barbara. "A Comparative Perspective on the Leninist Legacy in Eastern Europe," *Comparative Political Studies*, Vol. 28, No. 2, July 1995, 239–74.

[3] Hanson, Stephen. "The Leninist Legacy and Institutional Change," *Comparative Political Studies*, July 1995, 306–14, p. 311. See also Pridham, Geoffrey, and Lewis, Paul G., eds. *Stabilising Fragile Democracies: Comparing New Party Systems in Southern and Eastern Europe*. London: Routledge, 1996.

[4] Crawford and Lijphart 1995, p. 176.

Specifying the Legacies

If communist legacies are defined as the patterns of behavior, cognition, and organization with roots in the authoritarian regime that persist despite a change in the conditions that gave rise to them, three separate tests assess the impact of a given legacy on post-1989 party development. First, does the party consistently exhibit the given behavior or organizational pattern? If it does not, a "legacy" explanation becomes a tenuous and wishful description of what *might* have happened rather than a specification of an actual causal factor.[5] The imprecision inherent in some of the existing accounts of the "Leninist legacy" has led to unwarranted assumptions – for example, many so-called sociological legacies of communism turned out on closer inspection to be short-term responses.[6]

Second, can we identify a transmission mechanism? Some structural, individual, or ideational means must be discernible for the legacy to affect the party directly. Many of the mechanisms of replication and transmission of the legacies of the socialist regimes have remained underspecified. Both critics and advocates of the legacy-centered approach seemed to assume that inertia or a nearly "automatic" replication will continue to make legacies relevant, but have not taken into consideration either a dynamic or a deliberate element. While legacies without an identifiable transmission mechanism may appear, they do not lend themselves easily to a systematic analysis.

Third, does a given pattern persist until the political disjuncture, such as the regime collapse of 1989? If it does not, such a legacy is less likely to affect subsequent political development directly. This concern with persistence further implies that it is necessary to trace when, if ever, the legacies stop being relevant, and what determines why some are more tenacious than others. Despite their concern with the past, many students of the historical influences on the political status quo have not taken into account the time horizons, or the political "half-lives," of a given political legacy. Yet some inheritances from the old regime, such as a distorted price system, can disappear immediately, while others, such as patterns of labor relations, can continue for much longer periods of time.

[5] Elster, Jan. *Political Psychology.* Cambridge, UK: Cambridge University Press, 1993, p. 161.
[6] Kolarska-Bobińska, Lena. "Social Interests, Egalitarian Attitudes, and the Change of Economic Order," *Social Research*, Vol. 55, No. 1–2, Spring/Summer 1988: 111–38.

If they satisfy these conditions, legacies can influence political action in three different ways. First, they delineate the set of feasible actions: The lack of certain skills or networks makes some political decisions impossible. Second, they also provide the patterns and templates for evaluating both strategies and other actors: The historical record confers both cognitive biases and reputations that make some declarations credible. Finally, by providing a cognitive shortcut (as a ready source of information), they lower the transaction costs of decision making, relative to the other bases for evaluation.[7]

All three are especially relevant in the fluid and confusing political environment that follows a regime collapse. Regime transitions are periods of intense elite learning, but also of the use and reification of prior information and skills. Political actors, whether voters, party leaders, or policymakers, would seek credible sources of information that require the least investment of time and effort. If a persistent, stable, and transmitted legacy could provide information or a template regarding a political decision with less time and effort invested than other options (such as seeking international templates, delving into party programs, etc.), then it would be likely to influence decision making.

For example, a party leader could choose to advance his or her own cohort, whose familiar skills and abilities the leader trust, rather than attempt to recruit a whole new set of leaders from the outside. Similarly, a plethora of political parties with vague programs could make policy-based voting decisions difficult. Thus, a voter would rely on the historical divide between "the communist party state" and the "opposition" and label parties according to their roots rather than laboriously sift through the parties' numerous, and vague, programmatic declarations. As the political situation stabilized, however, the profiles of political actors become clearer and more settled, and the consequences of political choices more predictable. Legacies are then less likely to influence decision making directly. Instead, the patterns they initially set into motion, now translated into organizational and institutional choices, would begin to structure politics.

Certain legacies are more likely to persist than others – the more they are an irretrievably sunk cost, and the more "expensive" they are to change, the more they will be sustained. For example, individual education, skills,

---

[7] Rationality itself, after all, involves the realization that obtaining all pertinent information may not be cost-effective or rational. Dennett, Daniel. *Elbow Room: The Varieties of Free Will Worth Wanting.* Cambridge, MA: MIT Press, 1993.

and expertise would be more likely to persist than reputations. It is difficult to "discard" one's prior experiences, and acquiring additional skills or expertise requires relatively high effort. The regime transition could in fact fortify portable skills, since existing skills will define the set of feasible options for a given individual – and once a strategic choice is made, its implementation will often require the same skills and experiences that led the individual to adopt this strategy in the first place. Reputations, on the other hand, are continually updated, and new information is relatively cheaper to acquire (especially in the case of political parties, where all the competitors are constantly "pushing" information at the electorate, through campaigns, press conferences and releases, and public statements). The relevance of the usable past for voters and for other parties is thus more likely to wane as the communist successors develop new, consistent behaviors that eventually alter their past image.

These criteria allow us to reexamine several prior analyses of the legacies of communism. Disaggregating these patterns is the first step in ascertaining which actually mattered, and which lacked the consistency, transmission mechanisms, and persistence to make a difference. First, the parties' antidemocratic history and their authoritarian style of ruling and governing have been said to preclude success in democratic competition. Yet, paradoxically, the same party organizations responsible for the stagnation of state socialist regimes created a set of dynamic and skilled party elites. Those parties that regenerated after 1989 were surprisingly catholic in their recruitment of elites and increasingly tolerant of internal dissent. What mattered, then, was not only the opponent public governance, but also the persistent patterns of elite recruitment that underlied it.

Second, the longstanding resistance to communism in countries such as Poland was said to have eliminated the successor parties as political competitors in a freely elected party system.[8] After all, the party was widely repudiated by the populace, and the imposition of the communist regime in Poland was likened to "placing a saddle on a cow," in Josef Stalin's rustic phrasing. However, this public antagonism had a very different effect on the party itself. The more the party had to respond to an antagonistic society, the more it could develop experience with policy innovation, negotiation, and justification. Tracing the transmission of a given legacy and its effects on specific actors thus holds surprising conclusions.

---

[8] See Lech Wałęsa, quoted in *Życie Warszawy*, 2 February 1990, or Zubek, Voytek. "Poland's Party Self-Destructs," *Orbis*, Vol. 34, Spring 1990: 179–94.

Third, the Czech party's domestic roots, its postwar popular support, and the secularism of the populace favored the Czechoslovak communist party immediately after World War II. Some scholars thus predicted that this initial popular support meant that the party would succeed in the post-1989 polity. However, the initial support in Czechoslovakia for the communists rapidly subsided after the party's brutal coup in 1948 and even more so after the 1968–70 crackdown, so that very little remained by 1989. Without taking into account the ebbing strength of this legacy over time, we may be led to the wrong conclusion.

Fourth, the historical absence of social democratic parties has been used to explain why the Polish and Hungarian communist parties were able to regenerate, if the trade-off between communist and social democratic support on the Left holds.[9] Social democrats were active in the prewar Czech Republic, and once rebuilt after 1989, the party constituted the traditional Left alternative to the Czech communists. As a result, the Czech communist party was unable to become a more moderate competitor, it is argued, because the social democrats already occupied the centrist Left space. The Polish and Hungarian parties faced no such historical competition, and so could remake themselves into social democratic parties. However, this analysis ignores the weakness of the social democrats in the Czech Republic from 1989 to 1993, precisely the time when the other parties regenerated. Having barely reconstituted themselves (they were obliterated after World War II), and with many of their potential leaders in the Civic Forum opposition mass movement (including Valtr Komárek, Jan Kavan, and others), the Czech social democrats were simply not a real threat to the communists until they gained strength in 1993. Legacies thus cannot readily influence postcommunist development without mechanisms of transmission.

More generally, while some legacies of the interwar era persisted through to the post-1989 period, the configurations of parties and electorates prior to World War II had less influence on the communist parties' structures and practices.[10] After 1945, the polities differed from their prewar predecessors in crucial respects. First, the political leadership and

---

[9] Przeworski, Adam, and Sprague, John. *Paper Stones: A History of Electoral Socialism.* Chicago: University of Chicago Press, 1986.

[10] For an argument that the configuration of bourgeois-socialist cleavages and representation had a decisive influence on postwar communist systems and post-1989 democratic politics, see Kitschelt, Herbert, Mansfeldová, Zdenka, Markowski, Radosław, and Tóka, Gábor. *Post-Communist Party Systems.* Cambridge, UK: Cambridge University Press, 1999.

the intelligentsia had been weakened and even physically liquidated during the immense devastation of World War II, as in Poland.[11] Even if their experiences and skills diffused to other politicians, these patterns do not provide clear causal chains. The mechanisms of transmission from one period to the next are rather tenuous (the Czech Republic being a partial exception to this rule).

Second, even where the political elites and parties were not devastated, as in the Czech Republic, the communist parties repeatedly changed form and substance in the interwar period. For example, if we are to extrapolate Czech party strategies from the interwar to the postwar period, should the relevant reference point be the democratic, mass, moderate Czech communist party of 1918–25, or the authoritarian, radical, and Leninist Czech communist party of 1926–38[12]?

Third, the Polish and Hungarian communist parties were extremely weak in the interwar period, and this weakness may have led them to greater caution after World War II.[13] However, prewar strength was not necessarily a reliable predictor of postwar strategy. On the one hand, the Czech party's pre-1926 domestic support should have led the party to accept greater pluralism and reform efforts in the communist period, since the party felt assured of greater support. On the other, its weakness after 1926 should have led the party to reject free elections in 1946. That neither happened suggests that past patterns of bourgeois-socialist cleavages and representation were neither sustained, nor did they inform postwar strategy. In short, the continuities between the pre- and postwar regimes were neither as consistent nor as systematically persistent as the postwar patterns.

Which legacies *do* matter, then? For the communist parties, the key legacies were the elite political resources, established by the communist practices of elite recruitment, policy reform, and negotiation with the opposition. As a result, the parties entered the transition to democracy

---

[11] Gross, Jan. "The Social Consequences of War: Preliminaries to the Study of Imposition of Communist Regimes in East Central Europe," *East European Politics and Societies*, Vol. 3, No. 2, Spring 1989, 198–214.

[12] Prior to World War II, the Czech party functioned for several years as a mass party in the democratic Czech Republic, rather than as a traditional communist organization, focused on secretive cells and a strict discipline. Under its congenial leader Bohumil Šměral, the KSČ resembled a social democratic party á la the Austrian or German Social Democrats. Ultimately, Comintern felt compelled to purge the party and return it to the fold by instituting a new leader, Klement Gottwald, in 1926.

[13] I am indebted to Herbert Kitschelt for this point.

with distinct configurations of elite "portable skills" (elite perceptions, experiences, and expertise) and "usable pasts" (the sets of shared historical references that resonated with the populace), which arose in the communist era. While there were changes over time – most notably, with the post-Stalinist "thaw," which relaxed ideological demands and gave the parties greater leeway – these general patterns persisted throughout the postwar period.

To examine the effects of organizational practices, this chapter compares both how different parties responded to similar exogenous shocks and how similar parties can differ in outcomes. First, the Polish and Hungarian parties followed distinct policies of societal engagement and elite advancement: The Hungarian party entered into a "social contract" after 1956 that minimized public conflict, promoted extensive economic and political reforms, and coopted the intelligentsia into the party. Meanwhile, the Polish party faced greater and more continual public conflict, was more cautious in liberalizing the economy and the polity, and fostered competition and pluralism within its own ranks instead of coopting the intelligentsia. Yet both parties had to respond to lengthy negotiations that eventually forced them to exit from power.

Second, ostensibly similar parties differed in their responses. Thus, the Slovak party shared a common history with the Czech, under the umbrella of the Czechoslovak communist party. Nevertheless, its trajectory after 1989 differed considerably. Such comparisons, therefore, are very well suited to determining which legacies matter, how, and when, both in the regeneration of the communist successor parties and in other instances of organizational transformation.

Communist Takeovers and Regime Crises

If communist organizational practices were the key to the formation of elite resources, the communist capture of power after World War II initially determined these practices. In addition to establishing the monopoly control of politics, authority over political and economic decision making, administration, and adjudication, these takeovers first delineated the relationship between the party and the society. Specifically, if the party came to power through popular mobilization, it saw its organization as a means of establishing and retaining its power. It would subsequently try to ensure the purity and loyalty of this important asset, which brought the party to power and subsequently would ensure its rule. If, instead, the party was "imported" from the outside by the Soviet Union, it tended to view organization as less relevant to its maintenance of power. Without the legitimation of an initial electoral victory, such a communist party would be more likely to rely on elite cooptation and societal engagement to maintain its rule.

Thus, the takeovers encouraged the parties to reach distinct conclusions regarding the kind of party organization that would best establish the parties' authority. As a result, the parties adopted different organizational practices: policies of recruitment, willingness to negotiate with society, and willingness to respond with policy reform. Other factors, such as the differences in the relationship with the Soviet Union[14] or the distinct political cultures involved,[15] certainly affected postwar political developments. However, as the critical formative moments, the initial takeovers had the greatest influence on the choice of these organizational practices and hence on subsequent elite political resources.

Regime crises, in turn, reinforced these patterns and ensured that the parties' organizational practices would be sustained until, and through, 1989. Where the party elites saw the party organization as the guarantee of the party's authority and control over society, they naturally saw it as responsible for the failings of the communist regime, and thus set out to "improve" its reliability after regime crises. Where the parties discounted the party members, on the other hand, the crisis response consisted of removing the elite "culprits" – the discredited party leaders – and of engaging society through further reforms and negotiation, however meager in effect. The responses to regime crises thus not only reflected party cleavages, patterns of popular mobilization, and international pressures,[16] but the parties' organization and control over society.

If the takeovers established these practices and the crises reinforced them, their cumulative effects were greatest during the era of late state socialism, the 1970s and 1980s, for two reasons. First, the more recent the historical memories, the more likely they were to influence popular perceptions of the party. For example, the Polish party elites, whose most

---

[14] Bunce, Valerie. *Subversive Institutions*. Cambridge, UK: Cambridge University Press, 1999a.

[15] Holmes, Leslie. *Politics in the Communist World*. Oxford, UK: Clarendon Press, 1986. White, Stephen, Gardener, John, and Schöpflin, George. *Communist Political Systems*. New York: St. Martin's Press, 1982.

[16] See Ekiert, Grzegorz. *The State Against Society*. Princeton, NJ: Princeton University Press, 1996.

recent regime crisis was in 1980–1, were held far more accountable for the crisis than the elites of the Hungarian party, whose major crisis occurred in 1956. Second, the cohorts of elites currently leading the communist successor parties advanced through the communist organizations during those two decades, gaining the experiences and skills that proved crucial after 1989. Nonetheless, since the 1970s and 1980s both resulted from and reinforced the outcomes of earlier organizational practices, they cannot be viewed separately from the rest of the postwar era.

Thus, the postwar communist period shaped both the elites' portable skills and their usable past. Postwar takeovers of power set the stage for subsequent organizational strategies and practices pursued by the communist parties. Subsequently, the levels of reform and societal negotiation ebbed and flowed, as such efforts were pursued, only for the parties to backtrack. However, even as these reforms and negotiation efforts themselves were not cumulative, the skills and experiences gained by the elites were.

Organizational Practices

First, earlier policies of elite recruitment shaped the composition and skills of the elite cohorts of 1989. These policies consisted of elite advancement, leadership turnover, and, to a lesser extent, internal party pluralism, which have proven important in other contexts.[17] They fall into two ideal types. In "closed" or "intramural" recruitment, elites are recruited from the lower echelons within the organization itself. Leadership turnover is minimized, as is the existence of various ideological divisions or debates. This type of recruitment prizes stability and predictability, since it replicates the same set of values and practices from one level of the hierarchy to the next. Closed patterns of elite advancement have led to orthodox, cautious, and largely conservative elites in other political systems.

In contrast, in "open" or "extramural" recruitment, elites can be brought into the party "horizontally," from correspondingly high positions in other organizations, and they frequently change places within the organization. Such recruitment tolerates differences in opinion and favors diversity in individual experience and skill, promoting pragmatism and innovation.[18] Higher rates of leadership turnover also promote innovative

[17] Dogan, Mattei. *Pathways to Power*. Boulder, CO: Westview Press, 1989, p. 3.
[18] Waltz, Kenneth. *Foreign Policy and Democratic Politics*. New Haven, CT: Yale University Press, 1967, p. 46ff.

and flexible policy making,[19] and top leadership requires these attributes.[20] Open recruitment also keeps the elites from entrenching themselves in any position for too long and creates competition for prized positions. In turn, competition itself trains potential leaders in the skills required in the political system to which they belong[21] – and, as these cases show, in political systems that are radically different.

Given the differences in their recruitment policies, the parties had fostered different degrees of innovation and flexibility in their mid-level and top cadres. To summarize the patterns of party recruitment, the Polish and Hungarian parties recruited from the outside, using skill, style, and pragmatism as criteria, while the Czechoslovak party[22] advanced its elites from within, using ideological loyalty as the chief criterion. While they ironically allowed the rise of reformist Slovak elites through their strict control over the party, the Czech party leaders stifled their potential to put forth elites with practical, portable skills, who could lead a nonideological, competitive democratic party. Since the successor party leaders were all in these ranks in the 1980s, these party policies directly affected the leaders' capabilities.

Second, although no party radically transformed the economy or the polity, the Polish and Hungarian parties made several attempts to alleviate the more egregious shortcomings of the system, both by policy reform and negotiation with the opposition. The content of these policy experiments, however inadequate their results, was perhaps not as important as the willingness of the party actors to respond to a captive audience – the societies under communist regimes. The more a party promoted policy innovation prior to 1989, the more it fostered pragmatism and flexibility in policy making. The more it had subsequently implemented these innovations, the more experience the party elites received in overcoming administrative reluctance, organizational entrenchment, and other institutional and political barriers to party regeneration. Implementing reforms

---

[19] Putnam, Robert. *The Comparative Study of Political Beliefs.* Englewood Cliffs, NJ: Prentice Hall, 1976, p. 6, and Putnam, Robert. *The Beliefs of Politicians.* New Haven, CT: Yale University Press, 1973, p. 147.

[20] Ralf Dahrendorf. *Society and Democracy in Germany.* New York: W.W. Norton & Co., 1967, p. 225.

[21] Easton, David. *Systems Analysis of Political Life.* New York: John Wiley & Sons, 1965.

[22] Much as there was a Soviet Communist Party and various parties in the republics but no Russian Communist Party, similarly there existed a Czechoslovak Communist Party and a Slovak Communist Party but no Czech counterpart on the republican level.

also gave future elites considerable experience in responding to public concerns, and in convincing skeptics within both society and the party.

Finally, negotiation with the opposition and answering societal demands allowed the party mid-level elites to identify societal priorities, formulate responsive appeals, and convincingly address opponents within the party and within society. Such negotiation could even result in a tacit consensus between the more moderate elements within both the party and the opposition, as we will see in the Hungarian case and the aftermath of the revolution of 1956. The more consistently conflictual this relationship, on the other hand, the deeper and more persistent the post-1989 divide between the postcommunist and the postopposition camps.

To summarize the differences in public policy, the Czechoslovak party clamped down on any reform or liberalization (with the notable exception of the Slovak reform proposals) as a threat to its rule, and refused to negotiate. In contrast, the Polish and Hungarian parties continually dabbled in policy reform and negotiation, to gain societal acquiescence. The following sections turn to the individual cases to examine the origin of the parties' organizational practices, their persistence, and the differences among the parties.

Czechoslovakia

The Czechoslovak Communist Party (Komunistická Strana Československa, KSČ) captured power as a mass political party, with extensive organizational networks and a large party membership. Using these to mobilize voters, it won over 40% of the vote in the free elections in 1946[23] and wrested a leading role in the government coalition that followed. Dissatisfied with the pace of political change, the party fomented a crisis among its coalition partners in February 1948 (several noncommunist ministers resigned, without naming replacements) and took over power completely in a coup d'etat. Since it relied on its twenty thousand organizations and almost 2.5 million party members (or over 25% of the adult population) for electoral support, to eliminate political competitors and to mobilize

[23] The KSČ received a considerably smaller percentage of the vote in Slovakia. The party's high Czech support has been explained as a function of the banning of the Agrarian Party, the pro-Russian sentiment following liberation, and the gains in areas where Germans had been expelled following the war. Suda, Zdenek. *Zealots and Rebels: A History of the Communist Party of Czechoslovakia*. Stanford, CA: Hoover Institution Press, 1980, p. 196ff.

forces during the coup, the KSČ continued to emphasize its mass party character, even as it did away with elections.

Having successfully emerged from domestic competition, the party's leaders considered the party's structures and members the mainstay of their power. As Central Committee members argued, "the strength of our party rests in organization, whereas the strength of other parties rests on tradition."[24] A large, loyal membership was both an enormous political resource and the only proof that the party needed of its legitimacy. It was also a way of "crowding out" other political forces – other political parties had also sought mass party membership, and the KSČ saw its gains as their losses.

As a result, the KSČ leadership subsequently counted on the "saturation" of society by party members and structures to help establish party authority as legitimate and to maintain its control of Czechoslovakia. A large, committed, ideologically pure membership would guarantee the party's sustained control over society and retain the same structures that brought the party into power in the free elections of 1946. Table 1.1 details Czech party membership data.

Therefore, as befitted the vanguard of the workers, the party pursued the "proper" blue-collar members. The percentage of Czechoslovak party members in the white collar/intellectual sectors peaked at less than a third – the KSČ was the one party to insist on its "working-class" character until the very end. As a result, the Czech intelligentsia and white-collar workers were the group most eager to join the party, but faced the highest ideological barriers to doing so.[25] Even in the late 1980s, when well-educated technocrats dominated the party apparat and nomenklatura in Poland and in Hungary, the KSČ proudly noted that nearly 90% of its apparat came from communist, worker families.[26]

---

[24] SÚA Fond 01, sv 2 aj 12 2. Diskuse k referatu S. Gottwalda. 30.5.1946. Souček and Švermová.

[25] Wightman, Gordon, and Brown, Archie. "Changes in the Level of Membership and Social Composition of the Communist Party of Czechoslovakia, 1945–73," *Soviet Studies*, July 1975: 396–417, pp. 409–10. Czech white-collar workers had considerable incentives to join the party – employment in the state sector was made exclusively the provenance of the party, as was advancement within its ranks. The KSČ had wanted to recruit blue-collar workers but had fewer incentives for blue-collar workers to join, and far fewer sanctions to keep them from leaving. For example, while white-collar workers were demoted to menial jobs if they were expelled from the party, blue-collar workers faced no such punishments.

[26] *Život Strany*, No. 11, 1988.

Table 1.1. *Czech communist party membership.*

KSČ (Czech component)	1945	1950	1955	1965	1970	1980	1985
Membership:	17,500	2,200,000	1,370,000	1,400,000	900,000	1,152,000	1,240,400
Percentage of population	.2%	25.3%	16.5%	14.3%	10.1%	11.1%	12%
Organizations	14,000	26,400	35,100	38,881	33,579	34,300	35,000
Composition[a] (%)							
Blue collar	68.0%	38.4%	40.7%	32.9%	26.1%	30.0%	
Professional	4.5%		31.0%	23.0%	33.1%		
Agricultural	27.5%		6.7%				
Apparat			6,500	8,700	4,500	4,000	14,000
Nomenklatura			250,000		100,000	260,000	

Note: [a] The Czechoslovak party was unusually secretive about its composition – many of the files in the archives are marked "top secret," and much of the information was never released. In contrast, the Polish party published the data both in its statistical yearbooks and in the party press.

Source: SÚA, Fondy 02 and 04 (ÚV KSČ and Předsednictvo KSČ), Prague. *Yearbook on International Communist Affairs*. Stanford: Hoover Institution Press, 1966–91. Staar Richard. *Communist Regimes in Eastern Europe*. Stanford, CA: Hoover Institution Press, 1988, interview with Vasil Mohorita, 14 November 1996.

Concerned with the purity of party ranks,[27] Czech communist leaders purged their membership regularly, and at higher rates than any other party. For example, in 1948–51, two purges cast out 750,000 members, or 32% of party members.[28] In the most radical purge, the "normalization" drive of 1969–70 eliminated a third of the party's members and decimated the party intellectuals. The Czech party still railed against "non-Leninist thinking" within the party as late as 1988, and insisted that it was "wholly natural and logical that the party demands . . . Bolshevization."[29]

Finally, Czech party membership rates were twice as high as those in the neighboring countries.[30] By 1949, the Czech party had succeeded in

[27] SA Fond ÚV KSS Predsednictvo. 1981/1541/81-3.2 Karton č. 1596. As late as 1981, the Czechoslovak Communist Party still spoke of "characteristic care for the upholding of party rules, ensuring the discipline of the communist and purity of party ranks."

[28] Kaplan, Karel. *Political Persecution in Czechoslovakia*. Research project "Crises in Soviet-Type Systems," No. 3. Köln: Index, 1983.

[29] Gustav Husák, 11 December 1971, *Život Strany*, and *Život Strany*, No. 5, 1976.

[30] At the time of its takeover in Czechoslovakia in February 1948, the KSČ numbered 2.5 million members, or over 25.3% of the Czech population and 9.1% of the Slovak. Afterwards, anywhere from 13 to 16% of Czechs were in the party (prior to the debilitating Prague Spring purge), as were 6–7% of the Slovaks.

infusing society with party organizations – only 3.4% of Czech communities were without party organizations a year after the communist takeover.[31] Similarly, only 3.3% of the communities were without a party organization in Slovakia by 1954.[32] By 1989, a party organization existed for every 286 Czechs and for every 400 Slovaks. As a party journal explained as late as in the mid-1970s, "an effort must be made to ensure that there is no factory, no important workplace, and no community where there is not a primary organization of the Czechoslovak Communist Party."[33]

The Czechoslovak party was also perhaps the most persistent and successful in making society dependent on the party, in areas as basic as education and employment.[34] Membership in the orthodox Communist Youth Union was a prerequisite for higher education throughout the period, and "political criteria [were] always applied" in selection for both high school and university.[35] Five hundred and fifty thousand jobs were directly vetted by Czechoslovak party organs in the mid-1980s,[36] in contrast with 270,000 in Poland (with over twice the working population of Czechoslovakia) or the even smaller number in Hungary during the same time period.[37] Czechs and Slovaks were not allowed to travel as freely as Poles or Hungarians, and were subject to humiliating interviews, courtesy of the State Security Agency, after their return.[38] Censorship was also far more severe, as subscriptions to many Western journals were forbidden and domestic publications were under stricter control than in either Poland or Hungary.

---

[31] Kaplan, Karel. *Útváření generální linie výstavby socialismu v Československu; od února do IX sjezdu KSČ*. Praha: Academia, 1966, p. 166. Thus, four hundred Czech villages had no party organizations in 1949. At the time, there were 11,695 such communities in the Czech Lands and 3,361 in Slovakia.

[32] SA ÚV KSS Sekretariat. 1954/Inf a./54-7.9 Karton č. 91.

[33] *Život Strany*, No. 15, 1976, p. 12.

[34] Ulč, Otto. *Politics in Czechoslovakia*. San Francisco: W. H. Freeman and Co, 1974, p. 105.

[35] Kaplan 1983, p. 6.

[36] Renner, Hans. *A History of Czechoslovakia Since 1945*. London: Routledge, 1989, p. 111. For Polish figures, see *Polityka*, 2 September 1989. More conservative figures (Kaplan, Karel. *Áparat ÚV KSČ v letech 1948–68*. Prague: Sešity Ústavu Pro Soudobé Dějiny, Sv. 10, 1993) place the number of Czechoslovak nomenklatura posts at 180,000–250,000.

[37] The Hungarian system differed in that while the direct nomenklatura ranged from ten thousand (in the mid-1980s) to ninety thousand, the party held discretionary "advisory" rights to an additional 350,000 posts.

[38] For example, over 1 million Hungarians had traveled abroad in 1970, and over 5 million did so in 1980. Over 870,000 Poles traveled abroad in 1970, and nearly 7 million did in 1980. In contrast, the figures for Czechoslovakia are 400,000 and 870,000, respectively.

The party's response to regime crisis also reflected its understanding of the party organization as the mainstay of its rule. The major reform movement, the Prague Spring of 1968, began within the party, partly because the party had so penetrated society that by that point few centers of independent thought existed outside of the party, unlike the relatively free academic departments and scientific institutes in Poland and Hungary. The Spring began with the formulation of reform alternatives by three committees attached to the central party leadership in the 1960s. Reformists, such as Ota Šik, came to influence policy. The suggestions for improving the economy eventually led to calls for political reform, the ascension of the reformist Alexander Dubček into the party leadership, and eventually an unprecedented renewal of both the party and its relationship to the society.[39] For the first time since 1946, the party began to regain legitimacy and to allow pluralism within the party and within society.

After the Soviet-led invasion crushed the Prague Spring, however, all these gains were reversed. Since the impetus for the Czech liberalization had come from within the party, the party's "treachery" was punished. The leadership reasoned that without a reliable membership, it could not count on an effective public loyalty. Therefore, the Czechoslovak response focused on cleansing the membership ranks and clamping down on any "dangerous" initiatives. The result was both a renewed ideologization of party life and an increased fear of pluralism in the party leadership. Entire academic institutes and departments were summarily eliminated during the "normalization" campaign of 1968–70, the press and media were enervated completely, and constant "loyalty checks" made party members acutely aware of the party leadership's desire for ideological reliability.[40] In the most dramatic purge in the history of state socialism, following the Prague Spring, over 28% of KSČ members were expelled from the party within a year.[41] Moreover, expulsion meant not only loss of party membership, but of employment and schooling opportunities as well, not

[39] See Skilling, H. Gordon. *Czechoslovakia's Interrupted Revolution*. Princeton, NJ: Princeton University Press, 1976. Renner, Hans. *Dějiny Československa po roku 1945*. Bratislava: SAP, 1993. Kusín, Vladimír V. *The Czechoslovak Reform Movement, 1968*. Santa Barbara, CA, ABC-Clio, 1973. Kusín, Vladimír V. *The Intellectual Origins of the Prague Spring: The Development of Reformist Ideas in Czechoslovakia, 1956–1967*. Cambridge, UK: Cambridge University Press, 1971.
[40] Jancar, Barbara Wolfe. *Czechoslovakia and the Absolute Monopoly of Power*. New York: Praeger, 1971, p. 125.
[41] Wightman and Brown 1975: p. 408.

only for the expellees but their entire families.[42] The purge was designed to prevent any future reformist deviations in the party, but it also left a lasting trauma for much of society, whose bargaining power vis-à-vis the party was curtailed, and whose faith in the party's legitimacy was irrevocably gone.

The subsequent policies of societal oppression and policy stagnation were to demonstrate that the party was once again fully in control. Since 1968 itself was a party reform, the party did not consider any further political or economic reforms, for fear of a similarly disastrous loss of control over society. The party document after 1969, "The Lessons of the Crisis Development in the party and society after the thirteenth congress of the KSČ" (*Poučení z krizového vývoje ve straně a společnosti po XIII. sjezdu KSČ*) denounced any attempt at political or economic reform, either then or in the future. As late as 1989, the KSČ leader Miloš Jakeš argued that any revision or attempt to come to terms with the events of 1968 would mean that the party would fall apart.[43]

The one achievement of the Prague Spring was the federalization of Czechoslovakia, which partly addressed the earlier Czech domination of Slovakia under the auspices of "the Czechoslovak People's Socialist Republic." The communist party did relatively poorly in the 1946 elections in Slovakia, and never organized as thoroughly as the Czech party: The membership rate at the time of the 1948 takeover was 9.1% of adult Slovaks, about a third of the rates in the Czech lands (see Table 1.2). Nor were the Slovak party members or leaders seen as particularly committed to establishing communist rule. Therefore, the Slovak communist party was rapidly forced to join the Czech party, and the Czechs centralized control over the Slovak party.[44] In having to cede almost all its authority to the

[42] As Timothy Garton Ash put it lyrically, "that window cleaner over there: his thesis was on Wittengstein. Ask your waiter about Kafka: before his trial, he lecture on *The Trial*. Yes, the nightwatchman is reading Aristotle. Your coal will be delivered by an ordained priest of the Czech brethren. Kiss the milkman's ring: he is your bishop." (*The Uses of Adversity*: New York: Vintage, 1990, p. 63.)
[43] Interview in *Pártelet*, February 1989, quoted in Tökés, Rudolf. *Hungary's Negotiated Revolution*. Cambridge, UK: Cambridge University Press, 1996, p. 316.
[44] The Slovak communists played a considerable role in the Slovak National Uprising, directed against the Hitlerite puppet government of wartime Slovakia, led by Monsignor Jozef Tiso. The considerable gains they made were lost, however, when they actively participated in the "Prague agreements," which ceded Slovak autonomy to Prague and then made the Slovak communist party a part of the Prague-centered Czechoslovak Communist Party.

Table 1.2. *Slovak communist party membership.*

KSS	1945	1950	1955	1960	1965	1970	1980	1985
Membership:	16,500	230,000	200,000	250,000	300,000	300,000	388,000	436,000
Percentage of population	.5%	6.8%	5.4%	6%	6.8%	6%	7.9%	8.5%
Organizations		8,600	9,400	9,700	10,000	10,600	11,700	12,500
Composition (%)								
Blue collar	72.5%	51.3%	39.4%	37.5%	34.4%	29.9%		
Professional		17.3%	11.6%	15.9%	20.9%	22.9%		
Agricultural		17.3%	11.6%	11.6%	8.3%	8.3%		
Apparat			2,300		2,100	1,300	1,600	3,000
Nomenklatura						18,400		21,000

Source: SNA, Sekretariat and Predsednictvo ÚV KSS files, Bratislava. *Yearbook on International Communist Affairs*. 1966–91. Staar. 1988.

Prague center, the Slovak communists became an instrument of the Czech leadership. As a result, the Slovak branch was a subservient and stagnant party backwater until 1968 and the federalization of the country.

After 1968, however, the Czech party allowed the Slovaks some administrative autonomy, largely as a result of Slovak lobbying. Since the Slovak party was not as active in the Prague Spring,[45] Slovak party members were not purged as heavily. While districts where 20% of members were expelled were put forth as examples, others, such as the intellectual center in Bratislava, only had a tiny percentage of expellees.[46] Those who were expelled could also count on support from many of their old comrades. Moreover, since the intelligentsia was so small and well-connected in Slovakia, the party hesitated to punish intellectuals. As a result, Slovaks grew in relative importance in the party (for example, both the new KSČ leader after 1968 and the new mayor of Prague were Slovaks), and the Slovak republic became the main beneficiary of post-1968 policies. Thus, the Slovak party could gain some public support, given its fulfillment of national aspirations, and preserve a more ideologically diverse membership. After 1989, many of these Slovak communists dispersed into the new

---

[45] *Yearbook on International Communist Affairs*. Stanford, CA: Hoover Institution Press, 1966, p. 50.
[46] Politologický Kabinet SAV. *Slovenská Spoločnost v krizových rokoch 1967–1970*. Zbornik studii III. Bratislava: SAV 1992, p. 186.

political parties, blurring the divide between the communist party and the rest of society.

Elite Advancement Policies

The conservative Czech party leaders deliberately replicated a pattern of "closed" elite advancement – elites could rise only within and through the party ranks. The purges and recruitment policies of the Czech communist party rewarded neither education nor extramural experience, but ideological loyalty. Anxious to reassert control, and suspicious of any innovations that smacked of the 1968 reform movement, the party promoted only "safe" comrades, tested by years, if not decades, of party work. Prospective members had to apply directly to the party and could be rejected on ideological grounds. Advancement occurred mostly through progression upward in the party, into increasingly ideologically stagnant elite layers, so that conformist and orthodox members were the primary ones to advance in the party. The overwhelming majority of Czech and Slovak leaders were long-time party activists.[47] Although education levels increased over time, party leaders had no international experience, and their schooling was at either the Prague or the Moscow party schools.[48] The youth organization, completely under party control after 1968, provided no reformist elites. As a result, the Czech party elites in the 1980s were ideologically hidebound, and eventually unable to keep up with the transition of 1989.

Ironically, in their desire to control the Czechoslovak party, the Czech leadership created the space for Slovak reform potential. The strict centralization of power in the Czechoslovak communist party meant that as orders flowed from Prague to the Slovak regional party heads, Bratislava (the capital of Slovakia) was largely neglected by party supervision and control commissions. The Slovak elites who led the party after 1989 arose through an oversight – they spent most of the 1970s and 1980s in the Marxist-Leninist Institute of the Central Committee of the KSS, the Slovak party's main theoretical and programmatic organ, far away from both party supervision and access to party decision making.

[47] Wolchik, Sharon. "Economic Performance and Political Change in Czechoslovakia," in Bukowski, Charles, and Cichock, Mark, eds. *Prospects for Change in Socialist Systems*. New York: Praeger, 1987, p. 48.
[48] Kaplan 1993, p. 13.

Several younger party pragmatists quietly worked at the Institute and enjoyed relative freedom to travel abroad and a library fully stocked with Western journals and books, at a time when access to travel and foreign media was severely curtailed. They were led by Professor Viliam Plevza, whose ambitions had by several accounts extended well beyond the Institute.[50] Under Plevza's direction, the Institute research teams had come up with several reform documents, which circulated widely among both the Institute research staff and some of the younger apparat members. These young scholars were unable to advance into the party's leadership prior to 1989, and thus gained far more theoretical than practical experience in policy making and implementation. Nevertheless, they were ready to assume power, immediately after November 1989, at a time when most older, established party officials were either too disoriented or frightened to take charge.

While the Czech party and its institutes stagnated,[49] pockets of Slovak reformists could thus survive. However, these clusters of Slovak reformism remained an exception to the general rule of ideological stagnation and lack of policy innovation. In its effort to prevent the resurrection of "right-wing opportunism," the KSČ Politburo did not turn over its mid-level cadres and did not bring in any new members (unless an incumbent died) until 1987, when Jakeš's dogmatic wing of the party took over from the conservative pragmatic Gustav Husák.[51] As a result, an average of only 13% of the Politburo leadership changed every year (16% if we include the changes made in 1968) in the last two decades of communist rule (see Table 1.3), less than half the rates in Poland. Moreover, elites who left did so as a result of retirement or death – there was minimal horizontal movement to other positions.

Nor did the party allow internal pluralism. Any reform-minded party member bold enough to attempt to disseminate his or her views would be rewarded with both expulsion and loss of employment. Instead of capital-

---

[49] An exception is the Institute of Economic Planning, where the likes of Václav Klaus and Vladimír Dlouhý first became prominent. This same institute also employed Miloslav Ransdorf, currently the Czech successor's party main apologist. Unlike the Slovak Institute of Marxism-Leninism, however, the Institute of Economic Planning had no direct elite ties that would allow its members to ascend to the top of the successor party immediately.

[50] Žiak, Miloš. *Slovensko: Od komunizmu kam?* Bratislava: Archa, 1996, p. 28–9, and interviews with Peter Weiss.

[51] Josef Blahož in Lawson, Kay, ed. *How Political Parties Work: Perspectives from Within.* Westport, CT: Praeger, 1994, p. 230.

Table 1.3. *Changes in the Czechoslovak politburo.*

KSČ	Members and candidates	Number of new members	Percentage of change
1966	15	1	6.6%
1968	14, 28, 23	5, 21, 6	45.6%[a]
1970	14	3	21.4%
1971	13	2	15.4%
1977[b]	13	1	7.7%
1978[c]	13	1	7.7%
1986	17	3	17.6%
1987	17	2	11.8%
1988	17	2	11.1%
Average			16%

Notes: [a] Average of 35.7%, 75%, 26.1% changes.
[b] No changes between 1972 and 1977.
[c] No changes between 1979 and 1985.
Source: Yearbook on International Communist Affairs. 1966–91.

izing on the reform potential of 1968, the party deliberately eliminated its residues, partly because of its fear that party foment would once again destabilize the polity. In the 1980s, following both the rise of the opposition Charter '77 and Polish Solidarity, the party rank and file grew increasingly dissatisfied with the stagnation, and produced several localized, informal discussion clubs.[52] These, however, had neither the connections to the party elite nor the access to decision making to become full-fledged reform alternatives. Instead, they largely foundered at the local level or were kept out of the largely unchanged decision making structures. Therefore, party reformists in 1989, though they could now openly voice their concerns and offer alternatives, had little access to the central power structures. The more reactionary elites, with little commitment to party transformation, instead took over power in 1989.

Public Policy Reform and Negotiation

In Czechoslovakia, 1968 marked the only real economic or political reforms undertaken by the party-state. Prior to this time, the orthodox leadership

---

[52] For more on these groups and their fates after 1989, see Grzymała-Busse, Anna. "Reform Efforts in the Czech and Slovak Communist Parties and their Successors, 1988–1993," *East European Politics and Societies*, Fall 1998: 442–71.

of Klement Gottwald stuck closely to the Soviet line. There was no political or economic "thaw," seen in Poland or Hungary after Stalin's demise in 1953. Instead, Stalinist political oppression and the extremes of communist economic centralization "lasted long after the death of Stalin and in many aspects was not basically modified until 1968."[53] After the brief interlude of reform in 1968, Czechoslovak public policy stagnated again as the party feared another loss of control over society. There was no need for greater pluralism or reform, the leadership reasoned, since the party had been legitimated decisively in 1948. There was no need to test this image by liberalizing the economic or political strictures. Fears of the destabilizing effects of competing policy initiatives and leadership changeover were only confirmed by the nature of the Prague Spring. As the last party secretary, Jakeš, explained, "the anti-socialist opposition would rise up whenever the party changed its policies or self-criticized."[54]

The "normalizing" leadership that assumed power in late 1968 had little truck with reform or societal negotiation. The Husák government neither allowed policy innovation, nor did it have the elites to implement and justify it. The electoral law of 1967, which provided for a modicum of electoral choice, was repealed in 1971.[55] Nor did the party engage in even a pretense of pluralism: It presented a single-party list throughout the post–Prague Spring era. Although the party no longer enforced society's loyalty to the party by the 1980s, it displayed little tolerance of dissent. Instead, it zealously prosecuted such degenerates as the Plastic People of the Universe, a rock band whose chief "antisocialist transgression" appears to have been its penchant for long hair and unintelligible lyrics. The result was an ever-deepening divide between the communist party and the society.

Despite pressure from Mikhail Gorbachev's Soviet Union, the party instituted no changes in either the economy or the polity until the announcement of minor reforms in 1987, which were not implemented.[56] The collectivization of agriculture continued, with little evidence of the

---

[53] Skilling, Gordon H. "Stalinism and Czechoslovak Political Culture," in Tucker, Robert, ed. *Stalinism*. New York; W.W. Norton, 1977, p. 268.

[54] Jakeš, Miloš. *Dva Roky Generalním Tajemnikem*. Praha: Dokumenty, 1996, p. 103.

[55] Ulč, Otto. "Legislative Politics in Czechoslovakia," in Nelson, Daniel, and White, Stephen, eds. *Communist Legislatures in Comparative Perspective*. New York: SUNY Press, 1982.

[56] See Dawisha, Karen. *Eastern Europe, Gorbachev, and Reform*. Cambridge, UK: Cambridge University Press, 1988.

Poland

autonomy and private production eventually tolerated (and even encouraged) by the Hungarian or Polish parties. Subsidized oil prices kept the
economy going until the mid-1970s, when the Czechoslovak economy,
too, began to grind down. Even then, no reforms were forthcoming.

On the other hand, throughout the post-1968 era, Slovakia was better
off than the Czech lands. Economic policies continued to promote the
industrialization and urbanization of the rural Slovak republic, and political repression was not as severe in the Slovak republic as it was in the
Czech. Much of the normalization-era budget went to developing
Slovakia.[57] The Slovak party's mid-level elites also had more experience
with policy innovation, thanks to the efforts of the Marxist-Leninist Institute. The party had also struck something of a societal contract as well,
bound up with national aspirations of Slovaks. However, in both the Slovak
and in the Czech parties, the orthodox party elites were in charge of party
implementation and allowed little experience to the up-and-coming
younger elites. Nor did they engage in any societal negotiation. Thus,
the Czechoslovak party appeared completely out of touch with society. Its
elites had neither recent experiences in pluralizing the polity or the
economy, nor could they point to a shared record of negotiation, response,
or reform.

Poland

Imported from Moscow and supported by the Soviet Army, the Polish
communist party was painfully aware of its lack of support after World
War II. In their analyses, party leaders admitted that the Soviet presence
was "crucial" to its coming to power.[58] Party leaders therefore never
allowed a free election. As one enraged Politburo member explained in
February 1946, "we cannot allow 'loose' elections and an unfettered mobilization of fascist elements . . . we cannot allow a repeat of the Hungarian
experiment [in free elections]."[59] The Polish party thus came to power

[57] I am indebted to Andrew Schwartz for this point.
[58] AAN, 295/II-2/KC 20-26. 5. 1945. See Kochański, Aleksander, ed. *Protokoły posiedzeń Biura
Politycznego KC PPR 1944–45*. Warsaw: ISP PAN, 1992, p. 81ff.
[59] AAN 295/IV-2 K1-123 PPR KC. CKKP: protokoły i sprawozdania 1946–8. In immediate postwar Poland, "fascist" was the term used by communists to describe all independent political actors, including the World War II resistance groupings, the London
government in exile, and members of political parties. By 1947, party leader Władysław
Gomułka did not even speak about a pretense of elections, but referred to the capture of
power as a "social revolution" and an "overthrow of the government."

41

through electoral fraud and coalitional chicanery, faced with popular distrust and enmity.

Not surprisingly, therefore, the Polish party regarded its newly recruited members as unreliable and uncommitted.[60] Party members were as suspect in their loyalties as they were irrelevant to the takeover.[61] Polish party officials did not even know how many members the party had in late 1945. While the chaos at the end of the war may be partly responsible, their Czech counterparts had precise figures by that point.[62] Nor did the Polish leaders treat the party membership as a source of legitimization of their power. Instead, they complained that any increase in numbers weakens the party,[63] and argued that past mass membership drives were "inseparable" from loss of quality.[64] As a result, the party never pursued the sort of mass, committed membership that the Czech party did – by 1948, the Polish PZPR managed to recruit only 4.3% of the population, and subsequently averaged about 5.4% of the adult population as its members (see Table 1.4).[65]

In contrast to the Czech saturation of society with party organizations and representatives, a fourth of Polish villages had no party organization, as late as 1987.[66] Instead, the party ceded its presence in the villages to the United Peasants' Party (Zjednoczone Stronnictwo Ludowe, ZSL), its

---

[60] Palczak, Andrzej. *Procesy Stalinizacji w Polsce w latach 1947–56*. Zabrze: Wydawnictwo APEX, 1996, p. 33. AAN 295/IV-1 PPR KC. Early in the postwar era, the Chair of the Central Party Revision Commission noted that the influx of religious Roman Catholics into the party was especially frustrating. In another instance, party secretaries were reported to have started a collection campaign for a church monstrance among the workers entrusted to their care – and collected a "staggering sum." (295/IV-2: 20.2.1946 meeting of KC PPR KKKP.)

[61] Polish party officials did not even know how many members were actually in the party in late 1945, while their Czech counterparts had precise figures by that point. AAN 295/I/20.

[62] AAN 295/I/20.

[63] Władysław Gomułka, in AAN 295/II-1. 6-7.7.1945. KC Plenum. A few days later, Gomułka acknowledged that a real mass party, if it could be achieved, would be "useful" in elections. AAN 295/II-3/11-12.7. 1945.

[64] Edward Babiuch, quoted in Pomian, Grażyna, ed. *Protokoły tzw. Komisji Grabskiego*. Międzyzakładowa Struktura "Solidarności," 1987, p. 28.

[65] AAN 237/VII-3783. The average is of party membership from 1948 to 1986, using figures from AAN 295 and 237 files, and *Yearbook on International Communist Affairs*. Stanford, CA: Stanford University Press, 1966–91.

[66] In 1958, over half of Polish villages were without party organizations, a portion that decreased to 29% by 1965. This translated into twenty-one thousand out of forty-one thousand villages without party organizations, down to twelve thousand villages without organizations in 1965. *Nowe Drogi*, 1987. The Peasants' Party was to be the chief representative of the countryside and its interests.

Table 1.4. *Polish communist party membership.*

PZPR	1945	1950	1955	1960	1965	1970	1980	1985
Membership:	20,000	1,360,000	1,340,000	1,270,000	3,155,000	3,200,000	3,000,000	2,100,000
Percentage of population	.8%	5.5%	4.9%	4.3%	5.9%	6.8%	8.1%	5.6%
Organizations:	25,000	19,800–48,000[a]	20,000	52,000	67,000	72,000	74,000	75,000
Composition (%)								
Blue collar	64.5%	50.6%	39.8%	40.3%	40.1%	40.3%	45.9%	30.0%
Professional	7.1%	28.9%	39.2%	42.9%	42.7%	42.5%	33.2%	41.5%
Agricultural	24.1%	14.1%	18.4%	11.8%	11.7%	11.6%	9.4%	7.3%
Apparat		10,000	16,000	8,000	8,000		11,000	12,000
Nomenklatura			70,000			100,000	160,000	270,000

Note: [a] The party conducted both a purge and a membership drive during this time.

Source: AAN, 295 and 237 file (PPR and PZPR), Warsaw. *Yearbook on International Communist Affairs.* Stanford, CA: Hoover Institution Press, 1966–91. Staar. 1988. DeWeydenthal, Jan *The Communists of Poland.* Stanford, CA: Hoover Institution Press, 1986.

agricultural satellite party, in a way that the Czechoslovak party never did to the corresponding ČSL. By 1989, there was a basic communist party organization for every five hundred Poles, in contrast to one for every 286 Czechs. The number of central party apparat employees also reflected these differences – by 1965, there were more central party apparat workers in the Czech lands than in Poland (despite the fact that Poland's population was over 3.5 times the size of the Czech), and these differences persisted.[67] Nor did the party make society as dependent on loyalty to communism for either schooling or employment; for example, by the late 1980s, party membership figures among the students verged on the comic – in 1987, the party reported 879 student members among its 2 million–plus ranks.[68]

The regime crises reflected the loose coupling between party and society, and the lack of the party's reliance on its organization. Poles repeatedly poured out onto the streets in protest in 1956, 1968, 1970, and 1976. In the most dramatic, and most sustained, opposition movement against communist rule, they founded and then joined en masse the independent trade union Solidarity, which claimed 10 million members, or over a third of the adult population, during 1980–1. In what was both a historical irony and evidence of the party's laxity, over 35% of the Polish communist party members joined Solidarity, while 45% expressed pro-Solidarity sentiment in public opinion surveys.[69] The Solidarity movement, though self-limiting, exerted enormous pressure on the party-state to transform not only the economy but also the polity. The military crackdown on Solidarity that began on 13 December 1981, and the imposition of martial law, left a bitter distrust between society and the party. Occurring as it did only a few years before the democratic transition, the Solidarity era remained alive in the memories of both the party elites and the populace to persist as a regime divide after 1989.

Instead of purging members, the party reacted to these crises by exchanging party leaders (in 1956, 1970, and 1981). Polish party publica-

---

[67] Due to the dominance of the Czech party center over its supposed partner in the Czechoslovak federation, the Slovak aparat was a relatively smaller fraction of the total. Despite the 3:2 parity that was to reflect the population differences, the Slovak aparat size was often a fourth of the Czech. For example, see Fond 02/4, sv. 30 aj 50 bod 9, 20.12.1968, SÚA, Prague.

[68] Sułek, Antoni. "The Polish United Worker's Party: From Mobilisation to Non-Representation," *Soviet Studies*, July 1990: 499–511, p. 503

[69] Mason, David. "The Polish Party in Crisis, 1980–1982," *Slavic Review*, Spring 1984: p. 37.

tions openly blamed leaders for the party crises,[70] and party congresses were held to castigate those held responsible.[71] The PZPR also attempted to become more responsive and to "consult" with society, through freer elections and referenda in the 1980s. Nonetheless, the conflict between the party and society persisted, and the decade culminated in the Round Table negotiations of 1989, brought about by yet another wave of strikes in the fall of 1988.

Elite Advancement Policies

Even during the otherwise ideology-bound Stalinist era, the Polish PZPR unofficially tried to enlist the intelligentsia.[72] By 1966, party journal *Trybuna Ludu* argued that "the scientist, the engineer or the doctor, the teacher or the economist are wanted in the party."[73] Within a decade, official Polish party recruitment policies stopped favoring proletarian origins, and party workers became increasingly better educated by the 1970s.[74] Moreover, the party purged far fewer of its members than the Czech party. By the 1970s, a tacit understanding emerged between party members and their leaders, so that the vast majority of party members attended religious services, baptized their children, and even openly joined the opposition.[75]

Even more significantly for their fate after 1989, the Polish party pursued the youth organization leaders. The PZPR was eager to rebuild its cadres and revitalize its image with these young Turks, surprisingly well-educated in politicking and hungry for a chance to exercise their skills. The youth groups underwent several incarnations, with the Socialist Union of Polish Students (Socjalistyczny Związek Studentów Polskich, SZSP) as

---

[70] *Nowe Drogi*, No. 1/2, 1981.

[71] Grzybowski, Leszek. *Milczenie Ideologów*. Warszawa: Krajowa Agencja Wydawnicza, 1985.

[72] AAN AZHP 295/III, 23.11.1948, and AAN 295/II-3 11-12.VII.1945 Plenum KC.

[73] *Trybuna Ludu*, 8 July 1966.

[74] Wasilewski, Jacek. "The Patterns of Bureaucratic Elite Recruitment in Poland in the 1970s and 1980s," *Soviet Studies*, No. 4, 1990: 743–57, p. 747.

[75] This is not to say that the Polish party had not lashed out against internal dissent. In 1981, General Jaruzelski purged both the orthodox and the reformist "wings" in the party. Moreover, the PZPR had earlier made employment and schooling dependent on party loyalties – in 1945, Polish Politburo member Roman Żambrowski argued that no one can get a job without party membership (AAN 295/IV-1). However, he went on to argue that this policy backfired – the people were getting increasingly resentful, while the party gained no political benefit.

the organization that dominated the 1970s and early 1980s. This party youth auxiliary served as both a candidate pool and training ground for future elites in a setting marked less by ideology than by pragmatic problem solving, democratic voting procedures, and political bargaining and coalition forming as the key to attaining leadership roles. Thus, the SZSP's official statutes made it clear that the organization was open to both "believers and non-believers," and the union emphasized learning political and economic skills, such as trade law or political mobilization, rather than Marxist ideology. The party funded the youth organizations as part of the budgets of individual academic institutions, rather than that of a centralized structure, which gave the local organizations considerable autonomy. To advance in the youth organizations, potential leaders had to win secret-ballot elections, form effective coalitions, and subsequently log-roll and horse-trade to achieve their aims as leaders. The regional structure further meant that the future elites would learn how to win successive elections, manipulate coalitions, and achieve higher positions while learning legal and administrative norms.[76] In short, the youth organizations acted as a "school for democracy."[77]

Many of the future party leaders advanced in these parallel organizations. Throughout the 1970s, the leaders of the youth organization moved into lower leadership positions in the party and advanced from there. By 1986, for example, 35% of the first secretaries had been youth organization leaders,[78] and 80% of high-ranking party bureaucrats had belonged to the youth organization in Poland.[79] Extramural advancement became so prevalent that only six out of the twenty-four party Politburo members in 1987 had advanced from within, and even these were more educated,

---

[76] *Rzeczpospolita*, 13–14 April 1996: p. 3. Youth organization members, for example, learned trade laws long before anyone else had, giving them a considerable advantage when the market was liberalized in 1990.

[77] Wilk, Ewa. "Ordynacka rządzi Polską," *Polityka*: 23 December 1995: 20–6. At the same time, the pre-1989 opposition may have received a very different "training." Karol Modzelewski argues that the conspiratorial conditions under which the opposition worked in Poland and in the Czech Republic meant that "taking great personal risks, they develop a special type of loyalty. Conspiracy unites those who struggle together. . . . it was already evident that the most important reference point for Solidarity's leaders was its own political elite rather than their social base among workers." Modelewski 1994: p. 69.

[78] Lewis, Paul. *Political Authority and Party Secretaries in Poland 1975–1986*. Cambridge, UK: Cambridge University Press, 1989: p. 294.

[79] Wasilewski 1990, p. 749–50.

Table 1.5. *Changes in the Polish politburo.*

PZPR	Members and candidates	Number of new members	Percentage of change
1970	16	5	31.2%
1971	15	4	27.0%
1975	16	2	12.5%
1977	16	2	12.5%
1980	19	6	31.6%
1981	17	13	76.5%
1986	19	8	42.1%
1987	19	1	5.0%
1988	22	12	54.5%
Average			32.5%

Source: *Yearbook on International Communist Affairs.* Stanford, CA: Hoover Institution Press, 1966–91.

pragmatic elites, in keeping with the standard set by the youth organization graduates.[80]

Nor did the elites stagnate in their positions. An average of 32.5% of the Politburo leadership changed every year in Poland, over twice the rates of Czechoslovak turnover (see Table 1.5). Moreover, while the removed Czech elites either retired into obscurity or simply died, the Polish elites were part of a constant shifting of personnel from one party position to another. Edward Gierek, the Polish party leader from 1968 to 1980, instituted the "cadre carousel" and constantly "parachuted" appointees from one region to another.

The party also allowed a degree of internal pluralism, even if many in the top elite were often opposed. In response to the rise of Solidarity in 1980, hundreds of Polish party organizations formed networks autonomous of the national leadership (the "horizontal movements") and presented programmatic proposals to the Ninth Party Congress in July 1981. Delegates were largely chosen democratically by their basic organizations, and a real exchange of views took place (as opposed to the standard scripted speeches, dutifully followed by "stormy applause"). The new Central Committee elected by the Congress consisted of a majority of new

[80] Wasilewski, Jacek, ed. *Konsolidacja Elit Politycznych w Polsce 1991–1993.* Warsaw: PAN ISP, 1994.

members, beholden to their constituent rank and file and not to party leaders.[81] Only twenty-one out of the previous two hundred Central Committee members were reelected. At the same time, over 50% of the first secretaries of the basic organizations were changed, as were 38% at the factory, town, and commune levels.[82] Although the horizontal movements were quashed as part of the pacification of society following the imposition of martial law in December 1981, they established the generation of politicians active in democratic Polish politics today.

Faced with more social ferment, the party itself reactivated reform currents: The December 1988 Tenth Plenum specifically encouraged local organizations to aid the party by facilitating reform currents and platforms. As a result, many of these groupings arose locally, but with considerable elite ties. Throughout 1989, over two hundred reformist platforms arose, garnering over 80% of the delegates at the founding congress of the successor in January 1990.[83] The Polish party thus had at its disposal a plethora of options for both organizational strategies and public policy programs.

Nonetheless, these efforts faced two main limitations. First, the Polish party reformists had never organized themselves clearly, or at many levels, prior to the transition. Both ineffectuality and stagnation in the upper echelons of the Polish party, as well as resistance and obstruction at the regional levels, prevented reformists from gaining more power in the party.[84] This was precisely why party leaders (both General Wojciech Jaruzelski and then Mieczysław Rakowski) turned to the mid-level cohort in the 1988–9 negotiations – they were unusually reformist and pragmatic in their orientation, skilled in innovating and implementing party policies, and capable of convincing both colleagues and opponents.

Second, mindful of the repeated conflict with the party, the Polish opposition did nothing to support reform efforts within the communist party. The Polish party members repeatedly revolted against its leadership, but found no support from the ranks of the opposition,[85] the result

---

[81] Hahn, Werner. *Democracy in a Communist Party*. New York: Columbia University Press, 1987, p. 128.

[82] Lewis 1989: p. 132.

[83] *Trybuna Ludu*, 23 June 89, 1 December 89, interview with Sławomir Wiatr, 27 May 1997, Warsaw.

[84] Lewis 1989.

[85] "Kappa." *Partia Stanu Wojennego*. Warsaw: Samizdat, 1984. Available at the National Library, Warsaw, p. 7.

of the antagonism reinforced by 1980–1. As a result, the divide between the former communist party and the former opposition would seem as insurmountable in the 1990s as it was a decade earlier.

Public Policy Reform and Negotiation

The waves of public protests in Poland brought in new leadership teams, each of which had an incentive to establish credibility by responding to the public's demands. From the viewpoint of consumers, the Polish economy was the worst in the region: Constant shortages of basic consumer goods, lengthy queues, and ration cards for basic foodstuffs such as sugar or meat persisted throughout the late 1970s and worsened in the 1980s. Cycles of "reform" economic policies began in the 1960s, designed to increase the supply of consumer goods, lower prices, and reverse the economic decline endemic under the socialist shortage economies.[86] Protests over price hikes in 1970 and in 1976 were followed by relaxed wage policies, and "positive measures were enacted, usually immediately after leadership change or a particularly painful economic failure."[87] The party focused on "large economic organizations" in the reforms of 1972, linking salaries to performance, reducing direct targets, and introducing more flexible pricing. Although this effort was abandoned in 1975, the party continued reforms of producer goods' prices and the reorganization of foreign trade throughout the 1970s. In the 1980s, a series of reforms and concessions followed, to reduce inflation and provide a more rational pricing system. Party economists borrowed from their Hungarian counterparts, as the Polish reforms in the 1980s were based on the New Economic Mechanism (NEM) policies.[88]

In the political realm, quasiliberalization and administrative centralization followed each other. After martial law was instituted on 13 December 1981 to crush Solidarity, the party briefly arrested thousands, instituted

---

[86] Some of the means were less than successful in the longer term: Edward Gierek in 1970s Poland, for example, initially bought off the populace by importing foodstuffs and consumer goods. That he used Western investment loans to do so meant that Poland acquired an enormous foreign debt with little productive means to pay it off.

[87] Brus, Włodzimierz. "Economy and Politics: the Fatal Link," in Brumberg, Abraham, ed. *Poland: Genesis of a Revolution.* New York: Random House, 1983: 26–41, p. 30.

[88] Korboński, Andrzej. "Poland: 1918–1990," in Joseph Held, ed. *The Columbia History of Eastern Europe in the Twentieth Century.* New York; Columbia University Press, 1992: 229–76, p. 264.

curfews, and tightened censorship. However, the party did not engage in the kind of long-term repression favored by the Czechoslovak party.[89] Once martial law was lifted in 1983, new local and national elections were held, in 1984 and 1985. These mandated multiple candidacies, in a modest liberalization, but they never went as far as the Hungarian experiments in political pluralism. Nonetheless, the state began to gain autonomy of its own, and separate its organization, personnel, and policies from the party's.[90]

Mindful of the lessons of 1970 and 1976, when the lack of real consultation prompted a popular uproar over price hikes (consumer prices were unexpectedly raised despite tight wage policies), the Polish party engaged in what it termed "extensive consultation with society." Some informal negotiations followed the 1968, 1970, and 1976 unrests, as the party attempted to coopt the opposition, and the party continued to conduct talks with the Roman Catholic Church. Party efforts to anticipate the popular reaction included the 1987 referendum on further economic reform. Formal negotiations followed both the rise of Solidarity and the wave of strikes that began in August 1988, culminating in the Round Table negotiations. The deep regime divide, however, meant that these negotiations would be conflictual, and did not lead to sustained cooperation between the two camps.

Although they never fully opened up the political space in Poland, and the state-society conflict from 1981 continued to fester, these efforts were an attempt to justify party policies and to make them more palatable. As a result, the Polish communist party mid-level membership entered 1989 with a set of portable skills gained in their years of negotiating with the opposition and their cyclical reform efforts. Its past, in turn, was a record both of the conflict between party and society, but also of administrative reforms and negotiations.

Hungary

The Hungarian Communist Party (Magyar Komuniszta Párt, MKP, subsequently the Magyar Szocialista Munkás Párt, MSzMP)[91] also received

---

[89] Fifteen thousand were arrested in total, and several incidents of police brutality followed.
[90] Ekiert 1996, p. 274.
[91] The party changed its name to the Hungarian Workers Party (MDP) in June 1948, and then again in 1956 to the Hungarian Socialist Workers' Party (MSzMP).

little public support after World War II.[92] It was widely seen as a Soviet import, foreign to Hungarian political traditions.[93] (The Hungarian Communist Party had led the ill-fated and short-lived Hungarian Soviet Republic in 1919, which unleashed an enormous backlash against communism.) Like the KSČ, the Hungarian party competed in free elections after World War II, but received only 16.9% of the vote to the winning Smallholders' Party's 57% in the elections of 1945. The elections themselves were conducted under considerable shadows of doubt. No international supervision was allowed, and only Soviet observers ensured the fairness of the elections. Furthermore, the Soviet military commander in Hungary at the time initially threatened to increase the army presence from six hundred thousand to 3 million and to starve the country unless a favorable result emerged.[94] Subsequently, the Hungarian communists became part of the ruling coalition due chiefly to the presence of the Soviet Army.[95] Backed by Soviet intimidation, the party then resorted to an internecine war of attrition ("salami tactics") within the government coalition to increase the party's share of power and eliminate its coalition partners.

Since its capture of power relied chiefly on Soviet intimidation, coalitional trickery, and elite deception, the party had less use for an extensive and mobilized membership or for organization as the mainstay of its power. There was only one party organization for every 417 Hungarians, a rate that was far lower than in Czechoslovakia. In contrast to the 25.3% of Czech adults who were party members, the Hungarian party membership peaked at 12.3% of the adult population in 1948 (see Table 1.6). Afterwards, the membership declined to an average of 6% of adult Hungarians.

In contrast to the Czech obsession with ideological purity, the Hungarian party purged far fewer members and displayed less concern

---

[92] Even the parties' names are revealing. While the Czech party was known as the Czechoslovak Communist Party, the Polish one was first known as the Polish Workers' Party and then the Polish United Workers' Party, whereas the Hungarian communist party called itself first the Hungarian Workers' Party and then the Hungarian Socialist Workers' Party.

[93] Molnar, Miklós. *From Béla Kun to János Kádár*. New York: St. Martin's Press, 1990, p. 129.

[94] Kovrig, Bennett. *Communism in Hungary*. Stanford, CA: Hoover Institution Press, 1979, pp. 179–80.

[95] As early as fall 1944, the Soviet delegation demanded that the party would be in any and all postwar governing coalitions. Molnar 1990, p. 99. Elections themselves were held only because the Soviets insisted that Hungary fulfill this condition of international recognition. Kovrig 1979, p. 176.

Table 1.6. *Hungarian communist party membership.*

MSzMP	1945	1950	1955	1960	1965	1970	1980	1985
Membership:	2,000 to 220,000	829,000	860,000	498,000	584,000	627,000	810,000	870,000
Percentage of population	2.4%	8.9%	8.6%	5%	5.7%	6.2%	7.6%	8%
Organizations	1,500	9,500	16,500	16,800	18,000	18,000	24,000	25,400
Composition (%)								
Blue collar	42.6%				34.9%	41.7%	35.6%	35.5%
Professional	4.8%				38.2%	38.1%	41.3%	42.4%
Agricultural	39.4%				7.8%	20.0%	6.3%	7.8%
Apparat				11,500		7,000	10,000	7,000
Nomenklatura						10,000	90,000	

Source: Open Society Archives, Free Europe Press, 114.28 file, CEU, Budapest, Kovrig 1979, and Tökés 1996.

with the members' ideological loyalty.[96] Thus, while purges and show trials in Stalinist Hungary were among the most vicious persecutions of party *elites*, they were never matched by a zeal regarding ideological purity of the *members*. To wit, the Czechoslovak party conducted two major purges during the height of the Stalinist period, in 1948–51, which cast out 750,000 members, or 32% of the party membership.[97] The Polish party purged 300,000 members, or 20%. But the Hungarian party purged "only" 179,000 members, amounting to 16% of the membership, during the same period. Only 20.5% of the KSČ members who left did so of their own accord, in contrast with 35% of the Polish members and 42% of the Hungarian departures.[98] Consequently, while party members were purged in Hungary, the rates of (and reasons for) these purges were different from those in Czechoslovakia. The Hungarian party spoke of the "dialectic

[96] This is not to say that the Polish and Hungarian parties were simply hands-off managers without either influence or power. They were in full control of the government, the repressive apparatus, and the military. (The party used all of these to resolve domestic crises, as the Rajk show trials in 1948–9 and the executions of two thousand Hungarians after the 1956 uprising, the shooting of striking workers in 1970 and 1976 in Poland, and the institution of martial law in Poland in 1980 all show.)
[97] Kaplan 1983.
[98] SÚA Fond 02/4 sv 15 aj 20 bod 1. 29.11.1971. These figures include many members who were pressured to "resign." Most of these were blue-collar workers, who had little to fear from party resignations.

impossibility" of reconciling its leading role with mass membership, and limited itself to issuing vague declarations rather than pursuing a committed mass membership.[99]

The regime crisis, when it came in 1956, showed how fragile this organization was, and pointed to further negotiation and reform as an alternative way to build social stability. The 1956 popular uprising was a massive protest against the communist regime. It was violently and rapidly put down by a Soviet invasion. The party, which proved itself unable to control the situation and collapsed from within, dissolved.[100] Once the party refounded itself, a recruitment drive followed, but it paid little attention to the party's composition, and was seen as secondary to rebuilding the security forces.[101] As the newly installed Hungarian leader, János Kádár first pursued a policy of extreme repression, and then advanced a "social contract" of sorts with the society: The provision of consumer goods and a limited political pluralism (whose boundaries expanded with time) were exchanged for societal acquiescence. The party sought to coopt those who might have been a force against it, both by giving the intelligentsia considerable incentives to join and by implementing this "social contract." Hungarian party officials went out of their way to emphasize that expulsion or being struck from the membership lists carried no penalties,[102] and Kádár himself emphasized that the party brought in large numbers of nonparty experts into both the state administration and the economic sphere. The regime divide blurred, as mistrust slowly evolved into a shared recognition of the inherent limitations of the socialist system and its reform.

Elite Advancement Policies

Instead, the party resorted to a cyclical liberalization of economic policies and cautious negotiation with society. To do so, the Hungarian party pursued "technical experts" rather than blue-collar workers. As one scholar summarized, "the MSzMP was indeed extremely successful in incorporating qualified technical experts, professionals, and bureaucrats into the

---

[99] *Partelet*, I. 1973.
[100] See Kovrig 1979 and Molnar 1990.
[101] Kovrig 1979, p. 319.
[102] All the communist parties under consideration made the somewhat Talmudic distinction between being expelled and being struck off from party lists: The latter often entailed fewer sanctions and allowed for (very slim, in the Czech case) possibility of return to the party.

party organization. In contrast, strong ideological control, stringent cadre policies, and persistent anti-intellectual bias underlie the relatively weak effects of education in Czechoslovakia."[103]

Thus, the Hungarian party deliberately pursued the cooptation of the intelligentsia and administrative technocrats, especially in the 1970s and 1980s. It offered considerable incentives to join the party to these groups, whose know-how and experience made them valuable in formulating and implementing the party's reform policies. The more educated the functionary, the higher his or her chances for advancement. After 1956, the party emphasized its recruitment of intelligentsia,[104] as nonparty members were offered grants and positions in higher administration. At the same time, to advance in the Ministry of Interior, Foreign Affairs Ministry, or other important governmental departments, one had to join the party. Party positions were paid very well, and so many nonparty technocrats, who spent the first decade or so of their career in local administration, then made the horizontal move to the far more lucrative party structures. The move was made easier by the lack of stigma attached to party membership, and the minimal requirements made of party members. The result was that, despite occasional crackdowns, the party actually had an over-representation of intellectuals in its ranks, in stark contrast with the KSČ's anti-intellectual bias – by 1989, over half of the Hungarian party members were white-collar workers.[105] In short, the party promoted the rise of non-ideological, experienced professional administrators, who would prove key to its post-1989 development.

The "revolving door" personnel policies of the Hungarian party also meant that the cadres and mid-level elites received a variety of experiences in their advancement and gained considerable flexibility and diversity in their abilities. Kádár was notorious for constantly appointing and reappointing mid-level party leaders to different positions, following a policy of "lateral moves" designed to give the appointees experience in different areas (and to ensure that his power remained consolidated).[106] As a result, the top leadership's annual turnover rates averaged 25% in Hungary, less

---

[103] Wong, Raymond Sin-Kwok. "The Social Composition of the Czechoslovak and Hungarian Communist Parties in the 1980s," *Social Forces*, September 1996: 61–90, pp. 77–8.

[104] O'Neil, Patrick. "Revolution from Within: Institutional Analysis, Transitions from Authoritarianism, and the Case of Hungary," *World Politics*, July 1996: 579–603.

[105] Tőkés, Rudolf. *Hungary's Negotiated Revolution*. Cambridge, UK: Cambridge University Press, 1996, pp. 140–1, 109.

[106] Open Society Archives, Hungary File: Personnel Changes, 4 December 1980, MTI report.

Table 1.7. *Changes in the Hungarian politburo.*

MSzP	Members and candidates	Number of new members	Percentage of change
1965	15	2	13.3%
1970	13[a]	3	23.1%
1974	13	1	7.7%
1975	13	4	30.8%
1980	13	3	23.1%
1985	13	3	23.1%
1986	13	1	7.7%
1987	13	3	23.1%
1988	11	8	72.7%
Average			25%

Note: [a] Candidate memberships abolished after this year.
Source: Yearbook on International Communist Affairs. 1966–91.

than in Poland but significantly higher than in Czechoslovakia (see Table 1.7). Thus, while the top elites in the Politburo averaged fifteen years in office,[107] the mid-level cadres from which the future elites would be drawn were constantly recirculated.

Once the aftershocks from 1956 subsided, the 1962 "alliance policy" announced that "those who are not against us, are for us." Lowering ideological demands of the populace, the policy also allowed more internal party pluralism. Party leaders insisted on the necessity of debates within the local organizations.[108] Party elections were now to be held by secret ballot, the party committees were enjoined to apply resolutions to the local conditions, and "communists in nonparty state and social organizations were instructed to resort to persuasion to implement the party line."[109] The concept of "constructive opposition" was already developed by the late 1960s, and included some pluralism of expression, especially from party auxiliaries such as trade unions. By 1983, competitive elections were held within the party for county-level party secretaries, and in the Academy of Sciences, trade unions, and cooperative farms, with the result that 20% of the officially sponsored candidates were not elected.[110]

[107] Tökés 1996, p. 58.
[108] *Partelet*, June 1982.
[109] Kovrig 1979, p. 355.
[110] White, Stephen. "Economic Performance and Communist Legitimacy," *World Politics*, Vol. 38, No. 3, April 1986: 462–82, p. 473.

As a result, an openly reformist wing of the party leadership had formed by the late 1980s, and found considerable support both within and outside the party.[111] Three separate layers of reformists arose: First, a grassroots movement of local reformists within the party developed. Although well organized, they had no formal access to power. However, they were able to forge alliances with some of the reformers in the party elite (such as Imre Pozsgay), who then acted as their political "godfathers," attending national meetings of the reform movement, speaking out in their favor, and promoting reform ideas. This reform wing within the party leadership itself coalesced by the fall of 1989, forming the second layer of reformers in the party. Third, the diffuse administrative intelligentsia had increasingly become politicized, and turned to reforming the party as a way to preserve their position. As a result, reformists were directly in the seat of power, and they were present at all levels.

By 1987, party leaders agreed the government would leave alone opposition organizations such as the Hungarian Democratic Forum so long as they served the "interests of socialism," at least on paper.[112] Several lower-level party elite members supported these dissident groupings, and even attended their meetings, forming numerous personal ties to opposition leaders and networks of mutual support between party and opposition reformists, in stark contrast to the public suspicion between the two groups in Poland. As a result, the liberals among Hungarian communist successor party could credibly run as reformists and democrats by the first free elections in 1990. Although the center did not encourage reform platforms as actively as the Polish party, seven platforms were present at the founding congress of the successor party in October 1989, each with its own set of policy proposals. The Reformist Alliance, the largest of the lot, claimed a third of the delegates.

Public Policy Reform and Negotiation

The Hungarian party had done the most to implement political and economic reform policies prior to 1989. The party sought to regain social peace through reforms, and had the technocratic cadres to implement these policies after 1956. By 1968, NEM freed up some prices, allowed

[111] Open Society Archives, Judith Pataki, 24 May 1989.
[112] Radio Free Europe Situation Report, 3 June 1988.

enterprise managers greater nominal autonomy, and provided for a more flexible labor market. The party abolished the short-term command system. The bureaucracy continued to decide the entry and exit of firms, selected the managers, and set wages. Market mechanisms, however, decided the output, choice of technology, and many of the prices.[113] NEM was reversed in 1973, but new reforms were introduced in a piecemeal fashion. Subsequent economic liberalization dropped detailed directives, induced incentives for better performance on the local level, and invited local enterprises and coops to draw up their own plans. By 1982, personal income tax was introduced, and the government officially recognized a second, private economy.[114] After the initial recollectivization of agriculture following 1956, cooperatives were once again given autonomy.[115]

These policies were both a response to the 1956 tragedy and to the country's worsening economic conditions in the late 1960s and early 1970s. The cycles of reform and retrenchment also showed responsiveness to societal demands: The second economy boomed throughout this period, and the party did not attempt to erase this capitalist blight. In 1972, as growth slowed down, the party attempted to tighten the agricultural policy, but once this led to shortages and protests, immediately loosened its grip. In its agricultural policies after 1968, the party allowed both autonomy for the cooperative enterprises and a great deal of private entrepreneurship.[116]

In the political sphere, the Hungarian party dabbled with liberalization. From 1966 on, the electoral law provided for multiple candidacies in the single-member parliamentary constituencies.[117] Further liberalization of the national election law in 1983, which mandated multicandidate lists and allowed two independents to enter Parliament, despite the inconsistencies in the electoral system and election fraud.[118] In 1985, the first

[113] Kornai, János. "The Hungarian Reform Process: Visions, Hopes, and Reality," in Nee, Victor, and Stark, David, eds. *Remaking the Economic Institutions of Socialism*. Stanford, CA: Stanford University Press, 1989: 32–94.

[114] Tökés 1996, p. 113.

[115] Korboński 1992.

[116] See Szelenyi, Iván. *Socialist Entrepreneurs*. Madison, WI: University of Wisconsin Press, 1988.

[117] Kovrig 1979, p. 383.

[118] Kis, János. *Politics in Hungary: For a Democratic Alternative*. Boulder, CO: Social Science Monographs, distributed by Columbia University Press, 1989, p. 156.

parliamentary elections with two or more candidates in each district were held – and thirty-five out of the seventy-one unauthorized "spontaneously nominated" candidates were elected.[119] Even more importantly, the 1970s and 1980s saw the growing autonomy of the state from the party structures, unprecedented in the communist world.[120] As a result, the Hungarian party entered the democratic transition with both extensive elite skills and a record of response and reform that helped to minimize the regime divide.

To sum up, the parties continued to implement organizational practices that followed from their capture of power. For the Czechoslovak Communist Party, the trauma of the postwar elections led the party to value stability above all else. The KSČ both counted on its membership to maintain its control and was suspicious of any pluralist overtures. It hence emphasized membership size and purity, denounced reformist efforts, and clamped down on the members after political crises. Having gained legitimacy once, the leadership saw no need to negotiate with society or otherwise demonstrate responsiveness. The irony was that the party with the highest levels of initial political legitimacy became the one to repress its society far more than its counterparts.

In contrast, the parties who rode into power on Soviet tanks and had little legitimacy on their own right were the first to relax repression and to allow some degree of economic and political reform. For the Polish and Hungarian parties, their initial lack of support led to redoubled efforts to gain societal acceptance through constant efforts to demonstrate responsiveness. They thus neither made extensive inroads into society, nor did they have much use for party membership. Instead, they focused on leadership change and policy adjustment. While the reform policies often backtracked before lurching ahead again, the underlying patterns of the party state-society relationship remained. Since there was no initial mass legitimization, these parties constantly bargained with society in an attempt to keep social peace.

The Legacies and Their Results

These organizational practices framed the transition to democracy – they not only determined the elite resources, but the pace of the regime collapse, and the degree to which the transition was negotiated and

---

[119] Tökés 1996, p. 189.
[120] Tökés 1996, p. 155.

gradual. The willingness to respond to society's demands with policy tinkering and societal engagement increased the likelihood of a negotiated transition in 1989, rather than a forced capitulation. In turn, whether the party-state capitulated or engaged in lengthy bargaining gave the party itself additional time in which to adapt itself to the new political system and the demands it would make on the party organization, leadership, and members. Thus, rather than a prolonged transition simply causing party regeneration, the same forces determined both the character of the transition and the party's chances for regeneration. For their part, elite resources determined both the parties' understanding of what had to be done during the transition and of what strategies would best allow the parties to adapt to their changed circumstances. Thus, the more the party had earlier engaged in policy innovation, and the more pragmatist its future elites, the more it understood democracy as competition, and 1989 as the collapse of the regime.

Almost immediately, the differences became apparent. The Czechoslovak Communist Party refused to engage society or its representatives, and consequently did not engage in lengthy negotiations after the dramatic popular upsurge of November 1989, but in crisis control. The party's Extraordinary Congress was held barely a month after the Velvet Revolution, three weeks after the party was summarily removed from power, but long before the June 1990 elections could convince it of the necessity of change. As a result, its rapid capitulation left the party with little time to prepare for a transformation. Given the chaos surrounding the party's capitulation of power in November 1989, many regional delegates to the Extraordinary Congress of the Czech party in December did not even know that the regime had collapsed.

This sequence of events made the presence of strong reform alternatives within the party crucial – and in the Czech party's case, scarce. As we will see in the next chapter, the new party leaders had little to offer beyond the promise of gradual change toward "reform socialism," and no ability to change the party radically. The general secretary from 25 November to 21 December 1989, Karel Urbanek, was a veteran of the party apparat. His successors at the Congress, Vasil Mohorita and Ladislav Adamec, were the heads of the ossified Communist Youth League and the Deputy Prime Minister of the last communist government, respectively. They had few administrative or political skills. The new first secretary, Mohorita had been the chair of the Communist Youth Union, a conservative organization run by the party, and a member of the Central Committee Secretariat.

His youth (he was thirty-seven when he assumed power in the party) was not enough to guarantee a commitment or skill in reform. Meanwhile, new party chair Adamec was a long-time member of the Central Committee and its Presidium, and responded to the events of November 1989 by calling for greater attention to "improving socialism." These new elites, having spent most of their professional lives in the highly orthodox party apparat, could neither envision nor implement a dramatic party transformation.[121]

Since old apparatchiks failed, the party then turned to inexperienced unknowns. The party chair after October 1990, Jiří Svoboda, had been in the party since 1975. A film director, he was also the chair of the Communist Union of Filmmakers. He had earlier been expelled from theatre school for "reformist deviations" in 1963. Svoboda claimed to be a cofounder of the Civic Forum, having been present at its founding, but had few other reformist commitments or administrative experiences. His main qualification was that he was "untainted" by earlier activism in the Communist Party. These leaders could neither envision extensive reform, nor could they implement it.

For the Czech party, 1989 was a replay of the Prague Spring of 1968, and the clear necessity was to defend socialism in face of another onslaught. Given their limited engagement with society prior to 1989, and the firm ideological discipline within their ranks, party elites were unable to articulate a vision of radical transformation. The year 1968 was the one reference point. Even as the government was falling, the conclusion throughout the winter of 1989–90 was that 1989 was another opportunity to *reform* communism.[122] Similarly, for the Czech party leaders, steeped in the tradition of the "true socialist mass party," the advent of democracy meant internal democracy within the party rather than free competition with other parties.

Czech party leaders therefore talked of a "programmatic return to 1968,"[123] and both the party leadership and nascent reformist groupings called on reformist members expelled in 1968 to rejoin the party. As late as the spring of 1990, by which point the party's power had long collapsed

---

[121] Interview with Jaroslav Ortman, 7 November 1996, and interview with Jaromír Sedlak, 5 November 1996, both in Prague.

[122] See the memoirs of Miloš Jakeš (*Dva Roky Generalním Tajemnikem*. Praha: Dokumenty, 1996*)* and Miroslav Šťepan (*Zpoved vězne sametové revoluce*. Praha: grafit, 1991).

[123] Jiří Machalik, the Secretary of the Central Committee of the KSC, *Rudé Právo*, 31 January 1990.

and the Civic Forum now governed in the Government of National Understanding, 1968 was reinterpreted to carry forth the "best communist traditions" and was put forth as the template for party action.[124] Party elites talked of regaining "socialism with a human face," using the slogans of 1968, and the new party guiding document was named "The Action Program," just as the 1968 one had been. However, these calls could not resonate within either the party or the society, given the party's consistent and deliberate rejection of the 1968 reforms in the two decades that followed them. The result was the emphasis on the party and its history to the detriment of new party programs and reorganization, a choice made all the more poignant in light of the party's lack of a usable past, which could have made historical claims valuable.

The Slovak party, like its Czech master, also refused to negotiate with society and similarly capitulated in November 1989. However, it had a ready (if small) pool of reformists at the Marxist-Leninist Institute, and the chaos within the party that surrounded the rapid transition allowed them to enter the party's decision-making structures. Moreover, these new elites gained time to regenerate the party by consistently arguing that the federation with the Czech party was keeping the Slovak wing from developing its potential. During 1990, as the Czech and Slovak conflicts grew, the Slovak party continued to extricate itself from Czech domination, splitting formally by 1991. In so doing, the new party leaders were able to consolidate their internal reform efforts, while arguing to the public that they had always intended greater reform under communism, but were stymied by Czech intransigence.

The future leaders of the Slovak communist party successor, Pavol Kanis and Peter Weiss, entered the public arena through a spirited defense of their party's right to exist, in television debates and press articles during and after the Velvet Revolution. In the process, these leaders gained both publicity and popular approval. As young, well-educated, and personable party members (and since their mentor, a reliable older party member, vouched for them, thus reassuring any remaining old elites), they were the ideal candidates to represent the Slovak party in late 1989. They assumed the leadership on 20 January 1990, joined by other reformists such as Brigita Schmögnerová (from the Institute) and Milan Ftáčnik (from the mathematics faculty of Comenius University in Bratislava). It was under

---

[124] Ladislav Adamec, Party Chair, *Naše Prace*, 17 March 1990.

their direction that the Slovak communist party then adopted its decisions to disassociate itself from the KSČ, change its name, reregister the membership, and reform its image in 1990–1.

Prior to 1989, these Slovak mid-level elites could neither implement policy nor build wider consensus around it, but continued to construct reform policy proposals. As we will see in the next chapters, this lack of experience hurt the elites' ability to compete in democratic politics. They did not appeal to broad groupings in society, nor could they easily persuade the electorate. Nevertheless, their experience in policy innovation made them considerably more pragmatic and cohesive than their older colleagues, convinced them to centralize the party organization immediately, and gave credibility to their reform proposals after 1989.

The Polish and Hungarian parties had few illusions regarding the relevance of party membership as a source of support or the extent of change necessary. Democracy meant *electoral competition*, not internal discussion. Having already been challenged by society, these parties' leaders understood that they were faced with considerable competition as political actors, and that under the new conditions after 1989, this competition was now given free rein. In short, they saw that 1989 was not a change *within* the system but *of* it. Although the parties gave up power reluctantly, they understood that the political changes meant they would have to compete with other political actors and abandon any appeals to continuing the past regime or its practices.

Thus, the Polish and Hungarian parties abandoned any pretense of defending the Marxist ideal. Reformist factions within each party immediately saw 1989 as the opportunity to remake the parties. The slow, lengthy Round Table negotiations of 1989, initiated by the parties themselves (however reluctantly), gave the Hungarian and Polish parties plenty of time in which to prepare for the necessary changes ahead. Those changes occurred at Extraordinary Congresses of October 1989 and January 1990, respectively. The parties took full advantage of this period to formulate strategies of organizational reform and to ensure that they would be implemented.

In addition, these parties did not labor under delusions of popular support. As if the years of social conflict were not enough, the disastrous elections of June 1989 dissipated any doubts the Polish party may have had about its monopoly on public support. Further signals came in September 1989, when the opposition successfully called for further changes in the Round Table agreements (using the opposition activist Adam Michnik's famous formula: "your president, our prime minister"). The party knew that it had very little popular support left and approached its upcoming January 1990 congress accordingly. This reality only reinforced the call made earlier by Polish reformists for the separation of state and party and for the radical transformation of the latter.[125]

As a result of the party's recruitment policies, the new party leadership in 1990 consisted almost exclusively of youth organization alumni.[126] The first leader of the Polish successor party, Aleksander Kwaśniewski, graduated from the youth organization to become the government's minister of youth in the 1980s. Kwaśniewski's career path was typical of his cohort. As a college student, he joined the youth organization. In 1976, he was elected the youth organization's leader at the University of Gdańsk and joined the party a year later. He was then elected to successive ranks of the SZSP leadership, becoming part of the national leadership (1977–82). After the SZSP was dissolved, Kwaśniewski became the editor of the youth organization's weekly and then its daily newspaper. He was picked to become the new minister of youth in the government of Zbigniew Messner (1985–7), where he was also a member of the Olympic Committee. Kwaśniewski continued in the government, becoming a member of the government leadership until September 1989, during the biggest period of unrest and policy pressures. As a government representative in the Round Table negotiations, he chaired the Social and Political Committee. He was thirty-five when he assumed power in the party.

Similarly, Leszek Jaśkiewicz and Jerzy Szmajdziński, two other SZSP leaders, were both elected in secret and direct ballots in 1981 and the late 1980s, respectively.[127] Several postcommunist leaders in Poland, including two prime ministers and the president, were also members, as were numerous ministers, ambassadors, and other leading politicians after 1989.[128]

---

[125] Zbigniew Madej, *Polityka*, 6 August 1988. Jacek Zdrojewski, quoted in *Trybuna Ludu*, 16 January 1989.

[126] The notable exception was Leszek Miller, an ostensible representative of the conservatives within the party.

[127] *Trybuna Ludu*, 27 April 1981.

[128] These include such SdRP and post-1989 government notables as Aleksander Kwaśniewski, Józef Oleksy, Włodzimierz Cimoszewicz, Grzegorz Kołodko, Dariusz Rosati, Marek Borowski, Ryszard Czarny, Marek Siwiec, Jerzy Koźminski, Jerzy

These new leaders had been earlier selected for their political skill and had considerable experience in conceptualizing and implementing reform. They realized the importance of broad support, organizational centralization, and discipline, and had the ability to overcome opposition and convince a reluctant public. At the same time, however, they had to contend with the persistence of the post-1981 divide between party and society, and the charges of betrayal it brought.

In Hungary, radical change was also seen as inevitable. By 1988, one of the Hungarian party leaders had already argued that "no progress is possible without a transformation of the entire structure of socialism," and the first of these moves would be the separation of party and state.[129] The Hungarian party also had the benefit of mutual support between party and opposition reformists as a result of the party's liberal policies.[130] By February 1989, even the party's ruling elite acknowledged that the party had to "face up to a new situation, in which participation in policy-making depended not only on the party."[131] A month later, the Hungarian Central Committee admitted the necessity of a multiparty system and other political liberalization.[132]

The Hungarian elites were perhaps the most qualified and experienced. The forefront of the reformists, Miklós Németh, Imre Pozsgay, and Rezsô Nyers (the prime minister and the ministers of state), were all experienced administrators. The post-1990 leader of the Hungarian party, Gyula Horn, was the foreign minister in the late 1980s. In his ascent to the party leadership in 1990 at the relatively young age of fifty-eight, Horn followed a path typical of the mid-level elites of the Hungarian Communist Party. After graduating from the Don-Rostov College of Economics and Finance in 1954, he became a senior clerk in the Ministry of Finance, joining the

Szmajdziński, Bogusław Liberadzki, Jerzy Kropiwnicki, Stefan Olszowski, Hieronim Kubiak, and Manfred Gorywoda. A related source of party cadres was the Central School of Planning and Statistics (Szkoła Główna Planowania i Statystyki, SGPiS), which produced such future government leaders as Leszek Balcerowicz, Dariusz Rosati, Grzegorz Kołodko, and Andrzej Olechowski. The SZSP youth organization was especially powerful at the SGPiS.

[129] *Radio Free Europe Situation Reports*. Imre Pozsgay, cited 2 May 1988.

[130] "Kappa." *Partia Stanu Wojennego*. Warsaw: Samizdat, 1984, p. 7.

[131] János Berecz, quoted in Open Society Archives: Hungary: Party: Local File, 7 February 1989.

[132] *Radio Free Europe Situation Reports*, 22 March 1989. Károly Grósz was quoted as saying that the party "wanted to participate in politics not from a position of dominance, but in competition with others, and would assume the role of a ruling party only if it won the support of a majority of the population."

party later that year. Advancing in the government ranks to increasingly responsible positions at the Ministry of Foreign Affairs, he served as a diplomatic attaché and then an embassy diplomat. He then made the horizontal move to the party leadership, advancing in 1969 to the mid-level position of the head of the International Relations Department at the party. From there, he became the under-secretary for foreign affairs. Moving again to the government, he became the minister of foreign affairs in 1988, personally opening the border for the first time (snapping the barbed wires himself) and allowing thousands of East Germans to escape to the West. The one blot on this résumé was his role in the revolutionary uprising of 1956 – Horn was a member of the party militia groups that helped to put down the popular revolution.

Other new Hungarian party representatives had similarly high experience in government and in administration. Of the forty-three representatives of the MSzP in the first freely elected Hungarian parliament, five were former ministers and three were former state secretaries. Given their administrative reform experience as mid-level communist elites (state positions were second in rank to equivalent jobs in the party), these new elites were well positioned to transform the party, and had the skills and experience to do so. Moreover, they had at their disposal the most favorable usable past in the region: a record of the "social contract" between society and a relatively responsive party.

Therefore, as the parties geared up for their last congresses as communist parties, at which their regenerative strategies would be decided, they had at their disposal distinct configurations of both elite portable skills and usable pasts. As a result, the Czech party relied on its members and a relatively tired ideology, because it had few skilled elites or reform experience and a limited usable past. The Slovak party had a set of skilled new elites, but these had only untested policy proposals and little administrative know-how. The Polish party relied on its youthful elites and their earlier politicking experience, while the Hungarian party had not only a set of experienced, skilled elites, but also a usable past of political and economic liberalization. As we will see in the next chapter, these configurations would determine the success of the parties' adaptive strategies.

Conclusion: Communist Legacies Reexamined

The three communist organizational practices examined in this chapter – elite advancement, policy reform, and negotiation with the opposition

– had wide-ranging effects. They not only affected the paths these parties would take in 1989, by influencing the trajectories of regime collapse and the transition to democracy, but they established the elite skills and usable pasts with which the parties would pursue regeneration.

Patterns of elite recruitment and advancement had the most direct influence on the cohorts of elites that would progress in the parties and become the new party leadership in 1989. The more the party recruited from the outside, recirculated its elites, and allowed a measure of internal party pluralism, the greater the chances that pragmatic, experienced individuals could ascend in the party. These sorts of elites were most likely to be able to transform the parties in 1989. Ironically, then, the same policies of lax ideological standards and cooptation of the capable that allowed the parties to rule as monopolists also enabled the parties to transform and compete successfully when democracy arrived.

The innovation and implementation of public policies produced further elite resources. Policy innovation reinforced the importance of cohesion and streamlining, without which ideas could neither be disseminated nor implemented. Implementing policy reforms gave the elites skill in overcoming internal opposition, and gave them the rhetorical tools and experience in convincing opponents and building coalitions. Even if these reforms did not prevent the economic slide or the popular resentment against the parties' political monopoly, they gave the mid-level elites valuable experience in building internal consensus, publicly defending policy, persuading a reluctant society, and overcoming administrative hurdles. Since the economies of all these countries experienced their biggest downturn in the 1980s, the pressures for policy reform were then at their greatest. Those elites who withstood these imperatives to restructure would also resist the pressures to transform themselves in 1989. Negotiation with the opposition and society enabled the party elites to respond to public concerns and emphasized building broad public coalitions. The less adversarial this relationship, the more widely accepted the communist successor parties after 1989. Thus, these recent experiences in administration and politicking were readily portable to the new institutional setting after 1989.

Hence, these legacies of communism were not merely the logical preconditions for party transformation. By fostering flexibility and innovation, they enlarged the set of possible strategic options and promoted greater skill in making and implementing organizational decisions. The more versatile the elites, the more choices they had regarding organizational form, program orientation, electorates to be addressed, and so on.

This analysis suggests two broader points regarding *ancien regime* legacies and their effects. First, the legacies were replicated not through inertia but through deliberate action. Party politicians used party history both in its symbolic dimensions and as a template for further action. Older party leaders advocated the rise of the very men they had promoted earlier. Past developments were used to justify actions to party members and to the broader polity, as political leaders claimed they were reasserting the true character of their parties. Programmatic alternatives developed earlier were now the template for the new party programs. Thus, attitudes and practices were not simply replicated because alternatives were difficult to envision, expensive, and increasingly so.[133] Dominant groups within organizations also actively sought to reproduce the legacies and entrench themselves.

Second, disaggregating the legacies of communism into specific patterns of elite advancement, policy innovation, and societal negotiation also moves us beyond the assertion that "history matters" and instead shows us precisely *how* it did so. Even a collapsed and discredited regime leaves behind legacies that may not be readily visible, but that nevertheless exert a powerful influence on political development. Disaggregation also shows us *when* and *why* a given legacy stops influencing political developments – when it is no longer the "cheapest" way to orient decision making, as the new policies it has set into motion consolidate and are established enough to exert their own influence. Differentiating among the various inheritances of the communist era thus allows us to trace the dynamics of the linkages between two supposedly discrete regimes and eras.

As we will see in the next chapters, the elite resources produced by the communist organizational practices determined the extent and pace of the organizational transformation of the parties, the credibility of their

---

[133] See Pierson, Paul. "Increasing Returns, Path Dependence, and the Study of Politics," *American Political Science Review*, June 2000: 251–67. Arthur, Brian. *Increasing Returns and Path Dependence in Economy.* Ann Arbor, MI: University of Michigan Press, 1994. North, Douglass. *Institutions, Institutional Change, and Economic Performance* Cambridge, UK: Cambridge University Press, 1990. Steinmo, Sven, Thelen, Kathleen, and Longstreth, Frank, eds. *Structuring Politics: Historical Institutionalism in Comparative Analysis* (Cambridge, UK: Cambridge University Press, 1992).

electoral appeals, and the cleavages that continued to drive democratic competition and cooperation after 1989. Thus, these legacies of communism heavily influenced both the method, pace, and content of party transformations, and the relative success of these strategies in the parties' transition to democracy.

2

Breaking with the Past, Reorganizing for the Future

Even with the advantages of elite political resources, party regeneration was far from inevitable. It required an enormous transformation of the communist parties' organizations from tools of authoritarian rule to instruments of democratic competition. Once they were forced out of power, these parties now had to signal their new intentions, obtain strategic flexibility, and steel themselves for further programmatic, electoral, and parliamentary transformation. To that end, early and rapid centralization of the organization and a symbolic break with the past were crucial. One resulting irony was that success in democracy often involved profoundly undemocratic organizational means: weakening or eliminating party membership, abolishing internal debates, and reducing local autonomy.

Organizational transformation was a response to the parties' radically changed circumstances. The more the parties were discredited, and the greater the opposition they faced, the bigger the change required, both to function in a democracy and to convince the public of the parties' new intentions. The regime collapse and the parties' chaotic exit from power led to both administrative turnover and a clear signal of a dramatic change in the status quo, allowing change in policy and within organizations (Kingdon 1984). However, the communist parties first had to extricate themselves from tangled webs of organizational structures, which were as unwieldy as they were vast (see Table 2.1).

There were three main reasons for this organizational sprawl throughout the communist era. First, the parties held a monopoly on legislative, executive, and judicial decisions and administration. Second, the structures of the parties duplicated those of the state – the real center of power lay in the communist party departments that corresponded to the government ministries, multiplying the party bureaucracy. Finally, in an attempt to

Table 2.1. *Communist party organizations by 1988.*

Party	Members	Local cells	Central party employees	Nomenklatura (positions vetted by party)	Bureaucratization (ratio of party bureaucrats to member s in 1985)
Czech KSČ	1,250,000	35,000	10,500	550,000	1 to 119
Slovak KSS	450,000	12,500	3,000	21,000	1 to 150
Polish PZPR	2,100,000	75,000	12,000	270,000	1 to 175
Hungarian MSzMP	870,000	25,400	5,800	90,000 central 350,000 advisory	1 to 150

Source: "Informace o stavu členské zakladny a základních organizací, klubů, v KSČS k 30.6.1990," ÚV KSS Sekretariat Files, Bratislava. Henzler, Marek. "Drabina," *Polityka,* 14 May 1988; *Rocznik Statystyczny.* Warsaw: GUS, 1989 and 1990, and Open Society Archive, Party Life, and Personnel Files, Budapest.

coopt the population, the communist parties functioned much like amorphous mass parties, with large memberships, welfare services, and auxiliary organizations.

After 1989, such strategies of "mass incorporation" were no longer tenable. First, the new democratic governments outlawed party organizations in the workplace and obliterated the duplicate party-state structures. The parties had to renounce both their symbolic "leading role" in society and their executive organizations, such as their militia.[1] Second, without access to patronage networks and enormous state funding, the parties could not afford to retain their massive bureaucracies and auxiliary organizations. Third, the parties had to signal their new intentions credibly and consistently to potential voters and coalition partners, and the more the old organizational forms were retained, the less credible these signals. Nor, as it turned out, could the old organizational forms sustain the strategic flexibility or further transformations needed for party regeneration.

Given these incentives, each party under consideration attempted to modify its organizational structures. The substance of organizational transformation consisted of four key decisions: the entrance of new elites into the party leadership, the extent to which these leaders pursued centralization, the party's break with its past, and the pace of these transformations. The direction and scope of these changes depended on both the new elites' portable skills and the kind of usable past the elites had at their disposal.

Elite Turnover

First, organizational transformation required that skilled and change-minded elites would take over power in the parties. Strong and capable leadership has been found in other cases to lead to a change in the party structure and new party identity.[2] Elite abilities mattered more than either the elites' relative categorization as "standpatters," "liberal reformers," and "democratic reformers" (Ishiyama 1995) or their ideological commitment.

---

[1] The Hungarian party gave up its leading role during the Extraordinary Congress on 6 October 1989, while the Czechoslovak party did so on 29 November 1989, the East German on 1 December 1989, the Polish on 29 December 1989, and the Bulgarian on 15 January 1990. The parties disbanded their militia as follows: Hungarian on 20 October 1989; Polish on 23 November 1989; Bulgarian on 25 November 1989; East German on 17 December 1989; and Czechoslovak on 21 December 1989.

[2] Kopecký, Petr. "Developing Party Organizations in East-Central Europe," *Party Politics*, Vol. 1, No. 4, 1995: 515–35, p. 521.

Table 2.2. *Bureaucratic attrition and elite turnover during the transition.*

	Party bureaucracy: the apparat in 1990–8	1990–8 apparat in 1988%	New elites in top party leadership in 1989%
KSČM	180	1.7%	95.8%
SDL'	100	3.0%	96.8%
SdRP	110	.9%	94.7%
MSzP	300	5.2%	84.8%

Source: Interviews with Peter Magvaši, 27 January 1997, Bratislava; Jozef Heller, Prague; György Földes, 25 March 1997, Budapest; and Dariusz Klimaszewski, 12 May 1997, Warsaw. *Polityka*, 10 February 1990.

First, such categories are fluid: Not only do they change their relative meaning depending on the temporal and political context, but many party leaders fell into different categories over time, depending on the issue involved. Second, strong ideological commitments were both fleeting and rare, especially where the parties had engaged in negotiation and reform. And, without concomitant political skill, even the most committed reformists could achieve little, as we will see. Instead, the cumulative skills, experiences, and pragmatism of the new elites, gained earlier in the communist parties, allowed them both to envision and to implement transformation.

For their part, many of the old party leaders had little chance of staying on. The chaos and rapid changes of the transition meant that the old elites were discredited and largely helpless. Their power on the decline, many feared potential repercussions for their role in maintaining the authoritarian system. Many resisted change and were consequently forced out of the parties.[3] As a result, as Table 2.2 shows, the transition to democracy was also a time for a bureaucratic exodus and massive elite turnover in the parties.

The new elites thus had unprecedented opportunities and enormous amounts of discretionary power during 1989–90. Both within the parties and in the broader transitional environment, politics focused almost

[3] As Pauline Jones Luong argues, elites tend to support innovation where they perceive their relative power to be increasing, and resist changing the status quo and its distribution of power where they perceive their power to be declining. Jones Luong, Pauline. *Institutional Change and Political Continuity in Post-Soviet Central Asia: Power, Perceptions, and Pacts.* Cambridge, UK: Cambridge University Press, forthcoming.

72

exclusively on the level of the national elites, who both made the initial bargains in the democratic transition and then enforced them.[4] Moreover, the postcommunist elites, along with only a few of the opposition elites, were the most experienced politicians and administrators in the country.[5] Their cohort dominated at all levels of the parties: executive committees, parliamentary representation, and regional bodies. Their resulting consolidation of power had such lasting impact that where the parties regenerated, the same set of leaders who advanced in 1989 continued to lead the parties a decade later.

Centralization

How these new elites would take advantage of these opportunities depended on their portable skills and experiences. Their first two tasks during 1989–90 were to centralize the party organizations and to break with the past decisively – by changing the party's name, program, symbols, and public representatives. Capable and experienced elites made centralization far more likely to begin early and to succeed. Party centralization itself consisted of a) streamlining the party by getting rid of intermediate party layers, multiple sources of decisions, and overlapping authorities within the party, and b) vertical integration, or establishing a hierarchy of control dominated by the top elite.

As such, this post-1989 centralization differed from the fabled "democratic centralism" and the hierarchy of decision making in the communist parties, in two critical aspects. First, the parties no longer had to contend with overlapping roles and extensive organizations – such as the double administration of both the state and the party, the various auxiliary groups, and so on. They were free to function as parties qua democratic competitors and potential governors, not as political monopolists. Even when they subsequently allied themselves with trade unions or other political actors after 1989, the successor parties could control these alliances because of their superior access to votes and to power. Second, the parties were now free to establish their own hierarchy of power, instead of contending with the rule from above by the Soviet communist party and the structures that

---

[4] Ekiert, Grzegorz. "Peculiarities of Post-Communist Politics: The Case of Poland," *Studies in Comparative Communism*, December 1992: 341–61, p. 353. Racz, Barnabas. "The Socialist-Left Opposition in Hungary," *Europe-Asia Studies*, No. 4, 1993: 647–70: p. 650.

[5] Interview with Gustaw Herling-Grudziński, *Wprost*, 7 September 1997. Zielonka, Jan. "New Institutions in the Old Bloc," *Journal of Democracy*, Winter 1994: 87–104, pp. 92–3.

it established (which frequently had been sources of obstruction and resistance to the implementation of various policies).

Streamlining could minimize the various constituencies and factions that made it more difficult to pursue coherent electoral strategies, respond to the broader electorate, or appear united and effective. These barriers to transformation existed on several levels within the party, ranging from the individual orthodox leaders and regional party offices, to committed party members, to opinion platforms. Old regional and local leaders within the party feared losing their socioeconomic status and, often, the livelihood that came with a party position. The less convertible their skills, the less likely they were to favor party transformation. Orthodox ideologues could crowd out the pragmatists, discourage new ones from joining, and, given power, squelch reform. The party membership, its size and power within the party, presented another possible problem.[6] Reducing the influence of the rank and file and of internal dissent greatly facilitated party transformation in other parties, such as the Spanish PSOE and in the Italian PCI.[7] Finally, opinion platforms fomented reformist ideas and promoted greater party transformation *prior* to the Extraordinary Congresses. *After* the Congresses, however, the extent to which they were given access to decision making was inversely related to the consolidation of elite power and party reform. If left to persist in the party, these barriers could brake further party transformation.

For its part, vertical integration could bring party decision making under the new elite's control, leading to both greater efficiency in implementing party decisions and to greater dependence of all party representatives on the central leadership. Otherwise, the larger the organization, the weaker the control exercised by the leadership.[8] Openly competing views or diffuse decision making within the party could increase uncertainty for other parties and for voters attempting to evaluate the communist successor party's new stances and image. Moreover, vertical integration would reinforce other party policies, including reform, since it increases the impact of its leaders and their decisions.[9]

---

[6] Hellman, Stephen. *Italian Communism in Transition*. Oxford, UK: Oxford University Press, 1988. Kopecký, 1995, p. 521.

[7] Gillespie, Richard. *The Spanish Socialist Party: A History of Factionalism*. Oxford, UK: Clarendon Press, 1989, p. 301. See also Hellman, Stephen. *Organization and Ideology in Four Italian Communist Federations*. PhD. dissertation, Yale University, 1973, p. 260.

[8] Downs, Anthony. *Inside Bureaucracy*. Prospect Heights, IL: Waveland Press, 1994.

[9] Aldrich, Howard. *Organizations and Environments*. Englewood Cliffs: Prentice Hall, 1979, p. 19.

While no single organizational model guarantees success, centralized "electoral" parties[10] have had considerably higher strategic flexibility. Elsewhere, centralization promoted efficiency in seeking votes and in formulating coalitions, and reduced the costs of decision making for the party.[11] Conversely, the more numerous the organizational layers that would decide party policy, the longer it to could take the party to respond to the changing environment.[12] The greater the lag in the response, in turn, the more the competitors could take advantage of the lags in the party's response.

Moreover, patterns of adaptation to changing political contexts of the West European social democratic parties further suggest that the more robust the party competition,[13] the greater the value of centralized organization.[14] Where parties sought to maximize votes, they could ill afford to pander to policy-oriented members and activists.[15] Increased political competition demanded rapid flexibility: The more parties competed on the national level, with multimember districts (and national party lists), national media campaigns, state funding of parties, and fluid

---

[10] Political parties are categorized on the basis of their goals – office, policy, votes, or internal democracy – and the means with which they pursue these goals – ideology, members, media campaigns, or alliances with auxiliary organizations. Several "ideal types" have arisen: the *mass party*, with its pursuit of offices and policy that delivers material incentives to its members, using member mobilization and class-based ideology as electoral tools; the lean *electoral party*, with its pursuit of votes via media campaigns with minimal use of ideology or members; and the hybrid *"catch-all" party*, the result of a welfarist policy consensus that undercut class-based voting, with its large memberships but lack of clear-cut ideology, alliances with external actors such as unions, not seeking specific policies or socially based constituencies but votes and office. See also, Koole Ruud, "Cadre, Catch-all, or Cartel? A Comment on the Notion of the Cartel Party," *Party Politics*, No. 4, 1996: 507–23, and especially pp. 520–1.

[11] Strom, Kaare. "A Behavioral Theory of Competitive Political Parties," *American Journal of Political Science*, Vol. 34, No. 2, May 1990, p. 577.

[12] Kitschelt, Herbert. *The Transformation of European Social Democracy*. Cambridge, UK: Cambridge University Press, 1994, p. 212. Panebianco, Angelo. *Political Parties: Organization and Power*. Cambridge, UK: Cambridge University Press, 1988. Sjöblom, Gunnar. "Political Change and Political Accountability," in Daalder, Hans, and Mair, Peter, eds. *Western European Party Systems*. London: Sage Publications: pp. 370–403. Strom 1990.

[13] That is, the greater the number and strength of parties that could reasonably hope to achieve office: for example, where there is one strong party and dozens of fragmented and narrowly supported parties, the competition is not particularly robust.

[14] Kitschelt 1994, p. 231. Gunther, Richard, Sani, Giacomo, and Shabad, Goldie. *Spain After Franco: The Making of a Competitive Party System*. Berkeley, CA: University of California Press, 1988, pp. 409–10. See also Hellman 1988.

[15] Tsebelis, George. *Nested Games*. Berkeley, UK: University of California Press, 1990.

electorates, the smaller the chance of electoral success for decentralized parties.[16]

These were the same conditions encountered in the countries under examination: All had multimember districting and national party lists, competition took place on the national level, and all received some form of state subventions. Party competition was characterized by the primacy of parliamentary representation and low popular identification with parties.[17] The democratic transition had also demobilized the electorate, and parties "floated" above society.[18] Thus, in the posttransition context, parties had neither the incentives nor the resources to slowly build up loyal, specific constituencies. Given such contexts, we can hypothesize that in East Central Europe after 1989, streamlined and vertically integrated parties would be better able to pursue voters effectively, even if they forsook extensive networks of members and organizations.

For parties to benefit from centralization in both elections and in the parliament, however, their new elites had to have skill and experience in responding to societal demands. Otherwise, centralization could lead to insulation from critical electoral and parliamentary signals, if elites were unable to read and to respond to them. Moreover, organizational centralization per se required considerable administrative skill – in a newly centralized party, an already strained center would assume additional responsibilities for the running of the parliamentary bureau and of the regional organizations, while risking member alienation and accusations of nondemocratic practices.

Elites with extensive portable skills in policy innovation and negotiation would be more likely to pursue successfully a centralized party model. The more skilled and experienced these new elites, the less they had to rely on other political party assets – such as party members, local organizational presence, or extensive activist networks – to build their power

---

[16] Von Beyme, Klaus. *Political Parties in Western Democracies*. Aldershot, UK: Gower, 1985, p. 171.

[17] For example, 68% of Poles polled saw no local party activity, due to the shift of party political activity to Warsaw (*Rzeczpospolita*, 28–9 August, 1993). See also Ekiert, Grzegorz. "Democratization Processes in East Central Europe: Theoretical Reconsiderations," *British Journal of Political Science*, July 1991: 285–313. Lomax, Bill. "Impediments to Democratization in East-Central Europe," in Wightman, Gordon, ed. *Party Formation in East Central Europe*. Aldershot, UK: Edward Elgar, 1995, p. 121. Körösényi, András. "Stable or Fragile Democracy? Political Cleavages and Party System in Hungary," *Government and Opposition*, Winter 1993: 87–104, p. 96. See also Ware, Alan. *The Logic of Party Democracy*. London: MacMillan, 1979.

[18] Racz, 1993, p. 650.

within the party or to gain a popular support base. Their parties could then retain both local mobilization efforts and alliances with unions and civil society organizations, but did not have to rely on them – and, as we will see, could easily shed these alliances at will, as the SdRP did in 1999 and the MSzP did in 1998. In fact, all the parties under consideration had more extensive memberships and organizational networks than their competitors (see Table 2.3). However, they *relied* on these only where they had few other political assets, such as responsive programs, attractive candidates, or appealing electoral campaigns. As a result, these parties grew to resemble catch-all parties found in Western Europe, with their still-sizeable but inactive memberships, centralized organization, and, as we will see, cross-cutting appeals and vague ideology.

In contrast, parties with fewer elite assets were more likely to retain the more decentralized, member-heavy organization. As Martin Shefter has argued, the fewer financial or political resources of a given party, the greater its reliance on mass memberships.[19] Such parties, dependent on loyal members and activists as they are, would risk losing these supporters (without necessarily attracting new ones) if they changed their policies or programs. With few assets and less hope of attracting a broad electorate, these elites could instead attempt to maximize existing supporter loyalty. As a result, they would be more likely to retain existing party organizations, symbols, and appeals, without breaking either with the organizational forms or the symbolic past treasured by their supporters. The resulting party organization resembled that of the mass integration parties found in Western Europe, with their reliance on a large and active membership for voter mobilization, more decentralized leadership, narrowly based appeals, and relatively coherent (if often unpopular) ideology.

Breaking with the Past

Centralization was the structural side of party metamorphosis, but this rebirth also consisted of a symbolic aspect. Breaking with the past consisted of denouncing the symbolic dimension of the party identity: its name, symbols, and historical justifications. Although the communist experience was a source of portable elite skills and a usable past, most of the parties' past forms and actions had outlived whatever usefulness and

---

[19] Shefter, Martin. *Political Parties and the State: The American Experience*. Princeton, NJ: Princeton University Press, 1994.

Table 2.3. *Party memberships and local organizations, 1992–9.*

Czech parties	Members	Local cells
KSČM	200,000	6,900
ČSSD	18,000	1,500
KDU-ČSL	80,000	2,240
ODA	2,500	200
ODS	22,000	1,400
SPR-RSČ	55,000	2,000

Source: Party interviews, spring 1999 and fall 1996. *Hospodarské Noviny,* 2 December 1995.

Slovak parties	Members	Local cells
SDĽ	35,000	2,000
HZDS	45,000	2–3,000
DU	5,000	200
KDH	28,000	2,000
SNS	7,600	1,500

Source: Party interviews, spring 1999 and winter 1997.

Polish parties	Members	Local cells
SdRP	60,000	2,400
PSL	200,000[a]	2,000
UW	20,000	375
ZChN	6,000	26 regional[b]
KPN	19,000	175

[a] These figures may be exaggerated, since the party retained its pre-1989 membership rolls.
[b] No register of local organizations is available.

Source: Party interviews, spring 1999 and summer 1997. *Wprost,* 21 March 1993.

Hungarian parties	Members	Local cells
MSzP	40,000	2,500
SzDSz	16–34,000	759
Fidesz	15,000	325
MDF	27,000	820
FKGP	50–60,000	N/A
KDNP	28,000	885

Source: Lomax, Bill. "The Structure and Organization of Hungary's Political Parties," in Lewis, Paul, ed. *Party Structure and Organization in East-Central Europe,* Cheltenham, UK: Edward Elgar, 1996.

legitimacy they once had. Denouncing former misdoings and crimes signaled to both current and potential supporters that the party recognized why it was so discredited, and that it acknowledged responsibility for its history. Breaking with the past could be taken as far as the dissolution of the party, which led to greater party unity and elite consolidation (since the new members and organizations would have to commit their support to the new leadership).

However, if it alone represented the party's efforts to transform, breaking with the past could lead to charges of the party trying to get away with making opportunistic changes that were not credible or sustainable.[20] For outside observers, if unaccompanied by organizational centralization, self-criticism and denunciations of past organizational forms were little more than a smoke screen and a cynical attempt to regain support without fundamentally changing. For the party members, such renunciation could be perceived as a denial of their accomplishments and the ideology to which they were loyal for so many years. For their part, dissolution or member reregistration was likely to decimate the membership, and thus would eliminate the parties' ability to mobilize support on the ground through local organizations and member volunteers – a ready pool of supporters, who would also mobilize the vote in labor-intensive but inexpensive campaigning. Therefore, breaking with the past was a counterproductive strategy for parties that either depended on or wished to retain their members and immediate circle of supporters.

The more a party had earlier refused to transform public policy or enter into negotiations, the more it needed to break with the past and centralize, to signal change and to gain the flexibility necessary to change its unpopular stances. However, the practices of policy stagnation and the failure to negotiate with the opposition also gave rise to limited elite skills and experiences. This lack of skill in turn meant a lower likelihood of either a break with the past or centralization, as such elites turned to the party members and organizational continuity to compensate. The ironic result was that the more tainted the party's past, and the greater the necessity of a break, the less likely the party was to apologize for this history.

Where the parties were able to break symbolically with the past, they signaled a readiness to change their political methods and outlooks. They

[20] Wiatr, Jerzy. "From Communist Party to 'The Socialist-Democracy of the Polish Republic'," in Kay Lawson, ed., *How Political Parties Work: Perspectives from Within*. Westport, CT: Praeger, 1994.

were also able to offer reformist party members at least some guarantee that the orthodox communists would not dominate. Where the parties did not break with the past, not only did they become weaker competitors, but this disadvantage was further reinforced – militants are more likely to advance in parties that are weak competitively, where past moderation has not helped the party, or where the party is ignored or ostracized.[21]

The Timing of Transformation

These changes had to come quickly, early, and in a specific sequence to make party regeneration more sustainable and more credible. Thus, in contrast to many existing explanations, which view change as linear, equally feasible at any point in the organization's history, and unaffected by sequencing, the regeneration of the communist successors suggests instead that the timing and ordering of party transformation matters as much as the decision to implement it.[22] There were some very practical reasons for early change: The parties had to present a new program and as new an image as possible, in order to survive in elections. Even the most obstinate party optimists noticed the fate of the Polish party, which went unchanged to the June 1989 polls and lost every seat it could in that country's semifree elections. Moreover, early transformation was both camouflaged and justified by the chaos of the regime transition. If transformation occurred later, however, it was more likely to be seen as a "whitewash," or a naked grab for power driven by electoral exigencies and precious little commitment to reforming the party's role or redeeming its past.

Early changes proved to be the most decisive, given their self-reinforcing nature. First, the initial choices of organizational strategy, and consequently the political resources on which the party would rely, determined the available set of future party strategies. Organizational transformation involved large setup costs and self-fulfilling "adaptive expectations," further making it subject to such feedback effects.[23] Second,

---

[21] Kitschelt, Herbert. "The Law of Curvilinear Disparity Revisited," *Political Studies*, 1989a: 400–21, p. 407.

[22] Scholars have argued that early action was crucial to the *rise* of parties (Shefter 1994, p. 31. "Introduction," in LaPalombara, Joseph, and Weiner, Myron, eds. *Political Parties and Political Development*. Princeton, NJ: Princeton University Press, 1972 [1966]). However, this argument has not been made regarding party *transformation*.

[23] Pierson 2000.

these early actions also allowed the newly ascendant elites in the parties to assume their places and consolidate their power, and prevent the resurgence of orthodox rivals. Third, the parties also built their new reputations on early elite decisions – as we will see in the next chapters, the earlier the transformation, the greater the opportunities for sustained and consistent signaling of the parties' new commitments.

Sequencing the transformations proved equally important. Once the new elites got into power, they had to concurrently break with the past and transform the party organizations *before* they attempted to change either the programs or the electoral appeals of the party. There were two reasons to do so. First, without organizational streamlining, orthodox activists or members could contradict the appeals of reformist elites, resulting in inconsistent and heterogeneous signals to the electorate and to other parties. Second, where powerful opponents to reform remained in the party, they could defeat party regeneration, by sabotaging leadership decisions, mobilizing dissent within the party, or refusing to implement leadership decisions. Such opposition could cause the parties to backslide into outdated appeals and inflexible stances, as was the case with the Czech party. In short, the "when" of party regeneration affected its "how," in Charles Tilly's felicitous phrasing.[24]

Therefore, the Extraordinary Congresses, held in the fall and winter of 1989–90, were the crucial moments at which the most important of the new decisions would be made. For the communist middle-level elites themselves, the Extraordinary Congresses were an enormous opportunity to advance in the party organizations and put forth new policies. Those elites with experience in reform and negotiation already knew how discredited and in need of change both the political system and the parties had become. The more skilled they were, the more they moved to change party organizations and consolidate their reform programs. In contrast, less skilled party elites moved more cautiously and gradually, changing the party as little as possible and retaining much of the old structures. The differences among the new elites' implementation of party centralization, break with the past, and decisiveness of the changes are summarized in Table 2.4.

The following sections examine each party in turn and how its elite resources allowed the new leaders to answer the first challenges of

---

[24] Tilly, Charles. *Big Structures, Large Processes, Huge Comparisons*. New York: Russell Sage, 1984, p. 14.

Table 2.4. *Summary of organizational transformation.*

	Czech KSČM	Slovak SDĽ	Polish SdRP	Hungarian MSzP
Centralization	Minimal	Very high	Very high	High
Membership:				
1989	1,250,000	450,000	2,100,000	870,000
1992	200,000	45,000	60,000	40,000
1999	125,000	28,000	60,000	40,000
Break with the past	Minimal	Medium: unable to dissolve the party	Medium: did not apologize for the recent past	Very high: apologized for all of the communist past
Timing of transformation	Delayed	Immediate	Immediate	Immediate

regeneration: rapidly and decisively centralizing the party organization, and breaking with the discredited elements of its past. As we will see, these strategies produced new electoral and parliamentary opportunities, as well as considerable trade-offs in some cases.

The Czech KSČM

In 1989, the Czechoslovak Communist Party faced a dramatic popular upsurge, and an equally spectacular discreditation. Despite these stimuli, it did not decisively centralize or break with the past, and was far more reluctant to engage in organizational transformation than the other parties.

The party, which refused either to negotiate with society or to engage in any sort of preemptive reform, was forced to capitulate in November 1989. Its collapse of power began with the brutal repression of a legal student march in Prague on 17 November 1989 and the massive demonstrations that followed. Czech and Slovaks then united in a general strike set for 27 November. This brought the country to a standstill, and the party began a rushed series of meetings with the newly formed opposition (the Czech Civic Forum and the Slovak Public Against Violence).

Despite the mounting evidence of its lack of popular mandate – massive protests against the party's lack of response and its style of rule continued throughout November – internal party analyses concluded that it was the insufficient connection between party organs and members that led to the leadership's loss of control.[25] In response, the party planned to activate its members. Party veteran Karel Urbanek became the new party secretary on 25 November 1989, and the party adopted an "Action Program" on 1 December, which called for a return to the values of 1968 and the renewal of socialism. Once the government resigned, the party agreed to concede its leading role on 3 December. Two days later, it formed the new government with representatives of the opposition, sharing the minister-ial portfolios equally. Party leaders Miloš Jakeš and Miroslav Št'ĕpán reluc-tantly resigned, as responsible for the violent repression of the march.[26] Retiree-age members of the Central Committee were also asked to leave the leadership.

In an atmosphere of chaos and panic, the Czech party leadership announced the Extraordinary Congress for 20–1 December 1989, while simultaneously calling for retention of the workplace party organizations.[27] The Czech and Slovak parties, still united in the Czechoslovak federation, began to prepare for what became known as "the most bizarre party congress held,"[28] held little more than a month after the revolution. The members remained where they were – there were no mass departures in Czech party until the Extraordinary Congress.[29] Nor was there much momentum for reform within the party. The Democratic Forum of Com-munists (Demokratické Forum Komunistů, DFK) arose on the local level and valiantly argued for democratization of party life and a radical break with old party structures and practices.[30] Despite the thousands of rank and file members who joined, however, the DFK was unable to form any alliances with the elites, nor was it able to influence the party congress del-egates. At the Extraordinary Congress, for example, only forty-nine out of the sixteen hundred delegates were from the DFK. They were often simply drowned out by the other party delegates, who were chosen directly by the orthodox regional organizations.[31]

---

[25] Central Committee of the KSČ meeting, 24 November 1989, *Pravda*, 27 November 1989.
[26] Št'ĕpán was listed by John T. Ishiyama as one of the "standpatters" within the leadership who prevented the party from transforming. (Ishiyama, John T. "Communist Parties in Transition: Structures, Leaders, and Process of Democratization in Eastern Europe," *Comparetive Politics*, Vol. 27, January 1995: 147–66.) However, not only was he was out of the party by the time these decisions were made, but the elites' deference towards the members appears to have played a far greater role in braking party transformation.
[27] Suk, Pavel. *Kronos Listopad a Prosinec 1989*, Rukopis připravený do vydání. ÚSD: 1996.
[28] Jakeš 1996, p. 121.
[29] *Życie Partii*, 27 December 1989, No. 26, p. 11.
[30] Grzymała-Busse 1998.
[31] Suk 1996.

Centralization

Thus, the party's stated goal was gradually to "transform itself into a modern left party, which could answer to the voters on questions of both the present and future, while not diverging from the ideals and programmatic goals of the era when it was founded."[32] The conservative Executive Committee emphasized that democratization meant party decentralization, which in turn was equated with the new activization of members, and both ideological and organizational continuity.[33] The party's center was to coordinate only, as befitted a "modern left party."[34] The party did reject its earlier "Lessons of the Crisis Development," the main manifesto of the post-1968 repression, and voted to dissolve its militia. On the other hand, the old, pre-1989 leadership was *asked* to leave, rather than required to do so. As a result, 48 out of 109 Central Committee members elected in October 1990 were old party leaders. These stalwarts continued to exert a considerable role in the party.

The leadership structures were both large, and dominated by older activists and local representatives. The new Central Committee consisted of 140 members, most of whom were regional representatives, as well as representatives of the platforms (by March 1993, there were six), and a small minority of parliamentary representatives.[35] Furthermore, the party's organizational administration were not vertically integrated. The local and regional party organizations continued as the bastion of the most stalwart and hidebound party functionaries. The Czech party retained eight regional committees (*krajské výbory*), eighty-six local committees (*obvodné výbory*), and 14,500 basic organizations (*zavodní organizace*) over six months after the Extraordinary Congress.[36] In the name of party democracy in the Czech party, these organizations were given considerable powers, to the point that the regional committees were a "second center of power."[37]

Unfortunately for party reformers, the regional committees were the most conservative of the three layers, and were staffed largely by post-1968

---

[32] *KSČM v parlamentě*, p. 3.
[33] *Rudé Pravo*, 2 April 1990.
[34] *Naše Pravda*, Founding Congress of KSČM, 31 March 1990.
[35] For example, a March 1993 meeting of the Central Committee consisted of 117 members present, fifty-nine of whom were chairs of the regional organizations, twelve were parliamentary representatives, three were from the former Federal Parliament, and six represented opinion platforms.
[36] *Informace o stavu členské zakládny a zakládních organizaci klubu v KSČS k 30.6.90*. Prague: KSČS, 1990.
[37] Interview with Dušan Dorotin, 4 February 1997, Bratislava.

"normalizers." These party activists had few portable skills, having come up through the ranks at a particularly stagnant time in the party. They could not easily transfer to other political or economic spheres. Retaining their position, and the party's, was tantamount to preserving their livelihood, and so they took full advantage of their new, more powerful role. As a result, these activists braked change and acted as alternative sources of authority. By 1993, conflict emerged between the two layers, with the Central Committee complaining that it gave advice to the passive regional organizations, whose only response to the Central Committee was a number of attempts to evoke confrontation with the party leadership.[38]

These antireform regional leaders and functionaries dominated the Central Committee.[39] Their conservatism was apparent in party polls: Most wanted both the retention of the communist name, and the inclusion of all communists, including old leaders and discredited Secret Service functionaries, in the party.[40] Since they were also experienced politically, they were able to dominate local party discussions and select the congress representatives and local leaders they deemed most able to represent their views.[41] By the June 1993 Prostějov congress, the local organizations chose only orthodox members and regional leaders as congress delegates.[42]

The new party leadership insisted that the party was "reliant on a stable membership base."[43] With no reformist elites to put forth programmatic alternatives or experiences, and guided by the myth of the "socialist mass party," the Czech leaders saw the membership and its mobilization as the main chance at political survival, arguing that "the party has to be a mass party to be influential."[44] Without other political resources, such as skilled and attractive new elites, appealing programs, or local patronage networks, the party relied on its members as its main political asset. As a result, the

[38] *Zpráva ÚV KSČM o činnosti strany od 1. Sjezdu KSČM* (The report of the Central Committee of the KSČM about the activity of the party from the First Congress of the KSČM), *Dokumenty II. Sjezdu KSČM*, Praha: KSČM, 1993, p. 21.

[39] *Mlada Fronta Dnes*, 27 March 1993.

[40] "Zpráva komise o Vyhodnocení Vnitřostranické Diskuse" (The report of the commission on evaluating internal party discussion"), *Dokumenty III Sjezdu KSČM*, Praha: KSČM, 1993, p. 13.

[41] Interviews with Vasil Mohorita, Jiří Svoboda, Vera Žežulková, and Jozef Mecl, all in Prague, fall 1996.

[42] Interview with Stanislava Zajícová, SDL HQ, 2 October 1996, Prague.

[43] *Zpráva ÚV KSČM o činnosti strany od 1. Sjezdu KSČM . . .* 1993, p. 11.

[44] *Naše Pravda*, 20 September 1990.

emphasis was on deepening existing supporter loyalty, rather than broadening party support among other voters.

Activating and mobilizing the party members signaled reform for the new leaders. Becoming an electoral party would have been "in conflict with history and traditions . . . we do not want to make gains in public eyes at the cost of losing members."[45] Consequently, in article after article, and declaration after declaration, the membership was held to be the ultimate arbiter of party decisions. To give the members an incentive to stay, the party proposed that the members vet policy, form opinion platforms, and decide the party programs. The formal justification was that "party policy must arise from below, and all members of the party must share in a creative way in its formation."[46] As a result, the Czech party made major decisions via party referenda, polled the members continually, and heavily subsidized two newspapers exclusively for its members, arguing that "internal party democracy means that we will . . . base ourselves on the opinions and suggestions of the rank and file members and sympathizers far more than before."[47]

Hoping to retain its members, the Czech party continued without any reregistration. All communist parties had their local organizations both in the workplace (for the active labor force) and in local precincts (for retirees and those working at home). However, as the workplace organizations became delegalized after 1989, their worker members did not join the remaining street organizations. Even though the "party's main goal" was "to move from workplace to street organizations with minimal losses,"[48] the number of the party's organizations had dropped to 14,500, and its membership, to little over 560,000, within six months of the move from workplace to street organizations.[49]

These street organizations were the repose of the retiree members under the communist regime. Since these organizations were not dissolved in 1989, their membership continued automatically. As a result, an

---

[45] Jiří Svoboda, 28 May 1991, *Haló Noviny*.

[46] "Pisemná Zpráva ÚV KSČS pro 18. Sjezd KSČS," *Dokumenty 18. Sjezdu KSČS*. Praha, 3–4.11.1990. Praha: ÚV KSČS, 1990, p. 49.

[47] Report on the twelfth meeting of the Central Committee of the Party, Jiří Svoboda, *Haló Noviny*, 1 June 1992.

[48] Vasil Mohorita speech at the first meeting of the ÚV KSČ, *Pravda*, 9 January 1990.

[49] "Informace o stavu členske zakládny a zakládních organizaci, klubů v KSČS k 30.6.1990," ÚV KSČM. Praha: 1990.

estimated 80% of the party members by 1993 were pensioners.[50] They belonged to the generation of the "communist struggle," the ideologically committed party members who joined the party prior to its takeover of 1948. The vast majority were orthodox, loyal communists. By the second congress, in mid-December 1992, a plurality (37.4%) of the party members had joined before 1948, 18.2% between 1971 and 1980, and only .5% after 1990.[51] Party leaders lamented that these, the most experienced and loyal members, had little influence on the party prior to 1989.[52] Therefore, they argued, the proper response was the mobilization of these veterans of communism.[53] Unfortunately for party reformists, these members were also a deeply conservative and dissatisfied lot – by July 1993, 91% of them were not satisfied with the current political situation.[54] By 1995, 77% members thought there was more democracy prior to 1989.[55]

For all the conservatism of the members,[56] the Central Committee now existed only to fulfill their directives.[57] In relying on the party's membership, and giving it such an influence within the party, the Czech leaders effectively became the hostages of an army of communist stalwarts. These conservative members had little interest in organizational, ideological, or symbolic change, and effectively blocked any reform movements within the party.

By 1991, this problem was compounded by the return of the orthodox activists to the party, made possible by its lax and decentralized member registration. Given the minimal scrutiny of potential members and their views, orthodox activists began to return en masse beginning with the June 1990 elections.[58] Without a central register of members, with no oversight by the regional organizations, and given the orthodox leanings of the local and regional party officials, these orthodox forces had no problems growing.[59] They ensured that the KSČM would continue to function as a

---

[50] While retirees made up 25% of the Czech population, they formed anywhere from 60% to 80% of the party, according to party leaders, by March 1993. *Haló Noviny*, 6 March 1993.

[51] *Zpráva ÚV KSČM o činnosti strany od 1. Sjezdu KSČM . . .* 1993, p. 17.

[52] Jakeš 1996, pp. 83–4.

[53] Jakeš 1996, p. 115.

[54] STEM Polls, July 1993.

[55] Klub levicových sociologů a psychologů. "Zaverečná zpráva ze sociologického výzkumu levicove smyslějicích občanů České republiky" (The concluding report of the sociological research on left-thinking citizens of the Czech Republic), No. 13–1995, p. 8.

[56] Vasil Mohorita interview in *Nove Slovo*, 18 January 1990.

[57] Vasil Mohorita speech at the first meeting of the ÚV KSČ, *Pravda*, 9 January 1990.

[58] Interview with Jiří Svoboda, 24 October 1996, Prague.

[59] Jozef Mecl, *Rudé Pravo*, 22 January 1993. Confirmed by Oskar Krejčí, Victoria Publishing, 7 October 1996 interview, and Jozef Mecl, 11 October 1996 interview, both in Prague.

conservative communist party, not only through direct decisions on the party name, platforms, and congress delegates, but through constant pressure on the leadership.

This orthodox resurgence was furthered by the party's promotion of opinion platforms, initially to further member involvement. The Czech Eighteenth Congress concluded that "the party cannot dare, and cannot be, artificially united in its opinions. It has to create space for the free expression of opinions and constant discussion within itself."[60] Therefore, as of April 1990, these opinion platforms and factions could all create councils within the party, were admitted to Central Committee meetings, and were officially recognized in the formation of the party program and policy stances.

Officially, party platforms were to ensure the development and improvement of the program with new ideas. Unfortunately, as the party itself admitted, any reformist efforts met with little understanding, and often direct opposition, of the members.[61] Thus, the Democratic Left (Demokratická Levice, DL) arose in 1990 to push through reform within the party that would make the KSČM a more moderate left party. It was renounced immediately, and left the KSČM in mid-1991 to form the Democratic Party of Labor (Demokratická Strana Prace, DSP).[62] The same fate met the Democratic Forum of Communists (DFK), which arose in 1989, demanded dramatic change at the 1989 party congress, and then spent its remaining year in the party fighting accusations of betrayal and careerism.[63]

In contrast, orthodox platforms found support with the members.[64] The most notable of these was the "For Socialism" platform. Formed in the winter of 1992–3, this platform consolidated the efforts of many orthodox activists. It was led by Miroslav Šťěpan, the Prague party leader forced to resign after he brutally subdued the 17 November 1989 student march, and Jaromír Obzina, the former minister of interior. The platform's main

---

[60] "Pisemná Zpráva ÚV KSČS pro 18. Sjezd KSČS," *Dokumenty 18. Sjezdu KSČS*. Praha, 3–4.11.1990. Praha: ÚV KSČS, 1990, p. 49.

[61] *KSČM, Teze Zprávy ÚV KSČM o Činnosti Ústavujícího sjezdu KSČM do 1. Sjezdu KSČM* (Theses of the Report of the Central Committee of the KSČM about the activity of the Founding Congress of the KSČM to the the First Congress of the KSČM), ÚV KSČM, Prague: 1992, p. 4.

[62] DSP in turn then joined the Czech Social Democrats (ČSSD) as individual members in 1991.

[63] DFK members also largely either left politics or joined the ČSSD.

[64] Michael Kroh, *Naše Pravda*, 21 June 1990.

stated goal was a "renaissance of socialism," with North Korea as the role model.[65] Its unstated goal was the promotion of Šťěpan back into party leadership. Unlike the reform platforms, "For Socialism" was aided and abetted by regional party stalwarts, who, for example, readmitted Šťěpan to the party in February 1993, contrary to Jiří Svoboda's strict instructions that Šťěpan's membership be revoked.

A double standard applied: Reformists were ostracized for "dividing the party," while orthodox communists were protected.[66] The reformists' initial weakness was reinforced, since they were not only a minority, but one whose views were denounced. Hence, the policies designed to retain as many members as possible resulted in the rejection of the very groupings that could have remade the party into a more dynamic, modern political competitor. By giving a large role to the members and local representatives, the new elites did not vertically integrate the decision making. They also failed to streamline the party, retaining the old structures and institutionalizing the opinion platforms instead.

Breaking with the Past

Nor did the party break with its past, given its significance to the party members. The Czech leaders refused to part with the myth of the February 1948 takeover of power as a "great event,"[67] and beyond a few admissions of "Stalinist errors," defended the entire communist period as a time of social progress and economic advancement for the country. The party did not fully renounce its post-1968 repression or its forcible takeover of power in 1948. To do so would call into question the legitimacy of the entire postwar communist system in Czechoslovakia, so important to the party rank and file. Instead, the party extolled the glories of the old communists, did not disavow the hardliners among them, made use of the traditional communist hammer-and-sickle symbols, and continued to insist on a communist identity. The greatest concession was to argue that the party should now act as it did in the interwar Czech democracy: As late as 1993, prewar party performance was the standard by which its post-1989 leaders were measured.

[65] Jaromír Obzina, *Naše Pravda*, 12 February 1993.
[66] "Zpráva Ústřední Rozhodci Komise KSČM, Predložená III. Sjezdu KSČM" (The Report of the Central Deciding Commission of the KSČM), *Dokumenty III. Sjezdu KSČM*. Praha: KSČM, 1993.
[67] Jiří Machalik, *Naše Pravda*, 8 March 1990.

Nor was the question of the party's name settled at the Extraordinary Congress. By February 1990, a full-blown crisis erupted within the party. Although the name was changed from the "Communist Party of Czechoslovakia" to the "Communist Party of the Czech Lands and Moravia" in March 1990, this clearly did not satisfy party reformists. On the one hand, reformers in the parliamentary club argued that the name must change to reflect the dramatic collapse of the discredited communist system. On the other, the central party leadership argued that, "KSČM is, was, and will be, the communist party of Czechoslovakia. We will not take on a different name, and 95% of members agree with us."[68] Part of the argument for preserving the name was that it would satisfy the members. The other justification was that the "biggest and strongest European parties, the French, Italian, Portuguese, have retained their communist names."[69]

The subsequent November 1990 Congress was to have decided the question of the party name. Instead, however, the congress focused on other questions, thanks to a manipulation of the party agenda by the more conservative members of the Central Committee.[70] Eventually, with the agreement of the Central Committee, Svoboda declared a party referendum[71] in the name of the internal party democracy that was a consistent goal throughout his tenure.[72] He then deliberately contrasted the KSČM referendum with the Slovak party's "democracy from above."[73]

The referendum was scheduled for the fall of 1991. Given the membership's orthodoxy, the results were not difficult to predict – over 76% voted for retaining the communist name.[74] The referendum had other effects: On the one hand, it mobilized the moribund party membership. On the other, all other discussion stopped, and the name, more than ever, became the focus of the party's discussion.[75] Svoboda, unhappy with the referendum results, submitted another proposal to the members in April 1992 to change

[68] Jiří Michalik, "Jsme komunisty" ("We are communists"), *Naše Pravda*, 8 March 1990. The Central Committee eventually proposed a dual name, KSČM-Strana demokratického socialismu, to signal change without angering the members. (*KSČM, Teze Zprávy . . . 1992*, p. 14.)

[69] *KSČM, Teze Zprávy . . . 1992*, p. 14.

[70] Vasil Mohorita, *Rudé Pravo*, 23 February 1991. Michal Kraus, *Rudé Pravo*, 28 February 1991.

[71] Jiří Svoboda, *Haló Noviny*, 25 June 1991.

[72] Jiří Svoboda, "Levice to bude mít těžke" (The Left will have difficulties), *Haló Noviny*, 1 July 1992.

[73] *Nove Slovo*, 23 December 1996.

[74] *Zpráva ÚV KSČM o Činnosti strany od 1. Sjezdu KSČM . . . 1993*, p. 18.

[75] Ibid, p. 18.

the party name, but met with little support.[76] As the discussion dragged on, the Executive Committee members were unanimous in arguing that the membership base had to decide,[77] fully aware that by that point only 8% of members saw a name change as advised or even relevant.[78]

Thus, despite both internal and external stimuli, the party did not undergo streamlining or vertical integration. The reasons lie chiefly in the configuration of the new party elites and their political resources. First, the leaders had no experience or skill with which to devise or implement radical change. As a result of past recruiting practices, the new top leadership first consisted of old party apparatchiks (Urbanek, Mohorita, and Adamec), followed by an inexperienced unknown (Svoboda). The conservative Executive Committee dominated these leaders from the start, and neither Mohorita nor Svoboda had the political experience and the allies to fight against this domination.

Nor were they able to obtain support within the party, ostracized as they were for their moderate reformism.[79] Moreover, the new elites' view of party change was limited: By October 1990, Mohorita proclaimed that since there was no bust of Marx or Lenin in his office, and no communist classics in his library, the party had truly transformed itself. Finally, reformists were both isolated and inexperienced, and had no access to the party elites or its decision making. Although there were some proposals for radical reform, most notably from the DFK reformists, they were shelved by Urbanek and his successors.[80] Given the party's reliance on its members, the party could hardly jettison its organization or ideology.

Dissolution was never even proposed, either at the Extraordinary Congress, or subsequently.[81] It was "not a realistic path . . . especially if we want to retain a credible position in the June [1990] elections."[82] Party leader Mohorita argued that no dissolution was necessary, because once he and Adamec "had taken over the party, we did not have to do that . . . to the end I am convinced that it would have been a mistake to dissolve the party at that time."[83] Instead, the party's top priority was to retain as many of its members and structures as possible through the transition.

[76] *Haló Noviny*, 12 March 1993.
[77] *Haló Noviny*, 17 March 1993.
[78] Miloslav Randsorf, quoted in *Haló Noviny*, 26 April 1993.
[79] Interview with Vasil Mohorita, 14 October 1996.
[80] Interview with Vasil Mohorita, 14 November 1996.
[81] Interview with Jaroslav Ortman, 7 November 1996, Prague.
[82] Jiří Machalik, "Jsme komunisty" ("We are communists"), *Naše Pravda*, 8 March 1990.
[83] Interview with Vasil Mohorita, 14 November 1996.

The need for rapid organizational change was recognized only later – Svoboda eventually argued that the one time the party could have been transformed was from the end of 1989 to the beginning of 1990.[84] By the June 1990 elections, the old guard had begun to come back and the party itself was too satisfied with the election results to ponder "fixing what was not broken." At the same time, however, Svoboda argued that the first leadership could not have changed the party then, since attempting to transform the party prior to the June 1990 elections would have been "suicidal."[85] Party leaders repeated their commitment to the "proven paradigms" of both classical socialist democracy and classical communism.[86]

In short, the Czech elites' caution and hesitation in implementing organizational centralization and a break with the past reflected their lack of experience in formulating policy alternatives, negotiating with political competitors, and developing other political skills.[87] Their lack of portable skills or a usable past made the new party elites dependent on the conservative rank and file and vulnerable to domination by the orthodox Executive Committee. As a result, the few changes they implemented were piecemeal and gradual.

The Slovak SDĽ

In contrast, the Slovak component of the Czechoslovak party immediately called for radical reform, with greater autonomy for the Slovak party.[88] While the Czech party defended its presence in society and called for renewing socialism despite its enormous discreditation, the new Slovak leaders declared that "either the party fundamentally and immediately changes, or it will lose influence in society."[89] Consequently, they moved rapidly to centralize the party and to break with the past, even if they were

[84] Interview with Jiří Svoboda, 24 October 1996, Prague.
[85] Interview with Jiří Svoboda, 24 October 1996, Prague.
[86] *Haló Noviny*, 10 January 1991.
[87] The first leader of the party is perhaps the best illustration: Mohorita distinguished himself by chewing gum loudly during François Mitterand's visit to the Czech parliament, refusing to stand up for Margaret Thatcher, and making the ominous pronouncement that "the time of reconciliation has ended, and now the time for the struggle begins" in October 1990.
[88] There was no Czech party in the Czechoslovak federation until March 1990. Given the growing conflict between the two formations, the Slovak party unilaterally ended the federation in 1991 (*Rudé Pravo*, 2 September 1991).
[89] Peter Weiss, quoted in *Pravda*, 28 November 1989.

more limited in some of these efforts (such as dissolving the party) by their lower levels of experience and skill.

The Slovak reformers from the Marxist-Leninist Institute moved quickly and decisively to overhaul the party organization. In November 1989, Pavol Kanis, Peter Weiss, and others immediately formed an Action Committee (Akční Výbor, AV) consisting of twenty-four reformist members, to counter both the Czech domination and the stagnation of the Slovak Central Committee (Ustrední Výbor, UV).[90] As the Slovak old guard retreated, it made room for the new elites (largely because their well-connected mentor from the Marxist-Leninist Institute, Viliam Plevza, vouched for their acceptability). The interim leader of the Slovak party, Jan Široký, deliberately stepped aside to allow Weiss to take control, arguing that Weiss was "better able to lead the party into becoming a model left party."[91] He proposed Kanis and Weiss as party leaders.

The Action Committee quickly became the center of power within the party – once the old elites stepped back, it rapidly assumed many of their powers, and by 6 December, dissolved the Central Committee. Bypassing Prague, the local organizations, and its own Central Committee, the AV appointed a new party leadership and called the Extraordinary Congress – for 18 December, two days before the Czech party's congress.

At the Extraordinary Congress, new party leader Weiss made naming his Executive Committee (Výkonný Výbor) a condition of accepting the party leadership. As a result, twenty out of the fifty-six Executive Committee members were "his" people, while the others were largely reformist delegates to the congress. Only three of the new Central Committee served in a previous one, and none had served in the Executive Committee. Their average age was thirty-five.[92] Weiss thus both consolidated the reformists' authority in the party and deliberately introduced reformist cohorts into the leadership, including several reformist unknowns that went on to powerful positions in the government and in the party, such as Brigita Schmögnerová (the finance minister in the post-1998 government) and Milan Ftáčnik (the minister of education in the same government).

[90] In a letter to Urbanek, nominally the party's head, the AV wrote to demand autonomy for KSS and assert firm control over the Slovak party. Prague would now have to go through the AV leadership instead of directly reaching the Slovak regional organizations. *Pravda*, 8 December 1989.

[91] *Pravda*, 22 January 1990.

[92] *Pravda*, 21 December 1989.

Centralization

The new Slovak party elites centralized the leadership immediately.[93] The 260 Central Committee members of the Slovak party were reduced to 90 at the Extraordinary Congress,[94] and then even further. A two chamber leadership was initially founded, with a Central Committee and a Council of Regional Representatives. By mid-1992, this structure was made more hierarchical: The two were merged to form the Republican Council (Republikanská Rada), which now consisted of the parliamentary club, the local representatives (from the Obvodné Výbory), and fifteen mayors of major Slovak cities. Its Executive Committee (Výkonný Výbor Republikanskej Rady) consisted of twenty to twenty-five representatives of the Council, but the real party leadership, the Predsednictvo, which met weekly, consisted of the party chair, the six deputy chairs, and the parliamentary club chair. Two more people – a chair of the shadow government and of the council for local and regional politics – were added in 1994. Throughout this time, however, the party chair was given "Stalin-like powers."[95]

The Slovak transformation, as its leaders readily admitted, was a top-down affair, and as such, had to be administered accordingly. The emphasis was on vertical links between the center and local organizations, bypassing the mid-level entirely.[96] Thus, the four regional committees (*krajské výbory*) were immediately disbanded. Despite initial talk of basic organizations gaining power, Weiss rapidly began to assert vertical control over the party organization by mid-December 1989. The local committees (*obvodné výbory*) were given only a coordinating function, and the basic organizations now reported directly to the Central Committee. To make sure that there would be "no empty space in between"[97] the local and center organizations, an eleven-member team was formed by early 1990 to transmit Central Committee directives to the regional organizations and ensure that they were implemented.[98] As the party leaders

[93] *Pravda*, 9 December 1989, 11 December 1989.
[94] A delegate and member of the Central Committee elected at the Extraordinary Congress, Emilia Lončiková rather saltily commented that such a committee "was too large, and, in short, "worth s**t." KSS, *Zjazd KSS, konany v dnoch 20–21.10.1990 v Prešove*, II. Čast. Archiv SDĽ, Bratislava, p. 8.
[95] Interview with Juraj Janošovsky (DFK/ KSS'91), 3 February 1997.
[96] ÚV SDL meeting, 29 June 1991, *Pravda*. See also 18 December 1989 and 18 July 1991.
[97] ÚV SDL meeting on 29 June 1991, as reported in *Nove Slovo*, 18 July 1991.
[98] "Z uvodného vystupenia predsedu VV ÚV KSS Petra Weissa" (From the opening speech

explained, the point of organizational reform was "to connect the local organizations as tightly as possible to the Central Committee."[99] The new local committee leaders, dependent on the new party leadership for what little power was left to them, stood behind Weiss and deflected any attempts to swerve the party from its reformist course.[100]

Weiss continued to insist on quick and decisive change: "either we will quickly and thoroughly change the ideology, organization, and obviously, the name, to a modern left party with its own original identity, friendly and real national program and strong political personalities, as we approved at the Extraordinary Congress of the KSS, or we won't be able to get rid of all neostalinist ballast. We will then change into a sect, which will lose real influence in society."[101] The need for rapid organizational change, and for the elite impetus for it, became all the more apparent in the summer of 1990. By then, the will to transform the party had weakened – some party activists had argued that the success in the elections indicated that no real change was necessary.[102] By August 1991, Weiss argued that the "historical opportunity" for the KSČM to change had been lost.[103]

Yet for all the rapid changes, the Slovak party did not dissolve. Some leaders argued this would mean the reformists would not rejoin the party. More importantly, the party's inexperienced reformist elites felt vulnerable without a sizeable organization behind them[104] – they simply did not have the administrative skill to dissolve the party and go about founding its replacement. While they could gain power in the party, and knew what they had to do to assert it, these new elites were neither numerous nor skilled enough to dissolve the party and staff its structures with their own people. By the time the party could hold its first independent congress, in October 1990, party leader Weiss argued that it would be peculiar to dissolve the party then. The party had survived the June 1990 elections, and so the leadership felt more confident, even as the members grew complacent about party transformation.[105]

---

of the chair of the VV ÚV KSS Peter Weiss), KSS-SDĽ, *Dokumenty Zjazdu KSS-SDĽ Prešov, 20–21 Oktobra 1990*. Bratislava: ÚV KSS-SDĽ, 1990, p. 20.

[99] Pavol Bolvanský, *Pravda*, 18 December 1989.

[100] Thus Slovak DFK leaders complained that Weiss rejected the efforts of the DFK to decentralize the party.

[101] *Pravda*, 25 January 1990.

[102] "Z uvodného vystupenia predsedu VV ÚV KSS Petra Weissa..." 1990, p. 8.

[103] *Rudé Pravo*, 28 August 1991.

[104] "Z uvodného vystupenia predsedu VV ÚV KSS Petra Weissa..." 1990, p. 7.

[105] Interview with Peter Weiss, 7 February 1997, Bratislava.

Therefore, the leadership chose to reregister all its members in the fall of 1990, even if this would mean the "end of a mass party."[106] Weiss and others readily admitted that the members were both conservative and a hindrance to further reform. No attempt was made to encourage the party members to remain after the reregistration; Pavol Kanis even declared openly that he expected a maximum of 20% of the KSS members to join the new successor party, and a conservative party to arise to take care of the stalwarts.[107] As a condition of their reregistration, all members had to agree with the party's radical reform.[108] Local officials were to make sure each new member had agreed to the party's new program and orientation, and activists from the center constantly traveled to the regional organizations to convince the members.[109]

Because all members had to reregister, party membership declined from 400,000 to 190,000 prior to the reregistration, to little over 45,000 after the reregistration, decreasing further to about 25,000 after the 1994 national elections. However, party leaders remained satisfied with the fact that reregistration led the workers to leave the party, while the doctors, public administrators, and teachers reregistered – even if it had fewer members than the KSČM, the SDĽ retained a higher proportion of younger, more dynamic and educated members.[110] It was not until the 1994 electoral debacle, and the subsequent pressure from furious regional activists, that the leadership conceded that it needed to give more priority to the membership base. Even then, the leaders questioned the notion that the party's numerable membership was a comparative advantage over its competitors, since they had fewer members and yet received better results.[111]

Weiss repeatedly argued that the "voters will have the last word, and so it is necessary that party organs carefully consider whom they propose . . ."[112] As far as the leadership was concerned, unity based on conservatism was "useless."[113] It could only stand in the way of the party's electoral and parliamentary goals: Success was not measured by internal activity, but by

[106] Jozef Migaš, *Nove Slovo*, c. 35, 1991.
[107] Pavol Kanis, *Pravda*, 6 February 1990.
[108] Interview with Peter Weiss, *Naše Pravda*, 11 October 1990.
[109] Interview with Dušan Dorotin, 4 February 1997, Bratislava.
[110] Interview with Peter Magvaši, 27 January 1997, Bratislava.
[111] Interview with Peter Weiss, *Nove Slovo*, 2 January 1995.
[112] Peter Weiss, *Pravda*, 6 January 1990. See also *Pravda*, 27 January 1990.
[113] Peter Weiss, *Pravda*, 27 October 1990. See also KSS, *Zjazd KSS, konany v dnoch 20–21.10.1990 v Prešove*, I–II. Časť. Archiv SDĽ, Bratislava.

policy effects.[114] Therefore, prior to the October 1990 Congress in Prešov, the SDĽ encouraged platforms, in order to get rid of the orthodox communists under the guise of "making differences clear and strengthening differentiation."[115] The conservative Platform for Communist Defense (Platforma Komunistickej Obnovy, PKO) and the reformist Platform of a Socialist Orientation (Platforma Socialistickej Orientacie, PSO) arose, welcomed by the leadership because they identified those opposed to reform.[116] After the conservatives made themselves known, they were eliminated from the party. The more orthodox members left the SDĽ in disgust over the change in the party name and in its orientation. Some formed two communist parties in 1991, which then melded into the small Communist Party of Slovakia, which held no elected offices, and was not represented in the parliament. As in the Czech party, the orthodox former members also began to attempt to return after the 1990 elections. However, in the SDĽ, they were prevented from doing so on a large scale by the Central Committee and its strict membership requirements.[117]

At the October 1990 Congress itself, Weiss denounced the platforms as a substitute for real political discussion, and ended their recognition by the party statutes.[118] Party factions and platforms were then expressly forbidden by the new party leadership, much to the anger of the conservative party members, who denounced this move as "antidemocratic" and "reactionary."[119] The one serious split came with the formation of the Association of Slovak Workers (ZRS), led by Jan Ľuptak, who left the SDĽ in the spring of 1994.[120] In short, by forbidding "democratic expression" and not allowing party currents any say, the leadership consolidated its hold on party policy and ensured that alternative views would not become serious challenges.

Breaking with the Past

The Slovak party's break with its past was decisive. Even before the Extraordinary Congress, the AV declared the 1968 normalization "Lessons"

---

[114] Interview with Dušan Dorotin, 4 February 1997, Bratislava.

[115] *Pravda*, 26 February 1990.

[116] Gabriela Rothmayerová, *Pravda*, 30 Augusta 1990.

[117] *Pravda*, 16 July 1990.

[118] KSS, *Zjazd KSS, konany v dnoch 20–21.10.1990 v Prešove*, I-II. Časť. Archiv SDĽ, Bratislava, p. 15.

[119] Interview with Jan Zelinka, 8 February 1997, Bratislava.

[120] The ZRS joined the government of Vladimír Mečiar shortly after its formation in the fall of 1994, but disappeared from politics with its electoral drubbing in 1998.

document invalid, demanded that the party's Central Revision Commission investigate leadership corruption, suspended the Slovak party leaders, announced its plans for the immediate removal of party organizations from the workplace, and declared the party newspaper (*Nové Slovo*) independent. The party immediately changed its symbol to an abstract rendition of the SDĽ acronym, declared it had no ties to the communist movement, and disavowed discredited party representatives. In contrast to the Czech reliance on historical symbols and references, Weiss argued that the Slovak communist experiences prior to the 1948 takeover of power were of no use in the post-1989 situation: Society and civilization had changed too much.[121] To be fair, this move was made easier than it would have been in the Czech case, because the Slovak party could claim with some credibility that the Czech domination was responsible for the past injustices and misdoings.

The new elites saw the party's name as "the last link to the Czechoslovak Communist Party,"[122] and therefore acted to change it as soon as possible. At the Extraordinary Congress held in December 1989, the Slovak party had already put changing the name on the agenda.[123] On the same day in January 1990 that Czech leaders declared that change would not be credible,[124] Weiss argued that the name change was an "obvious" part of the larger restructuring of the party. The question of the name was not secondary to the program, but a prerequisite for credible transformation, one that would make the party acceptable to voters and possible coalition partners alike. It was a profound question of the party's identity. As one party reformist argued later, "the name change was the most difficult bit. Principles were easier to change, but the name was the party identity. For the party members, this would be the hardest thing to accept, and if they were allowed their say, the name would not be changed."[125] If put to a member referendum, especially prior to the reregistration, the result would be much as in the Czech party, and so one was never seriously considered.[126]

Instead, the leaders alone decided to change the party name. At the October 1990 congress, despite lobbying from KSČM's Svoboda to decide

---

[121] Peter Weiss, *Pravda*, 27 January 1990.
[122] Joerf Sebo, in *Nove Slovo*, 9 August 1990.
[123] *Pravda*, 18 December 1992.
[124] Peter Weiss, *Pravda*, 25 January 1990.
[125] Interview with Milan Ftáčnik, 31 January 1997, Bratislava.
[126] Interview with Milan Ftáčnik, SDĽ HQ, 31 January 1997. Interview with Peter Weiss, 23 February 1997, both in Bratislava.

the party name by referendum, the Slovak party leaders put the question on the congress agenda by simply asking which new name to adopt. As one member of the party leadership later explained, the name was changed because a majority of the parliamentary representatives and local party heads wanted the change – not because the members had any say in it.[127] The name was officially changed to the Strana Demokratickej Ľavici on 1 February, 1991, with nineteen out of twenty-one Executive Committee members voting for the change, and thirty out of the thirty-eight regional representatives concurring.[128]

In short, the Slovak party elites rapidly acted to change the party's structure and identity, and did so with little consultation of the party's members or activists. The new leaders had a profoundly reformist orientation, but not necessarily the administrative experience – nor were they particularly numerous within the party. As a result, they felt unable to dissolve the party. As we will see in the next chapters, the combination of aggressive vertical integration and streamlining tactics with the failure to refound the organization would subsequently precipitate conflict within the party.

The Polish SdRP

In Poland, the communist party was obliged to gradually negotiate its own exit. Given its extensive elite experience and skills, the party could centralize far more decisively than its Czech counterpart. On the other hand, given how recent the opposition-party conflict was, it could not fully denounce its past.

In August 1988, the PZPR responded to yet another wave of strikes with the Round Table negotiations between the government and representatives of the opposition Solidarity trade union-cum-social movement. Even as the negotiations got under way in February 1989, there was a similar, if limited, impetus to reform the party. Alarmed by the renewed unrest, the party held its Tenth Plenum in January 1989, where some leaders proposed a democratized mass party.[129] At the plenum, several meetings were held between the nascent reform movements within the party and its leadership.[130] Moreover, as part of an effort to rejuvenate the party, local committees were obliged not only to encourage but to *create*

---

[127] Dušan Dorotin, *Pravda*, 16 January 1991.
[128] *Rudé Pravo*, 28 January 1990.
[129] Grzybowski, Leszek. "Jaka Partia?" Warsaw: Książka i Wiedza, February 1989, p. 7.
[130] Interview with Zbigniew Siemiątkowski. *Rzeczpospolita*, 24 January 1994.

discussion clubs.[131] At the same time, however, the plenum's documents insisted on the necessity of workplace party organizations and intraparty democratic centralism.

The party was initially reluctant to engage in another round of negotiations with the opposition,[132] especially given the clear and persistent historical divide between "us, society," and "them, the party." Early versions of the proposed changes neither questioned the party's leading role nor the socialist nature of the system.[133] Solidarity was weak organizationally, and the negotiations were unprecedented, which limited the scope of the liberalization. After receiving repeated reassurances from Soviet leader Mikhail Gorbachev in the summer of 1989, however, the protracted negotiations culminated in political liberalization, the recognition of the trade union-cum-opposition movement, and semifree elections.

These elections, held on 4 June 1989, were an unmitigated catastrophe for the party. The party lost every seat it could: Not a single one of the newly elected one hundred senators was from the party, and all the freely contested seats in the parliament went to the opposition (35%). The party's national list was a disaster – no candidate gathered the support necessary in the first round. In a sublime understatement, party leaders admitted that they "did not take the changed situation into account."[134]

The elite finger-pointing began, as party leaders squabbled over mistakes made. They cited, for example, that the regional (*województwo*) committees named their own candidates, and this process led not only to too many party candidates competing with one opposition candidate, but to the selection of people who were not loyal to the party.[135] As a result, over five party candidates competed for every seat contested by a single opposition member.[136] These regional organizations were also blamed for misjudging and misreporting the political situation in the

[131] Grzybowski 1989, p. 5.
[132] As a weary party leader admitted, "let's face it, we do not really want a Round Table." Meeting of the KC PZPR Secretariat, 1 September 1988, in Perzkowski, Stanisław, ed. *Tajne dokumenty Biura Politycznego i Sekretariatu KC: Ostatni Rok Władzy, 1988–9*. London: Aneks, 1994, p. 219. A third of the Central Committee also voted against negotiations. Rakowski, Mieczysław. *Jak to sie stało*. Warsaw: BGW, 1991, p. 169.
[133] Proposal of "Nonconfrontational But Competitive" Electoral System, 16 February 1989, in Perzkowski 1994, p. 289.
[134] Rakowski 1991, p. 221.
[135] "Ocena kampanii wyborczej" (Evaluation of the Electoral Campaign), 25 July 1989, in Perzkowski 1989, p. 446.
[136] Document No. 55, Transcript of meeting of the Common Committee of the Government and Episcopate Representatives," 31 May 1988, in Perzkowski, 1989, p. 377.

country,[137] so that the national party could not properly address campaign shortcomings.

Given the enormity of the popular defeat, a party congress was announced within days of the election. Party members and activists were passive and resigned, "losing their will to fight." To mobilize them, party leader Mieczysław Rakowski traveled all over the country, and even reached out to the Socialist International for support.[138] In anticipation of the congress, several official commissions were formed, to resolve questions of the new party statutes, program, name, and the delegates, led by the Central Congress Commission (Centralna Komisja Zjazdowa, CKZ).

At the same time, the younger, middle-level elites saw their chance, and began to mobilize. Some had already left for other spheres, notably with the "spontaneous privatizations" of state-owned enterprises that occurred throughout 1998–9.[139] Those remaining in the party insisted on rapid change: "there's a suicidal feeling in the party leadership, that it's better to wait to see what Solidarity does, and then maybe in April have the congress. By April [1990] . . . there won't be anything left of the party except the apparat."[140] As a result of mid-level elite efforts, over two hundred party platforms arose, most pro-reform. Although they had few direct connections to the party leaders, they garnered over 80% of the delegates for the upcoming congress. The representatives of the July 8 Movement, perhaps the most influential of these, traveled constantly to mobilize local organizations, and united into an all-country organization by mid-October. As a result, over one thousand of the delegates at the congress (out of 1,474) had affiliated themselves with reformist platforms.

This greater number of reformist candidates and representatives was the result of the party's earlier policies of recruitment from the outside, and relative internal pluralism. The result of this reformist dominance at the congress was that the newly elected leaders could rely more on their own cohort, and the majority it gave them at the congress, instead of depending on the mentorship of elder party statesmen, as in Slovakia. On the other hand, the possibility of opinion differences and conflicts among

[137] Document No. 57, Transcript of the KC PZPR Secretariat, 5 June 1989, in Perzkowski 1989, p. 396.

[138] Sokorski, Włodzimierz. *Udana Klęska*. Warsaw: Savimpress, 1990, p. 74.

[139] Staniszkis, Jadwiga. *The Dynamics of Breakthrough in Central Europe*. Berkeley, CA: University of California Press, 1992.

[140] Kazimierz Kik, in "Sztandary i proporce" ("Banners and regimental flags"), *Polityka*, 30 September 1989.

the reformist cohorts also increased, as did their visibility, sometimes making the reformists an easy target.

Thus, party response to these reformist efforts varied: Many regional organizations blocked them, the vast majority of the parliamentarians supported them, and the Central Committee remained ambivalent.[141] Nevertheless, the party leadership hosted a series of press conferences to introduce the platforms officially, and called for greater party openness. By September, it was clear that the upcoming congress would be the last one for the Polish United Workers' Party.[142]

Dissolution was a foregone conclusion by November 1989. The six months between the party's electoral defeat and its congress meant that few in the party still deluded themselves that the electoral results were just a matter of "bad technical solutions."[143] As a result, the Extraordinary Congress, held 26–31 January 1990, simultaneously became the old party's last congress, and the founding congress of the successor. Former leaders of the party, while invited to those portions of the congress devoted to the PZPR, could not attend the *new* party's founding congress. Rakowski chose not to run for the chair of the new party, and encouraged other party elders to give up their places for the younger generation.[144] Party commissions, set up ahead of time, had already prepared the party's new statutes, name, program, and parliamentary strategy. The delegates "discussed" these issues, but made no changes to the committee proposals, and instead deferred to the earlier choices.

The election of the leadership was equally pro forma. The thirty-six-year-old Aleksander Kwaśniewski, a youth league activist, former youth minister, and the recipient of the greatest number of Senate votes in the Senate elections of all non-Solidarity candidates, became the "obvious choice."[145] He ran against two candidates, one of whom openly stated he was only a "straw man." Much like Weiss in Slovakia, Kwaśniewski agreed to run for the chair of the Head Council (Rada Naczelna, RN), but only on the condition that the newly elected leader would name 60 out of the 150 members of the RN. As he argued, "in this way we can ensure that representatives of the parliamentary club, the social democratic block, other platforms, and eminent intellectuals can all be in the RN . . . this will

---

[141] "Sztandary i proporce," *Polityka*, 30 September 1989.
[142] Rakowski, *Trybuna Ludu*, 23–4 September 1989.
[143] Interview with Aleksander Kwaśniewski, *Wprost*, 28 January 1990.
[144] *Trybuna Ludu*, 29 January 1990.
[145] *Trybuna Ludu*, 29 January 1990.

guarantee that the party will be an intellectual and organizational force from start, that it will be a good team."[146] Kwaśniewski won 90% of the votes, and got his wish. He named as leaders such reformists as Leszek Jaśkiewicz, Tomasz Nałęcz, and Zbigniew Siemiątkowski. Meanwhile, the regional organizations chose fifty candidates, and the congress delegates chose the rest.

The Polish party's leadership structures were deceptively large, with 150 members in the Head Council. The leadership was nominally "dual," in that the chair of the Head Council was to be the chair of the party, while the general secretary of the party, in charge of the more mundane affairs of the party, also led the Central Executive Committee (Centralny Komitet Wykonawczy, CKW). However, the latter was subject to the Head Council, as was the general secretary.[147] The Head Council itself had its agenda set by the party chair in close cooperation with a few deputies and parliamentarians. Regional organizations, formally part of the Head Council, were partially blamed for the electoral fiasco of 1989, and given formal representation but little real power. As a result, party spokespersons admitted that in the highly vertically integrated SdRP, "15–20 people decide about everything."[148]

While some debate occurred regarding the pace of the organizational streamlining,[149] the reformist consensus, led by the July 8 Movement, insisted not only on the party's dissolution but on subsequent member reregistration.[150] Prior to 1989, the Polish party membership was the largest in absolute figures (numbering over 2.1 million), but it was also notorious for its lack of ideological commitment. This lack of ideological loyalty was an additional disincentive to retaining a mass party. Some of the platforms had argued for a mass structure,[151] but Kwaśniewski and other party leaders prevailed. They repeatedly argued that "it is better to have 100,000 members and million voters, than vice versa."[152] Party leaders

[146] *Trybuna Ludu*, 30 January 1990.
[147] The RN could change the fourteen members of the CKW as it wished.
[148] *Polityka*, 14 September 1996.
[149] Stefan Opara, Warsaw Committee, *Trybuna Ludu*, 13 July 1989.
[150] Interview with Tomasz Nałęz, UP Sejm Office, 2 July 1997, Warsaw.
[151] Thus, the July 8 Movement "decidedly' wanted a mass party and close ties to the trade unions. "Interview with Leszek Jaśkiewicz and Tadeusz Nałęcz." [sic], *Nowe Drogi*, 11/12 1989: 6–23.
[152] Aleksander Kwaśniewski, in *Nove Slovo*, 22 March 1990, and in *Życie Warszawy*, 30 January 1990. Wojciech Wiśniewski quoted by AP, 12 February 1990. The membership grew by twenty thousand in the first two months of 1990, and stabilized at sixty thousand, well above all but one other party.

also openly announced that "the number of members or their functions do not matter as much as their influence."[153] Inactive party members were seen as useless, and so party leaders chose to force all members to reapply to the party, eliminating the most passive ones. Even those members were a second priority to the voters: "we prefer sympathizers, who support us,"[154] since "the era of mass parties is over."[155] Since all members wishing to rejoin the new party had to sign pledges of allegiance to the new program, the reform orientation, and the new leadership, the membership dropped to sixty thousand as a result.

Platforms were allowed to form, but none did – the leadership offered no recognition or material support to platform leaders.[156] Moreover, many of their members had either reintegrated into party structures or left the party for economic management positions. Party leaders paid lip service to "intra-party discussion" and occasionally instituted it, but admitted that such discussion had few results. This was in marked contrast to the other parties in Poland at the time, who gave their opinion currents considerable opportunity to voice their views and influence party policy. For example, it was not until 1994 that the mainstream Freedom Union eliminated the three wings that had become formalized in the party.[157]

The regional organizations, much-maligned and blamed for the 1989 electoral debacle, were dissolved in 1989–90. The new regional leaders were beholden to the center for their position, and at least initially threw their full weight behind the project of party transformation, on which their political careers depended. As they gained more local support and began to represent local interests, this consensus did not persist. However, by that point, 1991–2, the party's transformation was complete, and so their dissent presented little challenge. Similarly, when the more conservative members began to reassert themselves in mid-1991,[158] party leaders immediately lashed out, and never let members decide party policy.[159]

The relationship with the communist trade union successor, the All-Polish Alliance of Trade Unions (Ogólnopolskie Porozumienie Związków Zawodowych, OPZZ), underscored the party elites' ability to control the party and its political efforts. The SdRP retained ties to the

[153] Jacek Zdrojewski, Warsaw Party Committee, *Trybuna Ludu*, 16 January 1989.
[154] Andrzej Żelazowski, *Trybuna*, 18 March 1993.
[155] Andrzej Jaeschke, *Trybuna*, 4 February 1993.
[156] *Trybuna Ludu*, 23 August 1989.
[157] PAP, 9 April 1994.
[158] Igor Janke, *Życie Warszawy*, 3 December 1991.
[159] *Trybuna Ludu*, 16 December 1991.

OPZZ, and together they formed the Democratic Left Alliance (Sojusz Lewicy Demokratycznej, SLD) in the spring of 1991. The alliance ran in the elections of 1991 and 1993 together, with union candidates on the party ballot. On the face of it, then, the party's streamlining was belied by its continued association with a former auxiliary organization. However, because the trade union alliance was so decentralized,[160] the SdRP leadership took over strategic decision making, and was fully in charge of the coalition. As we will see later, the SdRP could both dominate and jettison this coalition readily enough.

Breaking with the Past

Nonetheless, the party did not denounce its controversial past, partly because the most salient events took place only eight years earlier, with the rise of Solidarity and the party's crackdown on the popular opposition movement. Moreover, the Polish party stood unable to condemn its repression of worker protests in 1976 and in 1981 – too many of its mid-level leaders and activists had been implicated, however tenuously. Even though some reformist leaders resigned in protest over the party's lack of condemnation of martial law and its past, the party did not denounce its past fully at any of its congresses.[161] Instead, Kwaśniewski argued that "we were all part of the [the communist] Polish People's Republic."[162] The conflicts between the party and society were too recent, and the new party elites and activists too involved, for the party's past actions to be condemned. They were to prove a considerable barrier to coalitions and parliamentary cooperation.

On the other hand, the party changed its symbols immediately, ceremoniously removing the flags of the PZPR at the Extraordinary Congress. Shortly thereafter, the party replaced the old symbols with the red rose of Social Democratic parties, to underscore its new commitment. The Polish party elites also knew ahead of time that the party name and program would be changed, even if the delegates did not know which name would be chosen.[163] As early as July 1989, party leaders from various wings all argued that while it was uncertain whether the party would be a mass or a parliamentary organization, the name and program would change at the

---

[160] *Rzeczpospolita*, 8 August 1990.
[161] *Życie Warszawy* 20 March 1993.
[162] Aleksander Kwaśniewski, in *Rzeczpospolita*, 3 September 1993.
[163] Interview with Dariusz Klimaszewski, 20 May 1997, Warsaw.

Extraordinary Congress.[164] A member referendum was held *before* the Extraordinary Congress, in the summer of 1989. The result of the referendum was that 72.1% of the members declared themselves in favor of changing PZPR into new party with new program, statute, and name (the Socialist Party of Poland being the top choice).[165] However, these suggestions regarding the party name were ignored, since the relevant committee had "its own ideas."[166] The result was that at the Congress itself, the main debate about the name revolved around the acronym, and whether it should be capitalized as SDRP or left as SdRP.[167] Similarly, the new program was approved immediately.[168] The program had been prepared ahead of time by the reformist Tomasz Nałęcz and his committee, and was approved by 1,106 delegates, with 66 against and 82 absent. Finally, the new centralized party statutes were approved, after minimal discussion. The result was a party "created from above."[169]

This is not to say that all change was orchestrated ahead of time and the outcomes predetermined. One of the most dramatic moments at the congress came when a group of reformers who saw the transformation as a whitewash broke away from the SdRP. Led by Tadeusz Fiszbach, a longtime party reformist from Gdańsk, they formed the Polish Social Democratic Union (Polska Unia Socjaldemokratyczna, PUS). About 140 people initially joined, and among its ranks were those removed from the party for their participation in the reformist "horizontal movements" of 1980–1. Of the parliamentary deputies present at the congress, about forty entered PUS, twenty-five the SdRP, and the rest remained undecided.[170] Meanwhile, the orthodox communists, left out of the SdRP, founded the Union of Polish Communists "Proletariat" (Związek Komunistów Polskich "Pro-

---

[164] "Co dalej z partią?" (Whither the party?), *Polityka*, 1 July 1989.
[165] Poll conducted 19–27 September 1989 on PZPR members, cited in *ycie Partii*, 18 October 1989.
[166] *Trybuna Ludu*, 22 January 1990.
[167] *Trybuna Ludu*, 30 January 1990.
[168] *Trybuna Ludu*, 29 January 1990.
[169] Interview with Dariusz Klimaszewski, 13 May 1997, Warsaw.
[170] By February 1990, the Union had a highly decentralized organizational structure and a program that emphasized the social democratic, nonclass based character of the party and cooperation with all democratic forces, including Solidarity (but not the SdRP) (*Rzeczpospolita*, 15 March 1990). PUS renounced both the practice of wholesale membership transfer, and the use of PZPR assets by the SdRP. In parliament, PUS had forty-two representatives. PUS split over the support by Fiszbach and the party's National Council of Lech Wałęsa's presidential candidacy in the fall of 1990. Several local organizations left in protest, and the party dissolved in July 1991 (1 August 1991, *Głos Poranny*).

letariat") in March 1990. Proletariat soon claimed about eighty basic organizations.[171] Officially registered in September 1990, the organization was unable to receive any electoral support. The reformist leaders of SdRP welcomed its rise, since it meant a clearer, more reformist profile for the main successor party. As Kwaśniewski revealingly declared, "I would happily welcome the rise of a communist party. It would be incredibly useful for [the SdRP]. I dream of this . . ."[172]

For all its rapid centralization, the Polish case reveals some of the limits of elite action. The elites' past experiences with reform and societal negotiation served them well in the organizational transformation of the parties, leading to a pragmatic dissolution and centralization of the party, with its disavowal of the party's members, regional organizations, name, and communist-era symbols. However, the recent history of the state-society relationship prevented even the reformists from renouncing the past, or the injustices perpetrated prior to 1989.

The Hungarian MSzP

In Hungary, the party's past reforming role, its active participation in the abolition of the party-state, and the genuine popularity of some of its leaders meant that the transition would be considerably less mired in conflict, and the party would be far less marginalized.[173] Not only had the party preempted and dampened opposition demands for reform, but considerable personal ties formed between the party reformists and the democratic opposition. Both the technocratic administrators and the intellectuals in party institutions increasingly agreed with the opposition that democratic reforms were required.[174] In short, the party was able to anticipate the transformation of the polity, and respond accordingly – its break with the past was more decisive than in any other case, and the need to centralize was considerably lower than in Poland or in the former Czechoslovakia.

---

[171] *Przedświt*, April 1990.
[172] Interview with Aleksander Kwaśniewski, *Przegląd Tygodniowy*, 14 October 1990. Ironically, the Związek Komunistów Polskich (ZKP) had already formed, and as of September 1990, officially registered, by the time of the interview.
[173] Kukorelli, István. " The Birth, Testing and Results of the 1989 Hungarian Electoral Law," *Soviet Studies*, No. 1, 1991: 137–56, p. 150.
[174] Szalai, Erzsébet. "The Metamorphosis of the Elites," in Király, Béla, ed. *Lawful Revolution in Hungary, 1989–94.* Boulder, CO: Social Science Monographs, distributed by Columbia University Press, 1995, p. 160.

By mid-1988, János Kádár and his fellow gerontocrats were already removed from their party positions. The new party head, Károly Grósz, emphasized that "socialist pluralism does not constrain the leading role of the party." László Németh still argued that was needed was a renewal of socialism, since the crisis was that of a model, not of the system.[175] By early 1989, however, it was "clear that MSzMP's government and parliament could not cope with the challenges set before it."[176] Moreover, the opposition had organized, in the Hungarian Democratic Forum (Magyar Demokrata Fórum, MDF) in September 1987, the League of Young Democrats (Fiatal Demokraták Szövetsége, Fidesz) in March 1988, and the Alliance of Free Democrats (Szabad Demokraták Szövetsége, SzDSz) in May–November 1988. Historical parties also began to resurrect themselves by the November 1988. By March 1989, while the Polish party still argued for representation exclusively within the one-party framework, the Hungarian Central Committee admitted the necessity of a multiparty system.[177]

The Round Table in Hungary, despite superficial similarities, differed from the one in Poland. Begun in March 1989, it was first a meeting among the opposition groups: The party did not meet with them until April. Unlike the Polish Round Table, where the lines between the united opposition and the government were clear, the Hungarian Round Table was trilateral, also involving representatives of unions and quasicivil society organizations (which were under the party's authority). Instead of a single opposition movement, five opposition groups participated, and they were relatively frail. Ironically, the opposition's weakness vis-à-vis the government radicalized the opposition's demands, and led to greater government concessions; the Polish Round Table had already occurred, and the opposition knew that it either had to negotiate free elections or it would begin to lose its legitimacy as representatives of the people.[178]

Negotiations broke down frequently, and while the communist party pressed for a presidential system with majority voting that would presum-

---

[175] Open Society Archives: Hungary: Government: Personalities File, 31 January 1989.
[176] Bozóki, András. "Hungary's Road to Systemic Change: The Opposition Roundtable," in Király, Béla, ed. *Lawful Revolution in Hungary, 1989–94.* Boulder, CO: Social Science Monographs, distributed by New York: Columbia University Press, 1995.
[177] Open Society Archives: Hungary: Party: Local File, 7 February 1989.
[178] For example, the first elections held in Hungary after 1989 were fully free, unlike the semifree election in Poland, with its system of seats reserved for the party. See Bruszt, László, and Stark, David. "Remaking the Political Field in Hungary," *Journal of International Affairs,* Summer 1991: 201–45.

ably reward its popular leaders, the smaller parties within the opposition wanted both a parliamentary system and proportional representation. The pressure began to mount, since the party's congress was scheduled for October 1989, and the reformists within the party had to show something at the congress to legitimize themselves.[179] Meanwhile, the relatively weak opposition split, as its moderates signed the Round Table agreement, and the radicals refused to do so, successfully pressing for a referendum on four additional issues.[180] In August 1989, the party proposed to remove itself from the workplace by June 1990 and from the army by the end of 1990.[181] After a burst of negotiations, fully free elections were scheduled for March 1990.[182]

The party's concessions were not enough for the party reformists, who increasingly organized themselves at all levels of the party. Of the various pro-reform factions, perhaps the most radical and comprehensive reform orientation was to be found in the Reform Circles.[183] The Circles first arose in November 1988. Founded by local activist intelligentsia, they spread throughout Hungary, and eventually numbered over 160, with one hundred thousand members. They demanded changing the "system structure in every sphere," including the separation of the party from the government, end of democratic centralism, freedom of opinion, and a name change for the party. They had also hoped to replace the party leadership.[184] Reformers within the party leadership acknowledged these efforts, and even attended some of the meetings.[185] Nevertheless, the Circles were often unable to engage their local party units in either discussion or alliances.

The Reform Circles were not to be confused with the reform wing of the party, which arose earlier but was more cautious in its proposals. Whereas the Circles had no formal ties to the party leadership, the reform wing was present throughout the Politburo and the Central Committee.

---

[179] Bozóki in Király 1995, p. 87.

[180] The referendum, held in the fall of 1989, asked four questions on the dissolution of the party militia, the return of party assets, the elimination of the party from the workplace, and the timing of presidential and party elections (in effect, whether the president could be from one party and the government from another).

[181] Open Society Archives: Hungary: Party: Local File, 29 August 1989.

[182] Bruszt and Stark 1991.

[183] Open Society Archives: Hungary: Party: Party Life File, 24 May 1989.

[184] *Radio Free Europe Situation Report*, 4 October 1989.

[185] Pál Vastagh, Rezsô Nyers, and Imre Pozsgay attended the Szeged meeting, and Miklós Németh and Mátyás Szűrös sent their greetings.

Therefore, the reform wing did not initially advocate greater party democracy or a change in leadership election procedures – as party leaders, they had little to gain from such changes, and could instead endanger their privileged positions. In short, while the Reform Circles wanted a change of the system, the reform wing wanted a change of the model.

These and other reformist platforms[186] played a key role at the Extraordinary Congress, held 6–9 October 1989, which transformed the MSzMP into the Hungarian Socialist Party, the MSzP. As in Poland, many of the party's skilled managers had already left for the new economic spheres. Unlike their Slovak counterparts, however, they were so numerous that out of the 1,276 delegates attending the congress, the reformist platforms claimed over 1,150. As a result, the Hungarian congress was even more dominated by reform platforms and their agitation than the others. It also took place in an atmosphere far more favorable than elsewhere: The party was not reacting to a defeat, it had prepared for the congress over many months, and the Left was seen as more legitimate in Hungary than elsewhere.[187] In short, the party was far less on the defensive than in the other cases examined here.

Early on the second day of the deliberations, the Reform Circles platform (now called the Reform Alliance) presented theses on forming a new party in the morning of 7 October 1989. The theses, deliberately phrased in "language general enough to be accepted,"[188] called for the dissolution of the party and a radical break with the MSzMP structure and program. As other delegates jumped on the bandwagon, the Reform Circles platform managed to push through the dissolution of the party that evening, with all but 197 out of the 1,276 delegates voting to create a new party. Party members were given a month in which to apply in writing to join the new party.[189] Renouncing its leading role in society, the MSzMP approved multiparty democracy and market reforms at the end of the congress.

The moderate reformist Rezsô Nyers was elected as party chair. László Németh, one of the most popular party leaders, declared he would abandon the party unless a slate of reformists was elected to the leader-

---

[186] Other platforms present at the congress included representatives of the youth, countryside autonomy, agricultural and food industries', workers section, and "For a Healthy Hungary."

[187] Interview with Attila Ágh, 19 March 1997, Budapest.

[188] Interview with Attila Ágh, 19 March 1997, Budapest.

[189] The deadline was extended until the end of 1989, since only tens of thousands joined by 10 November.

ship, much like Weiss and Kwaśniewski after him.[190] Given the support each of these leaders commanded, and the fact that each was seen as the only hope for the party's survival, Nyers, like the other new leaders, could effectively "blackmail" the Congress into compliance. The threat worked – the congress delegates voted that the chair would be elected by individual vote, and then would submit to the congress a list of his nominees for other leading posts.[191] As a result, the new party leadership was now both reformist and experienced.

Centralization

The Hungarian party had an active role in the dismantling of the communist bloc, and its reformist stances had been accepted for years. As a result, the party was not as discredited as the others and had greater initial acceptance. Consequently, it did not have to centralize quite as much as the others to retain competitiveness; its structures were neither as filled with orthodox obstructionists, nor were they as discredited as the others. Nonetheless, the MSzP streamlined and vertically integrated the organization considerably. The party leadership was a dual one, consisting of on the one hand the National Presidium, elected by the congress and the party manager, and on the other the National Steering Committee, consisting of elected and ex officio party activists, regional leaders, and parliamentarians. The party Presidium was carefully chosen: Not one of its members was unpopular or discredited. The Presidium at first had twenty-five members, and then decreased further as the party leaders consolidated their power to fifteen or so. It was in charge of tactical questions, party life, and practical decisions regarding government programs and policy. The 140-member National Steering Committee was in charge of party strategy and parliamentary policy, and of transmitting the views of party members and supporters.[192] It, too, decreased in number as time wore on, to about 115 members.

---

[190] Interview with György Földes, 25 March 1997. The next party leader, Gyula Horn, had close ties to both Németh and to Pozsgay, but not to Nyers. Nyers himself eventually became isolated in parliament after 1994, while Pozsgay's popularity dropped within the party after the fall 1990 referendum, since he was blamed for having negotiated away too many concessions. See Tamás, Bernard. *Party Competence: The Struggle for Political Survival in Post-Communist Hungary.* Book manuscript, 2000, p. 295.

[191] Open Society Archives: Hungary: Party: Congress File, 6 October 1989.

[192] MSZP. "The Hungarian Socialist Party." Budapest: MSZP, 1996.

With time, the Hungarian leadership deliberately gave the regional party centers more room to maneuver. The county-level organizations had a considerable say in the Presidium.[193] Specifically, the county party leadership selected the candidates for the territorial candidate lists. Yet these measures did not affect the party's overall centralization of decision making. The county party leaders initially spoke about possible alternatives to radical transformation, but were quickly trumped by the new elites – it was clear whose solutions would be implemented.[194] The national list was controlled by the party center, which also reserved the right to veto the county list decisions.[195] Moreover, local and regional interests were subjugated to the parliamentary leadership and its interests.[196] Therefore, the party's leadership was far more vertically integrated than that of the Czech party, but not as much as either the Slovak or the Polish party.

As part of the streamlining efforts, elites declared that "the focus of the new party should not be on its own membership, but on the population of Hungary as a whole."[197] Ninety percent of the party members in 1991 were transfers from the old party,[198] and while party leaders argued that they should not give up recruitment, given the smaller size and age of the party, they offered few incentives for new members to join.[199] The new members' sociodemographic characteristics further supported party reform: Over 50% of the new members had higher education, 25% lived in the cosmopolitan Budapest, and 45% were middle-aged.[200] By 1994, party leaders argued that "supported by almost 2 million voters, the MSzP has become a genuine catch-all party embracing left-wing ideals and capable of laying the foundation of a new social consensus Hungary badly needs."[201]

[193] Interview with György Földes, 25 March 1997, Budapest.
[194] Interview with Pal Tamás, 11 March 1997, Budapest.
[195] Racz, Barnabas. "Political Pluralisation in Hungary: The 1990 Elections," *Soviet Studies*, No. 1, 1991: 107–36, p. 126.
[196] Ilonszki, Gabriela. "Institutionalisation and Professionalisation in the First Parliament," in Ágh, Attila, and Kurtán, Sandor, eds. *The First Parliament*. Budapest: Centre for Democracy Studies, 1995, p. 196.
[197] Pozsgay, quoted by Open Society Archives: Hungary: Party: Congress File, 7 October 1989, Judith Pataki.
[198] Racz 1991, p. 126.
[199] Iván Vitányi, MTI, 30 June 1996.
[200] Ágh, Attila. "Organizational Change in the Hungarian Socialist Party," Hungarian Electronic Library (gopher://gopher.mek.iif.hu:7070/00/porta/szint/tarsad/politika/hungpol/agh76.hun), 1994a.
[201] Gyula Horn, MTI, 30 May 1994.

The leadership allowed opinion platforms and even financed them to some degree, paying for the travel of platform representatives and their speaker fees. Nevertheless, these remained amorphous and informal, more like groups sharing similar opinions than organized political factions, largely because they were more concerned with building links with regional party organizations than with directly fighting over party policy. By 1997, these organizations consisted of "Social-Democrats," who advocated cooperation with the liberals, "the People's Democratic Platform," a more traditionally leftist formation which had its roots in an eponymous platform at the Extraordinary Congress,[202] and the pro-union "Socialist platform." None had much influence, although the factional infighting delayed several policy initiatives, such as privatization, once the party was in government after 1994.[203] After the formation of the initial groupings, attempts to create new platforms did not succeed.[204]

Finally, in its relationship to the former communist trade union, National Confederation of the Hungarian Trade Unions (Magyar Szakszervezetek Országos Szövetsége, MSzOSz), the Hungarian successor party maintained even looser ties than its Polish counterpart. MSzOSz representatives ran on the party's ballot, but always under the MSzP label, never as a part of a formal electoral alliance. Moreover, unionists also ran on other party tickets, making the ties even more tenuous.

Breaking with the Past

Paradoxically, the 1989 Congress apologized more vigorously for a past that was by that point less objectionable than the Polish or Czechoslovak party history. The MSzP condemned its past mistakes more than any other party did, apologizing for its forcible merger with the social democrats after World War II, Stalinist repression, the 1956 suppression of the

---

[202] The People's Democratic Platform, led by András Bard, Tamás Krausz, Béla Sabry, and János Gonci, proposed a less radical set of reforms, with a continuation of, rather than a break with, the political developments that took place in Hungary after 1945, and a much more critical attitude toward the market and private ownership. Paradoxically, one reason for the moderation and gradualism of the PDP was the background of its leaders: As younger party members, their age distanced them from the crimes of the predecessor party, so they could promote a continuation of the previous system without implying support for the repression of the 1956 uprising.

[203] Oltay, Edith. "The Return of the Former Communists," *Transition*, 30 January 1995, p. 36. Interview with György Földes, 25 March 1997, Budapest.

[204] Interview with Vilmos Szabó, MSzP HQ, 19 March 1997, Budapest.

popular uprising (no longer called a counterrevolution), the party's inability in the mid-1970s to continue decentralizing reforms, the 1985 refusal by Kádár and his allies to liberalize further the decaying party system, and even the budget deficit.[205]

The party's new name, the Hungarian Socialist Party, had been discussed among the party's delegates prior to the Extraordinary Congress and voted upon immediately at the Congress. Nevertheless, partly because its Congress was the first in the region, the MSzP did not vote to remove the party from the workplace or dissolve its militia. As in Poland, the orthodox communists left immediately – they formed the Workers' Party (Munkáspárt, MP). Eventually taking with them an estimated one hundred thousand members, the MP consisted mostly of older, conservative communists.[206] Though the MP never gained electoral significance, its rise was welcomed by Pozsgay as "a real blessing," since it gave the MSzP "real" communists from which it could differentiate itself.[207]

The administrative experience of the new Hungarian elites and relatively low level of conflict with society allowed them to break with the objectionable elements of its past more than any other party did. Confident of their own capacities, the elites dissolved the party, streamlined it effectively, and integrated the party decision making, while allowing a modicum of regional initiative. At the same time, centralization did not have to go as far as in the Polish or Slovak cases, given the MSzP's greater initial acceptance among the electorate and other parties.

Timing and Sequencing

Of course, not all transformation occurred in 1989. However, change after the initial 1989–90 period was limited by three constraints. First, it would have to come at regularly scheduled party congresses or after elections. These periodic evaluations were anticipated (even if their outcomes were uncertain), so there was more opportunity for individuals and groups within the political party to attempt to buffer themselves from the rever-

---

[205] Documents of the Extraordinary Congress, quoted by Reuters, 9 October 1989.

[206] Its first Congress of December 1989 was organized by former party conservatives: János Berecz, Károly Grósz, and Frigyes Puja, the former CC secretary for ideology, the former general secretary and prime minister, and the former minister of foreign affairs, respectively.

[207] *Times of London*, 8 October 1989. These older communists also formed the János Kádár Society, which also attempted to transform itself into a party. Kádár's widow was apparently appalled.

berations that might have occurred.[208] Second, perhaps the most difficult task for the party elites was to change the party's public image: and unless organizational transformation was begun early and conducted consistently, it would be viewed with suspicion by both the voters and other political parties. Third, once the orthodox barriers reasserted themselves within the parties, change was more difficult to implement.

Consequently, the Czech party continued to maintain its communist identity, and as many structures as possible, in an effort to retain its supporters. The return of orthodox members and ideology was justified both by "democratic inclusion" and by continued references to the glorious achievements of "true," pre–World War II Czech communists. These orthodox returnees dominated the December 1992 congress,[209] and focused on the party's internal problems and the party name, to the exclusion of programmatic or electoral issues. The prevailing argument was that the party should focus on its members, and that it did not matter whether the program appealed to or addressed the citizens. In contrast to earlier documents, the congress denounced democratic socialism, the Socialist International, and social democratic experiences.[210]

Subsequently, a conflict erupted between the Central Committee and the party leader, Jiří Svoboda, who denounced the return of the orthodox activists to the party and to the leadership.[211] The reformist efforts were doomed by this struggle in the leadership, as the Central Committee argued that if the orthodox members were expelled, "extremist" reformists should also be removed.[212] Svoboda resigned the day before the June 1993 congress, arguing that he underestimated the old functionaries and their power, and the fact that any past reform was merely a temporary concession.[213] Despite similar initial opportunities for transformation, his lack of experience repeatedly translated itself into self-defeating decisions during his tenure – for example, the name referendum, or the promotion of party democracy that allowed the most bitter enemies of party reform to assume dominance in the party.

---

[208] See Powell, Walter, and DiMaggio, Paul, eds. *The New Institutionalism in Organizational Analysis*. Chicago: University of Chicago Press, 1991.

[209] *Mlada Fronta Dnes*, 30 March 1993.

[210] Interview with Jozef Mecl, *Rudé Pravo*, 26 June 1993.

[211] *Rudé Pravo*, 24 June 1993.

[212] *Mlada Fronta Dnes*, 30 March 1993.

[213] *Haló Noviny*, 26 June 1993.

Svoboda's resignation led to the departure of two reformist currents and the consolidation of the conservatives' power.[214] Several of the remaining leading moderates (most from the parliamentary representation of the party) left to form their own party, the Czech Party of the Democratic Left (Strana Demokratické Levice, SDL), led by Jozef Mecl. A few days later, other moderates, led by Jaroslav Ortman, formed the Left Bloc Party (Strana Levý Blok, SLB). The SLB claimed twenty-four out of the thirty-five KSČM parliamentarians, and received considerable state funding as well.[215]

The relatively more politically experienced new leadership, led by Miroslav Grebreniček, a former lecturer in the Party Higher School, now began belatedly to centralize the party in the fall of 1993. The center now was to control the regions more, parliamentary platforms were done away with, discussion of party programs by the members ended, and the Central Committee could now remove members at will. However, because earlier organizational decisions had made the party dependent on its members as the main base of its support, the party leaders did not wish to antagonize this narrow and ideologically committed base. The party's stances became more orthodox, with its earlier stances now labeled as a strategic, and temporary, "compromise."[216]

During the 1995 congress, the party further moved to integrate the organization vertically by increasing the direct contacts of the Central Committee with local organizations and party members.[217] The Executive Committee now numbered twenty-two, and the Central Committee had ninety-seven members. These changes, however, did not affect the party's ossified image, support, or ideological emphases. Nor did they necessarily have the desired effect – regional party centers continued to pursue their own policies, while in many cases, opinion platforms flourished

---

[214] *Mlada Fronta Dnes*, 30 March 1993.

[215] Law 424, which determined party funding, declared that the state would fund parties according to their parliamentary representation rather than according to their votes received. Hence, the SLB was able to take over the KSČM funds, or 3 billion Kčs.

[216] "Zpráva ÚV KSČM o vývoji ve straně od II. Sjezdu KSČM do III. Sjezdu KSČM" (The Report of the Central Committee About Developments in the party from the Second to the Third Congress), *Dokumenty III Sjezdu KSČM*, Praha: KSČM, 1993, p. 7. Miroslav Grebreniček, first meeting of the ÚV KSČM, *Haló Noviny*, 13 December 1995.

[217] "Zpráva ÚV KSČM IV. Sjezdu KSČM o činnosti Strany v Obdobi po III. Sjezdu (Červen 1993–prosinec 1995)" (Report of the Central Committee of the KSČM to the IV Congress KSČM About the Party's Activity in the Period After the III Congress (June 1993–December 1995), *Haló Noviny* (supplement), 18 December 1995, p. 8.

on the local level.[218] The possibility of party renewal had already been "brought to a standstill" by the earlier conflicts.[219] By 1999, and the party's Fifth Congress, the KSČM leadership formally declared that the party was a mass, communist party, and would continue to act as one, despite member attrition (the result of an increasingly aged and dying membership – the average age of the member was sixty-four years, compared to forty-six years in the SdRP, for example), worsened organizational activity, and the inability of the local organizations to cope with the mobilizational and informational tasks set forth.[220] Although the party found that "the importance of democratic centralism, solidarity, and party punishment, as well as control activity," had reasserted itself, it was too late to develop effective party discipline.[221]

The Czech case underlines the importance of both timing and sequencing. The attempts to broaden public appeals without concomitant organizational centralization, as we will see in the next chapter, were quickly reversed. Since the members were the party's chief political asset, the party retained much of its former ideology and structures to maximize their loyalty. As we will see, this strategy also affected the party's programs, electorates, and parliamentary performance.

The 1993 centralization efforts made little difference to the party's support base or choice of appeals, since the party's reputation had already consolidated. Moreover, since the party first attempted to change its appeals and then to change its organizational form, it was not until the December 1999 congress that the party could finally admit some wrongdoing in 1989 and moderate its positions on the communist past, Czech membership in international institutions, and the role of the market.

The Slovak party, on the other hand, retained its centralized organization until the debacle of the 1994 elections.[222] The relatively weak regional organizations then lashed out, demanding a greater activation of

---

[218] Miroslav Grebreniček, speech at the fourth meeting of the ÚV KSČM, *Haló Noviny*, 19 January 1994.

[219] *Dokumenty II Sjezdu KSČM*, p. 17.

[220] *Zpráva ÚV KSČM o Činnosti KSČM v obdobi po IV. Sjezdu v Liberci (prosinec 1995–prosinec 1999)* (The Report of the Central Committee about the Party's Activity in the period After the Fourth Congress in Liberec (December 1995–December 1999). Praha: ÚV KSČM, esp. pp. 30 and 65. Available also at the KSČM archive at http://www.kscm.cz.

[221] *Zpráva ÚV KSČM o činnosti KSČM v obdobi po IV. Sjezdu v Liberci (prosinec 1995–prosinec 1999)*. Praha: ÚV KSČM, p. 66.

[222] Interview with Peter Magvaši, SDĽ HQ, 27 January 1997, and interview with Peter Weiss, 23 February 1997, both in Bratislava.

the party membership and a strengthening of the regional party organizations. They argued that the enormous power and flexibility wielded by the elites in changing party programs to pursue different constituencies led to inconsistency and to a lack of responsiveness to the members' concerns. The 1995 congress changed the party rules, allowing for expulsion of inactive members, instituting more frequent party meetings, and permitting more frequent contact with the membership base. To accommodate the regional party centers further, the party founded a Council of Communal and Regional Policy, in addition to the Council of Practical Policy (the party's shadow government).[223]

However, despite these decentralizing moves, the party's real power center was still in Bratislava. The center continued to formulate party programs (introducing a three-tier program document structure in 1996), vet the national candidate lists, organize, and set the agenda for party congresses. The national leadership was the center of party struggles, as Peter Weiss was replaced in 1996, as part of the conflict between the "red managers" (the enterprise directors and businessmen who arose from the party nomenklatura), who wanted to join the ruling coalition no matter what its ideological stripe, and the initial 1989 reformists.[224] No further decentralization, nominal or otherwise, occurred after 1995.[225] Nor were there any subsequent major changes in the party programs, image, or tools of mobilization – it remained a pragmatic, electoral formation, despite insisting on closer ties to its membership.[226]

The Polish party consistently pursued further centralization. The SdRP held its second congress in March 1993, which further centralized the party's organization. The Presidium took over several functions of the National Council, which had already assumed several roles of the Central Executive Committee.[227] The party eliminated its auxiliary committees. The role of the general secretary was now limited, to eliminate the double leadership and the increasingly public conflict between the reformist Kwaśniewski and Leszek Miller, who led the "old apparat" faction. While the young reformists wanted to cut themselves off further from the compromising past of the party, Miller and the old apparat faction were convinced that if the party

[223] *Pravda*, 22 March 1995 and 20 May 1995.
[224] The conflict between Kanis and Weiss also grew at this time. *Nové Slovo bez respektu* č. 47, 21 November 1994.
[225] The party's RR did announce on 8 June 1996 that new regional party structures on the kraj level were to be set up to reflect the new administrative divisions of the country.
[226] *Dokumenty IV Sjezdu*, p. 35.
[227] *Biuletyn II Kongresu SdRP*, 20–1 March 1993.

did so, or changed its structure, the SdRP too would eventually disappear, as PUS had by July 1991.[228] Jerzy Szmajdziński became the general secretary, and Miller instead was convinced to run for one of the three vice chairs.

The party elites continued to disregard the membership. At subsequent congresses, for example, the program was simply approved by the congress, with minimal discussion on substantive issues (although the party did debate owning up to its past).[229] Party members complained, but supported the party anyway, "because to maintain unity any reason is a good one."[230] In 1996, Józey Oleksy explained, "we became a pragmatic party. A criticism of this today may be justified, but this does not mean that we could have done otherwise in 1989. We could not, and so after the dissolution of the PZPR we consciously became a non-ideological, pragmatic, electoral party."[231] He concluded that now the party had to mobilize its members more to retain their support between elections, and no longer simply function from election to election.

However, despite this announcement, no major changes were visible until 1999, when the party centralized again and united its electoral coalition into an eponymous new party, the Democratic Left Alliance (Sojusz Lewicy Demokratycznej, SLD). Miller, among other leaders, had consistently worked to streamline the party, and succeeded with remaking SLD from an electoral alliance into an even more centralized party, shedding its unionist connections. By 2000, fifteen out of the sixteen SLD regions were now led by Miller's people, who continued to implement central directives efficiently.[232] This transformation and the lack of challenges to this change within the party were made possible by the party's initial organizational dissolution and subsequent centralization, and the party's insistence on activist and member loyalty to the party leadership's program.

The Hungarian party's path also proved consistent. At its Fourth Congress in 1995, many observers expected a return to "Left values" after the party's implementation of austerity policies, but this did not come. Instead, the MSzP emphasized social peace as a key priority, and argued that the government would now try harder to explain its policies to the populace.[233] Even as the party continued to have platforms (as many as an estimated

---

[228] *Głos Poranny*, 18 November 1991.
[229] "Na Wieki Wieków" ("For Ever and Ever"), *Wprost*, 16 February 1997.
[230] *Rzeczpospolita*, 6 May 1994.
[231] *Trybuna*, 13 May 1996.
[232] *Wprost*, 19 March 2000, p. 44.
[233] MTI, 26 November 1995.

forty-eight in 1991[234]), their role and number decreased over time. The Fifth Congress, held in June 1997, did not challenge the leadership or Gyula Horn's centralized control. Leadership turnover meant that fifty-four persons cycled through the party's fifteen-member Presidium within the first nine years, but the centralized structures persisted.[235] It was not until after the 1998 elections (and the MSzP's loss therein) that the head of the MSzP's parliamentary grouping, László Kovacs, assumed the party leadership from Horn on 5 September 1998, but the party's overall ideological and organizational course continued.

These subsequent party congresses did not radically change the party organization, its image, or its electoral and coalitional appeals. Unlike 1989, there was neither the justification of a radically new political system, nor was there the opportunity provided by the chaos of the democratic transition. The key changes needed to be made early and decisively. Organizational decisions made after 1991 could consolidate earlier strategies and the elites who implemented them, but they produced minimal changes in the parties' structures and their public image. Moreover, unless the organizational transformations were undertaken *before* the parties attempted to change their image or their electoral appeals, the latter were neither credible nor easily sustainable.

If change was more dramatic early on, it also coalesced faster in some organizational spheres. For example, in the Czech communist party, the members were given considerable powers after 1989, while the competencies of the elites and the channels of decision making were still not fully worked out. As a result, Czech leaders "gave up" what were basic elite powers in the other parties, such as determining the party name or symbols. In the Slovak and Hungarian parties, on the other hand, the elites asserted and solidified their power far more rapidly, whereas the role and capacities of the members were still subject to occasional negotiation as late as 1994. As another example, where the parties had reregistered and dissolved, their membership took a far more precipitous drop after 1989 but stabilized rapidly (see Table 2.4). Where the no dissolution or reregistration occurred, gradual attrition meant the party would lose members each year, and thus lose its one of its remaining political assets.

---

[234] Gillespie, Richard, Waller, Michael, and Nieto, Lourdes Lopez, eds. *Factional Politics and Democratisation*. London: Frank Cass, 1995, p. 133.

[235] Ágh, Attila. "Party Formation Process and the 1998 Elections in Hungary: Defeat as Promoter of Change for the HSP," *East European Politics and Societies*, Winter 2000: 288–315, p. 309.

Conclusion

Consolidation in one area allowed change in another: Had it not been for the rapid influx of reformists into the party leadership, it would have been far more difficult to change the party symbols or programs. Furthermore, had the organizations not been centralized, the barriers to further transformation of public appeals and behavior would have reasserted themselves. Therefore, sequencing was crucial: if the parties wanted to sustain a broadening of their electoral and parliamentary appeals, they first had to transform the organizations. The more discredited the parties, and the more they pursued the broad vote rather than existing loyalties, the more imperative this sequence.

Conclusion

The parties' fall from power demanded that they adapt to their new environment and convince the electorate of this intention. Together, the replacement of the old leadership by new, reform-minded elites, centralization, a break with the party's past, and the early implementation of these strategies were the first steps in this process. This sequence reinforced the perception that the successor parties had both discontinued communist practices and beliefs and embarked on a new, democratic, path.

The often chaotic nature of the transition that began in 1989 and the extraordinary congresses held that year provided an important opportunity for party transformation. In all four cases, these congresses allowed new elites to assume the party leadership and to determine the future direction of the parties. Both elite individual skills and usable pasts made it possible to take advantage of these opportunities – the leaders' past organizational experiences both led them to desire the transformation of the parties' organizations, strategies, and ideals, and gave them the skills with which to implement it. Centralization then allowed the elites to consolidate their new power early and decisively by eliminating alternative sources of authority within the party, such as rival orthodox elites or regional party centers immediately in 1989. Elites with such portable skills could thus rearrange the distribution of power within the parties to their advantage.

The Czech party had few such assets. Convinced that any change would be untenable, the party's leaders considered but rejected radical transformation. Instead, the Czech elites saw the membership and its mobilization as the main chance at political survival, and thus purposefully reiterated the postwar policies of the Czechoslovak Communist Party.

These conservative members, in turn, had little interest in party adaptation, effectively blocked such reform, and ensured that the Czech party would continue to critique the new system from a communist vantage point.

In contrast, the Polish, Hungarian, and Slovak party leaderships recognized how discredited the huge communist organizations had become and had alternatives ready. To various degrees, depending on their elite resources, they disregarded the members and used their own expertise to set the congress agendas, change the party names and symbols, and streamline and integrate the parties. They thus deliberately replicated some of the policies of their communist predecessors, who also did not rely on party members, saw the party leadership as responsible for the party's fate, and paid little attention to ideological commitment.

Organizational transformation then had effects of its own. First, such changes often carried an enormous significance at a time when there was considerable policy consensus and little knowledge about the electorate's potential cleavages. Organizational changes signaled the party's new identity and thus served as a shortcut for voters – hence the controversies surrounding the party name.[236] Second, as we will see later, early centralization determined how easily the elites could achieve the other aspects of party regeneration – the clear and consistent articulation of new programs, electoral appeals, and parliamentary goals. Sequencing change differently made these new party appeals far less credible for the voters, and far more difficult for the parties to sustain.

---

[236] Bielasiak, Jack. "Substance and Process in the Development of Party Systems in East Central Europe," *Communist and Post-Communist Studies*, Vol. 30, No. 1, 1997: 23–44, p. 35.

3

Developing Programmatic Responsiveness

Once the communist successor parties began to change their organizations, they still had to convince both the voters and other parties of the sincerity of their metamorphosis, and of their ability to govern democratically. Voters had little faith in the parties at the outset – over four decades of communist repression left profound suspicions regarding the successors' motives and intentions after 1989. Yet without such public trust, the communist successors could not function as democratic parties – they would not be able to obtain electoral support, represent their chosen constituencies, or cooperate with other parties in the legislature.

Moreover, practical considerations mandated that the parties turn to the electorate to survive politically; the first free elections awaited most of the successor parties within a few months after the regime collapses in 1989.[1] The communist successors now had to persuade the public of their democratic intentions and their ability to respond to popular concerns – that despite the communist parties' history of duplicity, authoritarianism, and lack of real liberalization, the parties' new commitments to democracy and the free market were real. In other words, the communist successors would try to prove that they were now dedicated to the very political system their predecessors had spent nearly five decades attempting to eradicate. Moreover, they had to prove that despite their authoritarian past, they could now legislate, represent, and govern *well*: in a responsive and efficient manner. As we will see in the next chapter, while all the parties did relatively poorly in the first elections, their subsequent electoral success was directly predicated on their ability to convince the

[1] These were held in June 1990 in Czechoslovakia, March 1990 in Hungary, and October 1991 in Poland, with a presidential election in December 1990.

public that they were committed to democracy and to the market, and could administer the new regime competently and effectively, as a reliable alternative to the political parties emerging from the former anticommunist opposition.

Given their predecessors' records, some observers have assumed that the communist successors simply attempted to capitalize on nostalgia for the socialist era and its safety nets.[2] Yet despite concerns that the communist successor parties were simply populist[3] and authoritarian,[4] they all accepted democratic competition and repudiated their earlier claims of sole representation and power monopoly. Subsequently, however, the parties' programmatic transformations varied in both kind and degree. The Czech party changed its programs the least and retained much of its former appeals. The Slovak party transformed its programs, but did not offer a credible alternative to the voters. Finally, the Polish and Hungarian parties not only dramatically and credibly transformed their programs, but created new dimensions of competition. This chapter examines why we see this variation, and what it took for the parties to transform their programs convincingly.

To sway the electorate, programmatic appeals were the only real means, since the successor parties under consideration could not rely on either patronage or charismatic leaders. Parties could rely on clientelistic claims and retain intact patronage networks under one of two conditions. First, if they remained in power through the transition and were not formally forced out of power, successor parties could retain greater continuity in their organizational and patronage networks. For example, the Bulgarian and Romanian communist successors, who never ceded power fully during the transition years of 1989–91, could retain many of their clientelistic relationships. As a result, they did not have to develop responsive programs, since they could gain votes by offering direct material incentives to their supporters.

[2] Kimball, L. "Nostalgia Wins the Day in Poland," *New Statesman and Society*, 1 November 1993, pp. 20–1.

[3] Jasiewicz, Krzysztof. "Polish Politics on the Eve of the 1993 Elections," *Communist and Post-Communist Studies*, December 1993a: 387–411.

[4] Kitschelt, Herbert. "The Formation of Party Systems in East Central Europe," *Politics and Society*, March 1992: 7–50, p. 31. See also Kitschelt, "Party Systems in East Central Europe: Consolidation or Fluidity?" *Studies in Public Policy*, No. 241 (Glasgow: Univ. of Strathclyde) previously 1995b, pp. 84 and 94.

Second, for parties that were forced to exit from power, patronage networks could be sustained if they were localized and "apolitical" – that is, not tied to the regime. For example, the Polish Peasants' Party (Polskie Stronnictwo Ludowe, PSL), the former communist satellite, had extensive local networks, maintained through auxiliary organizations such as the volunteer firefighting brigades, which it was able to retain after 1989 as a "service to the community." Such brigades were still needed to fight village fires, and as such could not be simply disbanded as party organizations. As a result, the PSL was able to funnel considerable material resources through these networks, under the guise of providing necessary local services, and could thus rely more on clientelistic mobilization.

The Czech, Slovak, Polish, and Hungarian communist successor parties, on the other hand, had both national and highly politicized patronage networks – for example, the whole nomenklatura system. When they were forced to exit from power, they lost access to these structures of clientelistic mobilization. As a result, since they had neither functioning patronage networks nor charismatic leaders,[5] they instead had to use programmatic appeals. As a consequence, programs were so important to communist successor regeneration because they were the chief way to respond to electoral cleavages and to convince the electorate. They were a clear signal to the voters and to other parties of the communist successors' new intentions and commitments to new policy choices.

For their part, the past programs of the communist parties were not much to go on. Under communism, these programs were little more than a ritualistic listing of goals and ideology. They were not responsive to popular concerns or priorities, provided no real policy alternatives, and did not swerve from the party's ideological line. Thus, if they were to demonstrate that they were a reliable alternative to the political parties emerging from the former anticommunist opposition, the successors' programs after 1989 had to address these shortcomings.

Given this historical and institutional context, programmatic transformation was a major challenge for the communist successors. The new party programs had to become *responsive*: focused on the voters, policy-oriented, and flexible. Responsive programs would thus address the

---

[5] Personal connections and networks tied together many economic directors and political leaders. However, minimal clientelistic networks existed between the communist successor parties, out of power at all levels of government after 1989, and individual voters.

electorate (rather than internal party concerns), emphasize its policy priorities, and take up similar stances (as reflected by the congruity between the dominant themes in the party programs and public evaluations of "extremely important" government roles by the voters).[6] A party's appeals would not be responsive when the party's programs addressed only internal concerns, exhibited little congruence between the policy priorities of the party and the electorate, or failed to change when the electorates did. Thus, political parties had to respond to voter priorities, and to formulate programs and appeals that responded on multiple occasions to shifts in popular opinion and to the distinct opportunities presented by the countries' political environments.

At the same time, however, there were limits to the extent to which the parties would follow the broad electorate. Parties could be more flexible on stances they consider a matter of political pragmatism than on their "core beliefs," which are central to their identity and the retention of "core" supporters. On some issues, parties would stand fast, even if it meant not gaining additional supporters, in order to retain their identity and current support. The more confident a vote-maximizing party would be of support on other issues, the more it would retain a core belief, provided that taking this stance did not *reduce* its existing support. As a result, even when adopting a given political stance could have broadened a party's appeal, these considerations could steer the party in a different course. For example, the Polish SdRP retained its strong secular stance, while the SDL' consistently maintained its support for democratic reform, even when more populist claims could have swayed some voters.

Beyond addressing existing voter priorities, political parties could also create *new dimensions of competition*. Where the communist parties were discredited and forced to exit from power, political parties tended to converge in their rejection of the old system and in broad calls for reform. Under such conditions of general policy consensus, communist successor politicians tried to highlight other dimensions of competition. Instead of directly

---

[6] Unlike Ian Budge and Dennis J. Farlie, *Explaining and Predicting Elections*. (London: Allen & Unwin, 1983) and other practitioners of the "saliency" theory of issue-voting (see Robertson, David. *A Theory of Party Competition*. London: John Wiley & Sons, 1976), I argue that stances, as well as number of mentions, are relevant; otherwise, using the "saliency" measures, a party advocating a stance opposite to the desires of the entire population would be coded as "responsive," simply because it mentioned the issue in its program. For more details on the content analysis techniques used, party documents used, and the methodology of coding the party programs, please see Appendix A.

competing on existing dimensions (at the risk of being outflanked by other, more credible parties), communist successors could attempt to compete across these cleavages. Such efforts to create new, orthogonal axes of competition, dubbed "heresthetics" by William Riker (1986), privilege their creators ex ante: In effect, a party could set up the very standards on which other parties competed – the same standards which it could best fulfill.

Circumventing the existing policy cleavages with new ones that offered a comparative advantage to the communist successor parties was also a programmatic strategy that was most likely to be successful electorally. If the successor parties continued with their old communist appeals, they were likely to retain a core group of orthodox supporters, but were unlikely to convince the broader electorate. If they moderated their policy appeals, the successors depended on voters with similar priorities and stances for the core of their support, but still had to compete with other parties whose origins in the anticommunist opposition often made them more credible. Finally, too radical a programmatic turnaround might be perceived as an opportunistic "whitewashing" rather than an indication of real commitments. Creating credible new appeals that transcended existing cleavages, on the other hand, got around the problem of taking unpopular or noncredible stances on existing issues.

The less a party was able to compete on policy issues or create new ones, the more it emphasized its historical identity at expense of present appeals.[7] In turn, the greater the emphasis on doctrinal symbols, such as the party name or its logo, the less attention was paid to programmatic alternatives. Without a new political program, symbols and history took precedence, further precluding the formulation of new political or economic alternatives and continuing the cycle. Thus, where a successor party hoped to attract a broader electorate, it would try to become responsive to existing cleavages and, where it had the elite resources to do so, to create new bases for competition. If, in contrast, a party prioritized retaining its existing members as core supporters, it was more likely to try to retain its old ideology. The resulting variation in programmatic responsiveness is summarized in Table 3.1.

This variation in programmatic strategies has much to tell us both about the parties' policy commitments and the challenges that the parties faced in signaling these pledges. Reliance on party programs increased the elec-

---

[7] Waller, Michael. "Party Inheritances and Party Identities," in Pridham and Lewis 1996, p. 25.

Table 3.1. *Summary of variation in party programs, 1990–8.*

	Czech KSČM	Slovak SDĽ	Polish SdRP
Appealed to:	Existing party supporters.	Shifting constituencies.	Broad electorate.
Stances on economy	Not responsive to rest of electorate.	Responsive: Party supporters and party program shift together.	Responsive to both supporters and other voters.
Stances on secularism/ nationalism	Party responsive, but secularism not a relevant cleavage.	Party and electorate not very secular. In 1996, the party responds to supporters' secularism.	Party and its supporters very secular, far more so than the rest of the electorate.
	Some nationalist claims regarding Sudetenland.	Shifted views on Hungarian minority.	No nationalist claims.
Stances on managerial competence	Unable to claim managerial competence credibly.	Seen as more committed to democracy than competent.	Seen as highly competent and professional.
Creation of New Issues	"Autonomy," but neither credible nor resonant.	Democracy, but not resonant with voters.	Competence, both credible and resonant.

toral and parliamentary costs of changing stances,[8] since the betrayal of a public pledge would carry with it the risk of seeming dishonest or unpredictable to the voters.[9] More generally, programs reflect and respond to policy debates in developed democracies,[10] influence the political discus-

---

[8] Parties can (and often do) accept these costs, if they can become part of a coalition that blurs individual party responsibility for a given policy. However, given the low coalition potential of all three parties, the need for programmatic consistency is all the greater. I am indebted to Katarzyna Stanclik for this point.

[9] Budge, Ian. "The internal analyses of election programmes," in Budge, Ian, Robertson, David, Hearl, Derek, eds. *Ideology, Strategy, and Party Change: Spatial Analyses of Post-War Election Programmes in Nineteen Democracies.* Cambridge, UK: Cambridge University Press, 1987, p. 27. Dixit, Avinash, and Nalebuff, Barry. *Thinking Strategically.* New York: W.W. Norton, 1991.

[10] Budge and Farlie, 1983.

sion during electoral campaigns,[11] and set the policy agenda even when the parties do not enter government.[12] Such appeals provide a useful image of the party's main concerns and its normative visions, the issues it wishes to address, and its policy priorities. Put more elegantly, they are "a unique and authoritative statement of policy endorsed by the party as a whole at a certain point in time."[13] They do have their limits – critics have charged that they are not read or understood by the electorate, and largely designed to pacify activists rather than to provide a blueprint for party policy.[14] However, they were still the principal public document to commit the party to given stances and policies.

The emergent political parties in East Central Europe faced programmatic tasks that were as overwhelming as they were unprecedented – they were now called on to provide constructive answers to a slew of policy problems, while attempting to obtain support, engage their parliamentary colleagues, and build organizations on the ground. As inexperienced as they were in directly representing and answering to the voters, the parties also had to provide answers to the difficulties that arose from the post-1989 transformation of political boundaries, the new rules of political competition, and the conflicting demands of redistribution and economic liberalization.[15] The simultaneity of these transformations, their wide scope, and the resulting fluidity in the political and economic situation made accurate programmatic responses even more difficult than they would have been in an established political and economic system.

The successor parties consequently had to formulate coherent policy proposals and then overcome the higher coordination and information costs of transmitting and explaining them.[16] These tasks were made all the

---

[11] Budge et al. 1987.

[12] Klingemann, Hans-Dieter, Hofferbert, Richard, and Budge, Ian. *Parties, Policy, and Democracy*. Boulder, CO: Westview Press, 1994.

[13] Laver, Michael, and Budge, Ian. "Measuring Policy Distances and Modelling Coalition Formation," in Laver, Michael J., and Budge, Ian, eds. *Party Policy and Government Coalitions*. New York: Saint Martin's Press, 1992: 15–40, p. 17.

[14] Gallagher, Michael, Laver, Michael, and Mair, Peter. *Representative Government in Western Europe*. New York: McGraw-Hill, 1992, p. 128. On the other hand, 49% of Czech party members read the program, according to party polls (Klub levicových sociologů a psychologů "Zaverečná Zpráva ze sociologického výzkumu . . . ," No. 14-1995, November 1995, p. 8).

[15] Offe, Claus. "Capitalism and Democracy by Design? Democratic Theory Facing the Triple Transition in East Central Europe," *Social Research*, Vol. 59, No. 4, 1991: 865–92.

[16] Kitschelt 1995a, p. 449. Kitschelt, Herbert. "Formation of Party Cleavages in Post-Communist Democracies," *Party Politics*, October 1995a: 447–72.

more difficult for the communist successors by the general public antipathy toward the communists, the rejection of the old system, and the burden of their past. Therefore, the new programs also had to consistently accumulate evidence of the parties' transformation. As we will see, the response to these complicated challenges was predicated on elite resources and the organizational transformation they produced.

Organizational Bases for Programmatic Transformations

Earlier organizational transformations and the elites who led them were the main factors behind the variation in the parties' programmatic responsiveness. To be sure, the political environment – the demands of the post-1989 transformation and the fragility of the party system – exerted considerable pressure on the parties. Fragmented party competition was characterized by numerous parties that competed on orthogonal dimensions,[17] the volatility of the new democratic politics tended to promote vague appeals, and the crowding of parties could lead to centrifugal competition.[18] Nonetheless, differences in party responsiveness do not correspond to the levels of party system fragmentation structure alone (see Appendix C). For example, the Polish party system began with the highest initial fragmentation, and then consolidated rapidly after 1993. Yet the party's stances were responsive from the start, and this capacity has not altered much. Similarly, the Slovak party did not respond to the drop in party fragmentation in 1992–4 by increasing its responsiveness during this time.

Instead, while outside forces exerted pressure on party appeals, elite portable skills and the internal organizational streamlining and vertical integration they engendered determined whether and how the parties would respond to these demands. Where the program writers were few and united, party appeals were more likely to be coherent and flexible. In contrast, party democracy could hinder programmatic transformation.

---

[17] Inglehart, Ronald. *The Silent Revolution: Changing Values and Political Styles Among Western Publics*. Princeton, NJ: Princeton University Press, 1977. Kirchheimer, Otto. "The Transformation of the Western European Party Systems," in LaPalombara, Joseph, and Weiner, Myron, eds. *Political Parties and Political Development*. Princeton, NJ: Princeton University Press, 1972 (1966), p. 197. Przeworski and Sprague 1986. Kitschelt, 1994.

[18] Cox, Gary W. "Electoral Equilibrium Under Alternative Voting Institutions," *American Journal of Political Science*. February 1987: 82–108. Sartori, Giovanni. *Parties and Party Systems*. Cambridge, UK: Cambridge University Press, 1976.

Members' opinions would have to be canvassed, and members' support secured, taking up both time and resources. As various factions lobbied for the inclusion of their views, internal divisions and conflicts could further confuse the process of writing and disseminating party appeals.[19] Finally, where the party's members and core supporters were both powerful and different from the electorate in their views, they could prevent the party from tapping into the concerns of the broader electorate.[20]

For such efforts to be successful, the party elites making these appeals had to have the political skill and experience to pick a dimension that both resonated with the public and was credible. These leaders were now in charge of both reading the political situation and responding to it. The more the parties had earlier innovated, the greater their capacity to formulate new policy answers to the challenges of transition. Such parties had a considerable comparative advantage over other parties: their administrative experience and managerial expertise. Moreover, elites with prior negotiating experience could more easily tap into public concerns and present party programs that appealed to new electorates without alienating others.

Relatively experienced, innovative, pragmatic, and transformation-minded elites were especially important if the party would attempt to create new dimensions of competition. Where the parties broke with the past and centralized, they had the organizational wherewithal to become programmatically responsive. Where they had skilled elites, they not only stood a better chance of responding to the voters, but could more readily create new dimensions of competition.

If centralization determined the breadth and flexibility of party appeals, its early timing had two consequences. First, the elites had the most leeway to change radically the party appeals early in the party's transformation, during 1989–90. However, they could sustain these new signals only if they retained control over the party's strategic goals and programs through centralization. Thus, later efforts to centralize or decentralize, after 1990–1, made little difference to programmatic responsiveness. The Czech party centralized in 1993, yet its responsiveness took a dip at this

[19] Rose, Richard. *Do Parties Make a Difference?* Chatham, NJ: Chatham House, 1980, p. 147. Harmel, Robert, and Janda, Kenneth. "An Integrated Theory of Party Goals and Party Change," *Journal of Theoretical Politics*, Vol. 6, No. 3, 1994: 256–87, p. 265. See Strom, 1990.

[20] But see Schlesinger, Joseph. "On the Theory of Party Organization," *Journal of Politics*, May 1984: 369–400.

time. Similarly, the Slovak party decentralized somewhat in 1995, yet its programs have shown no change in their responsiveness.

Second, without an early and decisive organizational streamlining, orthodox activists and representatives could reenter the party and work from within to subvert the reformist agenda, by insisting on their input into programs or simply by making conflicting public declarations. The old party membership and apparat could not be relied upon to commit itself fully to reform – and the greater role they had in the organization, the more the program would reflect their priorities. Early organizational centralization made it possible for the elites to act consistently and prevented the subversion of elite signals. The earlier this organizational transformation, therefore, the more credible the renunciation of the communist past and the adoption of new appeals.

Voter Priorities and Social Cleavages

As a result of the parties' distinct organizational transformations, the programmatic responsiveness of the parties varied in their orientation toward the voters, their policy emphases, and their flexibility.

First, the parties differed in the extent to which they addressed the voters' public policy concerns, and the degree to which they instead concentrated on the party's internal life. Such "public policy issues" consist of the party's stances toward democracy, economy and economic reforms, "quality of life" issues (also known as "New Left" issues), international relations, administrative decentralization, nationalism, and regional autonomy. The category of "internal life" comprises references to the party members, party self-identity organizational issues, and self-defense against perceived threats to the party's existence.

The ratio of the party's emphases on internal to public issues is the first indicator of whether it intends to address widely held popular concerns or a narrow group of party activists and supporters.[21] Overall, the parties devoted about 80–87% of their programs to public issues, and about 11–16% to internal concerns. However, within individual parties, this emphasis differed considerably, as shown by Table 3.2. Where the party

---

[21] Arguably, an inward-looking program does not preclude programmatic responsiveness. A party could, for example, devote 20% of its program to its own concerns, and then use the remaining 80% to respond fully to the voters. Alternatively, a party could spend only a tiny fraction of its program on itself, and yet fail to respond to any public concerns.

Table 3.2. *Voter orientations and policy trade-offs.*

	Czech KSČM	Slovak SDĽ	Polish SdRP	Hungarian MSzP
Average percentage of programs spent on internal party issues	28.6%	10.8%	16.1%	
Member-voter trade-off[a]:	17.9	8.1	4.2	6.2

[a] Measured by the average gap between supporters and nonsupporters' priorities, in percent of poll respondents.

Source: Tóka, Gábor. "Party Systems and Electoral Alignments in East Central Europe." Machine-readable data. Central European University, 1992–6.
Source: Content analysis of party programs, see Appendix A.

leadership depended on the rank and file, and the membership was not contingent on acceptance of the program, the party paid less attention to its public policy and focused instead on the symbolic dimensions that concerned the members, such as the party name, symbols, and its history.

As a result, centralization also determined the potential trade-off between appealing to party supporters and the rest of the electorate. If the two groups differed considerably, reaching out to a broader electorate would mean losing the party's core supporters.[22] The parties' organizational criteria regarding membership institutionalized this trade-off. The more the party relied on members for political mobilization and support, the more it had to address their concerns and give them incentives for continued support. Where the parties first retained or allowed conservative communist members, and then tailored party programs to suit their demands, the gap between party supporters and rest of the voters grew, as did the alienation of the broader electorate. These parties' subsequent tendency to canvass the views of the members, rather than the broader electorate, further limited the sort of commitments and stances such parties could make.

In contrast, where the parties had first formulated responsive programs and then made membership contingent on their acceptance, the trade-off was minimized. Members had to agree to the parties' new moderate course to join the party. Assured of member support for the program, such parties could appeal to the broader electorate with less worry about losing existing support. Subsequently, such parties could rely on public opinion polls

[22] Przeworski and Sprague 1986.

of the broad potential electorate, rather than of existing sympathizers, since the two groups were more congruent.[23]

Thus, while existing analyses have often assumed that the trade-off between appealing to party activists and to voters[24] is constant and exogenous, it was largely of the parties' own making in the postcommunist context. It was also self-reinforcing – for example, a party with active and orthodox members, by making appeals that satisfied these members, would alienate the broader electorate. This would make the party ever more dependent on its membership and thus bound to orthodox stances. The high costs of building internal consensus on party programs in programmatic parties[25] meant that the less streamlined the party, the higher this trade-off (see Table 3.2).

Second, in the realm of public policy, three issue domains were critical to both the voters and to the parties: economic policy, secularism/nationalism, and administrative expertise. These issues have dominated both the party programs, and the public discussion, throughout the period after 1989 in the four countries. (The analysis of Hungarian party responsiveness is pursued in far less detail, as it replicates the Polish pattern in most programmatic outcomes.[26])

Economic Policy

Given the enormity of the economic transformation and the very real costs borne by the population, such as inflation or unemployment, it is not surprising that economic policies were the single most important issue for both the electorate and the political parties in East Central Europe after 1989.[27] Over three-quarters of all electorates under consideration saw the

[23] *Życie Warszawy*, 9 August 1993.
[24] See Aldrich, John. "A Downsian Spatial Model with Party Activism," *American Political Science Review*: 1983: 947–90. Robertson 1976, ch. 2. Tsebelis 1990. May, John D. "Opinion Structures of Political Parties: The Special Law of Curvilinear Disparity," *Political Studies* 21, 1973: 135–51. See also Wilson, James Q. *The Amateur Democrat*. Chicago: Chicago University Press, 1966. But see Kitschelt, 1989a, and Iversen, Torben. "The Logics of Electoral Politics: Spatial, Directional, and Mobilizational Effects," *Comparative Political Studies*, July 1994: 155–89, for a critique.
[25] Kitschelt, Herbert. p. 7.
[26] The Hungarian party did place less emphasis on secularism and more on antinationalism, as the latter issue was more salient in Hungarian politics. The other major difference was the Hungarian party's greater emphasis on economic redistribution.
[27] Kitschelt 1995b, p. 39.

Table 3.3. *Mean economic stances of party programs,*
1990–8.

Party	Average economic stance[a]	Variance
Czech	3.09	.224
Slovak	2.34	.269
Polish	2.80	.503

Note: [a] The scale is 1–4, with 1 as strongly pro–free market
and 4 as strongly pro-interventionist.

Source: Content analysis of party programs; see Appendix A.

economy as the crucial issue.[28] The broad category of "economic policy"
comprises four separate issue areas:

- First, the development of the free market, and the extent to which
  competition and market incentives should take the place of state regulation and control of the markets.
- Second, social policy: the scope of the welfare state and its provisions
  – redistributive taxes, pensions and benefits, full employment policies, health care, education, and housing.
- Third, private property rights and their development: the extent to
  which restitution and privatization should take the place of state
  ownership.
- Fourth, redistribution: the extent to which inequalities are acceptable, as opposed to the idea that social justice demanded equality of
  both opportunity and outcome.

The evolution of the parties' economic stances demonstrates two relationships hypothesized earlier. First, organizational centralization allowed
the parties to change their stances more readily than the retention of a
member-heavy, decentralized organization. As Table 3.3 shows, the Slovak
and Polish parties could more readily change their views (as shown by
the variance around the mean of the stances). The Polish party especially
could evolve its views to a strong support of economic reform, as a result
of its centralized, flexible program-writing mechanisms.

Second, the more centralized the party, the more easily it could pursue
a broad, pro-reform, strategy. Thus, the elites of Czech party, with its mass

[28] Kitschelt 1995a confirms this result.

Table 3.4. *Mean secular stances of party programs,*
1990–8.

Party	Average secular stance[a]	Variance
Czech	1.75	.200
Slovak	2.0	.222
Polish	1.17	.167

Note: [a] The scale is 1–4, with 1 as extremely secular, and 4 as extremely antisecular.

Source: Content analysis of party programs; see Appendix A.

party organization, initially held pro-reform views, but these were quickly obliterated as the orthodox activists returned to the party, and the leadership (never particularly committed to reform) was helpless to stop them. In contrast, the ultracentralized Slovak party's stances became more supportive of economic reform and the free market than the populist HZDS.

Secularism and Nationalism

The issues of secularism and nationalism were on an orthogonal dimension to those of economic reform and redistribution. They reflected a secondary dimension in East Central European politics that ran between secular, cosmopolitan, and liberal attitudes toward the separation of church and state, national identity, and civil rights on the one hand, and more religious, particularist, and authoritarian attitudes on the other.[29]

The parties' stances on secularism illustrate the significance of "core beliefs." Ironically, the more predominantly religious the country, the more secular the party, as Table 3.4 shows. However, the significance of these secular views varied – the success of a particular programmatic strategy was predicated on the elites' ability to read the electorate and respond without abrogating existing support.

The Czech communist successor held relatively mild secular views. Given the prevailing secularism of the Czech polity, such stances did not distinguish the party from its competitors, nor did they change the party's support among the relatively indifferent electorate.[30] In contrast, the Polish SdRP held stances that were far more secular than the Polish

[29] Kitschelt 1992. See also Evans and Whitefield 1993.
[30] Kitschelt 1995b, p. 82.

voters, 95% of whom identified themselves as Catholic. These secular views were at the core of the SdRP's identity as a modern, cosmopolitan party, and so the party consistently maintained this stance. Moderating secularism would not only lead to the loss of its secular core supporters, but also reduce the party's distinctiveness from centrist parties to its communist roots – not a facet the SdRP wished to emphasize. At the same time, given the intrusion of the Church into public life in 1990–2, retaining secularism gained the party votes. The Polish party was thus able not only to retain its core support, but to gain a broader electorate in 1993. In contrast, the Slovak party programs moderated their secularism to gain a wider electorate, but the elites were unable to justify this move to the party's existing supporters. The inconsistency served only to disappoint and alienate the party's core electorate, which was far more secular than the rest of the voters. As a result, in lurching from stance to stance, the SDĽ lost existing supporters without necessarily gaining new ones.

Expertise, Competent Managers, and the Creation of New Issues

If the parties could capitalize on a comparative advantage, they stood to create a new dimension of competition that did not conflict with a commitment to reform. Doing so, however, required skilled elites who could make such claims credibly, and the organizational centralization to give these elites the dominant voice in the party. One issue that fulfilled these requirements was managerial competence: It did not conflict with the reform program, did not commit the party to a particular policy stance, and could be made credible both by the successor parties' previous administrative experience and the first democratic governments' relative incompetence.

By 1993, an average of three fourths of the electorates agreed that the provision of competent managers by political parties was "extremely important for the country." Managerial competence became a crucial campaign issue, partly as a result both of the consensus on many policy issues and of the successor parties' efforts to create new bases for competition. Unlike purely policy stances, this issue was not a question of convictions or the content of policies but of the efficacy with which they would be carried out. Therefore, if a party could convincingly argue that it would implement policies effectively, it reinforced the rest of its message and stood to gain an even bigger electorate.

However, whether or not the communist successor parties could respond to this voter priority depended on the elite skills produced by the communist parties' earlier reform and response efforts. The more the parties had earlier reformed and implemented liberalizing economic and political policies, the more their new elites could claim administrative experience and managerial expertise that was portable to the democratic setting. Thus, parties with considerable elite resources could refer back to their administrative competence, ideological moderation, and managerial experience. In Poland and in Hungary, the successor parties were able to make competence a key electoral issue and credibly claim they could best provide managerial expertise. In Slovakia, the SDĽ also tried to make competence an electoral issue, but was less successful in convincing the electorate. In contrast, the Czech party also attempted to create a new dimension of party competition, economic autonomy. When this failed, since it was neither resonant nor credible, the party asserted it had competent managers, but could not buttress these claims. As a result, it returned to reiterating the party's history and symbols.

Thus, initial centralization heavily influenced the parties' voter orientation, policy emphases, and programmatic flexibility, while elite portable skills made possible the creation of new competitive dimensions. The sections that follow examine the identities and goals put forth by the individual parties, their programmatic appeals, their responsiveness, and the organizational factors that underlie them. This analysis does not claim to explain the development of political party systems after 1989, the full patterns of party positions, or their shifts. Rather, it focuses on one set of political parties and shows how their communist past and subsequent reorganization could allow them to transform their programmatic appeals and to respond to the very electorate whose demands they would not fulfill under communism.

The Czech KSČM

The Czech communist successor party faced a difficult situation. First, its earlier organizational choices bound it to its core of orthodox supporters, creating a considerable trade-off between appealing to party members and to the broader electorate. Second, an economically pro-market, and politically anticommunist, consensus dominated Czech democratic politics from the outset. The post-1989 order was dominated by the free market rhetoric of the Civic Democratic Party (Občanská Demokratická Strana, ODS) and its leader, Václav Klaus. Not only had the republic's elites agreed on the need for market reforms, but 88% of poll respondents declared that a market economy was "right for the country," the highest such percentage recorded in the region.[31] Moreover, this consensus had tangible results: Czech unemployment and inflation figures were the lowest in the region until the late 1990s.[32]

As a result, the KSČM desperately needed to create a new dimension of competition – but both its lack of portable elite skills and its organizational dependence on its narrow circle of supporters made such a strategy doubly difficult. The party could not issue responsive appeals and could not create new grounds for competition. The KSČM instead chose to retain many of its communist appeals and await the expansion of its support as the status quo worsened.

Consequently, the post-1989 Czech party elites proudly proclaimed the KSČM a communist party, insisting that "we are communists."[33] As one party official explained, "both the program and the identity of the party are contained in its very name."[34] This explicit programmatic continuation of the communist tradition[35] emphasized both the relevance of Marx and Engels and the importance of party democracy.[36] Above all, party programs were to be created "exclusively on the basis of a pluralism of opinions" within the party.[37] The party's preoccupation with members and platforms meant that its leaders then tailored the party program to appeal to the narrower circles of party members and affiliates rather than to the broad electorate. As party leaders argued, "we have to be careful that the gains in public eyes won't be bought at too dear a price of losing a part of the membership base."[38] For their part, the only groups concerned with

---

[31] William L. Miller, White, Stephen, and Heywood, Paul. *Values and Political Change in Postcommunist Europe*. New York: St. Martin's Press, 1998. The poll was taken in 1993.

[32] Thus, unemployment peaked at 4.1% in 1991, when it was nearly 12% in both Poland and in Slovakia. Inflation in 1990 was 18%, less than a tenth of what it was in Poland at the time. By 1995, it was 8%, still lower than Hungary's 28% or Poland's 22%. Data from Błażyca, George, "The Politics of the Economic Transformation," in White, Stephen, Batt, Judy, and Lewis, Paul, eds. *Developments in Central and East European Politics 2*. Durham, NC: Duke University Press, 1998.

[33] Jiří Machalik, *Naše Pravda*, 8 March 1990.

[34] Interview with Vera Žežulková, 24 September 1996.

[35] *Zpráva ÚV KSČM o činnosti strany od 1. Sjezdu KSČM* . . . 1993, p. 19.

[36] *Zpráva ÚV KSČM o činnosti strany od 1. Sjezdu KSČM* . . . 1993, pp. 26–7. "Písemná Zpráva ÚV KSČS pro 18. Sjezd KSČS" (Written Report of the Central Committee for the Eighteenth Congress of the Communist Party of Czechoslovakia), *Dokumenty 18. Sjezdu KSČS*, Praha, 3–4.11.1990. Praha: ÚV KSČS, 1990, p. 49.

[37] KSČM, *Teze Zprávy* . . . 1992, p. 3.

[38] Jiří Svoboda, fifth meeting of the Central Committee of the KSČM, *Haló Noviny*, 28 May 1991.

making the program more responsive, the reformist platforms, had to concentrate on fighting for their own survival within the party.[39]

At first, some of the early post-1989 documents argued that the party had to learn from the social democratic experience. At the founding congress, party leader Ladislav Adamec talked about the "valuable experiences" of the social democrats and how much they had to teach the party. Thus, even if they still relied on references to "Marxist humanism,"[40] the first party programs tended to support both political and economic reform in an attempt to respond to the changed political situation. As one party leader put it, "our program is a renewal of socialism, fully respecting the opinions and stances of the people."[41]

Shortly thereafter, however, these initial cautious commitments to reform were subverted by the party's decentralized structures. First, orthodox activists began to return to the party in 1990–1 and flood its leadership positions. They exploited intraparty democracy and began to use its consultative channels to return the party programs to a more orthodox stance. Their insistence on a return to communist appeals meant that the programs would not resonate within the broader public, which was far more satisfied at the time with return of the free market, democracy, and economic reforms.

Second, the members were at first chiefly concerned with the party name and party symbols in 1990–1, leaving the elites to formulate the program as they saw fit.[42] By early 1992, however, these questions were largely settled. As the rank and file turned their attention to the program, their main goal was to ensure that the program now reflected the party's communist name and orientation. The members criticized the relatively reformist early programs as "an attack on the communist party."[43] The failure to streamline the party organization decisively thus allowed the party's initial moderation to slide back into orthodoxy and into a denunciation of moderate left stances as destructive.

---

[39] Interviews with Vasil Mohorita, 14 October 1996, Marie Stiborová, 21 October 1996, and Michal Kraus, 22 October 1996, all in Prague.

[40] *Rude Pravo*, 31 March 1990.

[41] Ladislav Adamec, *Rude Pravo*, 6 January 1990.

[42] Neither regional meetings nor party congresses took up the question of the party's programs, and the party members devoted their energies instead to the discussion and eventual referendum on the party name. By December 1991, however, the question of the name had largely been settled in favor of the Communist Party of Bohemia and Moravia.

[43] Ivan Hruza in *Hálo Noviny*, 22 November 1992.

The Czech KSČM

With Miroslav Grebreniček's attempt to centralize party decision making in 1993, programmatic references to internal party democracy and the benefits of a "permanently mobilized" party ceased. The party kept its mass party structure, but no longer gave the members as much influence. For the first time, party programmatic documents were simply distributed to the local organizations *after* they had already been approved and formalized.[44] However, this belated centralization did not alter the orthodox course – reformists, most of whom were gone by 1993, were all denounced, and orthodox stalwarts crowed that the party now returned to its "rightful" course.[45]

Even after the 1993 centralization, membership still did not require agreement with the party program. Instead, the party statutes requested only that "members should recognize the program of the party and unite in accordance with it."[46] As a result, orthodox communists could join and become active in the party despite its initially reform-oriented programs. Since the conservative regional leaders were put in charge of funneling member wishes to the party center, they helped to ensure that the party programs assumed a more orthodox character.

Despite the goal of broad support,[47] the party did little to respond to the electorate. For one thing, the party's leaders were caught between the need to appear consistent to the party members and the desire to respond to the rest of the voters – the goals of the two groups diverged as the party insisted on retaining its members. It was unclear which appeals could satisfy both groups. As one critic of Svoboda put it, "the new party leaders were unable to deal with the party program. To succeed as a communist party, we needed new theory that provided alternatives to what the communist movement could no longer offer after 1989 – and these were not easy to find."[48]

By the time the party centralized, there were few voters beyond its core support group to whom the party could appeal with its policy stances. The

---

[44] "Jiří Hlad Answers Readers' Questions," *Naše Pravda*, 7 June 1995.
[45] "Zpráva ÚV KSČM IV. Sjezdu KSČM o Činnosti Strany v obdobi po III. Sjezdu (Červen 1993–prosinec 1995)" ("Report of the Central Committee of the KSČM to the IV Congress KSČM about the party's activity in the period after the III Congress (June 1993–December 1995), *Haló Noviny* (supplement), 18 December 1995, *Haló Noviny* (supplement), 18 December 1995, p. 6. See also V. Papěž, *Haló Noviny*, 5 February 1993.
[46] *Pravda*, 5 October 1992.
[47] Minutes of the Nymburk meeting, *Naše Pravda*, 13 February 1994.
[48] Interview with Miloslav Ransdorf, 26 September 1996.

141

Table 3.5. *Average gap in Political priorities between KSČM supporters and the rest of the electorate, 1992–6.*

Government roles considered important	Party supporters (%)	Rest of electorate (%)	Average gap
Helping private enterprise	16%	47%	31
Ensuring competent managers	77%	82%	5
Ensuring democracy	48%	61%	13
Lessening the economic burden	75%	54%	21
Maintaining political stability	58%	46%	12
Strengthening patriotism	54%	40%	14
Increasing pensions/benefits	72%	50%	22
Increasing the role of the church	5%	8%	3
Speeding up privatization	9%	34%	25
Reducing unemployment	41%	19%	22
Decommunization	13%	42%	29

Source: Tóka, 1992–6.

rest of the electorate had begun to endorse other parties, some of which had been unable to compete with the KSČM earlier. For example, the Social Democrats became a national force by 1993 and began to garner much of the moderate electorate concerned with the speed and extent of economic reform. As a result, after 1993, the KSČM had difficulty gaining new supporters and was no longer as responsive to its loyal ones. The centralization of 1993 did not increase programmatic responsiveness, even as it maintained the party's consistently critical stances and its censure of the free market.

Since the party did not centralize early on, it continued to rely on its core supporters, its members. This reinforced the narrowness of the party, since by 1993 the differences between the Czech party supporters and non-supporters were greater than in any other country studied (see Table 3.5).

On almost all issues (other than the priority given to competent managers and the low levels of support for increasing the role of the Church), party supporters and the rest of the polity seem to inhabit different worlds, and many of these gaps have not narrowed over time. Throughout 1990–6, the policies of the government led by the ODS, and the ability of the prime minister (Václav Klaus) to explain the new market reforms and gain popular backing for them, created a considerable pro-market and pro-reform consensus among the majority of the Czech electorate.[49] A considerable portion of the electorate (42%) also supported decommunization (the removal of communist officials from their posts) and the lustration policies of the Klaus governments (the banning of high-ranking communist officials from holding public office for several years after the transition to democracy). In contrast, the party's supporters were far more reluctant to support the free market reforms, to abandon the welfare state, or to decommunize, by margins of 22 to 31% (these margins were considerably higher than elsewhere in the region). Party supporters overall also tended to be older, more pessimistic, and less supportive of democracy than the rest of the electorate. Ideologically, 58% of the KSČM electorate saw itself as communist, while only 19% of the remaining Left electorate did.[50] They were clearly older than the rest of the adult Czech population: As early as 1990, almost half were retired, and over 40% were over sixty years old. Only 3% were businessmen or entrepreneurs. Around 90% explicitly saw themselves as Marxist.[51]

In contrast, less than a quarter of the Czech electorate was retired, and less than half of the Social Democratic electorate saw itself as Marxist.[52] As a result, the differences between the KSČM supporters and their nearest neighbor on the left-right axis, the Social Democrats (ČSSD), were greater than between any other two neighboring parties, either in the Czech Republic or elsewhere in the region.[53] Thus, appealing to one group was likely to reduce the support of the other. Party leaders recognized this dilemma, but felt bound by their commitment to the members.[54] Their

---

[49] Appel, Hilary. "The Ideological Determinants of Liberal Economic Reform: The Case of Privatization," *World Politics*, July 2000: 550–85. See also Orenstein, Mitchell. "Out of the Red: Economic Reform in Poland and in Czechoslovakia," Ann Arbor, MI: University of Michigon Press, 2001.

[50] KSČM, Klub levicových sociologů a psychologů "Zaverečná Zpráva ze sociologického výzkumu . . ." No. 14-1995 (November 1995), p. 8.

[51] Klub levicových sociologů a psychologů "Zaverečná Zpráva ze sociologického výzkumu . . . ," No. 13-1995.

[52] Klub levicových sociologů a psychologů "Zaverečná Zpráva ze sociologického výzkumu . . . ," No. 13-1995.

[53] Matejů, Peter and Vlachová, Klara. "The Crystallization of Political Attitudes and Political Spectrum in the Czech Republic," Working Paper of the Research Project "Social Trends," Institute of Sociology, Academy of Sciences of the Czech Republic, No. 9, 1997, and Markowski, Radosław. "Political Parties and Ideological Spaces in East Central Europe," *Communist and Post-Communist Studies*, No. 3, 1997: 221–54.

[54] *Haló Noviny*, 25 May 1991, fifth meeting of the Central Committee of the KSČM.

main hope, therefore, was that popular dissatisfaction with the pro-reform government would increase to such levels that the broader electorate would begin to converge with the party supporters in their pessimism and discontent.

Tailoring party appeals to the broader electorate was made more difficult, moreover, by the party's efforts to gauge public opinion. KSČM continued to canvass its sympathizers and members, to better fit its message to this audience. Unlike the other parties, which often used public surveys, the Czech party continued to distrust public opinion polls as politicized and misleading, "dominated by the liberal perspectives of their authors."[55] Instead, it conducted its own polling – but on its members only. This reinforced the existing orthodoxy and barred broader appeals, which further forced the elites to look to members for support. The party's would-be constituency, then, continued to be a rather narrow group of existing party supporters, who differed radically from the rest of the electorate.[56]

In short, the KSČM was beholden to its membership as a main source of support and mobilization, and the members demanded that the party stick to its orthodox ideology in its appeals. As a result, so long as most of the voters were satisfied with the political and economic reform developments, the party was unable to appeal to a broader electorate. The party's programs addressed a laundry list of potential voter groups – farmers, intelligentsia, youth, women, the ill, the "losers of the transition," and the elderly were all specifically addressed. However, a broad national electorate was mentioned only once, in 1992.[57] Not surprisingly, party leaders concluded that the central problem was not that of creating a more acceptable ideology, but of creating a new membership organization.[58]

Programmatic Responsiveness

For the KSČM, policy issues were secondary to internal party questions, given the costly trade-off between appealing to members and to the broader electorate, and the high expectations of the members, on whom the party was dependent. The Czech party programs were far more concerned with its internal party life than with public policy.

---

[55] Interviews with Miloslav Ransdorf, 24 September 1996, Prague.
[56] Klub levicových sociologů a psychologů, "Zaverečná Zpráva ze sociologického výzkumu. . . ." No. 6-1993.
[57] This was the election that was to decide on the split of Czechoslovakia.
[58] Interviews with Miloslav Ransdorf and Jozef Heller, Prague.

Anywhere from 10 to 20% of the first programs, in 1990 and in 1991, referred to the party members and to the party's self-identification as a mass party seeking to mobilize its supporters rather than to gain power (see Table 3.6). Such references peaked in 1992 and in 93, with nearly 24% of the program taken up by assertions of the party's identity. The name, and how to decide whether to change it, was the single most controversial issue within the party throughout 1989–93. Several congresses were spent discussing nothing but the party name, since most party activists and members saw the name as the equivalent to "all of the party's political line and orientations."[59] After 1993, the references to members did disappear, as the party attempted to address broader public policy issues, but these efforts came too late to broaden the party's support.

Economic Policy

Nor could the party retain its initially moderate economic stances. Although the party leaders repeatedly spoke of its 1989 program document as a "renewal of socialism,"[60] this first program, put forth in late 1989, was relatively supportive of free market reforms. Much of this support was theoretical – the Civic Forum government had not implemented any market reforms prior to the June 1990 elections, and the government coalition led by Klaus and the ODS would implement market reforms only in early 1991. Nevertheless, the program formulated for the Olomouc party congress in March 1990 moved the party's stance on the economic reforms (16% of the program) toward greater approval for the free market reforms, reflecting the initial power of the reformist platforms.

However, these stances could not be sustained. With the return of orthodox members and activists, new pressures arose on the leaders to comply with their conservative views.[61] Even as reformists argued that the Olomouc program "was the only basis for the party to build on,"[62] the orthodox returnees dominated the discussion with their calls for a return to "true communist values." Thus, beginning with 1992, the party's programs reacted against market reforms, calling for protectionist, interventionist, and redistributive measures. The party's next program, for the

---

[59] Interview with Vera Žežulková, 23 September 1996, Prague.
[60] *Rudé Pravo*, 1 December 1989. Ladislav Adamec, *Rudé Pravo*, 6 January 1990. Adamec, *Rudé Pravo*, 7 February 1990, and Vasil Mohorita, *Naše Pravda*, 31 March 1990.
[61] Vladimír Papež, *Naše Pravda*, 31 July 1992.
[62] Michael Kroh, *Rudé Pravo*, 21 June 1990.

Table 3.6. *Dominant themes in KSČM party programs in percentages.*

I.89	I.91	III.92	I.93	I.94	II.95	I.98
Self-identity 20.5%	New Left 23.3%	Self-identity 23.8%	Self-identity 23.8%	Economy 49.1%	Economy 45.8%	Economy 52%
Constitution 14.1%	Democracy 15.8%	Economy 21.1%	Economy 21.1%	New Left 16.4%	New Left 20.8%	New Left 24%
Democracy 12.7%	Economy 15.8%	New Left 21.1%	New Left 21.1%	International relations 9.1%	International relations 8.3%	International relations 14%
Members 9.5%	Self-identity 13.5%	International relations 13.2%	International relations 13.2%	Autonomy 7.3%	Democracy 8.3%	Autonomy 10%

Source: Content analysis of party programs; see Appendix A.

The Czech KSČM

Table 3.7. *Economic stances of the KSČM, 1989–98.*

KSČM program	Market	Welfare state	Private property	Redistribution
I.89	3	2	3	2.4
II.90	2	3	3	2.5
I.91	3.25	3	Not mentioned	Not mentioned
III.92	3	2.5	3	3.1
I.93	3	2.5	3	3.1
I.94	3.6	3.3	3.2	3.3
II.95	3	3.25	3	Not mentioned
I.98	3.4	3.4	3	2.3

Note: The scale is 1–4, with 1 being most supportive of the market, reduction of the welfare state, private property, and nonredistribution.
Source: Content analysis of party programs; see Appendix A.

December 1992 congress in Kladno, shifted stances even more (see Table 3.7). Content analyses of the programs shows a swing toward orthodox communist appeals, especially in the party's views on the welfare state and social policy, which went from a 2 to 3.4 (on a 1–4 scale, with 4 being extreme support for a full welfare state).

The reason for this shift was straightforward: While reformist platform representatives wrote these two first programs, new party leaders emphasized the importance of member input starting in November 1990. Over 5% of the program referred to Marxist and socialist ideas, to an unprecedented extent. Moreover, an identical program was adopted for the June 1993 congress in Prostějov (the same congress that ended the Svoboda leadership and brought in the more conservative Grebreniček leadership). Even after its members no longer had much of a say, the orthodox domination of the party meant that its 1994, 1995, and 1998 programs moved the party further away from its initial acceptance of the political and economic reforms in some regards.

Given the member-voter trade-off, such orthodoxy could appeal to members, but was unlikely to gain a broad electorate. Surveys showed that the most important issue for over 80% of the Czech party supporters was lessening the economic burden of the transition. Roughly a third to half of the nonsupporters saw helping private enterprise and speeding up privatization as very important government goals, but only a tenth to an eighth of party supporters shared these aims – so the party's emphases and stances, in their member-oriented suspicion of the market, would not appeal to the public during 1990–6.

Over time, some of these stances of party supporters moderated. They were less likely to see reducing unemployment, increasing pensions and benefits, or lessening the economic burden as extremely important. Party supporters grew slightly less threatened by the new system, and no longer saw the economic reforms and social changes as quite so threatening as they initially were. However, the post-1993 alienation of programs from members meant that the party's programs continued to espouse communist economic orthodoxies.

Secularism and Nationalism

The Czech party never made dramatic calls for secularism, and its stances on secularism were surprisingly mild compared to the Polish party's rather strident denunciations. The KSČM, functioning in a far more secularized and non-Catholic country, adopted a more moderate stance and acknowledged the Church's role in formulating public values and morality (but only in its programs; the party's press attacked religion in its cartoons and editorials). Moreover, content analysis shows that party programs mentioned religion far less often (1–6% of program mentions, to the Polish SdRP's 3.2–18%). Both its supporters and nonsupporters were very unlikely to demand a greater role for the churches, but the KSČM did not denounce the Church or its negligible influence in Czech society.[63]

Instead, the party attacked the claims of the Sudeten Germans (well over 2 million of whom were expelled from Czech border territories after World War II), who had clamored after 1989 for the return of their land and property. Since the KSČ had done especially well in elections in border districts prior to the war, this issue was of profound importance to the party's self-image. Accordingly, these emphases found considerable approval among the party's members, many of whom were old enough to remember the expulsions themselves. However, they found little resonance with other voters, who felt the Christian Democrats and the Civic Democratic Party would be better able to protect Czech interests.

---

[63] The KSČM was not alone in its religious indifference. All the other Czech parties, with the understandable exception of the Christian Democrats, ignored the religious dimension. Kitschelt 1995b, p. 82.

Expertise, Competent Managers, and the Creation of New Issues

The vast majority of both party supporters and nonsupporters agreed that competent managers were extremely important for the country, one of only two issues on which the two groups agreed. However, the public opinion polls showed that the Czech KSČM was also seen as the least competent party in the political arena, and the one least likely to achieve any of a host of government roles. Aside from a party leader's admonition in 1992 that "we too, have experts,"[64] the party did little to answer the call for administrative expertise. Doing so was made especially difficult given the apparent efficacy of the "government of technocrats" of Klaus, whose discipline and determination dominated Czech politics until 1997.

The party's one effort to create new grounds for competition failed. During 1991–2, among the party members and activists, the current supporting "autonomy" (*samosprava*) grew to dominate the party, and so party programs reflected this preference.[65] A throwback to the workers' self-management in communist Yugoslavia, autonomy was defined by party officials as both self-rule in various aspects of life (including the devolvement of government powers to local communities, and the devolvement of economic decision making to the factory floor) and economic autarky.[66] Accordingly, the party increasingly viewed this ill-defined concept as *the* solution to the economic problems facing the Czech Republic, taking up 10% of the program's contents by 1998. As party officials stated, autonomy was the core of the party's future programs and policies, the one issue that no other party took up on such a scale.[67] The KSČM leadership hoped that it would prove to be the decisive issue in the elections.

Samosprava, however, found little resonance with the electorate.[68] The emphasis on autonomy indicated not only the party's lack of responsiveness, since the party focused on an issue to which no one else paid much attention, but it also made the party's wider acceptance unlikely. The

---

[64] Jiří Svoboda, *Haló Noviny*, 1992.

[65] Radim Valenčik, *Pravda*, 10 April 1991, confirmed by Zdeněk Mlynář, *Rudé Pravo*, 1 June 1991. Jiří Svoboda, fifth meeting of the Central Committee of the KSČM, *Haló Noviny*, 28 May 1991. Miroslav Grebreniček, fifth meeting of the Central Committee of the KSČM, *Haló Noviny*, 26 March 1994. See also *KSČM, Teze Zprávy . . . 1992*, p. 18.

[66] Interviews with Vera Žežulková, 24 September 1996, and Miloslav Ransdorf, 26 September 1996, Prague.

[67] Svoboda, Jiří. "Levice to bude mít těžkě," *Haló Noviny*, 1 July 1992.

[68] Interviews with Vera Žežulková, 24 September 1996, and Miloslav Ransdorf, 26 September 1996, Prague.

communists were the only party to advance this issue, and it was never seen as an answer to the challenges of economic reform facing the Czech Republic after 1989. Nor was it credible – the KSČ had earlier denounced similar experiments in Yugoslavia, and had not experimented with such reform before 1989. Neither the broader electorate nor other parties in the parliament took seriously the party's ideas or its efforts to create new bases for competition.

By 1996–8, when controversies surrounding the funding of both the ČSSD and the ODS electoral campaigns surfaced, and when it became apparent that the voucher privatization program had serious deficits, the opportunity arose for alternative parties whose competence would better serve the country. However, the KSČM could not readily deliver on such expectations. By that point, it was seen as incompetent and had few attractive policy alternatives. Instead, much of its new support came in the form of protest against the complacency of the republic's ruling parties.

In short, the KSČM could neither respond to the electorate nor create new dimensions of competition. For many of its critics, the Czech party appeared out of touch with the broader society, had no usable recent experience in pluralizing the polity or the economy, and made claims to a "better future with human socialism" that verged on the absurd. Ultimately, this discreditation went so deeply as to convince the party leaders that the only rational strategy was to cling to its communist ideals since "no one will believe the change anyway."[69] As a result, the most credible set of appeals that the party made was its opposition to many of the features of the post-1989 system. These stances meant the KSČM would be most likely to succeed either as a protest party or in the event all other parties were discredited.

The Slovak SDĽ

In contrast, the Slovak party centralized its organization early on, and consequently acquired the flexibility to change its appeals and its addressed constituencies. As a result, the SDĽ was considerably more responsive than the KSCM, and faced far less of a trade off in its appeals. However, its limited elite skills made it less capable of creating new grounds for competition than either the Polish or the Hungarian parties.

[69] Radim Valenčik, KSČ spokesman, *Rudé Pravo*, 25 January 1990.

Compared to its Czech counterpart, the SDĽ also faced less of a united front against the communist regime. Slovak attitudes toward communism were far more ambiguous – not only had the communist system benefited the Slovak republic more than the Czech, industrializing the economy and providing for more autonomy within the Czechoslovak federation, but communists dispersed into almost all the political parties after 1989, and at high levels. Moreover, economic and political reform was likely to hurt Slovakia more than the Czech Republic, given the greater preponderance of heavy industry. For example, as early as 1990, President Václav Havel announced that Czechoslovakia would no longer produce explosives or armaments – but most of these enterprises were located in Slovakia. As a result, unlike the Czech Republic, the pro-reform, anticommunist consensus was far less clear.

Partly as a result, other cleavages characterized politics. The political spectrum in Slovakia after 1991 was characterized by a cleavage between "nonstandard" parties (populist, authoritarian, and nationalist) and "standard" democratic parties. Maneuvering between these two, and defending democracy, required considerable skill and flexibility. The Movement for a Democratic Slovakia (Hnutie za Demokratické Slovensko, HZDS) dominated the political scene during 1990–8. The HZDS was largely the political machine of its leader, Vladimír Mečiar, a former communist official and member of the Public Against Violence. Prime minister since the June 1990 elections, Mečiar became an increasingly populist and authoritarian leader in Slovakia. The HZDS preempted policy dialogue with its populist message and successfully changed the terms of the political debate to populism/nationalism versus democracy/liberalism. These stances, and the HZDS's confrontational tendencies, successfully forced the other parties to compete with the HZDS on the same bases.[70] "Nation-building" became the catch-word, and any opponents were perceived as "anti-Slovak." The SDĽ elites had neither the rhetorical experience nor the skills to counteract these claims by changing the terms of the debate to issues on which they could compete successfully.

Instead, the SDĽ saw its programmatic commitments to democracy as the main distinction between it and the HZDS. The latter had a similar

---

[70] Szomolányi, Soňa, and Mesežnikov, Grigorij, eds. *Slovakia: Parliamentary Elections 1994*. Bratislava: Slovak Political Science Association and Friedrich Ebert Foundation, 1995, pp. 106–7.

heritage, since many of its members and founders started their political career in the Communist Party of Slovakia. However, since the HZDS was often seen as undemocratic and authoritarian, the SDĽ emphasized its democratic commitments in its programs partly as a way to distinguish itself from the HZDS. The SDĽ's emphasis on its democratic credentials and its pragmatism differed from the other Slovak parties, which emphasized either populist/nationalist appeals (HZDS, ZRS, SNS), minority rights (the Hungarian coalition), or a traditional free market agenda (DEU, KDH).

The SDĽ firmly rejected communist ideology and insisted that any communists should join instead the orthodox splinters, such as KSS '91.[71] Party leader Peter Weiss repeatedly declared that "we are not a communist party."[72] Weiss went as far as to say that "we are for the market mechanisms and plural democracy . . . we do not want to be an ideological party."[73] The party repeatedly rejected a communist identity, and was among the first Slovak parties to speak out in favor of joining the North Atlantic Treaty Organization (NATO) and the European Union (EU), in mid-1993.[74] Under the Weiss leadership, the Slovak centralized the decision making within the party, largely emasculated the party membership, and focused above all on gaining votes. Changing the party name further led both the older communists and the voters to conclude that the party was no longer interested in pursuing its old goals.[75]

The Slovak party program became a major measure of how much the party had reformed in the eyes of its leaders.[76] Changing it "became the key to setting the stage for subsequent transformations."[77] Since the Slovak party was still in the federation with its burdensome Czech counterpart in 1990–1, its reformist leaders emphasized the programmatic differences between the two parties as a reason to split away from the Czech KSČM.[78] The program was thus a signal of its differentiation from the Czech party.[79] For the SDĽ elites, changing the program was a key goal, since it was a crucial tool for

[71] *Naše Pravda*, 1 July 1991.
[72] Interview with Peter Weiss, *Rudé Pravo*, 28 August 1991, and *Lidové Noviny*, 22 May 1992.
[73] Peter Weiss, *Pravda*, 24 January 1991.
[74] Interview with Peter Magvaši, 27 January 1997, Bratislava.
[75] Interview with Milan Ftáčnik, SDĽ HQ, 31 January 1997, Bratislava.
[76] *Nové Slovo*, 18 July 1991.
[77] Interview with Peter Magvaši, 27 January 1997.
[78] *Rudé Pravo*, 16 November 1991.
[79] Komunistická Strana Slovenska, *Zjazd KSS, konany v dnoch 20-21.1990 v Prešove*. I-II cast. Archiv SDĽ, Bratislava.

achieving two goals: cleansing the party of orthodox communist remainders, and consolidating the party's identity and its transformation.

At the party's congresses in December 1989 and in October 1990, the party elites made changing the program a priority.[80] The minutes of the first party congress show that the voting on the dramatically changed party program, first on the agenda, was virtually unanimous.[81] Unlike the other nascent parties, these elites argued, the Slovak successor party had at its disposal scientific analyses and recommendations,[82] which originated prior to 1989 (given the greater freedom and worse economic status quo in Slovakia than in the Czech lands).[83] Therefore, the party was able to formulate policy and address the broad concerns of voters, rather than focusing on the narrow circles of party members.[84] The new party leadership centralized program formulation, by putting the party's twenty-member Executive Committee in charge,[85] moving with both flexibility and unity of reformist purpose. As a result, the party could readily switch its addressed constituencies and pursued votes wherever it could.

The Slovak party elites then made agreement to the new program a prerequisite of member reregistration. Only those former communist party members who signed a pledge of agreement with the party's new program were allowed to join the new formation. As a result, the differences between the SDĽ supporters and rest of the Slovak electorate were considerably smaller than in the case of the Czech party (see Table 3.8). The SDĽ was supported by former Public Against Violence and even Christian Democratic voters, which had traditionally opposed the communist regime prior to 1989.[86]

As a result, while party supporters and nonsupporters initially varied in the political priority they gave privatization, the role of the Church, or

---

[80] Jan Široký argued that the key to a successful transformation is the change in the party program, and argued that Weiss is the comrade "theoretically best prepared to do so." *Rudé Pravo*, 23 January 1990. Also interview with Milan Ftáčnik, SDĽ HQ, 31 January 1997, Bratislava.

[81] The type of leadership and the statutes were similarly approved in haste. KSS. *Zjazd KSS, konany w dnoch 20-21.10.1998 v Prešove*. I-II. Cast. Archiv SDĽ, Bratislava.

[82] Interview with Peter Weiss, *Nové Slovo*, 1 March 1990.

[83] Interviews with Dušan Dorotin, 4 February 1997, and with Peter Weiss, 23 February 1997, SDĽ headquarters, Bratislava.

[84] *Pravda*, 5 January 1990, 14 August 1990.

[85] The VV consisted of the party leader, three deputy leaders, and fifteen or so members chosen by the party congress.

[86] Interview with Peter Weiss, *Pravda*, 22 May 1992.

Table 3.8. *Average gap in political priorities between SDĽ supporters and the rest of the electorate, 1992–6.*

Government roles considered important	By party supporters (%)	By the rest of the electorate (%)	Average gap
Helping private enterprise	27%	41%	14
Ensuring competent managers	82%	78%	4
Ensuring democracy	50%	55%	5
Lessening the economic burden	70%	66%	4
Maintaining political stability	68%	64%	4
Strengthening patriotism	31%	40%	9
Increasing pensions/benefits	58%	62%	4
Increasing the role of the church	5%	16%	11
Speeding up privatization	18%	27%	9
Reducing unemployment	80%	73%	7
Decommunization	11%	29%	18

Source: Tóka, 1992–6.

decommunization, their views converged far more than for the KSČM (see Table 3.8). Both groups shared similarly high concerns with the welfare safety net and competent managers, with considerable majorities emphasizing lessening the economic burden, increasing social benefits, and maintaining political stability.[87] Therefore, the Slovak successor party could appeal to both its immediate supporters and the rest of the electorate, having minimized the trade off through its earlier reregistration.

Whether or not the party could take advantage of this minimal trade off, however, was another matter. Despite its focus on the electorate, the SDĽ did not pursue any one group consistently. The SDĽ addressed several societal groupings in its programs and slogans, and it appealed to a group (for example, the workers in 1992) only to ignore it in subsequent programs. The party briefly mentioned those who suffered from the transition in 1990 and 1993. While it identified itself as a Left party, it sought

---

[87] Interestingly, the rates of both party supporters and nonsupporters who claim that "strengthening patriotism" is a very important political goal have dropped off over time. This indicates perhaps the growing weariness with the nationalist obsessions of the Slovak National Party (SNS), and to a lesser extent, the public rhetoric of the HZDS.

the support of the intelligentsia, educators, and white-collar professionals. Perhaps most surprisingly for a self-identified Left party, the SDĽ made direct appeals to the managers and enterprise directors, formalized in its 1996 program.[88] The party's elites simply did not have the experience in conducting negotiations or in implementing policy reforms that would make it easy to anticipate the electorate or to claim competence.

Nonetheless, the SDĽ emphasized public policy over any concerns with its internal life; content analysis shows that emphases on the latter dropped from a high of 18% in 1990 to zero mentions in 1993 and in 1994 (see Table 3.9). In 1995, its programs tentatively began to mention the party itself again, and devoted 5–10% of its program to self-identification that reassured the public of the party's skills and ability to reform the constitution and ensure democratic rule of law. The party programs thus tried to focus attention on the party's defense of democracy, an issue the SDĽ hoped would give it an advantage in electoral competition. Program contents also minimized references to members – after 3.6% mentions of the members in 1990, they disappeared from party programs until 1996, when they took up 2.1% of the program. Instead, the SDĽ emphasized its ties to the Socialist International and its modern Left identity.

After the party's poor performance in the 1994 elections, local leaders blamed the party's electoral failure on both a lack of the common touch and a program that was not addressed enough toward those who lost during the transition.[89] Party leaders promised greater attention to the alienated membership, a new, more people-friendly vocabulary, and new powers for the regional organizations. The Executive Committee of the party announced that it would now work on a new program and the organizational forms, to better reflect the Left character of the party, "lost" in both the government coalition with the Christian Democrats earlier in 1994 and in the electoral coalition that followed.[90]

---

[88] These new appeals came at the expense of a focus on labor and agricultural workers – and had earlier contributed to the rise of the splinter Association of Slovak Workers (ZRS) in March 1994.

[89] However, this was "not a question of rejecting reforms, but of organizing protest against their harmful forms." Announcement of the Republican Council of SDĽ meeting held to evaluate the election, *Nove Slovo*, 31 October 1994, pp. 28–9.

[90] The SDĽ was in the governing coalition that arose after the fall of the Mečiar government, from March to September 1994. A broad coalition of parties opposed to Mečiar's riding roughshod over both democratic rules and economic reform, it ranged from the SDĽ on one side to the Christian Democrats on the other. TASR, 29 October 1994.

Table 3.9. *Dominant themes in SDE party programs in percentages, 1990–6.*

1990 average	1991	1992	1993	1994	1995	1996
Economy 25%	Economy 32.8%	Economy 36.6%	Economy 44.5%	New Left 36.9%	Economy 35%	Economy 29.5%
International relations 14.3%	Constitution 11.4%	New Left 17%	International relations 14.8%	Economy 31.6%	Constitution 17.5%	New Left 14.8%
Self-identification 18%	Democracy 11.4%	Democracy 14.6%	Constitution 13.5%	Constitution 10.5%	New Left 15%	Status quo critique 10.2%
Democracy 13.5%	International relations 10%	Decentralization 9.8%	New Left 5.4%	Democracy 10.5%	Democracy 12.5%	Constitution 8.6%

Source: Content analysis of party programs; see Appendix A.

However, there was little immediate difference in the party's responsiveness. Although changing the program was to be a priority at the 1995 congress for the party elites,[91] congress delegates were so angry about the party's lack of internal mobilization that they largely ignored the party program.[92] As they turned the discussion to organizational questions, the party elites simply approved the existing programmatic line. When the party tried to regain its core group of supporters by making the program more secular in 1996, it found that its earlier coalition with the Christian Democrats had already damaged the credibility of the party's secular stance with SDĽ supporters.[93]

Economic Policy

The party also shifted back and forth in its economic views. At first, the SDĽ's programs grew increasingly supportive of economic reforms, the free market, and streamlining of the welfare state. By 1993, the party's leaders proudly considered the party more liberal than the ruling HZDS.[94] Content analysis shows that of the four parties under consideration, the Slovak party was overall the most supportive of free market competition, and the most willing to lower welfare state provisions. In 1995, however, the programs returned to greater criticism of the market, and of private property, stances last seen in 1990 (see Table 3.10).

This inconstancy led to accusations of *l'avirovanie*, perhaps best translated as "fishtailing" or "slaloming," by both domestic and international critics.[95] There were two reasons for this constant shifting. First, the SDĽ elites did not have earlier experience in negotiating with or addressing the opposition prior to 1989. As a result, the SDĽ elites were unable to "read" the broad electorate's underlying concerns, and instead pursued the conflicting economic interests of one group after another. Second, as a result of the dominant divide between democratic and nondemocratic parties, the electorate's economic views were both secondary and shifting. The SDĽ did have the centralization to mirror these changes, and did so avidly.

---

[91] TASR, 2 January 1995.
[92] *Dokumenty Tretieho Zjazdu SDĽ*, Poprad, 17–18.2. 1995, p. 5. Interview with Peter Magvaši, 27 January 1998, Bratislava.
[93] Interview with Peter Weiss, 27 February 1997, Bratislava.
[94] Peter Weiss, quoted in *Pravda*, 8 June 1993.
[95] *Narodna Obroda*, 23 May 1993. Vladimir Drozda, *Pravda*, 18 October 1995.

Table 3.10. *Economic stances of the SDĽ, 1990–6.*

Slovak SDĽ	Market	Welfare state	Private property	Redistribution
1990	2.1	3.5	2.25	2.3
1991	2.1	3.3	2.4	2.5
1992	2	2.7	2.3	Not mentioned
1993	1.3	2.4	1.8	2
1994	2.5	2.6	2	Not mentioned
1995	2.75	2.3	2.6	1
1996	2.25	2.5	2.6	2.8

Note: The scale is 1–4, with 1 being most supportive of the market, reduction of welfare state, private property, and nonredistribution.
Source: Content analysis of party programs; see Appendix A.

Thus, beginning in 1993, party supporters grew far more supportive of speeding up privatization than they had been, and both they and the broader electorate reduced their concern with lessening the economic burden. That year also saw a drop in the percentages of the electorate and party supporters concerned with increasing pensions and benefits. As the supporters converged with the broader electorate in their increasing support for the market in 1993, party programs also increased their support for free market initiatives and private property rights. The broader electorate's support for private enterprise peaked in 1994, to drop off to its former levels, and decreased even further in 1996. Accordingly, the 1995 program marked a return to more Leftist stances toward the state's role in the economy and the need for moderation of the market's effects.

Secularism and Nationalism

The SDĽ took a relatively mild secularist stance and insisted that the religious were welcome as party supporters and members. Party leaders noted with satisfaction that half of their supporters attended church.[96] This tolerance initially did not bother the more secular party supporters, and it also opened the door to gaining a broader electorate. However, once the SDĽ entered a governing coalition with the Christian Democrats in 1994, party activists lashed out against what they saw as a betrayal of Left secular

[96] Peter Weiss, *Lidové Noviny*, 22 May 1992.

ideas. The party's 1995 programs, however, continued the mild secular stance of the earlier documents. It was not until 1996 that the party finally answered with the stronger secular response its supporters had demanded.

On the other hand, the party occasionally toyed with nationalism and anti-Hungarian sentiment. The SDĽ's chief competitor, the HZDS, often used such appeals to redirect the economic complaints of many Slovaks, as did the right-wing Slovak National Party (Slovenská Narodná Strana, SNS). After the 1994 electoral debacle, the party's renewed interest in its members further provided an anti-Hungarian impetus, since many of the party's members shared these suspicions regarding the Hungarian minority. With a change in the party's leadership toward a more populist set of leaders in 1997, this impulse was no longer a matter of electoral expedience; when the party entered the negotiations with potential government coalition partners in 1998, its first demand was that the coalition exclude the Hungarian party. However, party leaders dropped the demand after it met with a considerable outcry from the media and party analysts.

Expertise, Competent Managers, and the Creation of New Issues

The Slovak electorate also placed a premium on competent managers, and the SDĽ tried to address these claims once, in 1994. The often-controversial nature of government politics in Slovakia made these claims especially urgent as the Mečiar government attempted to monopolize both the economy and the polity throughout 1992–8. However, while the SDĽ was generally perceived as committed to democracy and the rule of law, it was not seen as particularly competent. Not only did the party behave inconsistently after 1989 – adopting a variety of appeals, strategies, and identities – but its elites were not particularly skilled in changing the political debates. Nor could they point to previous administrative experience, its elites having been sequestered in a theoretical think-tank under communism, while the Slovak Communist Party itself was kept under Prague's thumb throughout the communist era.

Since its appeals did not transcend the economic cleavage, and instead addressed shifting constituencies on either side, other parties could exploit the SDĽ's stances. Most notably, the populism of the HZDS, dominant in Slovak politics from 1992 to 1998, transcended the existing cleavages in ways that the SDĽ could not. The HZDS did little to gain support for a policy program of economic reforms, and rarely bothered to debate them. Instead, it successfully emphasized both populist appeals and particularist policies that focused on limiting the rights of the Hungarian minority in Slovakia (about 10% of the population) and the influence of international institutions, such as the EU.

The HZDS turned the debate from the finer points of economic policy to the fundamental questions of what the new political system should look like and who could participate in it. The SDĽ, which had defined its support of democracy as a core value, could only respond with further defenses of democratic standards. Consequently, the SDĽ could not out-flank the HZDS. Nor, given its lack of elite skills, could it change the bases of political competition to a set of issues that would favor the SDĽ over its competitors: Its commitment to democracy was credible, but the elites did not articulate it in a way that would persuade the voters, who favored populist parties.

Organizational centralization thus allowed the party to pursue the electorate freely and respond with considerable flexibility. However, without experience in negotiation or policy implementation, the SDĽ elites could neither anticipate the voters' priorities or create new dimensions of competition. Responsive appeals came at the cost of alienating existing supporters – not because their views differed so much from the general electorate's, but because the party leaders deliberately, and repeatedly, snubbed them. Had the party possessed more skilled elites, it may have gotten around this dilemma by gradually broadening its addressed electorates and creating new dimensions of competition that transcended existing cleavages, instead of jumping from one group of potential voters to another.

The Polish SdRP

The Polish communist successor's considerable elite skills, and its rapid organizational transformation, mean that the party was responsive (unlike the KSČM) and consistent (unlike the SDĽ), while it created new grounds for competition with its credible appeals to competence and effectiveness.

The SdRP found itself in a political environment where its communist past was both an obstacle to any cooperation with the parties originating in the Solidarity camp, and a usable record that served the party well by the 1993 elections. While the division between the former communist and opposition camps ran deep, two other factors influenced the political cleavages found in Poland. First, despite the wide-ranging elite consensus on the need for market reforms and their early implementation, the first democratic governments could neither avoid the widespread popular pain they caused, nor could they convince the public they were administering the reforms competently. Second, the Roman Catholic Church, in trying to capitalize on its support in the 1980s, increased the pressure on the parliament in 1990–2 to restrict abortion, introduce religion into schools, and pursue governance in accord with Catholic teaching. The resulting controversies were fertile ground for building new dimensions of competition, focused on government stability, executive competence, and legislative independence. The SdRP elites, with their extensive political training, took advantage of these opportunities.

The Polish party elites pursued a steadily social democratic identity from the start. At the Extraordinary Congress, not only had the party's new name become the Social Democracy of Poland, but the outgoing party leader, Mieczysław Rakowski, identified himself as a long-time social democrat – "as many of us have been, even if not publicly, and even if we were not called that."[97] From the beginning of its existence, the party consistently pursued a message of moderation and professionalism, and their elites were well prepared, having arrived at the Round Table in 1989 with both general aims and concrete proposals, as even their opponents admitted.[98]

Within a month of its founding congress in January 1990, the Polish successor party leaders insisted on the primacy of voters over party members; as a party leader explained, "the SdRP will be a typical electoral party. Therefore it does not need ranks of members, but sympathizers, who will vote in the elections for its program."[99] Thus, after choosing the new leaders, the first party congress in January 1990 voted on the program (which had already been prepared by the reformist programmatic commission by October 1989). Once reformists were elected into the party leadership, agreement with the new, "radical,"[100] reform program was a foregone conclusion: Few delegates wanted to disagree with the leaders whom they had just elected.[101] Subsequently, functionaries of the Executive Committee wrote the party programs, with no consultation of the members. Once approved by the committee, the program was then sent

---

[97] *Trybuna Ludu*, 30 January 1990.
[98] Kurski, Jacek. *Lewy Czerwcowy*. Warsaw: Editions Spotkania, 1993.
[99] Interview with Zbigniew Siemiątkowski, *Dziennik Lubelski*, 28 February 1990.
[100] Jerzy Majka, *Trybuna Ludu*, 23 October 1989.
[101] Interview with Tomasz Nałęcz, 2 July 1997, Warsaw. Interview with Zygmunt Najdowski, 2 July 1997, Warsaw. AP wire, 12 February 1990.

out to local organizations. They could have their say on questions of party history, but could not change the political or economic policy stances.[102] Party statutes forced potential members to agree with the new leadership, its programmatic reforms, and the new character of the party immediately after the January 1990 congress.[103]

The initial trade off between appealing to party members and to the electorate was thus minimized. Party supporters remained steadfastly secular, and far more so than the rest of the electorate – in fact, the most powerful predictor of SdRP support was its pro-abortion and anti-Church stances (see Appendix B). Not surprisingly, party supporters were also more likely to oppose decommunization. However, the party's economic stances were far less controversial, and its claims of expertise were broadly welcomed. Both the immediate supporters and the rest of the electorate shared a concern with helping private enterprise, ensuring competent managers, maintaining political stability, increasing pensions, and reducing unemployment (see Table 3.11).

The SdRP consistently pursued a broad electoral base, instead of focusing on the Left's "natural" electorate. For example, party leaders declared that they were not going to seek the votes of unqualified workers, who supported the party far less than other social groups did, and who were more likely to vote for extremist nationalist parties.[104] Instead of appealing to any specific group, the party appealed to both the losers and the winners of the transition, and above all to those seeking "safety and stability."[105] Those who suffered from the transition made a brief appearance in the 1991 program as an intended constituency, but were not mentioned again as a specific constituency. Overall, the SdRP continued to broaden its electorate, denying class-based appeals in 1993, and increasingly appealing to *all* citizens of Poland.[106]

While the Czech party leaders saw the program as their link to the members, and the Slovak party leadership viewed it as evidence of the party's transformation, the Polish party leaders viewed the program instru-

---

[102] *Gazeta Wyborcza*, 1 July 1997. *Polityka*, 15 February 1997. *Wprost*, 16 February 1997.

[103] Interview with Andrzej Urbańczyk, *Gazeta Krakowska*, 29 January 1990.

[104] Włodzimierz Cimoszewicz, *Rzeczpospolita*, 14–5 August 1993.

[105] Pyszczek, Grzegorz. "Tematy kampanii wyborczej 1993 roku," in Wesołowski, Włodzimierz, and Panków, Irena, eds. *Świat elity politycznej*. Warsaw: Wydawnictwo IfiS PAN, 1995, p. 23.

[106] The emphasis on this broad electoral constituency steadily rose, until it took up nearly 10% of the program in 1997.

Table 3.11. *Average gap in political priorities between SdRP supporters and the rest of the electorate, 1992–5.*

Government roles considered important	By party supporters (%)	By the rest of the electorate (%)	Average gap
Helping private enterprise	29%	35%	6
Ensuring competent managers	87%	81%	6
Ensuring democracy	76%	74%	2
Lessening the economic burden	72%	67%	5
Maintaining political stability	71%	77%	6
Strengthening patriotism	69%	63%	6
Allowing abortion	66%	44%	22
Increasing pensions/benefits	76%	72%	4
Increasing the role of the church	1%	9%	8
Speeding up privatization	14%	19%	5
Reducing unemployment	86%	83%	3
Decommunization	10%	17%	7

Source: Tóka, 1992–6.

mentally. Programs were a means to electoral ends. As a party leader explained, "in order to achieve program goals, the party must rule, and it can only do so through elections – we are for parliamentary democracy. Therefore the party must be an effective tool for winning elections, with a program that reaches potential voters."[107] Similarly, Polish party leaders freely admitted that their program changed after 1993 because they entered the government, and "programs have to follow reality."[108]

Therefore, the Polish party programs were least concerned with its internal life. Even the first documents, from the January 1990 founding congress, consisted of only 12% references to its internal life in the main programmatic documents.[109] After this first assertion of the new party identity at the party's Extraordinary Congress, subsequent programs contained no references to its members, the party organization, or internal splits. While the SdRP focused anywhere from 7% to 11% of its first

[107] Interview with Aleksander Kwaśniewski, *Rzeczpospolita*, 29 January 1990.
[108] Interview with Józef Oleksy, 28 July 1998, Warsaw.
[109] Addresses by the new party leader and to the Left in Poland contain around 30% references to the party's new identity and the reform processes the party was undertaking.

programs on its members, it subsequently dropped such references, and instead addressed its would-be voters, in keeping with its stated goal of achieving voter support (see Table 3.12). Party members were no longer even mentioned after 1990. From the start, the SdRP's programs were far more concerned with broader policy issues and the party's qualifications in addressing these issues than in communicating with party members or examining internal concerns.

Polish party programs could pursue the voters with such relative freedom for two reasons. First, unlike the Czech party, the party was far more centralized, and so the leaders never had to reach internal party consensus with a vast network of activists, regional leaders, or members. Second, unlike the Slovak party, the SdRP elites had the skills and experience both to change and promote their programmatic stances without losing supporters. Their earlier experience in negotiating with the opposition and implementing public policy caused the new party elites to frame and "sell" their increasing support for market reforms as a way for the party both to appear responsible and gain greater support. Since the Polish party program evolved more steadily, and partly because the party suffered no unexpected electoral defeat, its program was not subject to attacks from within, as in the Slovak case. Therefore, the SdRP could expend more of its energies on formulating policy alternatives rather than having to focus on its self-identity and internal party life.

Economic Policy

The party prioritized economic issues, which took up from over a third to nearly a half of its programs. Initially, the SdRP's programs were far more skeptical of the free market than its Czech or Slovak counterparts. Unlike the former Czechoslovakia, where the free market reforms did not begin until January 1991, Poland had implemented its market reform program, the Balcerowicz plan, a full year earlier, in January 1990. The reforms were painful,[110] and the SdRP initially seemed willing to exploit this pain. The party began with a commitment at first to "third road" solutions in the party's first congress in 1990. As early as March 1990, however, the party

---

[110] The reforms made the złoty convertible, lowered trade barriers, and lowered state subsidies. As a result, unemployment shot up from seven thousand in 1989 to 2 million in 1990 (12%), real wages dropped by 20% in 1990 (and did not recover in 1991), and inflation increased from 25% in 1989 to 586% in 1990. See Mason, David S., "Poland," in White, Batt, and Lewis 1993, and Błażyca 1998.

Table 3.12. *Dominant themes in SdRP party programs in percentages, 1990–7.*

I.90	II.90	V.90	I.91	II.91	I.93	II.93	I.97
Economy 38.7%	Economy 28.6%	Economy 42.3%	Economy 48.2%	Democracy 16.3%	Economy 25.5%	Economy 29.2%	Economy 32.7%
New Left 22.6%	New Left 28.6%	Autonomy 9.5%	Status quo 15.3%	Economy 11.6%	International relations 17%	Democracy 14.6%	New Left 23.1%
International relations 9.7%	International relations 21.4%	Party past 7.7%	Autonomy 9.5%	New Left 11.6%	Democracy 17%	Coalition 12.2%	International relations 15.4%
Democracy 9.7%	Self-identity 10.7%	New Left 4.8%	Self-identity 5.9%	IR/past/autonomy 7% each	Expertise/secular/New Left 10.6% each	New Left 9.8%	Constitution 9.6%

Source: Content analysis of party programs; see Appendix A.

Table 3.13. *Economic stances of the SdRP, 1990–7.*

SdRP program	Market	Welfare state	Private property	Redistribution
I.90	2.3	4	2.3	3.3
II.90	3	3	3.3	
V.90	3.2	3.8	2.4	3.5
I.91	2.75	3.3	3.1	3.2
II.91	3	4	3	1
I.93	1.5	2.25	2.7	3.2
II.93	2.6	2.75		3.3
I.97	1.8	2.3	2	2

Note: The scale is 1–4, with 1 being most supportive of the market, reduction of welfare state, private property, and nonredistribution.

Source: Content analysis of party programs; see Appendix A.

increasingly supported economic reform, both in its parliamentary support of the Balcerowicz package and through the party's programs: When the party elites debated program stances in late February 1990, they decided to support a moderate "correction" of the Balcerowicz plans rather than a more fundamental "change" of the reforms.[111] By 1991, the party supported the free market with some government intervention to protect the interests of working people and increased its criticism of the status quo. The former reflected the pragmatist realization that market reforms were both inevitable and necessary, while the latter was a criticism of the post-Solidarity government.[112]

The party shifted several of its economic views between 1991 and 1993. Content analysis of the programs shows that its support for the welfare state dropped from 3.62 to 2.4 after 1991 (on a 1–4 scale; see Table 3.13). Similarly, the programs now adopted a decidedly more pro-market reform stance (from an average of 2.85 to 1.97). The party's 1993 program called for different forms of privatization, and for strategic intervention of the government in supporting certain enterprises and not allowing others to go bankrupt.

The party's victory in the 1993 elections led to an even more pro–economic reform stance. By April 1994, Kwaśniewski emphasized the need for "supporting economic reform by all parties."[113] The party's 1997

[111] *Trybuna Ludu*, 5 March 1990.
[112] Interview with Andrzej Żelazowski, 16 June 1997, Warsaw.
[113] *Życie Warszawy*, 21 October 1994.

program, developed over the course of 1996, marked an even bigger turn toward the free market, backing entry into the EU and other Western international structures. This program shifted considerably in favor of the free market and nixed expectations of government intervention, the welfare state, and redistributive efforts.

Meanwhile, Polish party supporters increased their endorsement for free market measures, but also remained concerned about providing a safety net along with those reforms. In the case of supporting private enterprises and privatization, the gaps between the two groups have diminished considerably, to differences of 0.2–3%. By 1995, party supporters were slightly *more* likely to support private enterprises, and slightly *less* likely to support increasing pensions and benefits than the rest of the respondents. Thus, the party, its electorate, and the general public all became more supportive of privatization and supporting private enterprises, and the party programs reflected those changing stances.

On the other hand, the broader electorate did retain its high concern with increasing pensions and benefits, and grew more anxious about reducing unemployment in 1993, after Poland began to experience the highest unemployment rates in the region. Yet party programs reflected less support for the welfare state, although they supported redistributive efforts until 1997. SdRP mirrored these worries less than its otherwise socially sensitive programs would suggest. One reason was that, since it had entered government, the SdRP was responsible for implementing economic reform, an experience that forced the party to adopt policies it had previously rejected. Therefore, subsequent programs had to account for the SdRP government's cut-backs in the welfare state. Moreover, the party leadership saw its economic stances as pragmatic and flexible, and argued that economic policy making demanded pragmatism.

Secularism and Nationalism

On the other hand, secularism was a "core belief."[114] The party insisted on a secular identity as part of its commitment to the new democratic system and as a way to reassure some of the party faithful without making populist or nostalgic claims. As early as the 1991 elections, the SdRP's

---

[114] Janusz Bugaj, *Gazeta Wyborcza*, 31 March 1993, interview with Józef Oleksy, 28 July 1998, Warsaw.

secularism was one of its most noted characteristics.[115] The party took up a call for the declericalization of public life, full separation of church and state, a completely secular educational, system the removal of any privileges accrued to the Church, and abortion rights.

For its part, the Polish Roman Catholic Church hierarchy attempted to influence public policy after 1989, both through its clumsy insistence on "instructions" to the voters during church services and through pressure on post-Solidarity political parties to heed Church teachings. In the series of controversies that followed in 1990–1, the parliament curtailed access to abortion rights and passed new laws instituting religious education in schools. Combined with the Church hierarchy's constant admonitions and offensive declarations,[116] the Church's actions were seen by a majority of the electorate as "interference" in normal politics.[117] As a result, the SdRP's indirect claims that the party would curb the power of the Church and not let it influence policy were appealing. They were also convincing, given the fact that the SdRP's predecessor had battled with the Church prior to 1989, and the SdRP had consistently remained opposed to a political role for the Church after 1989.[118]

Not surprisingly, the party's supporters were steadfastly secular – they were least likely by far to support increasing the role of the Church or religion. An even bigger difference lies in the supporters' and nonsupporters' stance toward abortion, and this gap increased over time. After the 1991–2 debate over abortion and the role of the Church in setting such policies, the party's electorate supported abortion even more vehemently. By 1995, nearly twice as many party supporters as the rest of the electorate saw allowing abortion as extremely important. The party's 1993 program reflected the cleavage that formed: It was unequivocal in its

[115] Jasiewicz, Krzysztof. "Polish Politics on the Eve of the 1993 Elections," *Communist and Post-Communist Studies*, December 1993a: 387–411.
[116] Several priests became notorious for their antisemitic and xenophobic stances, most notably Father Henryk Jankowski, who advised Solidarity during the 1980s.
[117] The Church's approval ratings went from 88% in 1989 to around 30% within two years. CBOS, "Społeczna Ocena Działalnosci Instytucji Politycznych." Komunikat z Badań. Warsaw, October 1990. By May 1993, four months before the election, 38% approved of the Church's role, and 54% disapproved. CBOS, "Instytucje publiczne w opinii społecznej," Komunikat z Badań. Warsaw, November 1994.
[118] Gebethner, Stanisław. *Wybory Parlamentarne 1991 i 1993 a Polska Scena Polityczna.* Warsaw: Wydawnictwo Sejmowe, 1995.

support of abortion, and its secular stances took up nearly 11% of the program.

For the Polish party leaders, secularism was central enough to the party's identity that its leaders refused to compromise it (even if not changing this stance limited some of the party's appeal).[119] As party leaders explained, although the party was willing to compromise on its program and had changed its economic and political stances readily, secularism was nonnegotiable.[120] Unlike the changes in the party's policy views, which could be explained by coalitional politics or the necessities of reform, party leaders felt any change in SdRP's secular stances would only alienate the party's supporters and risk the party's identity.[121] At the same time, given controversies during 1990–2 over abortion restrictions, the introduction of religion into schools, and the Church's increasingly strident demands for political influence, SdRP leaders argued that these stances would not limit its electoral appeal and would in fact only help to distinguish it from the rest of the political herd – which either supported the Church's role, or remained ambiguous.

Expertise, Competent Managers, and the Creation of New Issues

The successful emphasis on administrative "expertise" and managerial skills of the party was a trademark of the Polish party. Beginning with 1991, the Polish party programs began to emphasize the expertise of its cadres, consistently arguing that they could better formulate and implement public policy. Party programs increasingly highlighted the party's qualifications: its administrative expertise, its ranks of qualified technocrats, and its stable and moderate stances in comparison with the messy politics of the governmental coalitions. By 1993, content analysis shows that 9% of the program mentioned the party's efficacy, experience, and ability to "get things done professionally," in contrast to the inefficient and unprofessional squabbling of the post-1989 Solidarity activist-led governments. The SdRP repeatedly argued that the Solidarity governments led to a deterioration of the economic and political situation, and that calm, moderate, experienced leadership of the sort provided

---

[119] Interview with Józef Oleksy, 28 July 1998, Warsaw.
[120] *Gazeta Wyborcza*, 15 October 1996.
[121] *Rzeczpospolita*, 3 April 1995.

by the SdRP was necessary to keep both economic reforms and democracy afloat in Poland. Having already developed administrative cadres and skills under communism, the party argued it had the greatest managerial experience.

Given the chaotic nature of parliamentary and cabinet politics in Poland until 1993, these claims transcended the existing debates and found an especially receptive audience. Solidarity had begun to fragment viciously by 1990, aided by Wałęsa's pitting of elites against each other. The governments that followed the 1991 elections were as fractioned as they were unstable. In the highly fragmented first Polish parliament (twenty-nine parties had entered the parliament in 1991), Jan Krzysztof Bielecki first continued as prime minister, presiding over a centrist-liberal coalition consisting of post-Solidarity forces. The coalition was increasingly shaky, and fell two months after the September 1991 elections. Starting with December 1991, the government of Jan Olszewski initially formed a minority coalition dominated by Christian Democrat groupings. His government stalled on several policy questions, including the privatization program announced in June 1991, which he reviewed with considerable reluctance. In the meantime, this government began to cooperate increasingly with the Church, whose teachings were now held to be moral guides for the nation. After a disastrous attempt to hunt down communist collaborators in public life, Olszewski's government fell in July 1992.

Olszewski's successor, Hanna Suchocka, formed a coalition that included both the Christian Democrats and the centrist Democratic Union (UD), and the equally liberal Liberal-Democratic Congress (Kongres Liberalno-Demokratyczny) and Polish Economic Program (Polski Program Gospodarczy). The Christian Democrats and the centrist-liberals immediately clashed, both over the role of the Church in public life and over economic liberalization. Subsequently, the Christian Democrats proved an especially disruptive force in the parliament, routinely torpedoing proposals they saw as "antifamily" or anti-Church (or too brazenly "liberal" in their economic stances).

Not surprisingly, then, the SdRP's appeals to moderation and professionalism resonated with a public weary of the "Polish zoo" of post-1989 politics. Changing the grounds of party competition to that of party expertise forced the other parties to answer, and recast the political debate. And, since the SdRP could compete very well on this dimension, with its considerable discipline and administrative experience, the party not only tapped into voter concerns, but made itself a stronger competitor by setting up the very standards it was best suited to meet.[122]

These efforts to create new bases for competition were made possible by the party's immensely skilled elites, whose earlier negotiation experience allowed them to convincingly address the voters in terms they understood, and whose record made these efforts credible. After all, even SdRP's adversaries acknowledged that the party was extremely professional and superior in its competence.[123] Their more moderate colleagues wished that "the post-Solidarity forces would show the same sort of political culture, as does [Józef] Oleksy and his party colleagues in debates."[124] This consistently moderate and disciplined behavior made credible the party's call for evaluating parties on the basis of competence rather than slogans. As a result, its professionalism and secularism allowed the party to win the 1993 elections.[125]

In short, the SdRP's earlier organizational centralization allowed it to respond easily to the electorate. The party leaders could choose whom to address without worrying about the member-voter trade off, since organizational transformation preceded the issue of new appeals. Moreover, the party's gradual evolution toward a more pro-market stance and its consistent secularism and emphasis on competence were bolstered by the party's past record. As a result, while the Czech party struggled with responsiveness and the Slovak party with consistency, the Polish SdRP managed to compete effectively on existing grounds and create new attractive appeals.

The Hungarian MSzP

Similarly, although its record is not examined in detail here, the Hungarian MSzP also successfully pursued responsive appeals and created new standards of competition, of competent governance, and of professional moderation. The MSzP argued for a continuation of the market reforms, but with far more attention paid to their ill effects. The party also

---

[122] DiMaggio, Paul, and Powell, Walter. "The Iron Cage Revisited: Institutional Isomorphism and Collective Rationality in Organizational Fields," in Powell and DiMaggio 1991.

[123] *Gazeta Wyborcza*, 2 April 1993, quoting Sosnowski.

[124] Donald Tusk, in *Rzeczpospolita*, January 1993.

[125] Kitschelt 1995b, p. 97.

Table 3.14. *Average gap in political priorities between MSzP supporters the rest of the electorate, 1992-5.*

Government roles considered important	Party supporters (%)	Rest of the electorate (%)	Average gap
Helping private enterprise	57%	48%	9
Ensuring competent managers	94%	89%	5
Ensuring democracy	69%	71%	2
Lessening the economic burden	84%	81%	3
Maintaining political stability	71%	66%	5
Strengthening patriotism	35%	42%	7
Increasing pensions/benefits	81%	78%	3
Increasing the role of the church	8%	16%	8
Speeding up privatization	13%	19%	6
Reducing unemployment	89%	87%	2
Decommunization	14%	32%	18

Source: Tóka, 1992–6.

consistently identified itself with the modernizing/cosmopolitan/"urbanist" goals, instead of its traditional, often extremist, "ruralist" opposition. The party's appeals were all the more attractive in light of the greater support in Hungary for redistributive efforts,[126] and the enormous concern prompted by the instability and lack of discipline in the first democratic government during 1990–4.

Organizational streamlining minimized the trade-off between appealing to the party's core supporters and the broader electorate, and promoted a largely cohesive electoral campaign. Initially, the party's supporters were considerably less likely to support helping private enterprises or speeding up privatization, by an average of a ten-point margin. However, with time, this gap began to close down drastically (7% margin, down to 2% by 1996). Furthermore, however, there were few other differences between party supporters and nonsupporters, as Table 3.14 shows.

[126] For example, Hungary and Russia had the lowest rates of support for the free market, with only 64% declaring that the free market is right for their respective countries in 1993, compared with 88% in the Czech Republic and 79% in Slovakia. White, et al. 1998, p. 110.

Conclusion

Throughout 1990–8, the party's past experience led the party to formulate a set of responsive appeals, which paid attention to the specificities of the Hungarian political scene, and especially the greater need for economically redistributive arguments. The MSzP addressed a wide electorate, making "two basic economic arguments: that the government's approach toward economic transition had been unjust and that hostility toward state enterprises and the welfare state was self-defeating and inconsistent with fundamental social needs and preferences. In effect, the MSzP understood that the bulk of the population had been excluded from reaping the rewards of the economic transition and had only shouldered its burdens."[127] At the same time, however, the party sought to reassure the new businesspeople and entrepreneurs, and so some party leaders even announced that the party stood "closer to liberals that to the conservatives."[128] As party leader Gyula Horn argued in the 1994 campaign, "should the voters put their confidence in the MSzP, the socialists would form a government from competent and honest people, a government which will have a credible program based on experience and reality and will be able to lead the country out of the crisis."[129] Given its extensive elite skills in negotiation and policy implementation, the Hungarian party was able to make managerial competence the key political dimension, one that both resonated with the public and was made credible by the party's usable past and elite skills.

Conclusion

Despite the earlier verdicts that the parties would be unable to function as responsive democratic parties, the parties examined here made considerable, and consistent, commitments to democracy, party competition, and even a market economy. As this analysis shows, the responsiveness of party programs was dependent on earlier organizational decisions. Organizational centralization allowed the parties to focus on voters, address their policy concerns, and do so with flexibility. For their part, portable skills

---

[127] Barany, Zoltan. "Socialist-Liberal Government Stumbles Through Its First Year," *Transition*, 28 July 1995, p. 29.
[128] Iván Vitányi, quoted by MTI, 7 October 1994.
[129] Gyula Horn, speech at rally in Miskolc, 5 May 1994, MTI.

allowed the new elites both to "read" the electorate correctly, and to create credible new dimensions of competition.

With time, changing these programmatic trajectories grew more difficult, and the set of available options had consolidated. Nonetheless, the environment continued to exert considerable pressure and to present significant opportunities for parties flexible and credible enough to take advantage of them. All parties had to react to these constituencies, competitors, and ideological distributions. As we will see in the next chapter, some parties would not only respond, but succeed beyond anyone's expectations.

4

Convincing the Voters:
Campaigns and Elections

With the advent of democracy, the communist successor parties confronted a challenge their predecessors had long forgotten: free political competition. The communist successors had to cope with a profusion of polarized competitors, inchoate electoral institutions, and an electorate whose priorities and preferences were not fully clear. All these made formulating a winning electoral strategy difficult, and forming stable governing coalition even more so. Yet only an electoral victory or participation in a parliamentary coalition would give the parties their ultimate goal: a return to governance, this time in a democratic system.

The configuration of environmental conditions made certain electoral strategies especially likely to succeed. First, the parties had been forced to exit from power, and were largely discredited by 1989. They consequently could not rely either on patronage, appeals to nostalgia, or extremist ideologies. Second, the electorates were fluid – the preferences of the voters were often unclear, making narrow appeals riskier. Third, the electoral institutions placed a premium on attractive electoral personalities: national party lists (in the Czech Republic, Poland, and Hungary), single-member districts (in Hungary), and open party lists (in Poland). As we will see in this chapter, these conditions favored responsive appeals addressed to broad electorates, new dimensions of competition that got around the parties' discreditation, and cohesive national campaigns.

How well each party could cope with these environmental challenges, however, depended on elite political resources and earlier organizational transformation. These could produce both the cohesive campaigns and the cross-cutting appeals that would prove key to winning elections in postcommunist democracies. Thus, if the previous chapter examined the *prerequisites* for programmatic responsiveness and the creation of attractive new appeals, this chapter will analyze the *effects* of these trans-formations. The sections that follow first explore how the parties dis-seminated their views through their campaigns, and how these were constrained by earlier changes in party organizations and appeals. The sections then consider the claims that would prove most convincing to the voters, and the bases for the parties' electoral support.

Electoral Campaigns

All the parties wanted to maximize the votes they obtained. Party leaders openly declared that their priority was to win elections.[1] As even the member-obsessed Czech party leaders explained, "if we didn't want elec-toral success, we wouldn't be a political party,"[2] and argued that "a good electoral result will open roads to contacts with other leftist powers, the road to a leftist coalition, the road to a better socialist future."[3] Since all parties operated in systems with proportional representation, none had to gain an actual majority to win elections; depending on how fragmented the competition was, a party could win elections and form the governing coalition with as little as 12.3% of the vote, as the Democratic Union did in Poland in 1991.

To achieve these goals, effective electoral campaigns consisted of both responsive appeals (or better yet, heresthetic ones) and unified party cam-paigns. Where the parties were not discredited, where the electorates were already divided or committed, and where elections were localized, it was more feasible to tailor narrow appeals to these electorates and run locally popular but nationally unattractive candidates. However, given the numer-ous competing parties and electorates that were not loyal to any specific party, centralization and a break with the past allowed the communist successor parties to hedge their electoral bets.

First, centralization gave the party elites the flexibility to pursue new appeals, as we saw in the previous chapter. Given the lack of party loyal-ties, such flexibility was crucial to obtaining broad party support. Second, centralization gave the party leaders control over the selection of the party's candidates. The more the voters came in contact with professional,

[1] *Pravda*, interviews with Peter Weiss and Jan Široký, 6 January 1990, 22 January 1990.
[2] Vasil Mohorita, *Naše Pravda*, April 1990.
[3] Jiří Machalik, *Naše Pravda*, 8 March 1990. By 1995, the party wanted a 20% share of the vote in the 1996 elections (*Dokumenty IV Sjezdu*, p. 59).

attractive "new faces," the more credible the party's message of transformation and reform. The more centralized the party, the more its elites could pick such candidates and ensure that they would remain loyal to the party's message. Third, centralization made it possible for parties to use a variety of mobilization methods and retain a cohesive message. Initially, scholars predicted that since the successor parties had relatively extensive membership and organizational networks, they would rely on these assets.[4] However, this prediction did not hold up uniformly. Some parties had used their local networks more than others. Where the parties had centralized, the members and local organizations would loyally reinforce the party's message. Where the parties were not as centralized, the members had more autonomy and freedom to contradict the leaders, sowing confusion. As a result, the Hungarian and Czech parties both mobilized the voters directly, but obtained very different results. Thus, the *method* of mobilization mattered less than its *content*.

Organizational streamlining and vertical integration thus increased the coherence and clarity of the dissemination of party programs. In contrast, decentralized control of recruitment for national electoral office has often led to inflexibility in campaign strategies, given the transmission of local interests upward.[5] Without a centralized vetting mechanism, local organizations could easily put forth candidates and orchestrate campaigns contrary to the overall party's message.[6] Where powerful internal currents did exist, they tended to blur the party's image, as internal conflict confused the voters.[7]

Electoral Appeals and Election Outcomes

To win elections, the parties could not rely on appeals to old adherents, new interest groups, or narrow protest stances, but on appeals that successfully addressed broader electorates. These appeals were mandated by the nature of the postcommunist political context: Economic performance

---

[4] Marada, Radim. "Who's Right in Czech Politics?" *Constellations*, January 1995: 62–71. Lewis, Paul. "Political Institutionalisation and Party Development in Post-Communist Poland," *Europe-Asia Studies*, No. 5, 1994: 779–99. Dehnel-Sznyc, Małgorzata, and Stachura, Jadwiga. *Gry polityczne: orientacje na dziś*. Warsaw: Volumen 1991, p. 83.
[5] Kitschelt 1994, p. 231.
[6] In other words, these monitoring and veto mechanisms circumvent the principal-agent problem the central elites would otherwise face vis-à-vis the local party organizations.
[7] Barany 1995, p. 29.

and individual well-being were foremost on the minds of the voters, as we saw in the last chapter. Given how unsettling the economic and political transformations were, several social groups suffered greatly as a result of the dismantling of the socialist welfare state, full-employment policies, and social security. As a result, for all the elite consensus on reform, one primary social division arose between those who benefited from the old socialist welfare system (for example, state enterprise workers) and those who stood to gain from the new, free market status quo.

Given the Left provenance of the communist successor parties, there were strong reasons to expect them to exploit this divide and represent the "losers" of the transition.[8] Traditionally, Left parties (which is how the communist successors identified themselves) have been supported by the traditional trade union and labor milieu[9] and by those who stood to benefit from protective and redistributive economic policies,[10] such as the elderly, the uneducated, and the unemployed. Given the parties' ties to the old regime, their self-proclaimed Left orientations, and the system of proportional representation that rewards appealing to specific groups, their electorates should have consisted of narrow groups of traditional Left constituencies – trade unionists, those dependent on the welfare state, and labor rather than management.

However, there were three reasons why narrow, nostalgic, or traditional Left appeals would not have been a successful strategy for the communist successor parties under consideration. First, the communist successor

---

[8] Kitschelt 1992. Evans, Geoffrey, and Whitefield, Stephen. "Economic Ideology and Political Success," *Party Politics*, October 1995: 565–78. Ágh, Áttila. "The Hungarian Party System and Party Theory in the Transition of Central Europe," *Journal of Theoretical Politics*, April 1994b: 217–38. Bunce, Valerie, and Csanádi, Maria. "Uncertainty in Transition: Post-Communists in Hungary," *East European Politics and Societies*, Spring 1993: 240–73. Cotta, Maurizio. "Building Party System After the Dictatorship: The East European Cases in a Comparative Perspective," in Pridham, Geoffrey, and Vanhanen, Tatu eds. *Democratization in Eastern Europe: Domestic and International Perspectives*. London: Routledge, 1994. Zubek, Voytek. "The Reassertion of the Left in Post-Communist Poland," *Europe-Asia Studies*, No. 5, 1994: 801–37.

[9] Kitschelt 1994, p. 45, on trade unions, and Von Beyme 1985, p. 285, on secular support. See also Harrop, Martin, and Miller, William L. *Elections and Voters: A Comparative Introduction*. London: MacMillan, 1987, pp. 181 and 189, respectively.

[10] Kis, János. "Between Reform and Revolution," *Constellations*, 3, 1995: 399–421. Evans and Whitefield 1993, Przeworski Adam. *Democracy and the Market*. Cambridge, UK: Cambridge University Press, 1992. The concept of "Left" in the region has been problematic after 1989, since it combined both political and economic cleavages. "Left" here means the general economic project of the Left: redistribution, nationalization, a strong welfare state, and egalitarian social policies.

parties' options were especially limited. They could not renounce their past and simply embrace the free market. Denouncing their old stances completely and making a radical turnaround would not have been credible, and parties making such shifts in their ideology have been punished by the voters elsewhere.[11] Nor could they speak out against economic reform, since this would smack of attempting to retain the old system and would call into question the party's reinvention. Because the parties had been forced out of power, it would do little good to the parties' public support and credibility as transformed parties to promote a return to the old, discredited system. However, where the parties were not as discredited, they could more readily rely on appeals to nostalgia for the old system.

Second, both the elite consensus on the necessity of economic reform and the effect of international pressures made it difficult to appeal exclusively to either the winners or the losers of the transition. This policy consensus left little room for purely redistributive or class-based appeals. This was all the more the case since initial public support for free market reforms was bundled with popular anticommunism and support for democracy in the countries under consideration.[12] Parties could compete on *how* to implement the free market reforms, but not on *whether* to do so. Although the support for market reforms wavered after 1991, no new alternatives to market reforms arose. Where this consensus was missing, it was easier to run on protest appeals.

Third, competition was national, and the electorates were fluid. Thus, instead of relying on loyal, existing electorates who could be mobilized via localized campaigns, the communist successors had to rely on responding to a broad, national electorate and applying a variety of campaign methods. Where the parties mobilized locally or where the electorate had already been mobilized along clear cleavages (such as the ethnic lines made salient by Slobodan Milošević in much of the former Yugoslavia), voter encapsulation strategies could be more successful in capturing the electorate and its loyalty.

Therefore, creating and exploiting dominant new cleavages were the strategies most likely to be successful for the communist successor parties

[11] Tamás, Bernard. "Spatial Distance or Historical Division: When Does the Public Reject a Party's Ideological Shift?" Paper presented at the Annual Meeting of the American Political Science Association, Washington, DC, 31 August–3 September 2000.
[12] Bunce, Valerie. "The Political Economy of Post-Socialism," *Slavic Review*, Winter 1999: 756–93, p. 783.

under consideration. Where political competition was dominated by either a policy consensus or a principal party, such new cleavages could draw away voters. Where political competition was characterized by several cleavages or fragmented parties, straddling these cleavages could unite several groups in support for the party. Successful competitors in these post-authoritarian democracies consequently did not rely on a loyal and well-defined electoral constituency with specific interests. Instead, they appealed to categories that did not conflict with each other, expressed wide popular concerns, and tried to "exchange effectiveness in depth for a wider audience and more immediate electoral success."[13]

As we saw in the last chapter, promises of expertise and competent managers were especially attractive, since they refocused the debate to who would be better able to implement economic reform rather than whether to challenge the project and direction of economic reform. They reassured the new beneficiaries of the transition that the reforms would continue, but with greater efficiency, expertise, and sensitivity to those whom the new free market did not, or could not, benefit.

For their responsive programs and newly created cleavages to lead to electoral success, however, communist successor parties needed both skilled elites and time. The communist successor elites could not dictate the reactions of competing parties, changes in the economic and political climate, or the electorate's shifts. However, in centralized party organizations, they could control their parties' response to these challenges. Elite experience in negotiation and bargaining with society made it easier for the party leaders to read correctly which appeals would resonate and convince the electorate. Such experience would allow the elites to anticipate public reactions and to respond. Otherwise, their strategic flexibility could imply inconsistency, and elite centralization of the parties could result in deafness to the electorate and its needs.

Moreover, repeated interactions between parties and voters were needed to convince the latter of the parties' abilities and their sincerity. The *first* free elections were largely a referendum on the discredited communist regime. In all cases studied, the communist parties were trounced by the opposition in the first elections and roundly denounced as a spent political power. After forty-five years of communism, no matter how lax it became in its last years, few voters could possibly believe that their authoritarian rulers could now suddenly and enthusiastically administer a

---

[13] Kirchheimer 1966, p. 183.

Table 4.1. *Electoral campaigns and outcomes as of 2001.*

	Campaigns	Electorate	Vote in 1st elections (%)	Vote in 2nd elections (%)	Vote in 3rd and 4th elections (%)
Czech KSČM	Not cohesive	Protest voters	13 (1990)	14 (1992)	10 (1996) 10 (1998)
Slovak SDĽ	Cohesive	Narrow groups	13 (1990)	15 (1992) 10 (1994)	15 (1998)
Polish SdRP	Cohesive	Increasingly broad	12 (1991)	20 (1993)	27 (1997) 40 (2001)
Hungarian MSzP	Cohesive	Increasingly broad	11 (1990)	33 (1994)	32 (1998)

Source: Country Electoral Commissions and Tóka, Gábor. "Party Systems and Electoral Alignments in East Central Europe." Machine-readable data. Central European University, 1992–6.

democratic system. Their claims of moderation and competence were not yet credible.

Nonetheless, some successor parties were able to rebound and to gain both votes and acceptance in the subsequent elections, as Table 4.1 indicates. The details of these outcomes vary even further – from the new image of the Czech party as a credible protest party with a narrow but loyal vote, to the widespread recognition that the Hungarian party represented a "government of the experts" with broad national support.

These opportunities for the successor parties' electoral victories in the *second* round of free elections were the result of two developments. First, the new democratic governments were committed to change, but often unable to implement it effectively. Their enthusiasm for reform did not necessarily translate into expertise. The first elected governments after 1989 consisted of representatives of the earlier opposition to the communist regimes: the successors to Solidarity, Public Against Violence, Civic Forum, and the Hungarian Opposition Round Table. They were committed to a democratic system, but largely inexperienced in governing. As a result, the first four years of democratic rule were often marked by divisiveness and instability. Poland, for example, had five governments in four years.[14] The first Hungarian government, led by the Hungarian

---

[14] These were the governments of Tadeusz Mazowiecki, Jan Krzysztof Bielecki, Jan Olszewski, Waldemar Pawlak, and Hanna Suchocka. In all five governments, the centrist Democratic Union (later the Freedom Union) played a crucial role.

Democratic Forum, destabilized, as its nationalist splinters and irredentist statements both came under heavy criticism both at home and abroad.[15]

Second, these first democratic parliaments were unstable. Other parliamentary parties squabbled, brought out the specters of nationalism and clericalism, and were unable to maintain discipline or stability. Political parties fissioned constantly, while their members indulged in "political tourism" – traveling from party to party. For example, in the Czech Republic, seventy out of the two hundred representatives changed their party in 1990–2,[16] and thirty-seven further did so in 1992–4.[17] In Poland, sixty out of four hundred sixty MPs changed their parties in 1991–3.[18]

In contrast to this inexperience and instability, the Polish and Hungarian successor parties could point to their skill, responsiveness, and professionalism. They pledged to continue the reforms, but to do so more effectively and competently, with greater attention paid to their ill effects. They were voted back into power after a few years, because by then only they could credibly claim administrative experience and expertise. These parties were increasingly seen as the best providers of political stability, democracy, and competent managers, rather than of simply redistributive policies or greater welfare provisions. In short, their image was that of a credible reform alternative.

Thus, while the communist successors had far less time than the other parties to establish their new identity after 1989, these transformations would not bear fruit for several years. By the second round of elections, however, some successor parties could credibly point to their own commitment to democracy and reform – their public record showed they had supported economic restructuring and democratic reforms. Second, they could point to the other parties' shortcomings – and appear far more competent in comparison.

---

[15] Thus, István Csurka, an ultranationalist, was forced to leave MDF, and founded the Hungarian Justice and Life Party in the late summer of 1993. The hardliner József Torgyan split from the Smallholders party and formed his own party in 1991. Most notably, the prime minister, József Antall, announced that he was the "prime minister of 15 million Hungarians," infuriating Hungary's neighbors; only 10 million Hungarians reside within Hungary proper, and the rest form ethnic minorities in Slovakia, Romania, and the former Yugoslavia (Vojvodina).

[16] Mansfeldová, Zdenka. "The First Czech Parliament in the View of the Members of Parliament." Paper prepared for the International Conference on "The New Democratic Parliaments," 24–6 June, Ljubljana, Slovenia, p. 3.

[17] *Lidové Noviny*, 29 October 1994.

[18] *Wprost*, 24 January 1993. In the first eight months of the 1991–3 session alone, thirty-seven parliamentarians changed parties.

As a result, neither overwhelming nostalgia for the communist era nor the impoverished "losers of the transition" returned the successor parties to power. Instead, postcommunist parties gained votes and entered government where they attracted a broad, cross-cutting electorate.[19] Their voters thus included not only the "losers of the transition," but more importantly, its beneficiaries and the rising middle class, for whom the security and stability offered by the communist successor party governments were a welcome respite. In contrast, where they were unable to appeal to such a broad and inclusive electorate, the parties gained more limited support.

Two observations confirm the conclusion that the communist successor parties were brought back to power by broad and cross-cutting electorates, rather than by either a) narrow groups of the nostalgic, the impoverished, or the discontent, or b) favorable electoral institutions. First, the most vulnerable did not vote for the successor parties.[20] Even the orthodox Czech party's support was not correlated to economic development or urban residence after 1989.[21] Moreover, there seemed to be little "hidden" support for the postcommunists among the nonvoters; for example, the biggest segment of those demanding the outlawing of the Czech KSČM comes from the nonvoters.[22] Similarly, no new constituencies began to vote in 1993 and 1994 in Poland or in Hungary.[23]

Another potential constituency was identified in the trade unions, and the electoral coalitions they formed with the parties.[24] After all, the biggest

---

[19] Szelenyi, Iván, Fodor, Eva, and Hanley, Eric. "Left Turn in Post Communist Politics: Bringing Class Back In?" *East European Politics and Societies*, Winter 1997: 190–224, p. 220. Kovács, András. "Two Lectures on the Electoral Victory of the Hungarian Socialists," *Constellations*, January 1995, pp. 72–5, and, "Did the Losers Really Win? An Analysis of Electoral Behavior in Hungary in 1994," *Social Research*, Summer 1996: 511–29. Cline, Mary. "The Demographics of Party Support in Poland," *RFE/RL Research Report*, 10 September 1993. Wade, Larry, Lavelle, Peter, and Groth, Alexander. "Searching for Voting Patterns in Post-Communist Poland's Sejm Elections," *Communist and Post-Communist Studies*, December 1995: 411–25. Körösényi 1993. Tóka, Gábor. "Electoral Choices in East-Central Europe," in Pridham and Lewis 1996.

[20] This includes pensioners, unemployed, the least educated, and unskilled workers. Szelenyi, Fodor, and Hanley 1997, p. 220.

[21] Jehlička, Pety, Kostelecký, Tomaš, and Sýkora, Ludek in O'Loughlin, John, and van der Wusten, Herman, eds. *The New Political Geography of Eastern Europe*. London: Belhaven, 1993: 235–53.

[22] Wyman, Matthew, White, Stephen, Miller, Bill, and Heywood, Paul. "The Place of 'Party' in Post-Communist Europe," *Party Politics*, No. 4, 1995: 535–48, p. 545.

[23] Körösényi 1993: 87–104.

[24] Körösényi 1993. Waller, Michael. "Adaptation of the Former Communist Parties of East Central Europe," *Party Politics*, October 1995: 473–90. Orenstein, Mitchell. "A

electoral victors, the Polish SdRP and the Hungarian MSzP, both formed such alliances. Ostensibly, such coalitions appeared mutually beneficial. The parties stood to gain a workplace presence via the unions' local organizations, a buffer against union discontent, and a chance to broaden their electorate.[25] An alliance with the trade unions would reinforce the parties' message that they could finally bring about political stability – both Poland and Hungary had experienced labor unrest in the years immediately following the democratic transition.[26] For their part, the unions hoped to gain political representation, and the communist successors were their only likely allies.[27] Moreover, given the prevailing pattern of bilateral negotiations between the state and labor,[28] the greater the unions' access to the government, the better the terms the unions could negotiate.

However, the unions were nowhere near as powerful as their West European counterparts, despite a large nominal membership.[29] They were virtually nonexistent in the private sector,[30] and their power was curtailed either by legal challenges, as in Hungary, or by government actions, as in Poland, Slovakia, and in the Czech Republic.[31] Most importantly, the parties' support does not appear to have been predominantly unionist; as Table 4.2 shows, the victorious Hungarian and Polish parties were not

Genealogy of Communist Successor Parties in East-Central Europe and the Determinants of their Success," *East European Politics and Societies*, Fall 1998, Vol. 12, No. 3: 472–99.

[25] Interview with Földes György, 25 March 1997, Budapest.

[26] Ekiert, Grzegorz, and Kubik, Jan. "Contentious Politics in New Democracies: East Germany, Hungary, Poland, and Slovakia, 1989–93," *World Politics*, July 1998: 547–81. Ekiert and Kubik. "Collective Protest in Post-Communist Poland: A Research Report," *Communist and Post-Communist Studies*, June 1998: 91–117.

[27] In Hungary, for example, all parties *except* the postcommunists tried to obliterate MSzOSz and revert its assets to new unions. Reisch, Alfred. "Hungarian Socialist Party Looks Aheud," *PFE/RL Research Report*, 10 July 1992.

[28] Hausner, Jerzy. "Organizacje interesu i stosunki przemysłowe w krajach postsocjalistycznych." *Studia Polityczne*, XLIII, 1994: 10–26. Thirkell, John, Scase, Richard, and Vickerstaff, Sarah. *Labor Relations and Political Change in Eastern Europe: A Comparative Perspective*. Ithaca, NY: Cornell University Press, 1995. Pataki, Judith. "Former Communist Trade Union Strengthens Its Positions," *Report on Eastern Europe*, 5 July 1991.

[29] Membership of the successors to the official communist-era unions varied: 6 million (comprising 80% of the workforce) in the Czech ČSKOS, 6 million in the Polish OPZZ, 2 million in Solidarity, and 1–2.5 million in the Hungarian MSzOSz (the estimates vary considerably, from 1 million to 2–2.5 million). Cziria, Ludovit. "The Czech and Slovak Republics," in Thirkell, Scase, and Vickerstaff 1995.

[30] Hausner 1994.

[31] The unions could thus no longer dismiss employees, and played a far lesser role in the social fund boards. Workers councils were also abolished (Cziria 1995).

Table 4.2. *Union support for communist successor parties, 1992–6.*

Successor party	1992	1993	1994	1995	1996
Czech KSČM: party support from union members (%)	57%	56%	49%	37%	38%
Slovak SDL': party support from union members (%)	60%	56%	44%	50%	39%
Polish SdRP: party support from union members (%)	15%	25%	14%	12%	N/A
Hungarian MSzP: party support from union members (%)	43%	36%	33%	28%	N/A

Note: In both the Hungarian and Polish cells, numbers include support from both the communist successor union (the official electoral coalition partners of the SdRP and MSzP) and the anticommunist or neutral unions.

Source: Tóka, 1992–6. Data is shown for all years, rather than elections, to show trends in support.

dependent on union support. Ironically, where no alliances existed (and, notably, where labor was extremely weakly organized), in the Czech Republic and in Slovakia, union members tended to comprise a greater percentage of the party's supporters, according to public opinion surveys. While union membership tended in some analyses to predict communist successor party support, these parties could not, and did not, simply rely on the backing of organized labor.[32]

The evidence led scholars to conclude that "not a single socio-demographic variable appeared to have a consistent impact on post-communist party preference in any of the four countries."[33] Although their salience has been debated, the waning importance of these traditional sociodemographic factors was not unique to East Central Europe – over twenty years ago, scholars identified "New Left" cleavages in postindustrial societies.[34] Political discourse has expanded beyond "simple" economic

[32] Szczerbak, Aleks. "Interests and Values: Polish Parties and Their Electorates," *Europe-Asia Studies*, No. 8, Vol. 51, 1999, p. 1421. In 1992, OPZZ membership tended to increase support for SLD by 36%, and in 1997 those belonging to the communist-era trade unions supported the party at rates that were twenty-seven points higher than the national average.

[33] Tóka 1996, p. 114. See also Tóka, Gábor. "Party Appeals and Voter Loyalty in New Democracies," *Political Studies*, 1998: 589–610.

[34] Inglehart 1977.

redistribution. For example, the British Labour Party succeeded in 1997 largely because of the new support of professional and managerial constituencies rather than its traditional blue-collar electorate.[35]

Second, the structures of party competition also did not play the expected role. In other contexts, scholars have observed that the greater the number of competitors, the fewer the unoccupied stances on policy and ideology, and the greater the likelihood of challenges to the successor parties' claims and appeals. Therefore, communist successor parties should have succeeded where they faced weak competitors on the Left.[36] For example, the tiny social democratic parties in Poland and in Hungary presented no challenge to the successor parties' claim to social democratic identities. Successor parties should have done well where the party system revolved around a few large competitors, rather than a multitude of fragmented ones,[37] or where the electoral laws favored them (for example, where electoral thresholds privileged large parties).[38]

However, the Czech party faced no real competition on the left in 1989–93, yet it failed to transform itself or to increase its share of the vote. The Czech Social Democrats won only 4% in 1990 and barely cleared the 5% threshold for entry into parliament in 1992, but the Czech party neither took advantage of its competitor's weakness, nor was its support hurt by Social Democratic strength later on. As a result, the weakness of social democratic alternatives was not responsible for either the parties'

---

[35] King, Anthony, ed. *Britain at the Polls*. Chatham, NJ: Chatham House 1998. The swing vote in 1997 consisted above all of the young (20%), professional, managerial, and executives (22%), and white-collars (19%).

[36] Panebianco 1988, p. 267. Ishiyama 1995. Marada 1995. See also Zubek, Voytek. "The Fragmentation of Poland's Political Party System," *Communist and Post-Communist Studies*, March 1993: 47–71. Arato, Andrew. "Constitution and Continuity in the East European Transitions," *Constellations*, January 1994: 92–112. Millard, Frances. "The Shaping of the Polish Party System, 1989–93," *East European Politics and Societies*, Fall 1994a: 467–94.

[37] Millard 1994a. Millard, Frances. "The Polish Parliamentary Election of September, 1993," *Communist and Post-Communist Studies*, No. 3, 1994b. Arato, Andrew. "Two Lectures on the Electoral Victory of the Hungarian Socialists," *Constellations*, No. 1, 1995: 72–80. See also Sjöblom, Gunnar. "Political Change and Political Accountability," in Daalder, Hams, and Mair, Peter, eds. *Western European Part Systems*. London: Saye Publications, 1983: 370–403.

[38] Rae, Douglas. *The Political Consequences of Electoral Laws*. New Haven: Yale University Press, 1971. Taagepera, Rein, and Shugart, Matthew. *Seats and Votes*. New Haven, CT: Yale University Press, 1989. For a critique of Rae, see Lijphart, Arend. "The Political Consequences of Electoral Laws, 1945–85," *American Political Science Review*, Vol. 84, No. 2, June 1990: 481–96.

decisions to transform, or for their subsequent electoral appeals.[39] Competition and electoral laws may have made succeeding more difficult, but did not correlate fully with party regeneration; fractionalization, electoral thresholds, and districting failed to predict electoral performance.[40]

In short, these parties could not simply count on preexisting constituencies or on advantageous electoral institutions. Instead, their challenge was to create *new* bases of support. As a result, where they were successful in this endeavor, their electorates were far broader and more satisfied on average with the post-1989 status quo than the initial analyses predicted.[41]

The sections that follow examine the parties' campaign strategies and their electoral images and performance. Given the sophisticated analyses of the electoral competition and its development that are already available, this analysis does not aim to explain fully the patterns of electoral choice and competition after 1989 in East Central Europe.[42] The inferences drawn here are only about the successor parties and how they belied many expectations derived from the behavior of established democratic electorates and parties.[43] Multinomial logit regressions and machine learning

---

[39] Waller 1995a, Waller, Michael. "Starting Up Problems: Communists, Social Democrats, and Greens," in Wightman, Gordon, ed. *Party Formation in East-Central Europe*. Aldershot, UK: Edward Elgar, 1995b. Ishiyama 1995.

[40] Electoral thresholds magnified the volatility of the vote, but did not otherwise affect party regeneration. Moraski, Bryon, and Loewenberg, Gerhard. "The Effect of Legal Thresholds on the Revival of Former Communist Parties in East-Central Europe," paper presented at the Annual Meeting of the American Political Science Association, 28–31 August 1997, Washington, DC. Large district magnitude, which Katz 1980 argues leads to a multitude of parties and ideologized politics, should have led to difficulties in regeneration. However, it does not correlate with party adaptation (see Appendix C).

[41] Ágh 1994b, Bunce and Csanadi 1993, Cotta 1994, Evans and Whitefield 1995, Kitschelt 1992, Przeworski 1992, Zubek 1994.

[42] See Powers, Denise V, and Cox, James. "Echoes from the Past: The Relationship Between Satisfaction with Economic Reforms and Voting Behavior in Poland," *American Political Science Review*, September 1997: 617–33. Kitschelt et al. 1999. Miller, White, and Heywood 1998. Pridham and Lewis 1996, Tworzecki, Hubert, *Parties and Politics in Post 1989 Poland*. Boulder, CO: Westview Press, 1996. Tóka, Gábor. "*Political Parties and Democratic Consolidation in East Central Europe*." Glasgow: Center for the Study of Politics, 1997. Markowski, Radosław. "Political Competition and Ideological Dimensions in East Central Europe." Glasgow: Center for the Study of Politics, No. 257, 1995.

[43] These approaches owe much to the logic of spatial competition first set out by Downs 1957. See also Przeworski and Sprague 1986 on the specifics of the competition between communist and social democratic parties. Further emphasis on the environment in shaping organizations can be found in Aldrich 1979, p. 27.

algorithms analyzed the survey data, and an explanation of these data, techniques, and their limitations can be found in Appendix B.

The Czech KSČM

The Czech KSČM's strategy of organizational and programmatic continuity limited its appeal to the broad electorate and made its few broad appeals not credible. Unlike the Slovak, Polish, and Hungarian parties, it relied largely on a protest electorate, dissatisfied with post-1989 reform. The Czech communist successor could neither outflank the dominant Civic Democratic Party (ODS) of Václav Klaus, nor could it offer a credible policy alternative to the free market consensus.[44] Even when the Czech economy slid into a recession in 1996–7, partly as a result of the shortcomings of its earlier reforms, the communist successor was unable to benefit.

Electoral Campaigns

The party's electoral campaigns did little to help it gain support for its eventual goal of "systemic change, a deep, profound change of the capitalist system into a socialist one."[45] Neither the campaigns nor the candidates convinced the electorate of the party's ability to govern effectively.

The party's campaign slogans that "we too have experts" met with little resonance, as did its attempt to introduce "autonomy" as an electoral issue, as we saw in the last chapter. Nor were the campaign's appeals particularly successful – for example, another 1990 electoral slogan was to "Regain the trust of the people,"[46] but wags commented that the party could not regain what it never had. The party also stood "For a democratic socialist society" (1990) and insisted that "Socialism [is] the chance for the future" (1995–6), both of which tended to recall the communist past. Subsequently, party elites attempted to soften the party's public image – for example, its 1996 campaign featured a cartoon of several children dressed up as ghosts, with the familiar slogan "The specter of communism is haunting Europe," in

---

[44] Blahož, Josef, Brokl, Lubomír, and Mansfeldová, Zdenka. "Czech Political Parties and Cleavages after 1989," in Lawson, Kay, Römmele, Andrea, and Karasimeonov, Georgi, eds. *Cleavages, Parties, and Voters*. Westport, CT: Praeger, 1999, p. 136.

[45] *Zpráva ÚV KSČM o Činnosti KSČM v období po IV. Sjezdu v Liberci (prosinec 1995–prosinec 1999)*. Praha: ÚV KSČM, p. 21.

[46] *Rudé Pravo*, 30 January 1990.

an effort to make the party seem less threatening to the new democratic status quo. This, too, met with little broad support.

Nor was the party leadership able to establish control over the electoral campaigns. First, the party experienced infighting during the campaigns. By mid-1990, the public splits within the Czech KSČM made it unclear to the voters who "the real party" was – intraparty democracy blurred party identity in ways that made the party less attractive to voters.[47] Second, party candidates were initially chosen by the party leaders. Even if they were not otherwise particularly skilled in creating it, Mohorita and Adamec both wanted a more moderate image for the party. As a result, a wave of moderate reformists was allowed to enter the party's parliamentary representation, only to be forced to leave after forming opinion platforms that were rapidly ostracized by the orthodox members and activists.

To get around this problem, and to guarantee that the subsequent candidates would reflect the members' views, the Central Committee instituted primaries to choose local candidates for national office, and these were used in the 1992 elections.[48] As a result, conservative local organizations tended to push through their own candidates.[49] The result was the reinforcement of the party's orthodox image and the subsequent narrowing of the candidate pool for future elections. By the time the party centralized its structures somewhat in 1993, its leaders could only choose among orthodox communist candidates, as the reformists had already left the party.

Its organizational continuity also limited the effectiveness of the campaign tools at the party's disposal. Czech party leaders acknowledged that local organizations were "unreliable" and the elderly membership "almost unusable."[50] Nonetheless, they utilized both, given their lack of other political resources.[51] Members went door to door to mobilize voters, held demonstrations, and often prepared campaign materials themselves. These posters, flyers, and mimeos featured their own rather doctrinaire communist views, rather than the more diplomatically worded stances prepared by the party center. Given these conflicting signals, the party could not

[47] Ladislav Adamec, *Naše Pravda*, 24 July 1990.
[48] *Pravda*, 25 May 1991.
[49] Interview with Jozef Heller, KSČM HQ, 24 September 1996, Prague.
[50] Interview with Jozef Heller, 26 September 1997, Prague.
[51] *Zpráva ÚV KSČM o Činnosti KSČM v období po IV. Sjezdu v Liberci (prosinec 1995-prosinec 1999)*. Praha: ÚV KSČM, p. 35.

make convincing public declarations and appeals, as the party's own evaluation concluded by 1995.[52]

In fact, the party received its *worst* electoral performance in those districts where it had the most active local organizations – as party leaders admitted, the prospect of elderly communist pensioners extolling the virtues of centralized planning and one-party rule "sent the voters running to the ballot box to vote for any party except us."[53] Hence, the party did well above its national average in Tachov, Louny, Most, and Kutná Hora – where its organizations had been labeled "inactive and useless."[54] On the other hand, where it had had earlier identified strong local organizations, as in Liberec, České Budejovice, and Hradec Kralové, it had poor electoral results.[55] The one place where both organizations and electoral results were poor was Prague.

Moreover, these campaign strategies were not particularly successful in attracting a broad new electorate, necessary to win the elections – only 9% of its voters were influenced by the ubiquitous party meetings, and 45% by propaganda material stuffed into mailboxes.[56] As the party's Central Committee noted, the 1992 campaign used a fraction of the 1990 funds, yet the vote percentage did not change.[57] Not surprisingly, only 11% of the voters had decided to vote for the party in 1992 and 1996 as a result of the electoral campaign, less than any other party's supporters.[58] By 1999, the party acknowledged its minimal change in its mobilizational style or methods, and the continuing difficulties in broadening party activity beyond the membership base and the circle of sympathizers.[59]

Nor were its electoral coalitions effective in increasing the party's vote share. The KSČM formed an electoral coalition in 1992 with the Democratic Left (DL, Demokratická Levice, not to be confused with the epony-

---

[52] *Dokumenty IV Sjezdu*, p. 32.
[53] Interview with Vera Žežulková, 25 September 1997, confirmed by Miloslav Ransdorf and Jozef Heller.
[54] Thus, in 1992, when the party received 14% of the vote, it received over 20% in these districts. In 1996, when the party received 10% nationwide, it received as much as 16% and 18% in Tachov and Louny, respectively. Česky Statistický Uřad, *Volby do Poslanecké Snimovny Parlamentu Česke Republiky 1996*. Praha, June 1996.
[55] In 1992, these districts had under 11% of the vote, and in 1996, under 8%.
[56] Interview with Miloslav Ransdorf, 25 September 1997, Prague.
[57] Twelfth meeting of the UV KSČM, reported in *Haló Noviny*, 1 June 1992.
[58] *Mlada Fronta Dnes*, 2 February 1996.
[59] *Zpráva ÚV KSČM o Činnosti KSČM v obdobi po IV. Sjezdu v Liberci (prosinec 1995–prosinec 1999)*. Praha: ÚV KSČM, pp. 22–3.

mous reformist splinter), a small regional party headquartered in Brno. The two then formed the Left Bloc (Levý Blok – again, not to be confused with the Strana Levý Blok, the reformist splinter that left in 1993) electoral coalition in April 1992, along with twenty small auxiliary organizations (including such notables as the "Club of Progressive Architects," and "the Union of Freethinkers"). The coalition, however, did little to improve the electoral results in 1992, and disintegrated by the 1996 elections.

Party Image and Support

The KSČM's appeals, based as they were on a defense of the old socio-economic system and the members' views, held little appeal for the wider electorate. Any moderate electoral appeals were not bolstered by organizational transformation or a break with the past. As a result, the party could count on a loyal but narrow support base, largely limited to the party's members and those unhappy with the post-1989 changes and the political status quo. The party's best hope for increasing its electorate came from a worsening of the status quo, and increasing dissatisfaction with the democratic regime, rather than from its own policy appeals.

The KSČM elicited the most negative responses of all the parties under consideration. In every year of the poll, over 40% of respondents answered they liked "nothing" about it. The Czech party also had the highest rates of responses citing its lack of credibility and competence as the items most disliked about the party (see Table 4.3). Not surprisingly, 55% of the Czech adult population did not want the party in parliament, the highest such percentage received by any party.[60]

The KSČM was also consistently seen as the least likely to fulfill any one of a host of government roles. It was perceived as loosely committed to democracy; a third of those polled cited it as the party least likely to ensure democracy or to promote freedom of speech. It was also seen as the party least capable of providing effective administration – for the entire time of the polls, it had the dubious honor of being the party least likely to provide competent managers. The only mention of a possible policy accomplishment came in 1992, when the party was briefly seen as the most likely to reduce unemployment and inequalities. Subsequently, however, it was seen as incapable of achieving any of the redistributive goals

[60] STEM Poll, 26 May 1992, *Mlada Fronta Dnes*.

Table 4.3. *Popular perceptions of KSČM.*

KSČM	1992	1993	1994	1996
Items *most* liked about party	Nothing 46%	Nothing 45%	Nothing 43%	Nothing 42%
	Social policy 8%	Social policy 6%	Social policy 9%	Social policy 10%
	Credibility 4%	Credibility 4%	Program 5%	Program 5%
Items *least* liked about party	Credibility 16%	Credibility 20%	Credibility 18%	Credibility 11%
	Competence 7%	Style 11%	Style 11%	Specific members 4%
	Style 6%	Party structure 8%	Competence 7%	Program 4%

KSČM	1992	1993	1994	1996
As the party *most* likely to:				
Reduce unemployment	24%			
As the party *least* likely to:				
Decommunize	70%	76%	77%	74%
Help private enterprise	58%	50%	55%	56%
Increase the Church's role	60%	67%	53%	52%
Speed up privatization	60%	58%	58%	60%
Ensure democracy		31%	28%	31%
Provide competent managers	34%	29%	27%	24%

Source: Tóka, 1992–6.

traditionally favored by Left parties (of which the KSČM claimed to be a part). Even when the party's supporters demanded a rejection of the economic transformation and the free market and a return to the socialist welfare state,[61] the party was seen as least likely to be able to achieve these demands.

These stances moderated only slightly, and some negative perceptions actually increased in magnitude. As a result, the party's voters were both relatively few and hardly representative of the electorate. The Czech party

[61] In fact, the party made its claims more extreme with time, even as some of its supporters subsequently grew more accepting of the free market reforms.

Table 4.4. *Determinants of KSČM support, relative to the party's perceived chief competitor, ODS.*

Determinant	1992	1993	1994	1995	1996
Dissatisfaction with democracy	.84***	.92***	.94***	.87***	.91***
	(.77–.88)	(.87–.94)	(.90–.96)	(.82–.91)	(.88–.93)
Age	.66***	.66***	.69***	.74***	.67***
	(.60–.73)	(.60–.71)	(.63–.72)	(.68–.79)	(.63–.71)
Education levels	.53	.39**	.40**	.29***	.37***
	(.45–.60)	(.32–.45)	(.36–.53)	(.24–.35)	(.32–.43)
Secularism	.65**	.60**	.57*	.62***	.64***
	(.57–.73)	(.53–.66)	(.50–.74)	(.55–.68)	(.58–.70)

Note: Ninety-five percent confidence interval in parentheses. Statistically significant determinants of party support are shown as * at 90% confidence level, ** at 95% confidence level, and *** at 99%. Results are given in probabilities relative to the base category of support for the ODS. Thus, given increasing dissatisfaction with democracy, the probability of supporting the KSČM is 92% in 1993, relative to the probability of voting for the ODS.
Source: Tóka, 1992–6.

and its supporters were the "outliers" of Czech politics – generally older, increasingly dissatisfied with the democratic system, and not particularly well educated. KSČM supporters were also an unusually pessimistic lot, and considered the communist system superior to the post-1989 democracy.[62] In contrast, support for the ruling Civic Democratic Palm and Civic Democratic Alliance grew with satisfaction with democracy and with educational levels.[63] One of the variables most positively associated with support for the KSČM over the party that it perceived as its biggest rival, the ODS, was the KSČM's supporters' considerably higher dissatisfaction with democracy (see Table 4.4). The only group to be as discontent with democracy comprised the supporters of the extremist Republicans (SPR-RSČ).

[62] Among these supporters, 95% are unhappy with the market reforms and only 7% think the market is superior (compared to 52% of the Czech population). Among KSM supporters, 65% think the communist system superior and 87% think political developments are heading the wrong way (compared to 36% of the general population) in a 1992 poll by STEM. In July 1993, 90.8% were unsatisfied with the current poltiical situation.

[63] The support for the rival Social Democrats exhibited a steady "Left" identification, and its likelihood grew with residents in large urban areas. These supporters were also far more satisfied with free market reforms, although the Social Democratic electorate also expressed strong redistributive preferences.

Since both the party's image and support tended to center around a rejection of the new democratic status quo, the KSČM could count on political discontent as a source of its support. At the same time, the KSČM had neither the elite skills to make its claims of expertise and "autonomy" the decisive electoral issue, nor the usable past to make these claims credible. Thus, the party was unable to garner a broad electorate because its claims were too narrow and nostalgic, and its few moderate claims were not credible. The party was anything but a "party of the experts," while at the same time neither the "losers of the transition" nor the traditional Left electorate found the party's appeals compelling.[64]

On the other hand, the party's internal policies built up the most loyal electorate in the Czech Republic. As a result, one of the most frequent predictors for party support was a previous vote for the KSČM.[65] Forty-four percent of its supporters followed the party from election to election, compared to the ČSL's 30%, the ODS's 17%, and the Social Democrats' 8%.[66] In 1993, 74% of voters from 1992 would vote for the party again.[67] In 1996, 79% of voters had previously voted for the party.[68] Similarly, well over a half (58.7%) of KSČM voters in 1996 had already decided to vote for the party in the previous elections.[69] As a result, the party could count on a steady 10% of the electorate for support from election to election.

The KSČM's inability to expand its support beyond this faithful electorate allowed a social democratic party to arise independently of the communist successor, and succeed. Scholars have argued previously that a

[64] The party received 3% of the entrepreneurs' vote (the lowest such percentage of all the parties, compared to 54% for ODS), 6% of state employees (6%, second lowest, 38% ODS highest), 10% of workers (ČSSD got 32%), 3% of the wealthy and 11% of the poor (ODS got 50% and 32%, respectively), 4% of the young (KSČM got the lowest, with ODS highest at 35%), and 12% of over sixty-year-olds (ODS got 41%). *Mlada Fronta Dnes*, 3 June 1996.

[65] July 1993 STEM poll, February 1996 STEM poll, as reported in *Mlada Fronta Dnes*, 2 February 1996.

[66] *Dokumenty IV Sjezdu* KSČM, p. 38.

[67] Brokl, Lubomír, and Mansfeldová, Zdenka. "Political Parties and Their Programs," *East Europe 2000: The Czech Republic Background Studies*. Prague: Insititute of Sociology, Academy of Sciences of the Czech Republic, May 1993.

[68] *Mlada Fronta Dnes*, 2 February 1996.

[69] The only party whose supporters were similarly loyal was the ODS, with 55.9% of voters decided in previous elections and 18.4% during the campaign. In contrast, ČSSD had 25.7% voters decide in previous elections, 31.7% in the 1992–6 period, and 42.6% in the campaign. Vlachová, Klara. "Volby 1996 – více sila zvyku něž nové rozhodnutí" [Elections 1996 – more power of habit than a new decision], *Lidové Noviny*, 3 August 1996, p. 8.

strong social democracy would prevent the rise of a moderate communist party.[70] Thus, the KSČM was preempted by the Social Democrats' strong showings. However, these causal arrows may need to be reversed. The Social Democrats were an extremely weak party until 1993, barely clearing the 5% electoral threshold in 1992. By this point, the KSČM had already consolidated its orthodox communist appeals and image. Since it was perceived as incompetent, those voters who sought redistributive policies and ideological moderation eventually voted for the Social Democrats rather than the KSČM. In effect, the Social Democrats could become a strong party because the KSČM could not appeal to a broader electorate, rather than the other way around. By the time the consensus on market reform had ended by 1996, Social Democrats benefited from popular doubts. The KSČM was not a viable alternative either to the 1992–8 governments led by the ODS or to the Social Democrats.

Electoral Performance

As a result, so long as the electorate was satisfied with post-1989 developments, the party's support remained low. In 1990, in the first free election that was also an anticommunist plebiscite, the KSČM received a larger vote than any other communist successor, with nearly 13.2% of the vote (see Table 4.5). By the next elections, in 1992, it was clear that two distinct party systems were developing in Czechoslovakia – no parties campaigned in both the Czech lands and Slovakia.[71] Since the KSČM was the one party to speak out consistently against the partitioning of Czechoslovakia, it was also seen as the party least likely to lead to a rapid separation, by over 40% of those polled.[72] Some voters protested against the imminent division of the country by voting for the party, increasing its vote share to 14%.

Party leaders themselves argued that the "illusion of market successes" prevented a greater number of voters from supporting the party's attempts

---

[70] Przeworski and Sprague 1986.
[71] Nor did they have to, since the 5% party electoral threshold had to be cleared only in one republic.
[72] On the other hand, the ODS, the chief beneficiary of the split (since Klaus could now proceed with his policies with no objections from the Slovak parliament), was seen by nearly 70% as the party most likely to lead to a rapid separation. Tóka, Gábor. "Party Systems and Electoral Alignments in East Central Europe." Machine-readable data. Central European University, 1992–6.

Table 4.5. *Elections in the Czech Republic (government coalition in bold).*

Party	1990	1992	1996	1998
KSČM	13.2%	14.1%	10.3%	11%
ČSSD	4%	6.5%	26.4%	**32.3%**
KDU-ČSL	8.7%	**6.3%**	**8.1%**	9.0%
ODS	**49.5% (OF)**	29.7%	29.6%	27.7%
ODA	N/A	**5.9%**	**6.4%**	N/A
SPR-RSČ	N/A	5.9%	8.0%	3.9%
HSD-SMS	8.4%	5.9%	N/A	N/A
US	N/A	N/A	N/A	8.6%

Source: Czech Statistical Office elections server, http://www.volby.cz.

to slow down market reforms.[73] To resolve this problem, they planned to revitalize the local organizations and pay greater attention to mobilizing the voters. However, the party saw no need to change its appeals; in 1992, Václav Papěž, one of the hardliners, argued that part of the success of the party was that it did not "change its colors." In this view, the 1992 elections proved that a return to communist standards was the most viable course.[74]

Subsequently, however, between 1992 and 1996, the heyday of the Klaus era, the party lost 283,000 votes, and went from 14% to 10.3% of the vote. Nonetheless, KSČM leaders expressed satisfaction with the results of both the 1992 and 1996 elections, and saw them as a confirmation of its earlier policies – the name did not matter, so long as the party retained its members and internal democracy.[75]

The KSČM relied on a worsening political and economic situation to increase its support. So long as the aura of prosperity and successful reform surrounded the Klaus government, other parties could gain little support. When this halo of invincibility began to dissipate, during 1996–8, Czech economic performance worsened in comparison to other East European countries, banking and party funding scandals emerged, and a widespread mood of distrust in government appeared. However, the main beneficiary was the Czech Social Democratic Party. The Social Democrats went from less than 5% of the vote in 1990 to nearly 27% in 1996. The party gained

[73] Interview with Miloslav Ransdorf, 25 September 1996, Prague.
[74] V. Papěž, *Haló Noviny*, 31 July 1992.
[75] Interview with Miroslav Grebreniček, *Lidové Noviny*, 14 December 1992.

The Slovak SDĽ

326,410 votes in the early elections held in June 1998, for 32.3% of the vote. In contrast, the KSČM gained 32,414 votes from 1996 to 1998, going from 10.3% to 11%.[76]

Instead, voters tended to voice support for the party outside of elections, to protest the status quo. As campaign funding scandals rocked the ČSSD government in 1998–9 (similar scandals also affected its tacit supporter in government, the ODS) and new groupings demanded that the post-1989 politicians leave the political scene (such as the "Thank You, Now Leave" initiative of November 1999), the party gained as much as 20% support of those surveyed. This support was more in protest of the existing government, however, than in affirmation of the KSČM's positive policy offerings.

Thus, as a result of low organizational streamlining and vertical integration, the KSČM was unable to field broadly appealing candidates, and its campaign methods did little to convince the electorate or disseminate its message convincingly. The party's set of credible claims consisted of its suspicions regarding free market reform, international organizations, and the nature of the new democracy. For this strategy to bear fruit, the party would have to wait for the status quo to worsen.

The Slovak SDĽ

The Slovak party, operating in a political system marked by "nonstandard" political cleavages (that is, populist and nationalist claims on the one hand, and the more typical democratic parties on the other) championed political pragmatism, and explicitly denounced communism. Unlike the Czech party, its campaigns were cohesive. Unlike the Polish and Hungarian parties, however, it was unable to gain a broad electorate.

The Movement for a Democratic Slovakia's extensive populism and Mečiar's charisma made the HZDS a popular party in Slovakia – it won the 1990, 1992, and 1994 elections, despite the Mečiar governments being brought down briefly in 1991 and again, for six months, in 1994. On the other hand, Mečiar's attempts to shut down the free press, privatize enterprises by giving them away to political cronies, and make several antidemocratic moves made the party and its intentions deeply suspect for a sizeable fraction of the population. As a result, HZDS was increasingly seen as simultaneously most and least likely to achieve several political and

[76] Source: http://www.volby.cz.

economic goals, such as providing competent managers, lessening the economic burden, reducing unemployment, or ensuring political stability.

In responding to this dominance, the SDL' could not rely on nostalgia, given its democratic commitments. Nor, given the shifting electorates, could the party succeed with narrow appeals. At the same time, the lack of elite experience in negotiation and policy implementation made it difficult for the party to create the sort of new dimensions of competition that would broaden its support.

Electoral Campaigns

Despite its organizational centralization, the SDL' did not significantly increase its vote share, largely because the elites lacked experience in appealing to and convincing the public. Centralization without these concomitant elite experiences meant that the party campaign would be cohesive, but not necessarily effective. Elite mistakes, in fact, would have that much more impact, since the entire party would follow suit.

The party centralized the candidate selection and made it largely dependent on the central leadership's vetting.[77] However, the lack of elite experience in societal negotiation meant that the party often fielded candidates and rhetoric that were less than convincing to the broader electorate. For example, the party's leadership chose nationally unknown candidates, whom they found personally and intellectually attractive.[78] Local organizations protested in vain, and argued this was the main reason for the party's poor electoral performance in 1992 and 1994. Therefore, in 1995, the party's congress decided that regional conferences would be given additional say in proposing the candidates for the parliament. However, since the center leadership retained full veto power over the selection of candidates, it was able to push through its own selections. As a result, the party's candidates often stood accused of being aloof and unable to articulate the party's message to the "common man."

Second, the party's campaign slogans were also inconsistent. Its slogans often could have belonged to a right-wing party: From 1992 on, the party's main motto was, "To the able, their due. To the industrious, assurance." In 1994, its electoral coalition's slogan was, "Health, work, education, and safety for everyone," a more traditionally redistributive appeal, but it was

[77] RR SDL, in *Pravda*, 26 September 1992.
[78] Interview with Petr Magvaši, 27 January 1997, Bratislava.

accompanied by constant reassurances that the party disavowed tax-and-spend policies and would continue to implement market reforms. The party also used a vague appeal to competence by 1999: "Effective steps for future years."

At the same time, however, the party's organizational centralization made individual mobilization effective, where it was used. The earlier demands of loyalty during reregistration made the local party organizations into effective tools of electoral mobilization. As a result, where the SDĽ identified its strongest organization (greatest membership mobilization, interest in congress delegations, etc.), the party received the greatest support, in Prešov, Banská Bystrica, and Košice.[79]

The SDĽ's electoral coalition proved to be of little electoral value, because it obscured the SDĽ while diluting its message. The coalition that formed, Spoločna Voľba (Common Choice), also included the Agricultural Movement (Hospodarské Hnutie) and the Green Party of Slovakia (Strana Zelených Slovenska). The SDĽ expected the coalition to gain 25% of the vote, but Common Choice received only 10% of the votes in the September 1994 elections. Indeed, there were only two districts nationwide (both in Bratislava), where the coalition gained more votes than the SDĽ alone in 1992. Instead, there were several districts where the party experienced significant losses, and to parties the SDĽ had earlier rejected as extremist: its own splinter, the nationalist ZRS, the populist HZDS, and the orthodox Communist Party of Slovakia (Komunistická Strana Slovenska, KSS).[80] The news that the SDĽ retained the prodemocratic voters while the HZDS and ZRS gained the populist and nationalist electorate was cold comfort to party activists.[81] Centralization produced both elite control over the campaigns and flexibility. However, without more extensive elite experience, these attributes also led to inconsistency and isolation from the electorate.

[79] Thus, in 1992, when the party received 14% of the vote nationwide, it received 19% in Prešov, 15% in Banská Bystrica, and 21% in Košice. In 1994, when the nationwide vote was 10%, the party's vote was 12%, 11%, and 16%, respectively. In 1998, the nationwide vote was 14.7%, and 17%, 26%, and 15% in these districts, respectively. Source: Štatistický Úrad Slovenskej Republiky.

[80] Krivý, Vladimír. "The Parliamentary Elections 1994: The Profile of Supporters of the Political Parties, the Profile of Regions," in Szomolányi and Mesežnikov 1995.

[81] Bútorová, Zora. "The Citizen as Respondent and a Voter: Reflection on Election Polling," in Szomolányi and Mesežnikov 1995. Moreover, the SDĽ found its partners to be less than satisfactory as parliamentary allies – party leaders complained about their partners' absences in parliament and their lack of cooperation. *Nové Slovo* 29 April 1996.

Party Image and Support

The Slovak SDĽ hoped to obtain broad support, but its appeals pursued different narrow constituencies. The party shared a large part of its potentially broad electorate with the HZDS, and many of these voters saw the emphasis on democratic credentials as untoward attacks on the HZDS.[82] As a result, the SDĽ was unable to gain a broad electorate, both because of its programmatic shifts and because many voters were less concerned with democracy (the party's emphasis) than it was with stability and populist economics, the HZDS's forte. Moreover, this support was relatively unstable – the party's electoral fortunes rose and fell from election to election.

The SDĽ could not pursue a broad electorate with claims of competence or expertise, due to both its past and its less well-developed elite skills. First, without a record of negotiation and reform before 1989, doubts regarding the party's competence arose. The SDĽ had to rely on its own transformations after 1989 to gain a more favorable image. These, in turn, clearly committed the party to democracy and its defense. However, inconsistency made the party less reliable and consequently perceived as less competent. Such continual changes also alienated existing supporters. Moreover, the electorate was not particularly committed to democracy as its main priority.

Nonetheless, both its break with the past, and its democratic commitments meant that public perceptions of the SDĽ grew increasingly favorable with time. In 1990, the SDĽ started out as the most objectionable party in Slovakia. By 1992, however, it became the party most likely to maintain political stability (33% of those polled), and while only 11% of Czechs wanted to see the KSČM in parliament at the time, 51% of Slovaks approved of the SDĽ's parliamentary role.[83] Its professionalism and expertise were recognized as early as 1992 (44% of the respondents saw this as the party's strong suit, compared to 38% for HZDS), as was its social sensitivity (59% of respondents, compared to 40% for HZDS).[84] In 1993, it was also the party most likely to provide competent managers (gathering the largest share of those polled, 30%; see Table 4.6). If we take into account the "net"[85] values for the other years, it was also subsequently the

[82] Interview with Milan Ftáčnik, 31 January 1997, Bratislava.
[83] AISA poll, cited in *Mlada Fronta Dnes*, 26 May 1992.
[84] Centrum pre Socialnu analizu. *Slovensko pred volbami*. Bratislava: April 1992.
[85] By "net" I mean the difference between the "most likely" and "least likely" scores a given party would get. The HZDS is the one party that was seen as both most and least likely

Table 4.6. *Popular perceptions of* SDĽ.

SDĽ	1992	1993	1994	1996
Items *most* liked about party	Nothing 11%	Social policy 14%	Nothing 14%	Nothing 13%
	Party leader 10%	Nothing 11%	Competence 11%	Competence 11%
	Program 8%	Competence 9%	Program 9%	Program 8%
Items *least* liked about party	Credibility 14%	Performance 13%	Credibility 12%	Coalition acts 9%
	Nothing 12%	Credibility 12%	Performance 11%	Credibility 9%
	Performance 7%	Coalition acts 9%	Coalition acts 11%	Performance 9%

SDĽ	1992	1993	1994	1996
As the party *most* likely to:				
Increase benefits		40%		
Lessen economic burden		39%	20%	
Maintain stability		33%		
Provide competent managers		30%		
Ensure democracy		24%		25%
As the party *least* likely to:				
Decommunize	49%	66%	40%	48%
Increase the Church's role	47%	61%	39%	46%
Speed up privatization	23%			19%

Source: Tóka, 1992–6.

party most likely to supply competent managers. The SDĽ was also seen as the party most likely to lessen the economic burden and to increase pensions and benefits (net scores). SDĽ was lauded for its leaders, competence, program and social policy, even if its coalition behavior and lack of credibility were the two items most disliked about it.

to achieve several goals, and the SDĽ was also often mentioned as being both most and least likely to accomplish several goals after 1994. However, if we subtract the "least likely" form the "most likely," we get an adjusted "most likely" score that often makes the SDĽ the party that was more likely to achieve several goals.

Table 4.7. *Determinants of SDĽ support, relative to the party's perceived chief competitor, HZDS.*

Determinant	1992	1993	1994	1995	1996
Dissatisfaction with democracy	.66*** (.58–.73)	.73*** (.66–.78)	.66** (.55–.75)	.73*** (.69–.81)	.74*** (.64–.78)
Age	.57* (.51–.63)	.52 (.47–.57)	.52 (.45–.58)	.52 (.47–.57)	.50 (.45–.56)
Education levels	.59** (.53–.65)	.50 (.45–.56)	.53 (.45–.61)	.57* (.50–.61)	.50 (.45–.55)
Secularism	.61*** (.57–.65)	.57*** (.53–.60)	.56* (.50–.61)	.59*** (.55–.62)	.58*** (.55–.62)

Note: The 95% confidence interval is in parentheses. Statistically significant determinants of party support are shown as * at 90% confidence level, ** at 95% confidence level, and *** at 99%. Results are given in probabilities relative to the base category of support for the HZDS. Thus, given increasing dissatisfaction with democracy, the probability of supporting the 66% is 92% in 1992, relative to the probability of voting for the HZDS.
Source: Tóka, 1992–6.

As a result, SDĽ supporters tended to be younger and more moderate than KSČM supporters.[86] The SDĽ got more votes of the highly educated than any other party in Slovakia.[87] Party supporters were far more satisfied with democracy,[88] and their concrete political opinions tended to be centrist.[89] The loyalty of former communist party members dropped radically in 1994, and the party was never to recover its old levels of support after the its 1994 stay in government and its coalition with the Christian Democrats. Compared to its chief perceived competitor, the HZDS, SDĽ tended to be supported by voters who were more secular and dissatisfied with democracy – not surprising, given the SDĽ's constant critique of the shortcomings of the HZDS (see Table 4.7).

[86] Centrum pre Socialnu analizu 1992, and FOCUS, "Aktualne Problemy Slovenska na prelome roku 1995–6."

[87] The party got 18% of the highly educated vote, against an average 10.4% of the vote. Thirteen percent of Slovak society has higher education.

[88] In fact, despite the tumultuous history of party democracy in the independent Slovakia, dissatisfaction with democracy did not increase the likelihood of support for *any* of the parties. Support for parties such as the Slovak National Party, ostensibly a protest party, correlated with *satisfaction* with democracy, as did support for the Movement for Democratic Slovakia.

[89] FOCUS: *Current Problems of Slovakia*, Bratislava: May 1994.

Table 4.8. *Elections in Slovakia (government coalitions in bold).*

Party	1990	1992	1994	1998
SDĽ	13.8%	14.7%	10.4% (as SV)	**14.7%**
HZDS	**33.5 % (VPN)**	37.3%	**35.0%**	27%
SNS	11.0%	7.9%	**5.4%**	9.1%
ZRS	N/A	N/A	7.3%	1.3%
Hungarian Coalition	8.6%	7.9%	10.2%	**9.1%**
SDK	N/A	N/A	N/A	**26.3%**
Social Democrats	1.8%	4%	In SV	In SDK
KDH	19.0%	8.9%	10.1%	In SDK
DS	N/A	3.3%	3.4%	In SDK
DU	N/A	N/A	8.6%	In SDK
SOP	N/A	N/A	N/A	8.0%

Source: Statistical Office of the Slovak Republic.

Electoral Performance

The SDĽ's electoral record reflected the party's shifts (see Table 4.8). First, in the decade after communism, the party did not clear more than 15% of the vote. In 1990, in the anticommunist plebiscite that constituted the first free elections in Czechoslovakia, the party obtained 13.8% of the vote, comparable to the KSČM.[90] In 1992, the SDĽ obtained its highest share of the vote, with 14.7%. Unlike the KSČM, however, the SDĽ was not seen as the party most likely to keep Czechoslovakia from separating: Both the Christian Democrats and the Democratic Union were seen as more likely to do so.[91] Instead, the SDĽ was now seen as a credible alternative to the beginning of the HZDS domination and destabilization (the first HZDS government fell, partly as a result of the SDĽ standing up to its early abuses of power, in 1991).

However, the SDĽ's support then dipped to 10% after the SDĽ participated in the disastrous coalition with the Christian Democrats that brought down the Mečiar government in March 1994. Once it returned to power in the 1994 election, the HZDS government continued to run Slovakia in an increasingly authoritarian fashion, monopolizing public

---

[90] Parties competed separately in the Czech Lands and in Slovakia, and only had to clear the threshold in the constituent republics.
[91] Tóka, Gábor. "Party Systems and Electoral Alignments in East Central Europe." Machine-readable data. Central European University, 1992–6.

administration with its loyalists and restricting the rights of the Hungarian minority. In reaction to these excesses, the Modrá Koalícia (Blue Coalition), composed of several prodemocratic parties, formed in 1997 and began to gain strength.[92]

As a result, the HZDS monopoly was in question by 1998. Mečiar and his party were implicated in increasingly bizarre confrontations – for example, the 1997 kidnapping of the president's son to Austria by the secret police, apparently the result of the conflict between Mečiar and the president, Michael Kovač. The HZDS was also blamed for the irregularities that surrounded the May 1997 referendum on NATO entrance and the direct election of the president. Thus, a considerable opportunity opened up for parties promoting democracy, especially once the united and increasingly popular Slovak Democratic Coalition (Slovenská Demokratická Koalícia, SDK) arose out of the Blue Coalition in the spring of 1998. Mindful of the voters' apathy (and retaliation) to its coalitions in 1994, the SDĽ did not join the Blue Coalition or its successor, the SDK, in 1997–8, all the more so since the two were led by the Christian Democrats, the erstwhile governing partners of the SDĽ. Instead, it chose to run in the 1998 elections alone. However, without effective national campaigns and candidates, the SDĽ did not benefit as much as the democratic coalition formed by other parties. In the 1998 elections, the SDĽ again received 14.7% of the vote, while the SDK received nearly 27% of the vote.

Thus, the SDĽ became accepted as a party committed to democracy, and organizational centralization made the party's campaigns cohesive. However, the party's support remained narrow both because its candidates could not convincingly articulate their message and because the party changed its addressed constituency from year to year. The party could not make the same credible appeals to stability and competence as the Polish and Hungarian parties could – nor could it compete as an effective counterweight to the populism of the HZDS. As a result, its support continued to be highly unstable, and its electoral future uncertain, since the party could rely neither on a loyal circle of members nor on a sizeable electoral base.

[92] These were the Christian Democratic Movement (Krest'ansko–demokratické Hnutie, KDH), the Democratic Union (Demokratická Únia, DU), the Democratic Party (Demokratická Strana, DS), the Social Democratic Party of Slovakia (Sociálnodemokratická Strana Slovenska, SDSS), and the Green Party of Slovakia (Strana Zelených na Slovensku, SZS).

The Polish SdRP

Unlike the Czech or Slovak communist successors, the Polish SdRP gained a broad and stable electorate. Organizational centralization allowed the party to run cohesive campaigns, while its elite experience in negotiation and policy implementation made its appeals extremely convincing. In fact, the Polish communist successor party was the most successful electoral competitor among the four cases considered here.

Both centralization and elite skills made the SdRP an increasingly popular electoral choice in Poland – the party ran cohesive campaigns, with effective participation of the local organizations, and presented attractive candidates. It became identified with competence, stability, and secularism, made especially attractive in a country whose politics were dominated by legislative indecision, governmental instability, and the Church's incursions in 1990–2. At the same time, the party reassured the voters that it would not stop the reforms, but that it would temper their pace and ill effects. These were the appeals that brought the party back into power in 1993, with 20% of the vote, and again 2001, with over 40% of the vote.

Electoral Campaigns

In its campaigns, the Polish successor party continued to disseminate its message of competence and professionalism in a unified and coherent fashion. The SdRP gradually evolved its stances, rather than radically shifting them back and forth, so that it was not accused of inconsistency. The steady emphasis on competence and social protection steadily broadened the party's appeal to include new groups. Its subsequent electoral success – the party doubled its electorate from 1991 to 1993 – further fixed its trajectory of programmatic evolution and broadening support.

The party's centralization meant that the Executive Committee leadership nominated and approved *all* national candidates, while allowing local organizations to propose candidates for local office. At the same time, in campaigns for local office, especially in small villages, where localized majoritarian voting made personality more important, the party gave its candidates more leeway in their party identification – "the candidates can run as 'a friend of household pets' so long as they agree with the party program," as one party leader explained.[93] In the larger cities, where the

---

[93] Interview with Andrzej Żelazowski, 16 June 1997, Warsaw.

party ran its most prominent leaders, the SdRP personalities were the big winners in 1993 and 1997, carrying such major cities as Warsaw, Katowice, Łódź, Białystok, Gdańsk, and Bydgoszcz. In its national campaign, the party relied on the mass media, as well as on large-scale meetings with national leaders, rather than on individual voter mobilization,[94] having earlier denounced a mass party character.[95] At the same time, as a result of its organizational centralization, local mobilization was effective where it was used – the Polish party's strongest organizations, such as Katowice, Bydgoszcz, and Włocławek, saw the best electoral results as well.[96]

Centralization and extensive elite experience made for coherent and unified campaigns. The party constantly emphasized its moderation, professionalism, and expertise. In 1989, it proclaimed that "with us, there is greater certainty," and as early as 1990, the party argued that "voting for the . . . SdRP, you will support people who want radical reforms . . . but want to implement them with minimal social costs."[97] As one commentator noted, "during the lengthy and brutal presidential campaign of 1990 . . . the SdRP began to develop a political approach that it gradually brought to perfection, that of dignified restraint."[98] Even in the 1991 elections, the SdRP emphasized its goal of a "Poland of progress, law, and democracy," and its appeals to moderation, experience, and expertise consolidated after these elections. Whereas one of the party's 1991 slogans was "It cannot continue like this," its 1993 version proclaimed more ambiguously that "It does not have to be this way," suggesting a continuation of old policies but with more safety nets. By 1997, the party's electoral slogan was "A good today – a better tomorrow."

Its image and support already relatively certain, the SdRP made relatively little use of its electoral coalition, the Democratic Left Alliance

---

[94] Interview with Sławomir Wiatr, 27 May 1997, Warsaw. Nor did other parties in Poland employ these methods, leaving them for the likes of the Peasants' Party, the only real mass party that remained, and that had extensively saturated the countryside through volunteer fire departments, extension agents, and so on. Tomasz Nałęcz, *Rzeczpospolita* 14–5 August 1993.

[95] Leszek Miller, *Trybuna Ludu*, 21–2 October 1989. Rakowski called in vain for appeals to workers, using traditional mobilization methods. *Polityka*, 23 April 1994. See also Wiatr, Jerzy. *Krótki Sejm*. Warsaw: BGW, 1993, pp. 14–5.

[96] Interview with Andrzej Żelazowski, 16 June 1997. Thus, the party's coalition received 20% of the nationwide vote in 1993, but 29% from Bydgoszcz and 33% in Włocławek. In 1997, the party's nationwide average was 27%, but 37% in Bydgoszcz and 38% in Włocławek. Source: Państwowa Komisja Wyborcza.

[97] SdRP, *Dokumenty Programowe 1990–1991*, May 1990, p. 37.

[98] Zubek 1995, p. 290.

(Sojusz Lewicy Demokratycznej, SLD). The SLD formed around the presidential campaign of Włodzimierz Cimoszewicz, in the fall of 1990. Consisting of twenty-seven organizations, the SLD set its goals as "gain the party the greatest electoral result possible, and to show that other social organizations identify with the party."[99] First, to appear representative of broader society, the SdRP sought the support of various civil society organizations (most of whom had originated in the party's structures prior to 1989) and several small political parties.[100]

Second, the SdRP actively sought the support of eleven small trade unions and the main postcommunist trade union, the OPZZ. The OPZZ itself arose as a government-sponsored counterweight to Solidarity after martial law was imposed by the communist party in 1981. After 1989, Solidarity began to bear the blame for the hardships and austerity that followed the market reforms, since it supported the new governments that were made up of its political activists. Meanwhile, the OPZZ held on to its considerable material assets, was free to criticize the government, and presented itself as the real defender of labor.[101]

Despite obtaining sixty-one out of the 171 SLD parliamentary seats, the union found its role restricted in the coalition. First, the SdRP remained fully in control of the strategy of the coalition. The trade union complained it could not receive the access to decision making for which it had bargained. As a result, as early as 1991, the Movement of People of Labor (Ruch Ludzi Pracy, RLP) arose within the union, fueled by both the personal ambitions of its leaders and a slew of anti-SdRP grievances.[102] Second, the trade union's activities were limited within the coalition to fund-raising, rather than individual mobilization in the workplace.[103] The SdRP elites retained control over the party's campaigns, and used that control to limit

---

[99] Interview with Dariusz Klimaszewski, 20 May 1997, Warsaw.
[100] *Rzeczpospolita*, 22 June 1993. These included the orthodox Union of Polish Communists "Proletariat" (Związek Komunistów Polskich "Proletariat," ZKP), the Greens Party (Partia Zielonych), the Labor Party (Partia Pracy), and a splinter from the historical Polish Socialist Party (Polska Partia Socjalistyczna, PPS, led by Piotr Ikonowicz). The SdRP hoped that the latter especially would make the coalition more legitimate, since the PPS represented broad swathes of society in the prewar Polish democracy. Unfortunately, the coalition only decreased the credibility and popularity of Ikonowicz.
[101] Zubek, Voytek. "Phoenix out of the Ashes: the Rise to Power of Poland Post-Communist SdRP," *Communist and Post-Communist Studies*, No. 3, 1995: 275–303, p. 291.
[102] A faction with a similar name arose in the PZPR as early as 1988, becoming a small party of OPZZ (Ogólnopolskie Porozumienie Związków Zawodowych, All-Polish Trade Union Alliance) activists in January 1991. Interview with Lech Szymańczyk, 10 June 1997.
[103] Włodzimierz Cimoszewicz, *Rzeczpospolita*, 14–5 August 1993.

the vetting of candidates and to determine all campaign efforts. Moreover, the ties to the union loosened over time, until they were dissolved with the renaming of the party in 1999.

Party Image and Support

Achieving a distinct and consistent party image in Poland was made difficult by the greater number of competitors. Nonetheless, the SdRP was perceived as a clearly competent party early on. By 1992, it was seen as the party most likely to reduce unemployment, to increase pensions and benefits, and to lessen the economic burden (see Table 4.9). It was also consistently perceived to be the party most likely to ease the economic burden, increase pensions and benefits, and reduce unemployment. At the same time, SdRP became the party most likely to maintain political stability and to provide competent managers, competing with the centrist Freedom Union. It was also the party least likely to increase the role of the churches.

After the SdRP took power in 1993, the party's image moderated for the better: Its coalition partner, the Peasants' Party, was now the party least likely to help private enterprise or to speed up privatization. By 1996, after three years in government, the SdRP's image polarized: It was the party most and least likely to provide competent managers, ensure the freedom of speech, lessen the economic burden, and increase pensions and benefits. Some of the ambivalence about "competent managers" may also stem from the fact that the Polish successor party's cadres bore the brunt of dislike about the party: Its "old nomenklatura" was among what was most disliked about the party (by 7–12% of those polled).

In general, SdRP's image was that of a desirable party in the Polish system, and its steady message of professionalism and experience found a receptive audience. The party's appeals were so effective that 42% of those who voted for the SdRP coalition in 1993 did so because the party would govern more effectively.[104] The ideal political candidate in 1991 was an enterprise director in the communist era, educated, and experienced,[105]

---

[104] Marody, Mira. "Three Stages of Party System Emergence in Poland," *Communist and Post-Communist Studies*, No. 2, 1995: 263–70.

[105] Other positive characteristics were a Polish nationality and being from the area represented. The characteristics seen as most damning were SB (Stuzbor Bezpieczcinsthe, Polish secret police) informer (81%), SB officer (67%), and SB worker (63%), as was a lack of education beyond the basic (72%). PZPR activism was seen as a positive characteristic by 7%, as negative by 55%, and as irrelevant by 38%. OBOP, *Pożądane i niepożądane cechy kandydatów na posłów*, August 1991.

Table 4.9. *Popular perceptions of SdRP.*

SdRP	1992	1993	1994	1995
Items *most* liked about party	Nothing 15%	Nothing 8%	Nothing 14%	Nothing 19%
	Competence 5%	Program 3%	Competence 9%	Competence 9%
	Represents the lower strata 4%	Social Policy 3%	Party Leader 3%	Program 6%
Items *least* liked about party	Nomenklatura 12%	Nomenklatura 7%	Performance 10%	Nothing 15%
	Nothing 7%	Nothing 6%	Nothing 10%	Nomenklatura 11%
	Performance 5%	Credibility 3%	Nomenklatura 8%	Credibility 7%

SdRP	1992	1993	1994	1995
As party *most* likely to:				
Reduce unemployment	14%		19%	31%
Increase benefits	14%			
Lessen economic burden	13%	14%	13%	17%
Provide competent managers				22%
Maintain stability			16%	27%
Ensure democracy			17%	13%
As party *least* likely to:				
Increase the Church's role	32%	44%	45%	55%
Decommunize	32%	46%	47%	54%
Speed up privatization	16%			12%
Help private enterprise	15%			10%
Lessen the economic burden		15%		8%
Increase pensions				7%
Ensure democracy			7%	

Source: Tóka, 1992–6.

precisely the qualities emphasized by the SdRP. In 1996, Polish voters considered experience the most important characteristic for a party to have (51% of those polled), followed by honesty (49%), effectiveness (37%), and responsibility (36%). The SdRP fulfilled these expectations well: After over three years in the government, the SdRP was seen as the most experienced by 41% of the respondents, as the most effective by 23%, and as the most professional by 18%.[106] In contrast, the Freedom Union, its main competitor for the "professional" image, was seen as most experienced by 26% of the respondents, as professional by 19%, and as effective by only 6%. Therefore, it is not surprising that by 1993, half of the Polish electorate did not mind an SdRP victory, and 23% actively supported the idea.[107]

As a result of its consistently attractive appeals and unified campaigns, the party's support changed between 1989–93 and 1993–6. Prior to 1993, the SdRP electorate was fairly pessimistic about the political development of post-1989 Poland.[108] The 1991 electorate consisted mostly of the retired, former nomenklatura, and the "dissatisfied" (but did not include the workers).[109] By 1993, however, the party's electorate was the "modern" Poland.[110] It also crossed societal strata, as the party gained support across social groups. The white collar vote went from 12% to 24%, workers from 6% to 19%, managers 8% to 17%, and retirees 11% to 22%.[111] The tenuous links between social and economic characteristics and support for the SdRP loosened even further.[112] With time, the likelihood that dissatisfaction with democracy led to support for the party dropped off significantly. The 1993 electorate had also broadened to include new voters – 22% of those who voted for the first time in 1993 supported the SdRP coalition.[113]

By 1993, the party's support base not only was more optimistic, but consisted to a larger degree than any other party's supporters of the well-educated, wealthy, private businessmen, managers, and the intelligentsia.[114] The SLD voters in Poland were those with higher education and average to high incomes,[115] while the area of greatest support for the postcommunist presidential candidate, Aleksander Kwaśniewski, came from the

---

[106] OBOP, *Wizerunki partii politycznych*, 21–4 September 1996.

[107] Millard 1994b, p. 309.

[108] Interview with Halina Frańczak, Demoskop, 16 June 1997, Warsaw.

[109] Jasiewicz 1993a.

[110] Wade, Lavelle, and Groth 1995.

[111] *Rzeczpospolita*, 21 September 1993. In contrast, the UD received 17% of white collars, down from 22%, 7% of workers, down from 9%, lost 3% of managers, and retained 15% of retirees.

[112] Mateju̇, Petr. "In Search of Explanations for Recent Left-Turns in Post-Communist Countries," *International Review Of Comparative Public Policy*, Fall 1995.

[113] *Wprost*, 8 May 1994.

[114] CBOS, June 1993.

[115] Cline 1993, p. 18. This voter profile was matched, ironically enough, by voters of the Democratic Union.

economically most developed and successful region in Poland, the western Wielkopolska.[116] Older voters were less likely to vote for the party than in 1991, and the likelihood of an SdRP vote increased with education. In 1993, the party received the greatest share of the vote of the self-employed (including businesspeople and entrepreneurs) and of "specialists" (white-collar professionals).[117]

As a result, the SdRP increasingly began to share an electorate similar to that of its chief competitor, the centrist and pro-reform Freedom Union (Union Wolności, UW). Only the Freedom Union could compete with SdRP in the percentage of its well-educated or wealthy supporters,[118] and the two parties shared a well-off, educated, managerial constituency.[119] By 1993, 130,000 of the Freedom Union's 1991 supporters voted for the SLD, but only 12,000 SLD supporters from 1991 went over to the Freedom Union.[120] By 1995, the two parties' constituencies were differentiated chiefly by the SdRP's supporters' higher secularism (see Table 4.10). The UW and the SdRP electorates also varied in the degree to which they saw themselves as left wing or right wing and in their past party membership, but not in any other significant sociodemographic aspect.[121]

As a result of its earlier organizational centralization, the Polish communist successor party found that its supporters not only grew in number, but were increasingly representative of the broad electorate, converging almost fully in their views on the economy, the need for competent managers, and political stability. While the party's supporters had doubts about privatization, there were few accompanying demands for redistribution or for full employment.[122] Supporters of the SdRP were just as likely as other voters to agree that too many people relied on

---

[116] Wade, Lavelle, and Groth 1995 further argue that in the 1993 elections, the more developed, "modern," northwest Poland voted for the SLD, while unemployment had no statistical significance in determining the vote.

[117] Millard 1994b: p. 308. See also Sikorski, Radek. "How We Lost Poland," *Foreign Affairs*, September/October 1996.

[118] CBOS, *Preferencje Wyborcze w czerwcu 1993*, June 1993, *Elektoraty partii politycznych rok po wyborach*, October 1994, *Wybory Parlamentarne – potencjalne elektoraty*, June 1995.

[119] *Wprost*, 8 May 1994.

[120] The SLD also gained seventy thousand KPN voters (while KPN received five thousand of the SLD's), and seventy thousand PSL voters (while the latter gained forty thousand SLD supporters). *Rzeczpospolita*, 21 September 1993.

[121] See Markowski 1997. The probable supporters of the Peasant Party or the Christian Democrats were readily identifiable by their rural residence, their religiosity, anticommunist sentiment, and increasing "right" self-identification.

[122] CBOS, *Wyborcy Zwycięskich Partii: Komunikat z Badań*, December 1993.

Table 4.10. *Determinants of SdRP support, relative to the party's perceived chief competitor, UW/UD.*

Determinant	1992	1993	1994	1995
Dissatisfaction	.77***	.63***	.60*	.44
with democracy	(.68–.84)	(.56–.69)	(.52–.67)	(.35–.53)
Age	.52	.47	.57*	.52
	(.45–.60)	(.42–.53)	(.50–.64)	(.45–.59)
Education levels	.43*	.46	.45	.42
	(.35–.49)	(.40–.52)	(.39–.52)	(.35–.49)
Secularism	.55*	.58***	.54	.60***
	(.49–.60)	(.54–.63)	(.49–.59)	(.55–.65)

Note: The 95% confidence interval in parentheses. Statistically significant determinants of party support are shown as * at 90% confidence level, ** at 95% confidence level, and *** at 99%. Results are given in probabilities relative to the base category of support for the UW. Thus, given increasing dissatisfaction with democracy, the probability of supporting the SdRP is 77% in 1992, relative to the probability of voting for the UW.
Source: Tóka, 1992–6.

the state and that it was necessary to lower the role of the state in the economy.[123]

At the same time the party broadened its support, however, historical divisions continued to structure the party's image. On the one hand, a plurality of Poles thought the party has inherited the ideals and achievements of the old ruling communist party (47% compared to 31% who disagreed). An equally large group thought that the SdRP's main goal was to gain economic influence and material benefits for itself (44%). The SdRP was also the party least likely to strengthen patriotism, a reflection of the highly antagonistic historical relationship between "us, the society" and "them, the communist party." Nonetheless, a similarly high percentage thought that SdRP was a party of progressive people who wanted Poland to become a modern country (42%).[124]

Electoral Performance

Not surprisingly, the outcomes of the elections led to both increasing optimism and a sense of vindication, among the SdRP leaders – their transformation of the party's organization and appeals had borne fruit. In the

[123] CBOS, *Wyborcy Zwycięskich Partii: Komunikat z Badań*, December 1993.
[124] PAP, Demoskop Poll, 26 January 1996.

Table 4.11. *Elections in Poland (government coalitions in bold).*

	1991	1993	1997	2001
SLD	12.0%	**20.4%**	27.1%	**40.4%**
Social Democrats	0.5%	N/a	N/a	N/a
PSL	9.2%	**15.4%**	7.3%	8.9%
UD	**12.3%**	10.6%	**13.4%**	3.1%
ZChN	**9.0%**	6.4%	In AWS	N/a
PC	8.7%	4.4%	In AWS	N/a
KLD	**7.5%**	N/a[1]	N/a	N/a
KPN	7.6%	5.8%	In AWS	N/a
UP	4.7%	7.3%	4.2%	Electoral coalition with SLD
AWS	5.1%	4.9%	**33.8%**	5.6%
LPR	N/a	N/a	N/a	7.9%
Samoobrona	N/a	1.1%	.1%	10.2%
PiS	N/a	N/a	N/a	9.5%
PO	N/a	N/a	N/a	12.7%

Source: Central Electoral Commission, Poland.
[1] Joined UD 14.11.1993

first fully free elections in the fall of 1991, held with no election thresholds and a vote translation formula that favored small parties (Hare-Niemayer), its performance had already placed it second in an otherwise fragmented parliament, with 12% of the vote (see Table 4.11). Kwaśniewski argued in 1992 that the party would only improve its results – people were reevaluting the communist regime, the current governments were "incompetent and ineffective," and "in the chaos and . . . paranoia, more and more people want groupings and people that are pragmatic, serious, and unlikely to indulge in adventurism."[125] As it turned out, he was right.

As the post-Solidarity parties fought among themselves from 1990–3, the SdRP "claimed that it was an oasis of peace and of pragmatic and professional purpose, and promised that it would continue Poland's balanced socio-economic transformation."[126] The SdRP also emphasized its secularism, which found considerable resonance. Since the party's communist past was a major campaign issue, and the relationship to the pre-1989 regime was a major cleavage in the campaign, the SdRP and its coalition,

---

[125] Radio Zet interview with Aleksander Kwaśniewski, 7 October 1992.
[126] Zubek 1995, p. 293. The party's effective campaigning was best exemplified by a political cartoon showing a group of people in front of a TV, and one exclaiming, "Elections without communists would be like *Dynasty* without Alexis."

the SLD, was careful not to appear to be the party of nostalgia. Instead of issuing anti-reformist appeals or emphasizing references to the past, the party instead stressed the experience and moderation of its cadres, in contrast to the instability and gaffes of the post-Solidarity governments. The SdRP insisted that it would continue the economic and democratic reforms, while at the same time alleviating the hardships caused by the Solidarity-led governments. Partly as a result, the Peasants' Party (PSL) and others became seen as the "nostalgia" parties, while the SLD was identified with the continuation of reforms, but with greater sensitivity and competence.

As a result, the SdRP managed to transcend the issue of the pace and extent of free market reforms. It did so by creating a whole new cleavage for the other parties to compete on, that of managerial competence, which the party consistently emphasized. In other words, the party set a standard it was best prepared to fulfill: that of professionalism and administrative experience. Given the consensus surrounding market reforms, the SdRP could appear responsible and realistic, while at the same time it could offer those hurt by the transition the hope that better-administered reforms would be less painful.

Other parties simply could not compete as well. By 1993, not only had the party considerably increased its share of the vote to 20%, winning the plurality of votes and going on to form a government coalitions, but it had done so among a very broad and successful electorate. Moreover, it had done so in a different electoral system – the new electoral law for the 1993 elections included a 5% threshold, smaller districts, and a formula, the d'Hondt, that favored large parties.

Once in government, the SdRP managed to withstand allegations in the fall of 1995 that its prime minister, Józef Oleksy, was a Soviet spy. Other challenges included accusations of financial misdoings and an obstreper-ous coalition partner. The party not only withstood these difficulties, but claimed credit for more positive developments: Poland was the first country in the region to recover economically, in 1996, and the SdRP took considerable credit for this achievement. As a result, it not only retained its electorate in 1997, but gained voters in absolute terms. Moreover, the success and cohesion of its SLD coalition acted as a template for its com-petitors, prompting the Solidarity forces to form a similar coalition, after years of failed attempts to unite. It was this coalition, the Electoral Action Solidarity (Akcja Wyborcza Solidarność, AWS), that won the elections with 34% of the vote to the SLD's 27% in 1997.

Subsequently, the SdRP capitalized on the charges of ineffectiveness and corruption widely levied against the AWS government. Further promoting the image of SDL as the one stable political force, three new parties arose, taking away centrist votes from the Freedom Union and populist ones from the AWS. In the September 2001 elections, the SdRP's message of competence and expertise again won, this time with an astonishing 40.4% of the vote.

Neither the SdRP's appeals nor its electorate were based on socioeconomic or class divisions, giving little credence to the hypothesis that the party won the 1993 elections (or did so well in the 1997 elections) because it garnered the traditional "Left" electorate of workers, union members, and those who would benefit from redistributive policies. Instead, in the consensus surrounding economic reform, the party's ability to respond to the demand for administrative competence convinced both those who benefited and those who lost from the market transitions.

The Hungarian MSzP

Finally, the Hungarian party ran campaigns that were as cohesive as the Polish and Slovak parties, and relied on responsive and creative appeals that allowed it to win the 1994 elections and retain much of its support afterward.

The MSzP had a more traditionally "Left" profile, in that it argued for more redistributive policies. Accordingly, economic factors played a greater role in the Hungarian party's victory than in the SdRP's. Nevertheless, it too focused its appeals, and its self-definition, on the pragmatic and moderate solution of policy problems, and on the rejection of nationalist or otherwise ideologically driven appeals. It refrained from making nationalist statements, and instead pointedly called for moderation and pragmatic politics. The party stressed its professionalism and promised the voters a professional government of technocrats.[127] As a result, it rose above the existing cleavages (of religious particularism versus secularism, and traditionalists versus Westernizers), instead gaining a "double identity" as both a moderate redistributive and highly professional technocratic party.[128] The two communist successor electoral winners thus made claims that were theirs to make alone, transcending existing cleavages.

[127] Lengyel 1995.
[128] Márkus, György. "Cleavages and Parties in Hungary after 1989," in Lawson, et al., 1999, p. 152.

215

Electoral Campaigns

From the beginning, the MSzP pushed a steady message of pro-reform, pro-Western expertise as part of its appeal to modernizing Hungary.[129] As early as 1990, the party's slogans called the voters to "Choose the Secure Future," and "the Reliable Solution." Consequently, the reasons for voting for the MSzP in 1990 included support for "reform, [and a] preference for left, experienced leaders."[130] The MSzP "appealed to voters by projecting the image of a competent party capable of helping those hardest hit in the transition to a market economy while pressing ahead with economic reform and trying to integrate with Europe. Its 1994 slogan exhorted, "Let the Experts Govern." These slogans were made all the more appealing by the MDF-led government of 1990–4, which saw the rise of extremist and nationalist rhetoric and intragovernmental conflict. The conservative parties' campaigns, for their part, largely focused on the danger of a communist return and the need to settle accounts with the past."[131]

The MSzP relied on both a relatively more decentralized selection of candidates and centralized vetting mechanisms, which ensured both appealing candidates and cohesive local campaigns.[132] The local party decided the individual constituencies, the county organizations set the county lists, and the central leadership decided the national lists.[133] The electoral structure in Hungary mandated this mixed system – the Hungarian party system was a hybrid of 176 single-member majoritarian constituencies, and 210 national list candidates elected by proportional representation. Local politics became far more personalized, and the local party organizations could more easily pick the popular local candidate (knowing that if they failed in the elections, their subsequent decisions would be vetted by the center).

[129] Tamás, Bernard 2000.
[130] Tóka, Gábor. "Voting Behavior in 1990," in Tóka, Gábor, ed. *The 1990 Election to the Hungarian National Assembly*. Berlin: Sigma, 1995, p. 108. Reasons for voting for the MDF included its association with "balance, moderation, people's well-being, security," while for Fidesz (Fiatol Demokrotok Szövetsége, Alliance of Young Democracy), they were "good program, radicalism, expertise."
[131] Oltay, Edith. "The Return of the Former Communists," *Transition*, 30 January 1995, p. 30.
[132] Local organizations selected the candidates to run in the individual districts and for local office. While the national leadership did not usually change these decisions, it could ask the local organizations to "reconsider," and ensured itself informal veto power over future decisions.
[133] Racz 1993, p. 650.

Given its long history of reform and engagement, the party could place prominent and popular candidates on its national list as early as 1990. The first five places on its 1990 list were all nationally known figures: Imre Pozsgay, the head reformer, Rezsô Nyers, a prominent member of the government since 1960 and the MSzP's first leader after 1989, Gyula Horn, the foreign minister prior to 1989 and the subsequent MSzP leader, Mátyás Szûrös, a former parliamentarian and prominent Central Committee member, and Miklós Németh, the prime minister. In fact, in every election, the party had the deepest pool of qualifed and highly experienced candidates.[134]

The party's earlier transformation meant that the voters came in contact with a modern and moderate party running a unified campaign. The MSzP in 1994 "spent the least money on its campaign but its modest and professional style was attractive, and it had the largest and best organized party, with many disciplined activists."[135] The Hungarian party, with its greater mobilization of local activists than either the Polish or the Slovak parties, saw a direct correlation between the strength of its local organizations and electoral results – where the party had its strongest party organizations, in the counties of Somogy, Budapest, and Borsod-Abauj-Zemplen, it also received its best electoral results.[136]

Much as its Polish counterpart, the MSzP also formed a coalition with trade unions that was effectively controlled by the party. Following a pattern where Hungarian unions arose tied to the political parties,[137] the party took several trade union leaders onto its candidate lists in 1994. Six trade union officials stood for office under MSzP auspices, and the leader of the official communist-era trade union, Sándor Nagy, was the number two candidate on the MSzP electoral slate. The alliance was not a formal coalition, as it was in the Polish case – union leaders encouraged their

---

[134] Tamás, Bernard 2000.
[135] Ágh, Attila, and Kurtán, Sander, eds. *The First Parliament*. Budapest: Centre for Democracy Studies, 1995, p. 20.
[136] In 1990, with 11% of the nationwide vote, the party received 11% in Somogy, 13% in Budapest, and 14% in Borsod-Abauj-Zemplen. In 1994, with 33% of the nationwide vote, the party received 41%, 35%, and 40%, respectively.
[137] For example, the Alliance of Free Democrats formed a close alliance with the white-collar trade union Liga, and the Smallholders' Party formed an alliance with the farmers' association Parasztszövetsége. As a result, eighty parliamentarians were associated with Liga, even if these ties were weak. (Hughes, Stephen. "Living with the Past: Trade Unionism in Hungary Since Political Pluralism," *Industrial Relations Journal*. Winter 1992: 293–303.)

members to run on the slates of other parties as well.[138] Those who ran under MSzP auspices were subject to MSzP vetting and complied with party directives regarding the campaign.

Party Image and Support

The Hungarian elites moved quickly to transform the party's appeals, and to consistently signal the party's support for democracy and reform, with closer attention to Hungarian sensitivities to social redistribution and social nets. From the start, the Hungarian party reformists' administrative experience and policy knowledge enabled the party both to control the Round Table negotiations and rapidly formulate policy alternatives afterward.[139]

Subsequently, in an atmosphere increasingly dominated by the nationalist-religious outbursts from the ruling Hungarian Democratic Forum (MDF),[140] the MSzP made non-ideological, pragmatic appeals centering around efficient management. Ironically, both the SdRP and the MSzP benefited from the anticommunist rhetoric of the other parties – while not all citizens would agree with statements such as those of SdRP leader Aleksander Kwaśniewski that "we were all part of the "People's Republic,"[141] many voters were far more concerned with able management and competent policy making than they were with settling past accounts. In recasting the electoral debates to managerial competence and experience, the successor parties could "offer everything to everyone" – both the assurance the reforms would continue, and the hope that more effective administration would make them more efficient and less painful. Moreover, both the SdRP and the MSzP benefited from their earlier exclusion – they could not be held accountable for the often-incoherent policies of the first postcommunist governments. As a result of their isolation, they were could not take the blame for the government policies after 1989.

Unlike the SdRP, the MSzP could make far more direct references to its previous tenure in power prior to 1989, chiefly because the era of late

---

[138] Pataki, Judith. "Trade Unions' Role in Victory of Former Communists in Hungary," *RFE/RL Report*, 1 July 1994.

[139] Tőkés 1996, p. 208.

[140] Kitschelt claims that the SLD won due to its libertarian, secular stances, and the MSZP was similarly perceived as not being antimarket. Kitschelt 1995b, p. 97.

[141] Kwaśniewski, *Rzeczpospolita*, 3 September 1993.

communism in Hungary was more stable and more liberal than elsewhere. For all its shortcomings, "goulash communism" had meant no consumer shortages or destabilizing strikes, unlike the 1980s in Poland. Moreover, the defining crisis of the party's regime, and the oppression that followed, occurred over thirty years earlier, leaving fewer antagonisms. This shallower regime divide meant that, as one observer put it, "it was enough for Gyula Horn to say in 1994 that 'when I was in the government [1988–89] – wasn't it true that it was better then?' "[142] The Polish successors could not make these sorts of direct references, both because of the conflict between the party and society prior to 1989 and because the Polish economy of the 1970s and 1980s was continually wracked by shortages of basic goods and services.

Consequently, the Hungarian successor received broad support and a favorable image, even earlier and more decisively than the Polish SdRP. By 1993, it was the party most likely to provide competent managers, by a wide margin (15–24% of those polled), and by 1994, it became the party most likely to ensure political stability (18% of those polled; see Table 4.12). Since the provision of competent managers was seen as extremely important by over 90% of those polled, while the maintenance of political stability was seen as extremely important by over 60%, these perceived abilities of the MSzP resonated with the electorate.

The Hungarian successor consistently portrayed itself as the party of similarly pragmatic "experts,"[143] with a political style that is consistently "moderate and restrained."[144] The voters responded – the MSzP's image was based on its competence. It was consistently seen as the party most likely to reduce unemployment, increase pensions and benefits, and lessen the economic burden (25% of those polled, down to 12% by 1996). Again, since Hungarians considered these issues to be considerably more important than did their counterparts in the other countries studied, the Hungarian party's appeals resonated all the more.

Similarly, its redistributive stances resonated deeply with Hungarian society, for whom the post-1956 regime was marked by social stability and greater economic satisfaction than in Poland. The Hungarian party appeared traditionally "Left" in its commitment to redistribution and the welfare state. In the overall spectrum of Hungarian politics, however, these

[142] Interview with Rafał Wiśniewski, 19 March 1997, Budapest.
[143] Lengyel 1995, pp. 26–7.
[144] Barany 1995.

219

Table 4.12. *Popular perceptions of MSzP.*

MSzP	1992	1993	1994	1995
Items *most* liked about the party	Nothing 10%	Competence 12%		Nothing 29%
	Credibility 7%	Nothing 9%		Competence 15%
	Competence 7%	Party leader 7%		Program 6%
Items *least* liked about the party	Nothing 10%	Nothing 13%	Credibility 18%	Performance 19%
	Members 6%	Members 10%	Style 11%	Economic policy 13%
	Credibility 4%	Credibility 4%	Performance 7%	Credibility 9%

MSzP	1992	1993	1994	1995
As the party *most* likely to				
Increase benefits	18%	26%	26%	13%
Provide competent managers		15%	24%	17%
Lessen the economic burden			24%	13%
Maintain stability			18%	
Ensure democracy				8%
Reduce unemployment				13%
Maintain stability				19%
Speed up privatization				26%
As party *least* likely to				
Decommunize	32%	23%		29%
Increase the Church's role				
Speed up privatization	19%	20%		
Lessen the burden	15%	16%		20%
Increase benefits				17%
Reduce unemployment	17%			9%
Maintain stability				5%

Source: Tóka, 1992–6.

views did not make the party unusual.[145] *All* of Hungarian society was considerably more concerned with lessening the economic burden, increasing pensions and benefits, and reducing unemployment than the Poles, Czechs, or Slovaks. Redistributive appeals addressed not only the needs of a particular societal group, but more universal societal concerns. The MSzP was seen as most likely to address societal concerns on grounds of ideology *and* efficacy, rather than on its support for a particular group of the disadvantaged. The party, in short, was able to satisfy the demands of society with appeals to expertise and competence in implementing reforms.[146]

For the Hungarian party, as for the Polish and Slovak, government entry polarized popular opinion regarding the party. Once it entered government, the party was seen both as "most" and "least" likely to pursue a given goal on six out of the eleven stances examined. Moreover, while the MSzP started out in 1992 with its credibility and competence as the factors most liked about the party, these became the items *least* liked about the party in 1994 and afterward. By 1995, "nothing" was the most frequent response to the question of what was liked most about the party. However, that was also the most frequent answer to the question of what was *least* liked about the party, and performance/competence continued to be an important reason in favor of the MSzP (15.2% in 1995). Moreover, its orthodox splinter made the MSzP seem more moderate during the crucial election year of 1994 – the MSzMP (Hungarian Socialist Workers' Party, the acronym of the old communist party) became the most secular party and the least likely to pursue decommunization.[147]

Over time, the MSzP supporters were increasingly satisfied with democracy and saw the MSzP as a party of experts most likely to solve current problems.[148] As in the Polish case, a greater share of former communist party members supported the MSzP, but the party relied on them

---

[145] Markowski 1997.

[146] One could argue that the communist-era policies of promoting managerial competence and technocratic styles of administration actually created the standards by which the parties would be judged after 1989. Thus, the MSzP in a sense stacked the cards in its favor by promoting the very standards it was best able to satisfy.

[147] Not surprisingly, the MDF and the Smallholders (Független Kisgazdapárt, FKGP), two of the parties in the 1990–4 conservative government, were the ones seen mostly likely to decommunize, while their partner, the Christian Democrats (Keresztény Demokrata Néppárt, KDNP), were the party most likely to promote the role of the Church.

[148] Kovács 1996.

Table 4.13. *Determinants of MSzP support, relative to the party's perceived chief competitor, SzDSz.*

Determinant	1992	1993	1994	1995
Dissatisfaction with democracy	.65** (.56–.72)	.53 (.46–.59)	.55 (.48–.61)	.50 (.47–.62)
Age	.66*** (.59–.73)	.58** (.52–.64)	.58* (.51–.62)	.70*** (.66–.76)
Education levels	.58** (.53–.64)	.49 (.44–.53)	.44** (.40–.48)	.49 (.44–.53)
Secularism	.54 (.47–.60)	.51 (.46–.57)	.56* (.51–.60)	.56* (.52–.61)

Note: A 95% confidence interval is shown in parentheses. Statistically significant determinants of party support are shown as * at 90% confidence level, ** at 95% confidence level, and *** at 99%. Results are given in probabilities relative to the base category of support for the SzDSz. Thus, given increasing dissatisfaction with democracy, the probability of supporting the MSzP is 65% in 1992, relative to the probability of voting for the SzDSz.
Source: Tóka, 1992–6.

less and less. The party's supporters were more moderate and older than their Slovak counterparts, and union support dropped after 1994.[149] Compared to the party's biggest perceived competitor, the SzDSz, the likelihood of support for MSzP rose slightly with age and secularism, but was otherwise similar after 1992 (see Table 4.13).

Electoral Performance

The first free elections were dominated by the communist opposition in 1990, and specifically the Hungarian Democratic Forum (Magyar Demokrata Fórum, MDF). The MDF, with nearly 25% of the votes, went on to form the governing coalition with two other parties, and vigorously denounced the former communists in both the electoral campaign and in government. Nonetheless, the MSzP received support from both workers and the urban intelligentsia.[150] Already running on its message of professionalism and competence, the party received above-average support among administra-

[149] This profile differs from the younger, better-educated, dissatisfied supporters of Fidesz, or the young and urban SzDSz supporters, the religious Christian Democrat support base, and the slightly "right" MDF supporters who were satisfied with democracy.
[150] Kovács 1993, p. 269.

Table 4.14. *Elections in Hungary (government coalitions in bold).*

Party	1990	1994	1998
MSzP	10.5%	**33%**	32.3%
Social Democrats	3.0%	1.0%	0.1%
SzDSz	21.4%	**19.7%**	7.8%
Fidesz	8.6%	7%	**28.2%**
MDF	**24.7%**	12.0%	**3.1%**
FKGP	**11.7%**	8.8%	**13.7%**
KDNP	**6.5%**	7.5%	2.6%
MIEP	N/A	1.6%	5.5%
MP	3.7%	3.2%	4%

Source: Hungarian Ministry of Interior, http://www.election.hu/index.htm.

tive and professional sectors.[151] However, its overall support was less than 11%, placing it the fourth out of six parliamentary parties (see Table 4.14).

The government led by the MDF and its prime minister, József Antall, also included the Smallholders' Party (FKGP), and the Christian Democrats (KDNP). Within the coalition, the main problem was with the Smallholders' Party; disappointed by the lack of land reform (its main issue), the party shifted further to the right as József Törgyan attempted to take over the party and make it his political machine. Once he became party president in June 1991, Törgyan split the FKGP and then led a walkout of his faction from the coalition in early 1992. As if the FKGP's instability were not enough, the Christian Democrats publicly stated they could join the opposition by 1992.

The MDF coalition seemed alternatively meddling (as in its clumsy attempts to control the media) or ineffective (when the taxi-drivers' strike erupted in October 1990). Combined with the rise of István Csurka, whose nationalist and antisemitic announcements had mortified the more moderate MDF representatives in 1992 (but which were not condemned by Antall), the coalition was perceived as unstable and fractious. Finally, Antall's illness and subsequent death in December 1993 ended the MDF's career as a political force.

[151] Ágh, Attila. "Partial Consolidation of the East-Central European Parties," *Party Politics*, Vol. 1, No. 4, 1995a: pp. 491–514.

After four years of tumultuous MDF governance, the 1994 elections were dominated by the issue of party competence. Accordingly, the MSzP expanded its share of the vote by a factor of three. Managers and workers alike voted for the party.[152] It continued to receive the well-educated, administrative, and retired vote,[153] while it received below-average rates of support from the unemployed and unskilled workers.[154] Its popularity among the civil service white-collars led some to conclude that it was their support that tipped the scales.[155] The party's dominant supporters in Hungary were middle-aged, better-educated, white-collar workers living in the city, dominated by university graduates, professionals, and urban intellectuals.[156] The MSzP gained about 25% of each social strata, and had a more loyal core of supporters (26.3% from election to election) than any party except the Christian Democrats.[157] The Christian Democrats, in fact, received the traditional "Left" electorate – pensioners (62% of their voters) and unskilled workers. The latter also supported the MDF and the Smallholders (53% and 49% of their voters), while the Free Democrats gained skilled workers and lost the pensioner vote, and Fidesz increased in all strata.[158]

The MSzP retained its high rates of support throughout 1994–8.[159] In the 1998 election, the party obtained 32.3% of the vote but lost the election. Its coalition partner, the SzDSz, fared far less well, losing over half of its support. SzDSz party leader Ivan Petô had earlier had to resign in 1997, after a scandal erupted about an enormous payment he had made to a privatization consultant. As a result, Fidesz was able to form the new governing coalition, with 28% of the vote. Not surprisingly, given the MSzP's steady critique of Fidesz's competence, the rates of support for the

---

[152] Szelenyi, Fodor, and Hanley 1997, p. 219.

[153] Ágh 1995a, p. 509.

[154] Tóka, Gábor. "Parties and Their Voters in 1990 and 1994," in Bela Kiraly, ed. *Lawful Revolution in Hungary, 1989–1994.* Boulder, CO: Social Science Monographs, distributed by Columbia University Press, 1995.

[155] Szilagyi, Zsofia. "Communication Breakdown between the Government and the Public," *Transition,* 3 March 1996, p. 42. There were seven hundred thousand civil service employees in 1996, an increase from 1989.

[156] Ágh 1995a, p. 499, Kovács 1995.

[157] Ágh, Attila. "Defeat and Success as Promoters of Party Change," *Party Politics,* Vol. 3, No. 3, 1997a: 427–44.

[158] Kovács 1996.

[159] These ranged from from a high of 47% shortly after the 1994 elections, to 22% in the first quarter of 1997, to 34–39% right before the 1998 election. Data from Szonda Ipsos, http://www.szondaipsos.hu.

MSzP went as high as 47% by the end of 1999,[160] and staying above 40% tthroughout 2000–1.

Conclusion

The electoral resurgence of the communist successor parties was thus neither an exclusive function of post-1989 conditions nor of communist legacies alone,[161] but of how their electoral appeals could resonate against both the historical record and the contemporary political conditions.

Convincing the electorate consisted of two key developments. First, campaigns had to be cohesive and disseminate a consistent and appealing message. Effective campaigning depended on both attractive party candidates and the ability of the entire party to reinforce the party's messages. The national media campaigns and political advertising could only go so far, if the voters were discouraged or disappointed by ill-prepared candidates, fractious local politicking, or, worst of all, mobilizational efforts that belied the party's message of transformation and readiness to govern.

Second, the parties' appeals had to reassure their potential voters that they would continue the free market reforms, but with greater competence and sensitivity. The importance of such appeals was not unique to the communist successor parties, as "voting decisions are now more heavily influenced by voters' assessments of the main parties' relative managerial competence, by their issue preferences, and by their evaluations of the rival front-bench teams' leadership abilities."[162] The story of the British Labour Party's victory in 1997, after all, has been that of "the widespread belief among voters . . . that Labour is now the party of managerial competence."[163] Thus, given a general consensus on market reform, both the voters of one of the oldest democracies and the youngest responded less to appeals to socioeconomic class or ideological differences, and more to cross-cutting appeals of competence in administering policies.

---

[160] Percentages reflect support stated by those respondents who would vote. Data from Szonda Ipsos, http://www.szondaipsos.hu.

[161] Petr Mateju argues that in Poland and in Hungary, favorable attitudes to the Left stem from the regimes' slow disintegration prior to 1989 and account for the communist successor party vote. However, this explanation ignores the far greater conflict between party and society in Poland, and the constraints this conflict placed on the SdRP. Mateju, Petr. "In Search of Explanations for Recent Left-Turns in Post Communist Countries," *International Review Comparative Public Policy*, Fall 1995.

[162] King 1998, p. 221.

[163] King 1998, p. 243.

Organizational centralization and elite skills made these two developments feasible, while the parties' usable past made them credible. After all, the Czech communist successor also declared that "we too have experts," yet these claims were uniformly dismissed. Moreover, the more skilled a party's elites in formulating and implementing policy, and the more consistent the party's behavior, the more likely the party was to retain its support. Where they failed to convince the electorate that they were the most competent alternative available, government parties lost a sizeable portion of the vote – for example, the Hungarian MDF went from winning 42% of the vote to 12%, to 3% in successive elections.

In contrast, both the Polish and Hungarian parties retained much of their support in the third elections, in 1997–8. The Polish party was more successful in this arena – it gained votes in 1997, while the Hungarian party lost some in absolute numbers.[164] As we will see in the next chapter, part of the reason for the greater Polish success was the party's abler handling of the necessity of continued market reform and of the party's own coalitional conflicts. The robust economic performance during the party's governance only added luster to the rhetoric of administrative efficacy. The Hungarian party, meanwhile, was forced to go back on its redistributive electoral promises, and grappled with maintaining the appearance of coalitional cohesion. Another reason for the greater Polish success lies in the electoral alternatives: The Polish party appeared relatively more competent than its competitors, all of whom had been in government already. The Hungarian electorate, meanwhile, could vote for Fidesz in 1998, a popular and longstanding party that had not yet governed.

As the next chapter shows, however, convincing the electorate proved an easier task than winning over parliamentary colleagues, for whom the legacies of the past, and the post-1989 environment, often made cooperation with and acceptance of the communist successor parties especially difficult to stomach.

---

[164] The party received 2,815,169 votes in 1993, or 20.4%. In 1997, the SdRP received 3,551,224 votes, or 27.1%. The Hungarian MSzP received 1,781,504 votes in 1994, or 33%, and 1,476,235 votes, or 32.3%, in 1997. For the sake of comparison, the MSzP received 535,064 votes in 1990, while the SdRP received 1,344,820 in 1991.

5

Parliamentary Effectiveness and Coalitions

Parliamentary effectiveness was both crucial to the communist successor parties' access to decision-making and more difficult to achieve than any of the other dimensions of party regeneration. The task ahead was as daunting as it was significant – parliaments were central to post-1989 politics in the region, both because they were responsible for legislating the future shape of the political and economic systems and because they were the main wellspring for new political parties and their interactions.[1] The communist successors themselves immediately recognized that parliamentary performance would serve as one of the main standards by which they would be judged by voters and competitors alike. Given their initial electoral defeats and lack of alliances, the parliament was one arena in which the successor parties could prove themselves in the first few years following the democratic transition.

Parliamentary effectiveness consisted of acceptance by other parties and cohesiveness of the party's parliamentary grouping. Parliamentary acceptance is the extent to which a given party is able to establish cooperation with other parties and is considered for potential government posts and coalitions.[2] In the parliamentary systems considered here, such acceptance comprised the potential to participate in government and in opposition coalitions, informal party alliances, and membership in parliamentary committees. As we will see, the parties' historical record, and specifically the reputations engendered by the earlier conflict between the communist party and society, were chiefly responsible for their

---

[1] Ágh 1994b, p. 229.

[2] I define parliamentary acceptance by these indicators, rather than by the parties' success in pushing through policy proposals, because the latter is chiefly a function of government participation in parliamentary systems.

parliamentary acceptance – or lack thereof. The ironic result was that even otherwise completely transformed parties could be as unacceptable to potential partners as successors who retained communist appeals and structures. Consequently, the Polish party, for all its electoral appeal and transformation, could not be characterized as an "attractive" coalition partner.[3]

In turn, cohesion comprises working together for the goals of the group and parliamentary club unity: the lack of defections or expulsions.[4] Party elites with the political resources to centralize the party organizations could then enforce unity and discipline within their parliamentary clubs. Both cohesion and acceptance were needed for the parties to have an impact on parliamentary decisions and policy making. If they were isolated in parliament, even the most disciplined and cohesive parties stood little chance of forming coalitions or having their policy proposals taken seriously. On the other hand, the most accepted party in parliament could not hope to have a significant impact if its legislators continually left or entered the parliamentary club, formed their own, or could not be cajoled into voting the party line. As a result, while all the parties had a considerable parliamentary representation (see Table 5.1), their numerical strength did not necessarily correspond to either acceptance or cohesion.

Parliamentary Acceptance

Parliamentary acceptance was crucial for two reasons. First, since all the parties under consideration functioned in parliamentary systems with proportional representation, few competitors could hope to gain an outright majority of seats – and so the ability to form and join coalitions was essential to gaining access to governance. Second, even if the parties were excluded from coalitions, they could hope to influence policy through the parliamentary committees and legislative voting – and the more the parties were accepted, the more likely they were to gain both parity in committee representation and informal alliances in the process of voting on legislation. In short, access to governance ultimately depended on interparty

---

[3] Ishiyama 1995, pp. 160–1.

[4] In turn, parliamentary discipline consists of regularly accepting the leadership's commands. Below a certain level of cohesion, it is impossible to impose discipline, and above a certain level, there is little point in doing so, since the members already agree with the leadership. Bowler, Shaun, Farrell, David M., and Katz, Richard S. *Party Discipline and Parliamentary Government.* Columbus, OH: Ohio State Press, 1999, p. 5.

Table 5.1. *Summary of communist successor parliamentary effectiveness.*

	First term	Second term	Third term	Fourth term
Czech	30 seats (15%)	35 (17.5%)	22 (11%)	24 (12%)
Acceptance	Low: excluded from all coalitions	Low: excluded from all coalitions	Low: excluded from all coalitions	Low: excluded from all coalitions
Cohesion	Low (1990–2)	Low (1992–6)	High (1996–7)	High (1998–)
Slovak	22 seats (15%)	29 (19%)	18 (12%)	23 (15.5%)
Acceptance	Medium	Briefly a junior partner in the ruling coalition	Accepted by democratic parties	A junior partner in the ruling coalition
Cohesion	High (1990–2)	High (1992–4)	High (1994–8)	High (1998–)
Polish	173 seats (38%)	59 (13%)	171 (37%)	164 (36%)
Acceptance	Low: no allies	Low: no allies	Governed with another postcommunist party	Medium
Cohesion	Low (1989–91)	Medium (1991–3)	High (1993–7)	High (1997–)
Hungarian	34 seats (9%)	209 (54%)	134 (35%)	
Acceptance	Medium	Senior partner in a government with former 18 dissident party	High	
Cohesion	Low (1990–4)	High (1994–8)	High (1998–)	

Source: Parliamentary Institute records, Prague, Czech Republic. *Parlament Československé Republiky* and *Parlament České Republiky*, Poslanecká Sněmovna, Prague, 1990–6. Parliamentary Institute Records, Bratislava, Slovakia. *Národná Rada Slovenskej Republiky*, Bratislava: Chancery of the National Council of the Slovak Republic, 1996–8. Kancelaria Sejmu. *Sejm Rzeczpospolitej Polskiej: Informacja o Działaności Sejmu.* I Kadencja. Warsaw, October 1993. Ibid, II Kadencja, January 1997. Online at http://www.mkogy.hu.

cooperation, in the form of parliamentary coalitions, informal party alliances, and parliamentary committee representation.

Despite a host of ostensibly favorable conditions, the communist successor parties had great difficulty gaining such acceptance. In the first democratic parliaments, other parties were both inexperienced and fragmented. Precisely at a time when they were to play the greatest role in parliament, creating the laws that would radically transform the existing system, the new democratic parties had the fewest capacities – political experience, research abilities, or connections to other parliaments.[5] They were simultaneously involved in establishing their own structures, designing political institutions, and legislating new laws, "rebuilding the ship at sea."[6] Therefore, the expertise and discipline of the communist successor parties could make them valuable parliamentary partners. Yet the other parties rejected the expertise that the communist successors could provide as "tainted." Thus, the communist successors' past as the authoritarian rulers made them simultaneously the most experienced and the most discredited political actors after 1989.

Nor did parliamentary fragmentation make the communist successors more attractive as parliamentary partners. Theories of minimum winning coalitions suggest that parties are courted when their votes are needed – if a given party's seats are necessary for a coalition, it will be "accepted," irrespective of ideology.[7] However, if this expectation held, the unstable and undersized coalitions of the first Polish parliament should have invited the communist successor to join, and the minority government of the Czech Social Democrats in 1998 should have turned to the KSČM – and yet neither did. Even when the communist successors' votes could have stabilized shaky coalitions, such cooperation was rejected.

Nor did the nascent structure of the party system help the parties to become accepted and cohesive in parliament.[8] A fragmented party system can make it less likely for parties to cooperate and lead to frequent defec-

---

[5] Ágh, Attila, ed. *First Steps: The Emergence of East Central European Parliaments*. Budapest: Hungarian Centre of Democracy Studies, 1994c, p. 163.

[6] Elster, Jon, Offe, Klaus, and Presuss, Ulrich Klaus. *Institutional Design in Post-communist Societies: Rebuilding the Ship at Sea*. Cambridge, UK: Cambridge University Press, 1998.

[7] Strom, Kaare, Budge, Ian, and Laver, Michael J. "Constraints on Cabinet Formation in Parliamentary Democracies," *American Journal of Political Science*, May 1994, pp. 303–35.

[8] Olson, David, and Crowther, William. "Committees in New and Established Democratic Parliaments: Indicators of Institutionalization," paper presented at Midwest Political Science Association, Chicago, 22–6 April, 1998.

tions from their parliamentary clubs.[9] Yet despite similarly low levels of Czech and Slovak party system fragmentation, the KSČM and the SDĽ were treated very differently in their respective parliaments. Even when the Czech Civic Forum and the Polish Solidarity fragmented in 1990–1 and transformed into several smaller competitors, their successors were still united in their opposition to the communist past and the communist successors.

Ideological similarity or proximity also failed to make the communist successor parties more accepted. In established democracies, parties have tended to form coalitions and act in parliamentary concert where their ideologies are closely related and compatible.[10] Moderate parties make easy partners, and ideological changes have led to increased parliamentary acceptance for other parties.[11] As we have seen in the two previous chapters, some communist successor parties had programs, supporters, and images very similar to those of the centrist pro-reform parties. Yet even where they were the parties closest ideologically to the senior coalition partners, or where their support could have buttressed unstable and fragmented coalitions, communist successor parties were excluded from government coalitions or even from negotiations prior to their formation.

Instead, divisions within the parliament reflected the electoral competition between the opposition movements on one side and the communist parties on the other, and fell along a cleavage between the representatives of the new and old political orders. At a time when ideological and policy stances were often vague, this "regime divide" was the most salient parliamentary cleavage. As a result, the successor parties continued to be ostracized and isolated in the parliaments as the unwelcome remainders (and reminders) of the communist regime.

Such low parliamentary acceptance by parliamentary colleagues had two results. First, it meant great difficulties in entering electoral and government coalitions with other parties, without which the communist successor parties had little hope of governance in a parliamentary system.

[9] Malová, Darina. "The Institutionalization of Parliamentary Parties and Political Representation in Slovakia," paper presented for the Third Annual Conference on the Individual vs. the State, CEU, Budapest, 16–17 June 1995.

[10] Warwick, Paul. *Government Survival in Parliamentary Democracies*. Cambridge, UK: Cambridge University Press, 1994. Laver, Michael, and Schofield, Norman. *Multiparty Government: The Politics of Coalition in Europe*. Oxford, UK: Oxford University Press, 1990.

[11] Panebianco, Angelo. "The Italian Radicals: Old Wine in a New Bottle," in Kay Lawson and Peter Merkl, eds. *When Parties Fail*. Princeton, NJ: Princeton University Press, 1988: pp. 110–36, p. 118.

Second, it meant underrepresentation in the committees (despite the formal requirements of proportionality).[12] Since parliamentary committees were the chief source of legislative proposals and bills after the government,[13] and "policy expertise [was] concentrated to a great extent in committees,"[14] the lack of acceptance limited the parties' potential to formulate and shape policy.

What determined, then, whether the successor parties would overcome these formidable barriers? Above all, they had to convince their potential partners that the benefits of cooperation with the communist successors would outweigh the perceived costs of losing electoral or parliamentary support as a result of such cooperation. So long as either voters or other parties were perceived as likely to punish a party for cooperating with the communist successor, and so long as these costs outweighed the benefits of access to office, communist successor parties would have difficulty forming coalitions or gaining parliamentary acceptance.[15]

Whether or not the parties could overcome this obstacle, however, depended on the legacies of communist rule. All the parties in these new democracies needed to develop and to maintain their long-term reputational credibility, both with voters and with other parties.[16] Such credibility is acquired through repeated, consistent, and sustained electoral and parliamentary behavior,[17] and it is so crucial a concern that political parties have been found to pursue it even when doing so adversely affects their short-term goals.[18] For example, the SDĽ actually formed a coalition with

[12] Olson, David. "Paradoxes of Institutional Development: The New Democratic Parliaments of East Central Europe," *International Political Science Review*, Vol. 18, No. 4, 1997: 401–16.

[13] Remington, Thomas, ed. Parliaments in Transition. Boulder, CD: Westview Press, 1994, p. 46. Olson 1997. In each of the parliaments, the most important committees were the constitutional, budgetary, finance and privatization, and foreign relations committees.

[14] Ágh, Attila. "Parliamentary Committees in East Central Europe," in Longley, Lawrence, and Davidson, Roger, eds. *The New Roles of Parliamentary Committees*. Portland, OR: Frank Cass, 1998, p. 189.

[15] Of course, a variety of factors could potentially alter this calculus – international pressures, internal economic or political crises, or the rise of threats to democracy (arguably the case in Slovakia) could all favor cooperation.

[16] Laver, Michael, and Shepsle, Kenneth. *Making and Breaking Governments*. Cambridge, UK: Cambridge University Press, 1996.

[17] Dixit, and Nalebuff, 1991. Schelling, Thomas. *The Strategy of Conflict*. Cambridge, MA: Harvard University Press, 1960. Franklin, Mark, and Mackie, Thomas. "Familiarity and Inertia in the Formation of Governing Coalitions in Parliamentary Democracies," *British Journal of Political Science*, July 1983: 275–98 Laver and Shepsle 1996.

[18] Laver and Shepsle 1996, pp. 19 and 248. If such reputation becomes a key concern for parties, then it calls into question the perspective advocated by some analysts of parlia-

the party *farthest* away from it ideologically,[19] in order to protect and reinforce its reputation as a defender of democracy in Slovakia. Since the successor parties had no democratic record, their communist history would serve as the initial source of their democratic reputation. As a result, the extent of earlier negotiation with society and the ways in which the party responded to society determined the parties' usable pasts, and thus the kinds of claims a successor party could credibly make after 1989. After all, a commitment to democracy was that much more believable when made by a Round Table participant than by a former communist apparatchik who had denounced "bourgeois democracy" only a few years earlier.

Thus, the deeper the "regime divide," the higher the perceived costs of cooperation. As a result, ideological proximity could even act as an *obstacle* to coalition formation when the reputation of the *formateur* or the dominant party in the coalition would adversely affect the electoral support of its potential coalition partners.

The Czech party was underrepresented and ignored in coalition negotiations. Its pre-1989 record of squelching negotiations and oppressing the opposition simply eliminated it from consideration as a viable partner, often prompting other parties to treat the KSČM as both a political pariah and a scapegoat after 1989. This isolation was self-reinforcing – it meant the party could not convince the broad electorate or establish a different reputation necessary to overcome these barriers.

Similarly, the recent history of the conflict between the communist party and Solidarity in 1980–1 made parliamentary cooperation difficult to obtain for the Polish SdRP. While the electorate was willing to accept the party's rhetoric of expertise and moderation, its parliamentary partners proved far more difficult to convince. Other parties feared cooperating with the communist successor, because to do so would be to obliterate the clearest signal they could send the electorate: that they remained loyal to the ideals of the earlier anticommunist opposition prior to 1989. Consequently, all the successor forces of Solidarity rejected a coalition with the SdRP during 1989–2000. As SdRP leaders declared in 1991, "we have no

mentary behavior: that we should think of parliaments as single firms, established to monitor members in team production (in this case, of policy) to prevent opportunistic behavior. Saalfeld, Thomas. "Rational Choice Theory in Legislative Studies: Models of Politics without Romanticism," *Journal of Legislative Studies*, No. 1, 1995, pp. 32–64, p. 54. Parties are not concerned so much with the overall performance of the parliament, but with their ability to affect the outcome, and as such act more as firms competing with each other than as "members" of a single firm.

[19] Markowski 1997, p. 233.

illusions. There won't be any room in the new government for us. It will instead be probably formed by the various groupings still united by the word 'Solidarity.'"[20]

In Hungary, in contrast, the calculus was different. The party-society conflict was blurred by the existence of reformists and liberals on both sides, and their frequent cooperation. As a result, the Hungarian party was far more accepted in parliament than its partner in regeneration, the Polish SdRP, and had a far easier time forming a coalition across the regime divide.[21] Similarly, the diffusion of former communists into every party in Slovakia effectively mitigated the regime divide, highlighting other cleavages instead.

Parliamentary Cohesion

The parties' parliamentary isolation made their cohesion all the more important. Even if they were isolated, cohesive parties would be more likely to retain whatever access to power they did have.[22] First, the more cohesive the parties, the more powerful and formidable an opposition they could become within the parliament. Thus, even if they had not become fully accepted in parliament, they could become a force to be reckoned with. Second, such cohesion would also signal professionalism and competence to the electorate. Cohesive parties could hope eventually to gain the votes that would give them more seats in parliament and thus increase their chances of governance. Consistent parliamentary behavior would thus fortify other signals of transformation – such parliamentarians reinforced the message of professionalism and expertise, while disorganized or fragmented parliamentary clubs did little to signal transformation or readiness to govern.

Neither communist legacies nor parliamentary institutions alone determined the parties' parliamentary behavior. Some scholars argued that communist discipline, encapsulated in "democratic centralism" prior to 1989, should have provided a built-in advantage over other parties

---

[20] *Trybuna Ludu*, 31 October–1 November 1991.
[21] Moreover, the party's overwhelming victory in 1994 (its 33% of votes translated into 54% of seats) meant that the party had a majority on its own. The party proposed a coalition to get the two-thirds majority necessary for passing major legislation or making constitutional changes.
[22] The converse holds true only so far: A completely accepted, but fully incohesive partner, would be an unreliable, and thus far less attractive, potential coalition ally.

234

in maintaining parliamentary unity and discipline after the democratic transition.[23] This "traditional discipline" of the communist parties was expected to ensure their immediate efficacy and cohesion in parliament.[24] Communist successors would also benefit from the "tradition of exercising discipline over the rank and file [that] served these parties well."[25] Yet these expectations did not hold up as expected. There was no real discipline to be transmitted to the democratic system. First, the communist-era parliament itself functioned as a rubber stamp for the party's policy proposals. Second, with no competition or opposition in the communist-era parliaments, there was no real challenge to the artificial unity of the parliamentary party under communism.

Nor were the new democratic electoral institutions responsible. A decentralized system of party funding can undermine party discipline and cooperation, increasing factionalism by creating incentives for the formation of new parties.[26] Electoral laws also create their own incentives for parliamentary cohesion and acceptance; for example, party list systems tend to promote loyalty to the party, since party leaders determine the politician's future electoral and parliamentary opportunities (for example, through positions on candidate lists).[27] However, all four successor parties depended on state funding, which should have increased cohesion – yet they were less cohesive than other parliamentary parties early on, and showed variation in their parliamentary behavior. Moreover, members from single-member districts in the mixed electoral system in Hungary were as disciplined as their party list brethren.[28]

Instead, *all* the parties had considerable problems maintaining their cohesion immediately after 1989. The Polish and Hungarian clubs were initially far less stable than the other parties in their respective parliaments, as Table 5.2 shows. These high rates of turnover within the parliamentary

---

[23] See Gillespie, Waller, and Nieto 1995. Remington 1994. Laver and Schofield 1990.

[24] Olson, David M. "The Sundered State: Federalism and Parliament in Czechoslovakia," in Remington 1994, p. 104.

[25] Wade, Lavelle, and Groth, 1995, p. 412.

[26] Dodd, Lawrence. *Coalitions in Parliamentary Government.* Princeton, NJ: Princeton University Press, 1976. Laver and Schofield 1990, p. 156. Gillespie, Waller, and Nieto 1995, p. 10.

[27] Mayhew, David. *Congress: The Electoral Connection.* New Haven, CT: Yale University Press, 1974. Katz, Richard. *A Theory of Parties and Electoral Systems.* Baltimore: Johns Hopkins University Press, 1980.

[28] Morlang, Diana. "Socialists Building Capitalism: Electoral Laws and Party Discipline in Hungary," paper presented at the American Political Science Association Annual Meeting, Boston, 3–7 September 1998.

Table 5.2. *Turnover in parliamentary clubs (in percentages).*

	First term	Second term	Third term	Fourth term
Czech	(1990–2)	(1992–6)	(1996–7)	(1998–)
KSČM	22%	29%	0%	0%
Other parties	55%	26.8%	19%	N/A
Slovak	(1990–2)	(1992–4)	(1994–8)	(1998–)
SDĽ	0%	3.4%	0%	0%
Other parties	32.3%	17.2%	1.3%	N/A
Polish	(1989–91)	(1991–3)	(1993–7)	(1997–)
SdRP	41%[a]	5%	4.7%	0%
Other parties	25.4%	16.5%	14%	N/A
Hungarian	(1990–4)	(1994–8)	(1998–)	
MSzP	24%	0%	0%	
other parties	20%	22%	N/A	

Note: [a] From the parliamentary club of the PZPR to the parliamentary club of the Democratic Left.

Note: Average turnover is calculated by summing the seats *lost* by parties over the number of parties. Seats gained, and new parties formed, were not included, as they do not measure party unity but (new) party formation.

Source: Krause, Kevin Deegan. "System politických stran v České republice, demokracie a volby roku 1996" ("The Czech Political Party System, Democracy, and the 1996 Elections"), *Sociologický Časopis* (Czech Journal of Sociology), Vol. 32, No. 4 (Fall 1996), pp. 423–38. Kancelaria Sejmu. *Sejm Rzeczpospolitej Polskiej: Informacja o Działalności Sejmu*. I Kadencja. Warsaw, October 1993. Ibid, II Kadencja, January 1997. Ágh, Attila. "Party Discipline in the Hungarian Parliament," in Bowler, Farrell, and Katz, eds. 1999.

clubs were the result of the dissatisfaction and the departures among the elites.

The more centralized parties could overcome this initial disunity. First, the more the parties could impose sanctions on their representatives to ensure discipline, the more they could count on their parliamentarians' compliance. Second, the greater the overlap between the executive and the parliamentary leaderships of the party, the more disciplined and effective its parliamentary club. As a result, both the Polish and the Hungarian party clubs then stabilized – in 1994–8, there were no defections from the MSzP.[29] In the Polish case, only three out of sixty members resigned in

[29] Ágh 1994c.

Table 5.3. *Leadership overlap between the parliamentary and central leaderships, as of 1993.*

Organization	Central Leadership in parliament (%)	Parliamentarians in Central Leadership (%)
KSČM Central Committee	1.1% (13 out of 117)	37.1% (13 out of 35)
SDĽ Republican Council	24.7% (29 out of 116)	100%
SdRP National Council	49.0% (74 out of 150)	100%
MSzP National Committee[a]	24.3% (34 out of 140)	100%

Note: [a] Twenty out of the first twenty-five members of the MSzP Presidium were in the party parliamentary representation.

Source: Party leadership rolls and *Parlament Československé Republiky* and *Parlament České Republiky*. Poslanecká Sněmovna, Prague, 1990–6. *Národná Rada Slovenskej Republiky*. Bratislava: Chancery of the National Council of the Slovak Republic, 1996–8.

the 1991–3 period, and only 8 out of 171 in the 1993–7 period. In contrast, twenty-five out of the thirty-five KSČM parliamentarians left the party during the tumultuous summer of 1993 alone. As Table 5.3 shows, the most effective parliamentary party (the Polish) also had fused its leadership the most, while the most fractious and ineffective (the Czech) had far less overlap.

The fusion of party leadership with the parliamentary club also reinforced party reform. In all four parties, parliamentary representatives emerged as the biggest supporters of party adaptation and transformation. Given their daily interaction with representatives of other parties (and hence potential coalition partners), they generally viewed party transformation as the only way to overcome parliamentary isolation and irrelevance. The more responsive and pragmatic the successor party, they argued, the more seriously its proposals would be taken, and the less its past would be held against it. Where they were part of the central party leadership, these largely reformist parliamentarians led the successful regeneration of the parties; they could pursue the reformist agenda unhindered. Where, on the other hand, parliamentary reformers were denied access to party governance, party regeneration was hindered.

The parties' parliamentary performance both rested on the degree and extent of organizational centralization and reinforced its outcomes. The following sections examine first the parties' parliamentary acceptance, focusing on their coalition efforts and achievements, and then their cohesion as parliamentary actors.

The Czech KSČM

The KSČM's parliamentary exclusion echoed the party's lack of public support and reflected its lack of a usable past. The deep regime divide prevented the party from gaining coalitional acceptance, while its organizational decentralization first allowed extensive and lengthy discussions in the club and then promoted self-defeating conflict among the parliamentarians. As a result, the party had less parliamentary impact than any of the other parties discussed here.

Parliamentary Acceptance

The other parties excluded the KSČM *a priori* from any governing or electoral coalitions after 1989, putting them on par with the neofascist Republicans. The parliament was dominated from 1990 to 1997 by the Civic Democratic Party (ODS). As the main offshoot of the opposition movement Civic Forum, the ODS steadfastly refused to negotiate with the Czech communist successors – it had little reason to do so, given the availability of other coalition partners with a less controversial past and greater ideological proximity. The 1997 elections brought in the Social Democrats (ČSSD) into power, a party closer ideologically to the KSČM, but this result did little to alleviate the party's isolation. Instead of ruling in a coalition with the KSČM, the ČSSD chose to govern as a minority government, supported by the ODS.

The party continually complained of societal and parliamentary ostracism, and its elites admitted the KSČM had little chance of widespread acceptance.[30] As Ladislav Adamec, MP and erstwhile party head, admitted, "it is difficult to be in parliament, because of the barriers of deliberate isolation, deliberate abuse, and personal isolation."[31] Despite repeated efforts to establish good relations with other opposition parties, the KSČM was excluded from consideration as an equal, as late as 1995.[32] The party had difficulties in getting other parties to cooperate, even on the local level – party leaders declared that even in districts with good electoral results, the party had difficulty forming local coalitions.

This atmosphere of isolation was exacerbated by the conflation of market reform with anticommunism by Václav Klaus and the ODS.[33] As a result,

---

[30] *Dokumenty II Sjezdu* KSČM, p. 10.
[31] *Naše Pravda*, 13 May 1992.
[32] *Dokumenty IV Sjezdu* KSČM, p. 48.
[33] Appel 2000.

the Czech party's legislative proposals were kept off the agenda in several cases, prompting the party to declare that it would now pursue only policy proposals in "areas of interest."[34] The Prague district attorney even tried to shut down the party, under a 1990 law that forbade antidemocratic organizations. Another law in 1993 called the party a "criminal organization, antidemocratic and anti-human rights," and held the party responsible for the country's decline under communism.[35] Czech President Václav Havel also refused to meet with party representatives, even as he met with all of the other parties', including the extremist Republicans. Finally, the party complained that media coverage was either sparse or biased against it.[36] Party leaders argued that the party could not gain more support subsequently as a result of the "media blockade" and of its political isolation.[37]

Repeated efforts in 1990–2 to form alliances were rebuffed by potential partners in 1990–2, such as the Social Democrats, Jiří Dienstbier's Civic Movement (an offshoot of Civic Forum), and the Czech Socialist Party. Most importantly, the one party the KSČM had initially identified as an attractive coalition partner rejected it outright. The Social Democrats were led from 1990 to 1993 by Jiří Horák, who let in individual ex-communists into the Social Democrats, but denounced the very idea of cooperation with the communist successor party. By 1993, when the Social Democrats changed leaders, and the younger, more moderate Miloš Zeman took over, the KSČM had already refused to moderate its orthodox doctrine or transform its name or program, and had firmly established itself as a communist party, and was as such an unacceptable coalition partner.[38] Social Democratic leaders then declared that no

---

[34] *Dokumenty II Sjezdu* KSČM, p. 12.

[35] Vachudová, Milada Anna. "Divisions in the Czech Communist Party," *RFE/RL Report*, 17 September 1993: 28–33.

[36] During the 1996 electoral campaign, for example, the *Lidové Noviny* daily paper published the programmatic stances of all the parliamentary parties – except for the KSČM's. Grebreniček, moreover, received 133 minutes of air time during the campaign, less than any other parliamentary party leader. These numbers pale compared to the 708 minutes of Václav Klaus, and the rest of the parliamentary leaders, each of whom received over 200 minutes. *Lidové Noviny*, 14 May 1996. The KSČM received 7.1% of the airtime devoted to political parties. ODS received 30.7%, ODA 16.5%, the Republicans 1.3%, KDU-ČSL 8.9%, SD-LSNS 7%, and the two splinters of the KSČM, the LB and the SDL, 1% and 0, respectively. *Lidové Noviny*, 5 July 1996.

[37] *Dokumenty IV Sjezdu* KSČM, p. 33.

[38] Of course, there were internal considerations within the Social Democrats – the party could not approach the communists too closely, as that would blur their support and cause the defection of the anticommunist Social Democrats, while at the same time, Zeman could not be seen as a communist sympathizer. The history of the Czech Social

coalitions were possible with the communist successor due to "irreconcilable value differences" between the two parties and because the KSČM "lost its place among the system of democratic parties" in the Czech Republic.[39] As the Social Democrats announced in 1996, they did not "want to have anything in common with the KSČM."[40]

By 1995, given the attacks and isolation by other parties, the KSČM saw no chances of forming formal alliances within the parliament.[41] Similarly, the reformist splinters that arose from the KSČM argued that "we don't have the smallest chance to become a party of the ruling coalition because of our name, and our orientation, which is too rooted in the past."[42] These conclusions were underlined by two factors. First, the party had no "usable past" with which it could support its claims of expertise and commitment to democracy. Second, the party's representatives had no ties that could have mitigated the party's isolation – not only did a deep regime divide dominate the political cleavages, but there were no individual contacts or familiarity via earlier negotiations or meetings under communism, the result of a long communist policy of squelching and eliminating the opposition rather than engaging it. Moreover, the few reformists in the KSČM left by 1993, joining the other parties or forming parties of their own.

Similarly, although the parliament was to divide the committee assignments in proportion to party representation, the KSČM was kept out of the more important positions.[43] Despite receiving four vice-chairs of committees in 1990 as part of the Round Table agreements, the party was excluded from such important committees as the Constitutional, Mandate, or Human Rights committees. Committee chairs were elected on the floor, and so the party's lack of popularity weakened its position even further. From 1992 to 1997, despite holding 17.5% of the seats, the party was given *no* chairs of any committees. After the 1998 elections, the party held 12% of the seats in the parliament, but only 3% of the chairs (see Table 5.4). It continued to be underrepresented in the important Legislative and Mandate committees.

Democrats, with the forced merger with the communists in 1948, weighed heavily on both Social Democratic supporters and leaders.

[39] Petra Buzková, *Mlada Fronta Dnes*, 28 January 1993.

[40] *Mlada Fronta Dnes*, 20 August 1996.

[41] *Dokumenty IV Sjezdu*, p. 53.

[42] Interview with Josef Mecl, 14 October 1996, Prague.

[43] Olson, David. "The New Parliaments of New Democracies: The Experience of the Federal Assembly of the Czech and Slovak Federal Republic," in Ágh 1994c, p. 40.

The Czech KSČM

Table 5.4. *KSČM representation in parliament (two hundred seats).*

Seats and committee chairs	First term (1990–2)	Second term (1992–6)	Third term (1996–7)	Fourth term (1998–)
Committee chairs (%)	13%	0%	0%	3%
Seats (%)	15%	17.5%	11%	12%

Source: Parliamentary Institute records, Prague, Czech Republic. *Parlament Československé Republiky* and *Parlament České Republiky*, Poslanecká Sněmovna, Prague, 1990–6.

Given this lack of opportunities, the party declared it would look to a "broader left front" including unions, members of other parties, and cooperation between parties on the local and regional level, rather than inter-elite efforts.[44] These tactics and the defections of the reformists reinforced the party's image as unable to function effectively in a modern democratic party system. It also attempted to reach out to possible coalition partners through local efforts, summer camps, and mobilization of agricultural and blue-collar workers.[45] Both these attempts and the party's more traditional electoral and parliamentary activity met with little success – as the party concluded, the prevailing opinion was that "anything to do with the KSČM or its leadership is the biggest threat to democracy and the interests of the republic."[46]

Parliamentary Cohesion

The Czech party's parliamentary club, exposed to a far greater set of pressures than its colleagues within the party executive offices,[47] saw that the cause of its isolation in the parliament lay with the party itself. The parliamentary representation was the source of four separate reformist movements, which were immediately ostracized within the party: the DFK in 1990, the Demokratická Levice in 1992, and the Strana Levý Blok and Strana Demokratické Levice in 1993.[48] Even when they became independent parties, these offshoots were too closely identified with the KSČM,

[44] *Dokumenty IV Sjezdu*, p. 53.
[45] *Zpráva ÚV KSČM o Činnosti KSČM v obdobi po IV. Sjezdu v Liberci (prosinec 1995–prosinec 1999)*. Praha: ÚV KSČM, p. 30.
[46] *Dokumenty IV Sjezdu*, p. 32.
[47] Interview with Jiří Svoboda, 24 October 1996, Prague, and interview with Miloš Šťepán, *Naše Pravda*, 20 July 1991.
[48] Interview with Josef Mecl, 11 October 1996, Prague.

because they chose to break off so late, and so were also rejected from coalition negotiations.

The Czech party's parliamentary performance was not helped by its parliamentary disarray – there was no institutionalized mechanism by which the party could ensure its cohesion and unity. The KSČM parliamentary club split twice – once in 1991, when seven out of the thirty-two Czech National Council parliamentarians went over to the newly formed reformist Demokratická Levice, and in 1993, when twenty-five out of the thirty-five parliamentarians went over to the new reformist Strana Levý Blok. Moreover, the parliamentary club chair declared that the club would function as "a real place of discussion, on which base our representatives will take their stances."[49] Unfortunately, this discussion focused on ensuring representation of the diverse platforms, rather than on ensuring unity, and led to the constant airing of intraparty conflicts and opposing declarations.

The decentralized party had less ability to control parliamentary behavior, since the members demanded greater influence over the parliamentary club. Initially, the Czech party head was also the leader of the parliamentary club.[50] However, the leadership repeatedly argued that "party activity cannot be subjugated to parliamentary club interests."[51] Instead of fusing the parliamentary club leadership with the central party leadership, the party instead instituted a new rule in 1992 that forbade party leaders (specifically, Central Committee secretaries) from becoming parliamentarians, much less parliamentary clubs leaders.[52] The justification was that this would prevent the "overconcentration of functions." After the departure of the ten Strana Levý Blok faction parliamentarians in 1993, only two were in the party leadership. The Central Committee further stipulated that the parliamentary club was to tie itself more closely to members, rather than simply to constituencies, and reflect member wishes in its policy proposals. This fear of parliamentary autonomy also led the party to emphasize its extraparliamentary activity.

The party deliberately did not ensure any sort of party discipline or obedience: As the official party stance declared, the "party has not, and will not, determine how its parliamentarians vote."[53] Although the party

[49] Mohorita, quoted in *Rudé Pravo*, 31 January 1990.
[50] Interview with Vasil Mohorita, 14 November 1996, Prague.
[51] Jiří Svoboda, minutes of the fifth meeting of the Central Committee of the KSČM, 28 May 1991.
[52] *Zpráva ÚV KSČM o Činnosti strany od 1. Sjezdu KSČM* ... 1993, p. 19.
[53] KSČM, *Teze Zprávy* ... 1992, p. 2.

instituted formal vote discipline rules,[54] it did not monitor parliamentary performance. As a result, according to the former leader of the KSČ, Miloš Jakeš, the parliamentary club "did not cooperate at all with the Central Committee" throughout 1990–1.[55]

Since the two were not fused, the parliamentarians' reformist stances led to clashes with the national leadership.[56] The tensions between the parliamentarians and the executive grew throughout 1990 and 1991.[57] As a result, twenty-five out of the thirty-five representatives left the party in 1993 because "they saw life would be much easier if they were not associated with the communist party."[58] The party leadership lashed back and declared that "it is necessary above all to overcome the efforts of those who wanted . . . to change ideology and tactics to that of social democracy."[59] Not surprisingly, the leadership's efforts to bring the parliamentary club into the orthodox fold did little to foster greater acceptance for the party.

This lack of cohesion meant that internal conflicts translated into parliamentary club members voting against each other. During the 1990–2 term of the united Czechoslovak parliament, the Czech reformists were largely in the Federal Assembly, also considered by the KSČM representatives a more desirable location than the national parliamentary chambers. When the decision to break up Czechoslovakia was ratified in 1992, several attempts were made to move the Federal Assembly parliamentarians into a Temporary Senate, the precursor of the Senate chamber that would be finally founded for the 1996 elections. The National Council KSČM representatives, however, voted against this move, helping to leave the Federal Assembly MPs without a political home, but with considerable resentment and division among the two groups.[60]

The party's isolation only reinforced its lack of cohesion, by creating enormous incentives to defect from a party with little ability to make itself

---

[54] Kopecký, Petr. "Parties in the Czech Parliament: From transformative towards arena type of legislature," in Lewis 1996. The other party with such rules was the ODS.

[55] Jakeš 1996, p. 118.

[56] Such clashes occurred in the Czech Republic and in Hungary. In the latter case, the two were then fused, to allow more streamlined and centralized decision making. Poland had a similar crisis, but only in the June 1989–January 1990 period.

[57] *Zpráva ÚV KSČM o Činnosti strany od 1. Sjezdu KSČM . . .* 1993, p. 17.

[58] Interview with Vasil Mohorita, 14 October 1996, Prague.

[59] KSČM, *Dokumenty IV Sjezdu*, p. 19.

[60] The resentment that resulted pervaded even the reformists' efforts – for example, two reformist splinters (the LB and the SDL) formed along Federal Assembly/ Czech National Council lines.

more acceptable. The KSČM failed to gain parliamentary acceptance or to develop parliamentary cohesion, as a result of its lack of the elite skills necessary to transform the party's appeals, and of a usable past to make them credible. Consistently excluded in parliament, the KSČM could do little to become a viable coalition partner. Nor could it easily develop the kind of parliamentary unity, given all the departures of the MPs, that could have made it into an opposition force with which other parties would have to reckon.[61]

The Slovak SDĽ

Given the more ambiguous popular and parliamentary stances toward the communist past, the Slovak communist successor party gained parliamentary acceptance more easily than the KSČM. Thanks to its organizational centralization, the SDĽ also boasted far greater parliamentary cohesion. On the other hand, the party had to face the ruthless Movement for a Democratic Slovakia (HZDS), and its marginalization of parties not allied with the HZDS.

Parliamentary Acceptance

The SDĽ did not face as much isolation as a result of anticommunist cleavages – the regime divide was more shallow. Thus, former communists dispersed into all political parties, and the lines between the communist and opposition camps blurred. After all, Mečiar was only one of a host of communists who were first involved in the Public Against Violence opposition movement in 1989. Other ex-communists in government after 1992 included the president; the defense, interior, and foreign ministers; the chairs of Parliament and the Constitutional Court; and the attorney general. Given the prominence of so many former communists, few could capitalize on the communist/anticommunist divide. Moreover, the party claimed that it would have done much more for Slovakia under communism had it not been for Czech domination. These claims were reinforced again by the party's references to the post-1968 developments, and the Slovak party officials' protection of the Slovak intellectual and professional classes during "normalization."

---

[61] Mansfeldová 1996, p. 8. Nonetheless, both the ODS and the KSČM had the highest voting discipline until 1997, when it rose to 90–95% for all parties.

Initially, the SDĽ faced the same degree of informal isolation as its Czech counterpart.[62] Party leaders still complained in 1991 that their parliamentary colleagues expressed "only minimal acceptance and utilization of [SDĽ] expertise."[63] However, the dominance by the HZDS of the parliament meant that other parties scrambled to find candidates for coalitions to oppose the HZDS. Since the regime divide lines were blurred, the cleavage between "nonstandard" and "democratic" parties began to determine potential coalitions. Since the SDĽ was one of the few stable and consistent defenders of democracy within Slovakia, it rapidly became a valuable ally and was increasingly viewed as a viable partner by the "democratic" parties.[64]

Consequently, despite the opposition of some of the parties, the SDĽ was represented proportionately in the leadership of the committees from the outset: It received 14% of the seats and of the chairs in 1990–2, and close to 20% of seats and chairs in 1992–4. The committee chairs were not particularly strong in the Slovak parliament. However, they were elected by the floor in a secret ballot, and therefore the number of chairs signaled the party's acceptance in the legislature.[65] Unlike its Czech counterpart, the SDĽ was *overrepresented* in the Budgetary, Constitutional, and Economic committees, the most important ones in the Slovak National Council. For the most part, however, as with other parties in the Slovak parliament, the SDĽ was represented in the committees in proportion to its share of the seats (see Table 5.5).

Both sides of the political cleavage sought SDĽ as a coalition partner. Given the common roots in the Slovak Communist Party of both Mečiar and the SDĽ leaders, several leaders in both the HZDS and the SDĽ (such as Peter Magvaši, Lubomír Fogaš, and Pavol Kanis) felt an alliance between the two was a "natural" one.[66] Negotiations continued throughout the summer and fall of 1993. However, joining the HZDS in a coalition would have meant not only risking submission to a highly autocratic party, but

---

[62] Interview with Dušan Dorotin, 4 February 1997, Bratislava.

[63] *Nove Slovo*, 18 July 1991.

[64] *Pravda*, 27 September 1994.

[65] Malová, Darina, and Šivaková, Dana. "The National Council of the Slovak Republic: Between Democratic Transition and National State-Building," in Olson, David, and Norton, Philip, eds. *The New Parliaments of Central and Eastern Europe*. Portland, OR: Frank Cass, 1996.

[66] It would also stand to benefit the shared constituency of the two parties, the so-called "red managers" – former party directors who now managed newly privatized enterprises. However, by April 1995, such discussions became moot, as the HZDS no longer wanted to deal with SDĽ, and especially with Weiss. TASR, *Daily News Monitor*, 3 October 1994.

Table 5.5. *SDĽ representation in parliament (150 seats).*

Seats and committee chairs	First term (1990–2)	Second term (1992–4)	Third term (1994–8)	Fourth term (1998–)
Committee chairs (%)	14%	20%	0%	22%
Seats (%)	14.6%	19.3%	12%	15.3%

Source: Parliamentary Institute records, Bratislava, Slovakia. *Národná Rada Slovenskej Republiky*, Bratislava: Chancery of the National Council of the Slovak Republic, 1996–8.

also losing the SDĽ's hard-earned reputation as a protector of democracy and the rule of law in Slovakia.

Therefore, no formal alliance ever emerged – to enter a coalition with the HZDS would gain the SDĽ access to governance, but would mean losing the votes of those who saw the SDĽ as committed to democracy. Moreover, over 70% of the party's members were against the coalition, and the party congresses repeatedly decided against it.[67] Eventually, HZDS itself lost interest. The SDĽ thus demurred and remained in the opposition.[68] Sacrificing short-term access to power, it gained a long-term reputation as a party committed to democracy and the rule of law.[69]

Instead, the SDĽ and the Christian Democrats then joined to take over power from the Mečiar government after it fell in March 1994, and ruled until the elections in September that year.[70] Despite its self-identification as a Left party, the SDĽ implemented policies designed to speed up privatization, free up the market, and increase internal competition and foreign trade, and the party did so with the Christian Democrats, traditionally the anathema of both the communist and socialist movements. For their part, the tiny Slovak Social Democratic Party increasingly pressed the SDĽ for coalitional cooperation, culminating in the SDĽ forming and leading the Common Choice coalition with three small parties, including the SDSS, for the September 1994 elections. Given the SDĽ's leading role

[67] Interview with Milan Ftáčnik, 31 January 1997, Bratislava.
[68] The party's 1995 congress also voted against the coalition, further constraining the leaders.
[69] By November 1994, the Republican Council of the SDĽ set out the conditions under which it would enter the coalition, knowing that they would not be fulfilled: the removal of the nationalist Slovak National Party from the coalition, greater transparency in privatization, and no more attacks on the president. *Narodna Obroda*, 21 February 1996.
[70] Other coalition members included the HZDS splinters Alternative of Political Realism, Alliance of Democrats (both of which later joined to form the Democratic Union), and the National Democratic Party.

in the government from March 1994 to September 1994, the Social Democrats would lose little by joining the SDĽ, while the SDĽ hoped to gain more supporters by reaching out to other constituencies.

The results of the election, as we saw in the last chapter, were disastrous for the SDĽ electoral coalition. Mečiar and the HZDS returned to power in October 1994, after an absence of seven months. The new coalition also included the Slovak National Party (SNS) and the Association of the Workers of Slovakia (ZRS), two nemeses of the SDĽ. As a result, the SDĽ's situation worsened considerably. Because it stood fast and refused to cooperate publicly with the HZDS, the SDĽ was subject to the same discrimination as the other opposition parties after the September 1994 elections.

The new HZDS coalition immediately consolidated its power by eliminating the other parties' rights. Since the SDĽ was instrumental in removing Mečiar from office in March 1994, it was promptly punished for this after the 1994 elections. During the "night of long knives" of 3–4 November 1994, Mečiar and the HZDS purged any noncoalition government officials, committee chairs, secretaries, and so on. Furthermore, after the new HZDS-SNS-ZRS coalition took power, it took advantage of two loopholes in the committee assignment rules to gain an overwhelming majority in all but one committee.[71] The coalition decreased the memberships of ten out of the eleven committees, packing them with its own representatives.[72] The coalition then increased the size of the Environmental Committee, dumped the opposition MPs into it, and gave them a fourteen to five majority in that committee alone.[73] Not surprisingly, the SDĽ received no chairs or vice-chairs during the HZDS takeover in 1994–8. Four years of HZDS coalition rule began, characterized by corruption, populist attacks, and increasing international isolation.

The September 1998 elections removed Mečiar from power and brought the democratic SDK coalition to rule. By this point, the SDĽ had consolidated its democratic reputation, and so the party returned to its former significance.[74] After a four-year interlude, the SDĽ gained 15.3%

[71] The entire floor voted on the assignments of members to the committees, and so the coalition was able to pack the committees.

[72] The coalition then gave itself a super-majority in the sensitive Mandate and Immunity (nine to six), Constitutional (ten to five), and Economy and Privatization (eleven to six) committees.

[73] Olson 1997, p. 409.

[74] The majoritarian tendencies of the HZDS are illustrated by the assignments of parliamentary posts – the SDK government offered the HZDS one of four parliamentary vice

247

of the seats and 22% of the chairs. It once again joined the government, with the SDK and the Hungarian Coalition. There, the SDĽ gained nine ministries out of twenty-one, beyond the proportion to which its 15% electoral share entitled it.

Thus, the SDĽ was accepted by one group of political parties and not by another; but the distinctions between the two had less to do with the shallower regime divide, which lowered the cost of cooperation, than with the fundamental divide between democratic and nonstandard parties.

Parliamentary Cohesion

The Slovak party was able to maintain high cohesion among its the parliamentary club, which largely overlapped the party's national Executive Committee. The elites' lack of earlier experience in implementing policy left the party with less ability to convince the reluctant electorate, since the elites had no experience in justifying their stances to the public. However, their earlier experience in innovating policy made the elites realize the importance of cohesion and discipline, given the need for such unity to gain access to party higher-ups before 1989. Initially, the Executive Committee had oversight powers, so tensions between the two groups arose when the parliamentary club voted to remove Mečiar from power in 1994 without consulting with the Executive Committee.[75] As a result, the national executive body reasserted its control of the parliamentary club and fused decision making between the Executive Committee and the parliamentary club.[76] The chair of the parliamentary club was automatically included in the top leadership of the party, the Predsednictvo.[77]

Unlike the KSČM, the SDĽ put its most skilled representatives after the 1992 elections in the Slovak National Council, anticipating the split of the country.[78] As a result, unlike the tense situation among their Czech

chairs and a third of committee seats, but the HZDS refused, arguing that since it won a plurality of the vote in 1998, it deserved a majority of these posts. *Respekt* c. 45. 2–8 November 1998.
[75] Interview with Milan Ftáčnik, 31 January 1997, Bratislava.
[76] *Nové Slovo*, 12 March 1994.
[77] *Pravda*, 16 January 1994. The fusion of these powers furthered the leaders' immediate interests. During the subsequent negotiations with the HZDS over a potential coalition, Weiss insisted that while he supported the negotiations, only the fused parliamentary/executive body could make a final decision, and not the subsections that had been hinting at a possible coalition with their HZDS counterparts.
[78] Weiss in *Pravda*, 29 March 1992.

counterparts, there were few resentments to be aired after the split within the SDĽ – the Federal Assembly representatives, as political lightweights dependent fully on the SDĽ leadership for their political lives, disappeared from the political scene. Nor were there many expulsions or exits, given the extreme and rapid centralization and the hand-picked candidates loyal to party leaders. The Slovak party was numerically the most stable, losing only one member in 1994.[79]

In short, the shallower regime divide and the SDĽ's defense of democracy made the party an attractive coalition partner and relatively easily accepted in parliament. Its earlier centralization made it a cohesive party. This further reinforced its pro-reform image, and its coalition performance, even if, as we saw earlier, the party's inexperience led it sometimes to miscalculate both the bases for its support and the effect of its coalition cooperation.

The Polish SdRP

The SdRP perhaps best illustrates the different calculations of voters and of parliamentary parties – despite greater popular support, the party found less acceptance in parliament than its Slovak or Hungarian counterparts. Even centrist parties with whom the SdRP shared much of its ideology and policy proposals refused to form a coalition with the communist successor party. The party was both increasingly cohesive and considered the most professional among the Polish parliamentary parties. As one critic declared, its "only ideology is effective governance."[80] Nonetheless, the deep regime divide made it far less accepted in parliament than it had been in the voting booths.

The Polish communist successor was thus extremely cohesive, much as the Slovak and Hungarian parties were. However, despite its electoral popularity and democratic commitments, it was sometimes as ostracized as the Czech communist successor – the fresh memories of the party-society conflict created enormous parliamentary controversy in both cases.

[79] The one parliamentarian who left, Jan Ľuptak, formed the Association of Slovak Workers, a party that then joined the coalition with the HZDS in October 1994 and did its best to undermine the SDĽ.

[80] UW MP Andrzej Potocki, quoted in *Wprost*, 9 June 1996. The SdRP's cool professionalism and moderation was all the more accentuated by the radicalism and populism of its coalition partner, the Peasants' Party, PSL.

Parliamentary Acceptance

The Polish party faced the irony of electoral success without parliamentary acceptance – its eventual electoral success and its popularity were not reflected in the parliament. The SdRP was isolated in the Polish parliament, having polarized society into a communist and anticommunist camp during the Solidarity years of 1980–1, only nine years before the transition. From the start, it was seen largely as an outcast by the other parties – "for all significant parties, it was unacceptable at that time, and continued to remain unacceptable, to enter into any open alliance with or even to officially cooperate with the SdRP as the heir to the defunct communist party (PZPR)."[81] It was "on the parliamentary floor but not in the parliamentary game," in the words of one of its elder statesmen.[82] Despite its initial (and crucial) support for the Mazowiecki government, the SdRP was a "club excluded and isolated by other groups."[83] Many parliamentarians admitted that "there is parliament and there is the SLD (the SdRP's parliamentary club). No one allies themselves with SLD, no one cooperates."[84] It was even characterized as an "antisystem" party, as scholars saw a threat to the free market in the party's initially Leftist economic stances.[85] Its policy proposals were also ignored, even as the party supported the radical economic and political reforms of 1989–91, including the economic reform package of February 1992, in an attempt to appear "responsible" and gain greater acceptance.[86] The SdRP rather bitterly concluded that "sometimes we'd get the feeling that even if SLD proposed something that was most obvious and beneficial, it would still be rejected on the basis of its origins."[87]

From 1990 to 1993, the Polish parliament itself was a highly fragmented place: Not only had five governments formed and fallen in the first four years of its existence, but the parliamentary groupings proved very unstable. Yet despite the SLD's internal unity and professionalism, the party continued to be excluded, a priori, from consideration as a coalition

[81] Zubek 1993.
[82] Wiatr 1993, p. 37.
[83] Lelinska, Krystyna. "Sejm I kadencji w Świadomości posłów," in Wesołowski, Włodzimierz, and Panków, Irena, eds. *Świat elity politycznej*. Warsaw: IFiS PAN, 1995, p. 306. For similar accounts, see also Zubek 1995.
[84] *Rzeczpospolita*, January 1993.
[85] Wasilewski, Jacek, "Scena Polityczna," in Wasilewski 1994, pp. 39–40.
[86] Józef Oleksy, quoted in *Życie Warszawy*, 17 March 1993.
[87] Wiatr 1993, p. 35.

partner or parliamentary ally. In the 1991 elections, the SdRP came in a very close second to the Democratic Union (UD), whose ideology and supporters the SdRP had already begun to share. However, given its identity as a centrist post-Solidarity formation, the UD chose to form alliances with other post-Solidarity groupings, despite their fractious and unreliable nature, and studiously continued to ignore the communist successor party as a potential coalition partner. As a result, "the Left did not seek a place in government. Despite many programmatic similarities, no other party would dream of entering an alliance with the SLD. It merely hoped for a strong parliamentary presence."[88] Unlike the KSČM, however, the party did form some coalitions on the local level, where personal ties mattered more and trumped ideological considerations.[89]

The reasons for this isolation lie with the past party-society record, and the resulting regime divide. On the one hand, the party could easily, and credibly, claim professional expertise and managerial experience. On the other hand, the cleavage between postcommunist and anticommunist forces was deep, given the recent trauma of 1980–1, in which some of them played a role (unlike the distant events of 1956 in Hungary). The communists also faced a single opposition camp, Solidarity, instead of the several groupings in pre-1989 Hungary. Both factors led to the formation of a lasting cleavage in Polish politics between those who could forgive the party for its recent past and those who rejected its claims of transformation and identified instead with the 1980s opposition.

Instead of cooperating with the SdRP, parliamentary colleagues deliberately set out to divide the party, playing off wings of the party against each other and appealing to individuals rather than to the parliamentary club.[90] For example, worried about the SdRP's influence on Waldemar Pawlak, the Peasant Party's candidate for prime minister in June 1992, the parliament voted against the government he was attempting to form. Other parties, especially the right-wing confederation for an Independent Poland (Konfederacja Polski Niepodległej, KPN) and the Christian Democrats attacked individual SdRP parliamentarians, such as Leszek

---

[88] Millard, Frances. "The Polish Parliamentary Elections of October 1991," *Soviet Studies*, No. 5, 1992: 837–55, p. 843.

[89] The party ruled in local coalitions with the populist Peasants' Party (PSL), the Leftist Labour Union (UP), the neo-liberal Congress of Democratic Left (KLD), the centrist Democratic Union (UD), and the Polish Party of the Friends of Beer (PPPP), which combined a pro-market orientation with an ecological one ("because markets mean cheap beer, and clean water – good beer"). *Wprost*, 21 February 1993.

[90] Parties said to excel at this technique were the ZChN, UD, and KPN.

Table 5.6. *SdRP representation in parliament (460 seats).*

Seats and committee chairs	First term (1989–91)	Second term (1991–3)	Third term (1993–7)	Fourth term (1997–)
Committee chairs (%)		5% (vice-chairs)	26% (chairs)	23% (chairs)
Seats (%)	N/A	13%	37%	36%

Source: Kancelaria Sejmu. *Sejm Rzeczpospolitej Polskiej: Informacja o Działalności Sejmu.* I Kadencja. Warsaw, October 1993. Ibid, II Kadencja, January 1997, *Informator*, Wydawnictwo Sejmowe, 1990–7.

Miller or Izabella Sierakowska, as "party concrete."[91] Finally, the party had enormous problems gaining a favorable image in the media, unlike the post-Solidarity parties.[92]

Given this animosity, it was not suprising that even though the SdRP was the second-largest formation in the 1991–3 parliament,[93] it was not given a single chair of any of the committees, and given only five vice-chairs instead (out of seventy-four vice-chairs).[94] It had no representatives in the parliamentary leadership. Although its membership on committees was for the most part proportionate to the seats it had received (see Table 5.6), the party was underrepresented in the Rules and Parliamentary Affairs committees, as well as in the EU Committee. This underrepresentation stung all the more, given the fact that it was the SdRP's predecessor that initially allowed the committee system to gain many of its powers in the communist era.[95]

On the other hand, this initial discrimination allowed the party to "have the luxury of appearing moderate"[96] when the SdRP assumed power in 1993. The SLD club magnanimously gave eight out of twenty-five committee chairs to the opposition parties. As party leader Tadeusz Iwiński explained, "after 1993, we have exemplified democracy by giving the leadership of some committees to opposition representatives."[97] Nevertheless, the party, with 37% of the seats, dominated the Foreign Affairs and Social Policy committees, taking 48% and 44% of those seats, respectively.

[91] Wiatr 1993, p. 30.
[92] SdRP, *Biuletyn II Kongresu*, p. 3.
[93] The SdRP gained 12% of the vote and sixty seats, to the Democratic Union's sixty-two.
[94] Committee chairs were decided, as in the West, ahead of time by the party leaderships.
[95] Olson 1997, p. 409.
[96] "Konfitury," *Wprost*, 31 August 1997.
[97] "Konfitury," *Wprost*, 31 August 1997. As a result, the party could later claim that it "defeats its rivals, but does not destroy them," in the 1997 elections.

Once the SdRP won the 1993 elections, with 20% of the vote, it tried to avoid the inevitable coalition with the Peasants' Party (Polskie Stronnictwo Ludowe, PSL), a successor to the communist-era peasant party (and a fully subservient communist satellite prior to 1989).[98] The SdRP had already formed some local coalitions with the Democratic Union (Unia Demokratyczna, UD, which became known as the Unia Wolności, UW, after the UD and the Liberal Democratic Congress, KLD, united after the 1993 elections)[99] and tried to reach out several times to ally on the national level.[100] Immediately after the elections, SdRP leader Kwaśniewski thus repeatedly insisted that the Democratic Union would be the best partner for the SLD, as it would reassure the West of the new government's reformist continuity.[101] For its part, the leftist Labor Union (Unia Pracy, UP), with its Solidarity roots, responded that it would join the SdRP only if the Democratic Union would. Although the Labor Union had former communist reformers in its ranks, it argued that this "is the limit – one which we will not cross."[102] The Democratic Union, in turn, promptly responded that it would not join any coalitions with the communist successors, for fear of electoral backlash.[103]

Despite personal friendships between the political elites of these three parties, their shared experiences during the Round Table negotiations of 1989, and their shared views (especially on the role of the Church in Polish society, access to abortion, religion in schools, and foreign relations), the Labor Union and the Democratic/Freedom Union still could not afford an open alliance with the SdRP in 1993 or in the subsequent parliamentary term. While the three parties cooperated informally, especially on the new 1997 constitution, the UW and the UP avoided public association with the SdRP. For the Freedom Union, especially, its shared claims of expertise and managerial competence with the SdRP meant that one of the few things that distinguished it from the postcommunists was its origin in Solidarity. An open formal alliance with the SdRP, Freedom Union leaders feared, would eliminate their party from the political scene. Its

---

[98] Sojusz Lewicy Demokratycznej, *Nasz Program dla Polski: Trzy lata Pracy Parlamentarnej SLD*. Warsaw: SLD Parliamentary Club, 1996, p. 8.
[99] *Tygodnik Solidarność*, 5 August 1994.
[100] For example, it offered to stabilize the government of Hanna Suchocka, but she refused to negotiate with the party. *Rzeczpospolita*, 3 September 1993.
[101] *Rzeczpospolita*, 25–6 September 1993.
[102] *Sztandar*, quoting Wojciech Borowik of UP, 14 March 1996.
[103] *Trybuna Ludu*, 27–8 September 1993.

electorate was opposed to the communist successor, and flirting with the SdRP could only endanger the loyalty of Freedom Union voters, without gaining any new supporters. The communist era cleavage continued to structure politics, and the perceived costs of cooperation with the SdRP far outweighed the benefits.

Faced with this rejection from its first choice of partners, the SdRP was forced to form a government coalition with the Peasants' Party, with whom it shared a communist heritage but very few policy stances. The initial prognoses were dire: "this is a government for a few, maybe more than ten, months. The inevitable controversies loom, such as conflict over the budget, conflict with Belvedere [the president's palace], social protest, the attacks of the anticommunist-lustration groups, which remain currently divided but which will be consolidated by their common stance against the government."[104]

Differences immediately emerged, and persisted, over the Concordat with the Church, agricultural policy, local administration reform, and privatization.[105] From the start, the Peasants' Party (PSL) and the SdRP had very different economic and political aims. For the PSL, the priority was ensuring that its agricultural constituency would be protected from the market and international competition. Moreover, the PSL sought to consolidate its power by scotching administrative reform and further privatization, both of which would affect its holdings in banking, tobacco, and local government.[106] Partly as a result of these conflicting demands, only 25% of the large enterprises were privatized during the coalition's term in office while others remained financially shielded, agricultural reform was halted, and local government remained fragmented and disempowered.[107] As an outgoing finance minister put it, the Peasants' Party acted as a brake on reforms, "thinking only about how much it can grab for the peasants."[108] Moreover, the PSL continually criticized its coalition partner, treated the coalition as an endless source of patronage,[109] and refused to accept col-

---

[104] *Polityka*, 30 October 1993, p. 11.

[105] Sojusz Lewicy Demokratycznej, *Dwa Lata Pracy Parlamentarnej (19.9.1993–19.9.1995)*. Warsaw: SLD Parliamentary Club, 1995. This was despite the informal understanding that SdRP was in charge of the economy while the PSL concerned itself with state administration.

[106] *Rzeczpospolita*, 19 September 1994.

[107] "Plan Akcji," *Wprost*, 19 October 1997.

[108] Marek Borowski, resignation speech, *Gazeta Wyborcza*, 7 February 1994.

[109] For example, the PSL nominated, in twenty-two out of thirty cases, its own party activists to various posts. The SLD did so with only one out of eight. *Trybuna*, 7 February 1994.

lective responsibility for government actions,[110] knowing full well that the communist successor had no other potential coalition partners.[111]

Nonetheless, the SdRP found institutional solutions to the tensions within the coalition. First, on 15 November 1993, during the "night of settling coalition accounts," the SdRP demanded that both coalition partners must have a say in the decisions of the prime minister (at the time, Waldemar Pawlak, the PSL leader). As a result, the SdRP was able to "sell" its policies far more cohesively to the electorate, reduce the power of the worker councils, and promote the power of the management, despite PSL objections. The result was that the pro-reform course was maintained, and no major economic policy reversals occurred.[112]

Second, five representatives from each side would now form the "directorate" of the coalition, and each side could now call meetings of the directorate within twenty-four hours, preventing the Peasant Party from stonewalling and dodging issues, as it had begun to do. As a result, the communist successor-peasant coalition government lasted the entire term, from 1993 to 1997, in sharp contrast to the five governments that ruled Poland from 1989–93. Their government would not fall because members voted against their own proposals, did not bother to attend parliamentary meetings, or grossly miscalculated their own strength – as the opposition parties had done earlier.

At its 1996 conference, the SdRP declared that in future coalitions, its options consisted of the Peasants' Party, the centrist Freedom Union, or the leftist Labour Union.[113] The Freedom Union, for its part, declared that such a coalition would be possible only if "a massive disaster" occurred, and the rest of the political scene became extremely radicalized.[114] The Labour Union was an ally in the 2001 elections, but quickly declared it would form its own parliamentary club.[115] Nonetheless, the SdRP continued to be a dominant presence in parliament. After the 1997 elections, won by the Electoral Action Solidarity (Akcja Wyborcza Solidarność), the SdRP lost

[110] Sojusz Lewicy Demokratycznej, *Nasz Program dla Polski: Trzy lata Pracy Parlamentarnej SLD*. Warsaw: SLD Parliamentary Club, 1996, p. 15.
[111] The relationship between the two parties was so strained that when an SdRP parliamentarian tried to defend the coalition partner as a "good and solid one" at a party meeting, his sanity was promptly, and unequivocally, questioned. *Gazeta Wyborcza*, 7 November 1994. The exact query can be most charitably approximated as "did you fall off a Christmas tree?"
[112] Błażyca, George, and Rapacki, Ryszard. "Continuity and Change in Polish Economic Policy: The Impact of the 1993 Elections," *Europe-Asia Studies*, No. 1, 1996: 85–100.
[113] PAP, 20 May 1996.
[114] *Wprost*, 22 March 1998.
[115] *Donosy*, 26 September 2001.

only seven parliamentary seats, and held 164 out of the 460 seats, or 36%. It dominated the Construction and Consumer Affairs committees, and the all-important Economic Committee, with 50%, 43%, and 41% of the seats, respectively.[116]

Parliamentary Cohesion

The SdRP's parliamentary discipline and moderation reinforced the other signals sent out by the party. To achieve parliamentary discipline, the SdRP party elites fused the parliamentary and executive bodies immediately, since "if the party's main goal is to influence government, its representatives must have a considerable say in party decision making."[117]

Part of the reason was the early split that occurred between the parliamentary representation and the party executive after June 1989, and before the Extraordinary Congress. At the first meeting after the 1989 elections, the Central Committee outlined how the parliamentary club should vote, only to have its suggestions rejected outright.[118] The parliamentary club issued its own programmatic declaration, and began to act independently of the more conservative central leadership in the summer of 1989, much to the latter's surprise.[119] Moreover, the parliamentarians, having been elected to office, argued they had more legitimacy than the apparat.[120] The party's parliamentary leader Włodzimierz Cimoszewicz announced that "the party will end at the congress. We'll retain our mandates . . ."[121]

Another impetus for the fusion of the leaderships came from fears of further fission: The parliamentary club began after 1989 with 173 members, only to lose 71 of them to other parties in the first year and a half. The rival Polish Social Democratic Union, which formed at the January 1990 congress, took with it forty-three parliamentarians when it formed on 9 April 1990.

The result was that the party's Central Committee ceded all control to the parliamentary club,[122] and the parliamentary club became the chief

---

[116] Committees were assigned members by the Chancellor's Office of Sejm Committees. Van der Meer-Krok-Paszkowska, Jackiewicz, et al., 1998, "Committees in the Post-Communist Polish Sejm: Structure, Activity, and Members" in Longley, Lawrence, and Davidson, Roger, 1998, pp. 101–23, p. 107.

[117] Zbigniew Sobotka, *Trybuna Ludu*, 8 September 1989.

[118] Interview with Marek Król, *Wprost* offices, 17 July 1997, Poznań.

[119] Rakowski, Mieczysław. *Zanim Stanę Przed Trybunałem*. Warsaw: BGW, 1992, p. 123.

[120] Interview with Marek Król, *Wprost* offices, 17 July 1997, Poznań.

[121] *Trybuna Ludu*, 14 November 1989.

[122] Interview with Marek Król, 17 July 1997, Poznań.

decision maker within the party by the Extraordinary Congress.[123] Subsequently, the SdRP also joined the parliamentary bureaus with the party centers in twenty-eight out of forty-nine voivodeships, thereby increasing their funding, promoting greater unity, and ensuring the parliamentary bureau's control over the local party.[124] The center of the national party life, too, shifted to the parliament[125] – by 1993, only one of the six top leaders was not in the parliamentary club. The majority of the parliamentarians served, by 1994, as either the chairs and secretaries of the voivodeship party organizations or in the central SdRP leadership.[126] In 1999, when the SdRP transformed into the SLD, all 166 parliamentarians entered the National Council, along with 118 hand-picked candidates.

The party instituted an elaborate system of incentives and punishments to ensure voting discipline and cohesion. It employed a full range of the institutions designed to get rid of the principal-agent problem,[127] which included contract design, screening agents, monitoring their activity, and demanding that they account for their actions.[128] The parliamentary club issued a document, entitled "Principles of Behavior of the SLD Parliamentary Club," which declared that "the iron rule of the club is unity of voting." The document declared that the agenda would be exclusively set by the party leaders, that absences could be excused only with medical notes or with prior agreement of the leader, and that unless specifically exempted by a majority of the club, full voting discipline applied.[129] The resulting cohesion was a stark contrast to that of the other parties in parliament, whose lack of discipline was legendary, as the fall of the government of Hanna Suchocka in June 1993 exemplified – several government coalition MPs "pressed the wrong button," and voted no confidence in their own government.

SdRP party "coordinators" (basically, party whips) not only saw policy proposals through the various committees, but also told the MPs how to

---

[123] Gebethner, Stanislaw. "Parliamentary and Electoral Parties in Poland," in Lewis, Paul G., ed. *Party Structure and Organization in East-Central Europe*. Cheltenham, UK: Edward Elgar, 1996, p. 124.

[124] SdRP *Biuletyn*, II Congress SdRP, 20–1 March 1993, p. 1.

[125] Interview with Sławomir Wiatr, 27 May 1997, Warsaw.

[126] *Rzeczpospolita*, 6 May 1994.

[127] The problem consists of the difficulties in monitoring and ensuring compliance of agents delegated to performing tasks for the principal.

[128] Strom, Kaare. "Parliamentary Government and Legislative Organization," in Döring, Herbert, ed. *Parliaments and Majority Rule in Western Europe*. Frankfurt: Campus Verlag, 1995, p. 61.

[129] SLD. "Zasady postępowania Klubu Parlamentarnego SLD w Przyszłej Kadencji Sejmu," Warsaw, June 1997.

vote, all the more important given the high amount of baroque amendments attached to many bills.[130] Each parliamentarian was evaluated twice a year, and the results were made known to the other members of the club – positive evaluations would lead to nominations for chairs of extraordinary committes, vice-chairs of regular committees, and opportunities to serve as "coordinators."[131] Negative evaluations, or voting out of line, meant public castigations by the presidium, the club, and subsequently exclusion from party positions, the parliamentary club, and the party itself. As a result, by 1993, the SLD coalition maintained one of the most united voting records in the Polish parliament.[132] Five out of the fifteen most attentive MPs were from the SdRP,[133] and the party followed the decisions of Kwaśniewski even when they were not in keeping with the individual MPs' own interests.[134] Party elites were able to enforce discipline as a result of their earlier organizational centralization, which allowed them to set out the rules of parliamentary behavior, select MP candidates who would be loyal, and monitor their performance, retaining control of the system of incentives and punishments.

In short, the SdRP was highly successful in convincing the electorate, maintaining parliamentary cohesion, and demonstrating professionalism. Yet for all its electoral achievements (and it can be said to be the most successful party under consideration in this respect), the SdRP had less success in convincing other parliamentary parties to cooperate. Its past meant that the party could not gain the parliamentary acceptance it so badly sought, putting it in the ironical position of the party with the greatest electoral support, but with the least parliamentary reflection of this popular acceptance. Few parties were willing to forego their identity and support for cooperation with the SdRP. At the same time, the SdRP's legendary cohesion made it both a powerful force in the opposition and the senior partner in the first democratic government that was stable enough to last its entire term.

The Hungarian MSzP

Of the parties under consideration, the MSzP had achieved the greatest parliamentary success. Its history of negotiation and reform, combined with the tacit consensus between party and society after 1956, meant that it could be more readily accepted as a parliamentary actor. In fact, the

---

[130] Wiatr 1993, p. 35.
[131] Interview with Lech Szymańczyk, 8 July 1997, Warsaw.
[132] Wiatr 1993, p. 30.
[133] *Rzeczpospolita*, 23 June 1993.
[134] *Życie Warszawy*, 21 October 1994.

MSzP became the only communist successor party that readily formed a coalition with a party from its former opposition – the SzDSz. Furthermore, as befitted its image of competence and expertise, the MSzP was eventually among the most cohesive and effective parliamentary clubs.

Parliamentary Acceptance

The Hungarian party parliamentarians initially felt isolated in the parliament throughout 1990–3. The MSzP was not asked to join the governing coalition, despite the fact that its ideology and support base were often the closest to the individual coalition parties'.[135] However, the isolation was neither as severe nor as persistent as in Poland or in the Czech Republic. The other Hungarian political parties accepted the communist successor more readily, because the Hungarian party's past was nowhere near the liability that the Polish party's was. Moreover, all the parties shared a conviction in consensus building as a crucial prerequisite to social stability. As a result, less anticommunist consensus emerged from the recent communist past. In fact, the party had already liberalized electoral rules in the late communist era and had a more pluralist parliament for several years.[136] Thus, as early as 1990, the party had no problem obtaining committee seats and chairs in proportion to its representation (see Table 5.7).

The shared concerns after 1956 with social stability and consensus building made the MSzP's parliamentary acceptance even easier, if not assured. Other opposition parties welcomed the MSzP's exit from its political ghetto, even if they did not immediately seek cooperation with the MSzP.[137] The MSzP avoided direct confrontation with the MDF-led government during 1990–4 and instead focused on "acting responsibly in the parliament and displaying internal unity."[138] As the government-opposition conflicts increased, the MSzP and its insistence on moderation began to look increasingly attractive to the Hungarian parliamentary

[135] Markowski 1997. Szarvas, László. "Parties and Party-Factions in the Hungarian Parliament," Budapest Papers on Democratic Transition No. 34, Hungarian Electronic Library, 1992.

[136] By 1970, not only were 25% of the parliamentarians in the Hungarian parliament nonparty members, but so were 50% of the local officials. Formally noncommunist representatives sat in several other communist-era parliaments, but nowhere else were there so many nonparty government officials. As a result, by 1987, 56% of the populace thought parliament had a large role to play, belying its rubber-stamp reputation. Open Society Archives, Hungary: Government: Personalities Files, 24 September 1987.

[137] Reisch, Alfred A. "Hungarian Socialist Party Looks Ahead," RFE/RL, 29 March 1991.

[138] Reisch 1992, p. 25.

Table 5.7. *MSzP representation in parliament (386 seats).*

Seats and committee chairs	First term (1990–4)	Second term (1994–8)	Third term (1998–)
Committee chairs (%)	10%	43%	28%
Seats (%)	8.6%	54%	35%

Source: http://www.mkogy.hu, and Ágh, 1995.

groupings,[139] especially given its support for the economic and political reforms.

After winning the 1994 elections with 33% of the vote, the MSzP formed a governing coalition with the SzDSz, a liberal party arising from the pre-1989 opposition to the communist regime. Even though the MSzP held 54% of the seats, thanks to the disproportionality in the translation of votes to seats, it sought to form this coalition to gain the two-thirds supermajority needed to pass major laws, including constitutional changes. The MSzP took nine out of the twelve ministries, leaving Internal Affairs, Culture and Education, and Transport to the SzDSz. The SzDSz joined the MSzP coalition because it perceived that the benefits of cooperation outweighed future electoral costs. After all, SzDSz, had been assiduously ignored by the other parties – the Hungarian Democratic Forum (MDF), the Young Democrats (Fidesz), the Christian Democrats (KDNP) and the Independent Smallholders (FKGP). Joining the MSzP was the SzDSz's one chance for governance. Thus, despite the jailing of SzDSz members by the MSzP's predecessor prior to 1989 and the ideological distance between the MSzP and SzDSz,[140] the two parties could form a coalition.[141]

Once in government, the MSzP-SzDSz coalition began to dispute each other's policies and stances, leading observers to conclude it was unstable.[142] The SzDSz complained that Prime Minister Horn did not consult it and

[139] O'Neil 1996.
[140] Ideologically, the SzDSz was not necessarily the closest to the MSzP. Markowski 1997 argues that Fidesz was actually closest to the MSzP.
[141] Moreover, several SzDSz leaders, such as Tamás Bauer, Miklós Haraszti, and Ivan Peto, all had strongly Leftist views, and "many SzDSz leaders came from old party cadre families." Similarly, the MSzP's reformist elites had formed considerable personal ties to these future SzDSz elites earlier, in the late 1980s. Szelenyi, Szonja, Szelenyi, Iván, and Poster, Winifred. "Interests and Symbols in Post-Communist Political Culture: the Case of Hungary," *American Sociological Review*, June 1996: 466–77, p. 475.
[142] Barany 1995, p. 67.

overextended his powers.[143] The factions within MSzP, which had never been eliminated, also began to quarrel over economic policy. Horn and the left-wing faction failed to support Finance Minister László Békesi, who wanted to implement a financial austerity package.[144] As a result, Békesi resigned in March 1995, and the coalition stood accused of a "history of starting and dropping initiatives."[145] Nonetheless, the MSzP retained its voting cohesion. Its reputation as a professional, modernizing party did not suffer.

Despite the factional conflict, the coalition became known most notably for implementing the austerity package of Finance Minister Lajos Bokros to meet the demands of international financial associations in the spring of 1995. The package curbed both wages and the provisions of the welfare state, devaluing the currency, and introducing additional import duties.[146] As a result, there were no major retrograde changes in stabilization policy in Hungary after 1994; instead, the MSzP coalition attempted to scale back the welfare state sharply, through such instruments as means testing of child and maternity support, tuition fees for colleges, and fees for medical services. These were hardly the policies of a Leftist party, but they were presented as the necessary bitter medicine to get Hungary back on its modernizing track.[147]

Nor were the trade unionists in the party's parliamentary representation able to hinder these plans; less useful than predicted in the electoral campaigns, union representatives also achieved little in parliament. Seventy out of 209 MSzP deputies in the 1994–8 parliament were members of either MszOSz or its communist-era predecessor.[148] Horn attempted to get the MszOSz leader, Sándor Nagy, into the government in 1994, in order to balance Bokros and his austerity plans, and to offer alternative economic proposals that would lead Bokros to resign.[149] The plan backfired – Nagy had to resign from trade union leadership in November 1995 because the austerity measures of the government were implemented without consultation with the union.[150]

---

[143] Szilagyi 1996.

[144] Barany 1995, p. 65.

[145] Lengyel 1995.

[146] Szilagyi, Zofia. *Transition*, 22 March 1996, p. 41.

[147] Bartlett, David. "Democracy, Institutional Change, and Stabilisation Policy in Hungary," *Europe-Asia Studies*, No. 1, 1996: 47–83. The Constitutional Court later declared some of these policies unconstitutional.

[148] Pataki 1994, p. 4.

[149] Szilagyi 1996, p. 41.

[150] Ágh, Attila. "Parliaments as Policymaking Bodies in East Central Europe: The Case of Hungary," *International Political Science Review*, Vol. 18, No. 4, 1997b: 417–32, p. 423.

The coalitions with the unions did ensure, however, that both the Polish and Hungarian successor parties would be taken more seriously in parliament, even if they were in the opposition, since they could now represent the trade unions, quell incipient union protests, and so on. As a Polish party leader explained, "every government will speak with the unions, no government will talk to a party outside of the parliament. No party outside of the parliament can have any influence on policy development, but trade unions can."[151]

Parliamentary Cohesion

The Hungarian communist successor party's parliamentarians were not particularly cohesive at the outset, but the central leadership rapidly moved to remedy this situation. Convinced (and rightly so) that they would lose the 1990 elections, the parliamentarians initially wanted stability above all else, and so moved cautiously to assert their independence from the central party leadership.[152] The party's less-centralized structure led to jockeying for power between the regional party heads and the parliamentarians during 1989–91. Nor was the parliamentary club very stable: Eight out of the thirty-four MSzP parliamentarians resigned from the club during the first parliamentary term, including such party stars as Miklós Németh and Bokros.[153] However, by 1992, the MSzP top leadership coopted the regional party heads, and the resulting fusion and centralization reinforced the party's image as the most professional of all groupings.[154]

As early as 1990, all twenty members of the party's Presidium were on the national electoral list, tying together the fortunes of the party leadership and its parliamentary representation. Furthermore, of the first twenty-eight names on the national list (all of whom entered parliament), 57% had long administrative and party careers behind them, making the most politically experienced and administratively skilled of the parliamentary clubs.[155]

[151] Jerzy Szmajdziński, *Trybuna* 15–16 January 1994.
[152] Interview with György Földes, 25 March 1997, Budapest.
[153] Szarvas, László. "Personnel and Structural Changes in the First Hungarian Parliament," in Ágh and Kurtán 1995, p. 202.
[154] Vass, László. "Changes in Hungary's Governmental System," in Ágh 1994c, p. 196. Keri, László. "Decision-Making of the Government from the Point of View of Organizational Sociology," in Gombar, Csabá, et al., eds. *Balance: The Hungarian Government 1990–1994.* Budapest: Korridor Books, 1994, p. 83.
[155] Tamás, Bernard 2000, p. 209.

All the MSzP parliamentarians were subject to party discipline, whether or not they were party members – thus, trade unionists running on the MSzP ticket in 1994 had to answer to MSzP authorities first, rather than to their union constituencies.[156] As a result, the parliamentary club was unanimous, as early as 1990 and 1991, in 89% and 93% of its opinions, respectively.[157] Moreover, the party's stock of elite expertise meant that throughout 1990–4, in the first democratically elected parliament, its representatives were organized into working groups that approximated a shadow cabinet,[158] forming a basis for its future governance. Bigger conflicts did not occur until 1995. Given the strength of the prime ministership in Hungary, Horn had begun to propose and push through several economic reforms about which the parliamentarians had misgivings.[159] At the same time, he determined most of the party stances himself, angering the party Presidium and the informal party factions.[160] Nonetheless, given the party's statutes, he was able to continue to impose his will on the parliamentary club and on the party, maintaining both discipline and consistency.

As a result of the post-1956 consensus and the party's record of responding to and coopting the opposition, the Hungarian party had far fewer problems forming a coalition with a party stemming from the former anti-communist opposition than any other communist successor. At the same time, the party could not rest on its laurels, and had to work hard both to retain cohesion (in light of its lower levels of centralization) and to ensure the implementation of its policies.

Conclusion

In short, the communist successor parties were not nearly as cohesive during their first years in democratic parliaments, or as threatening to democracy, as some of their actions during the communist regime could

[156] Lomax, Bill. "The Structure and Organization of Hungary's Political Parties," in Lewis 1996, p. 31.

[157] Szarvas 1992, p. 5. Ironically, these are not the highest rates: The MDF had rates of 94% and 96% respectively, and among the opposition parties, the Federation of Young Democrats had rates of 92% and 95%, respectively.

[158] Ilonszki, Gabriela. "Institutionalization and Profesionalization in the First Parliament," in Ágh, Attila, ed. *The First Parliament: 1990–94.* Budapest: Hungarian Center for Democracy Foundation, 1995b, p. 196.

[159] MTI, 13 January 1996.

[160] Interview with György Földes, 25 March 1997, Budapest.

suggest. The communist successor parliamentarians had to *learn* discipline and cohesion, even if the process was made easier for those who had prior experience in negotiations with adversaries (as the Polish and Hungarian parties did). Early centralization made enforcing such cohesion much more feasible for the parties, and so organizational transformation formed the basis for parliamentary performance. Parliamentary effectiveness then reinforced other aspects of party behavior, and the perceptions thereof. For example, cohesion lent further credibility to the parties' claims of competence and transformation.[161]

Parliamentary acceptance, for its part, was largely a function of the parties' usable past and the reputations it engendered. These effects of the parties' communist past would wane as parliamentary and electoral records would eventually begin to serve as the basis for the voters and other parties, but they persisted for several years, for lack of other signals. Coalitions were consequently a function of the regime divide. Other parties hesitated to form coalitions with controversial partners, for fear of electoral repercussions. Where the regime divide was more shallow, other cleavages could determine party coalitions.

As a result, parliamentary colleagues were generally far harder to convince of the communist successors' acceptability than were the voters. The parliamentarians were led by different considerations than the electorate. Parties in parliament form alliances and vote on policy guided not only by programs or ideology, but keeping in mind they will have to justify these decisions to voters, party members and activists, and potential coalition partners. Voters, on the other hand, have little concern for their "reputation" in this sense – they do not have not publicly justify their decisions, nor do they worry about their identity as parties do.

In short, neither post-1989 conditions, such as party competition or parliamentary institutions, nor communist legacies alone determined the parties' parliamentary performance. Nor were the parties simply free to reinvent themselves and their image. Instead, the combination of their elite portable skills and their usable past, and the subsequent transformation of their organizations, allowed these parties to exploit successfully political competition and its shortcomings. As a result, the communist successor parties could eventually gain both electoral victory and parliamentary acceptance, finally succeeding in gaining legitimacy and governance in a system their predecessors had denounced for so long.

---

[161] Franklin and Mackie 1983. Laver and Shepsle 1996, p. 69.

Conclusion: Succeeding in Democracy

Few political actors have faced a more difficult task of reinventing and transforming themselves than the communist successor parties of East Central Europe after 1989. Yet, as we have seen, several of these disgraced *ancien regime* parties survived and succeeded in the new democratic system. Paradoxically, the reasons lie in the parties' discredited past: The same practices that made the parties' rule so inadequate during the communist era could become their salvation during the democratic transition and beyond.

These parties thus "redeemed the communist past" both by making amends for the most disgraceful elements of their history and by cashing in on their elite resources to remake themselves into successful democratic competitors and governors. In so doing, they confirmed the expectations presented at the outset of this study: The political resources at their disposal were directly rooted in the communist era, and these assets then influenced the parties' response to the challenges and difficulties of democratic politicking and transition politics. Thus, external policies of advancement within the communist party promoted elite pragmatism and technical know-how, experience with policy innovation led elites to realize the need for party transformation and centralization, while policy implementation and negotiation with the opposition promoted the formulation of responsive programs, new dimensions of competition, and effective electoral campaigns.

These portable skills and usable pasts determined whether the parties could embark on strategies of organizational transformation. These were of paramount importance for the public resurrection of discredited parties that were forced to exit from power. Organizational centralization and a break with the past allowed such parties to signal their change publicly,

265

become more flexible strategically, and further transform their appeals and behavior.

If this transformation came early and decisively, communist successor parties could then continue to metamorphosize into successful democratic competitors. They developed new, resonant, and credible appeals that straddled existing electoral divisions, made up for the collapse of the parties' patronage networks, and exploited the general pro-reform consensus. Such responsive appeals, together with cohesive campaigns, would serve the parties well in elections where the preferences of the electorate were poorly understood and the electoral institutions placed a premium on coherent national campaigns. The parliamentary isolation of the communist successor parties also mandated that they act cohesively in order to be taken seriously in the legislatures, and organizational centralization and elite skills made this strategy possible. The parties' usable past determined both the credibility of their various appeals and their attractiveness as potential parliamentary allies and coalition partners.

As a result of the differentials in elite resources, parties followed distinct trajectories after 1989. Both the Polish and Hungarian communist successors had transformed themselves radically and gained enormous popular support; however, the differences in their historical record meant that the Hungarian party became accepted in parliament and formed coalitions across the regime divide far more readily than its Polish counterpart. Similarly, while both the Slovak and Polish parties centralized considerably, the Polish party elites were far more experienced and skilled in policy implementation and public negotiation. As a result, they could "read" the electorate more readily and credibly make claims of expertise that gave them far greater electoral support than their Slovak equivalent could obtain. Therefore, the configurations of portable elite resources help to explain not only the strategies of party regeneration but their relative success.

In short, despite similar posttransition contexts, the extent to which the parties could take advantage of these opportunities depended on their elite resources. However, we have not yet seen how well this explanation would travel to other cases of posttransition party transformation, where the political and economic contexts differ considerably. Therefore, the sections that follow expand the empirical analysis, illustrate the limitations of the explanatory model employed, and examine the theoretical implications of the causes and processes of communist successor party regeneration.

Testing the Analysis

Moving beyond the immediate context of this study, we can test this explanation on two different sets of cases. The first set consists of cases where the parties did not have to regenerate fully in order to recover (or maintain) access to power. These cases thus challenge a basic premise of this study, that parties have to transform to govern again. The second set consists of authoritarian successor parties that faced a different form of regime collapse and transition. These included a new nation-state (the united Germany), a presidential system where parties were far less relevant (Russia), and noncommunist party collapse (South Africa). If, despite these differences, both sets of cases nevertheless demonstrate the same set of causal factors and mechanisms – elite skills resulting from authoritarian practice, their determination of party strategies, the need for early and decisive organizational and programmatic change, and the self-reinforcing nature of these changes – then the explanation is that much more robust and generalizable. In this section, I briefly examine these cases and the extent to which we observe similar processes and outcomes of party regeneration.

First, in Bulgaria, Romania, and Albania, the transition to democracy was less the collapse of a regime than a change in the political circumstances of the ruling parties. The strategy of organizational continuity and gradual programmatic change was both feasible and successful, since accepting democracy and formulating responsive programs were less relevant to the parties' subsequent electoral and parliamentary success. The parties were not as discredited, and so did not move the transform as much.

The Bulgarian communist party remained in control during the transition – it even had to help usher the opposition parties into existence.[1] Party elites staged a coup from within on 10 November 1989, as the relatively moderate Petûr Mladenov took over the party leadership from the aging stalwart, Todor Zhivkov. As in Poland, many new elites had earlier advanced through the youth organization and then assumed mid-level leadership positions in the communist party.[2] Thanks to the longstanding communist policy of coopting dissent and of instituting cycles of nominal reforms, the communist successor, the Bulgarian Socialist Party

---

[1] Karasimeonov, Georgi. "Bulgaria's New Party System," in Pridham and Lewis 1996, p. 255.

[2] Higley, John, Pakulski, Jan, and Wesołowski, Włodzimierz, eds. *Postcommunist Elites and Democracy in Eastern Europe*. Basingstoke, UK: MacMillan Press, 1998, p. 216.

(Balgarska Socialisticheska Partija, BSP), had "reserves of relatively well prepared and experienced professionals in all fields."[3] Several of these now entered the party leadership.

However, these new elites had no experience in negotiating with the opposition or implementing policy reform. Zhivkov's apparent "obsession with total loyalty"[4] limited their opportunities to gain such experiences. Moreover, the party's continuation in power meant no vacuum opened up at the very top. As a result, far fewer committed or skilled reformers could ascend.[5] Finally, since the party was not forced to exit from power or discredited, there were far fewer incentives to change either its structures or appeals.

Consequently, instead of making an early and decisive change, the party spread it out over two congresses, held in January 1990 and in September 1990. Neither had a particularly reformist orientation, and no major overhaul of the party's organization or appeals occurred. The party did own up to many of its past mistakes[6] at its first party congress in January 1990, and it discarded its communist symbols at the September 1990 congress.[7] Nonetheless, it did not dissolve, nor did it centralize: The 930,000 members (over 10% of the population) were retained, as was the party's mass structure. Opinion platforms were allowed, and a member referendum, not elite action, changed the party's name in April 1990. Elite reformists were "consistently defeated in their efforts to break completely with the party's past and appear[ed] to have only a limited influence over party policy formation."[8]

Instead, the BSP "tried to preserve its identity and its historical roots while at the same time slowly transforming its image from a totalitarian to a parliamentarian, social-democratically oriented party."[9] For much of its post-1989 existence, it relied on populism, nationalism, and clientelism.[10] Some scholars argued that the lack of left-wing alternatives was

[3] Karasimeonov 1996, p. 261.

[4] *Yearbook on International Communist Affairs*, Stanford, CA: Hoover Institution Press, 1979, p. 11.

[5] Szajkowski, Bogdan. *Political Parties of Eastern Europe, Russia, and the Successor States.* Harlow, Essex, UK: Longman, 1994, p. 94.

[6] Szajkowski, p. 98.

[7] Perry, Duncan. "The Bulgarian Socialist Party Congress: Conservatism Preserved," *RFE Report on Eastern Europe*, 26 October 1990, p. 8.

[8] Ishiyama 1995, p. 162.

[9] Karasimeonov 1996, p. 257.

[10] Troxel, Luan. "Socialist Persistence in the Bulgarian Elections of 1990–1," *East European Quarterly*, January 1993, p. 413.

responsible for the party's lack of transformation[11] – however, as we have seen in the Polish and Hungarian cases, such weak competition did not preclude party transformation elsewhere.

In addition to a weak opposition, the BSP also benefited from retaining its privileged access to patronage, state resources, and the media. As a result, in contrast to the dramatic electoral defeats in the first free elections in Czechoslovakia, Poland, or Hungary, the communist successor won the first free elections in June 1990, with 47% of the vote. Although it lost the second elections in October 1991, with 33% of the vote, to the increasingly powerful opposition Union of Democratic Force, which received 34%, the BSP won again in 1994. After the BSP lost power in 1997, no transformation followed these losses – without a regime collapse, and without a strong opposition to force it out of power, the party had few incentives to change.

Similarly, the communist party remained in power in Romania beyond 1989. The shadowy National Salvation Front (Frontul Salvarii Nationale, FSN), made up of communist party and military officials, staged a palace coup that removed Nikolai Ceauşescu from power in December 1989. The FSN retained full control of the state administration and proceeded to deny other parties access to material resources and to the media.[12] In an election rife with charges of intimidation and hindrance of the opposition, the FSN won 66% of the vote, and its presidential candidate, Ion Iliescu, received 85% of the votes.

The complete lack of reforms or engagement with the opposition under Ceauşescu produced few portable elite resources. Thus, although the new FSN leaders, such as Iliescu or Silviu Brucan, were initially considered to be relative reformists, they showed little commitment to democratic norms, much less to transforming the party to fit them.[13] The party neither centralized the organization nor broke with the past. Instead, its simply took over the assets of the Romanian communist party and retained its patronage networks. Nor did the FSN hold the sort of soul-searching congress that the other parties had, but instead held onto its old organization and appeals.

[11] Ishiyama, John. "Transitional Electoral Systems in Post-Communist Eastern Europe," *Political Science Quarterly*, No. 1, Vol. 112, 1997, pp. 108–9.
[12] Initially, the FSN claimed it would not contest the first free elections in 1990, but subsequently reneged on this agreement.
[13] Pasti, Vladimir. *The Challenges of Transition: Romania in Transition*. Boulder, CO: East European Monographs, 1997, p. 105.

The FSN then split in the spring of 1992, with the few reformists leaving the party and the conservative faction led by Iliescu eventually becoming the Party of Social Democracy of Romania (Partidul Democrației Sociale din România, PDSR) in July 1993. The PDSR continued to promulgate an anti-reform stance and never made a particular commitment to democracy – instead, it entered into coalitions with extremist and nationalist parties.[14] It eventually evolved a more socially sensitive platform, but the party continued to court antidemocratic parties and often played the nationalist card.[15] The weak democratic opposition both allowed the PDSR to retain power and provided inclusives for the communist governor to transform; the PDSR governed until the 1997 elections. In turn, the party's lack of elite resources meant there were few means with which to pursue party transformation.

Finally, the Albanian Party of Labor retained power outright, having insisted earlier that the transformations in the rest of the region would not affect its rule.[16] After a tumultuous year and a half, elections finally took place in March 1991. After waging a campaign of distortions, hoarding access to the media and campaign funds, and intimidating the opposition, the party won with 56% of the vote.[17] It did not exit from power until 1992.

Party elites had far fewer skills, and no usable past to speak of, after four decades of one of the harshest communist regimer in the region, under Enver Hoxha. A small group of reformers from the youth organization was both the smallest and least-supported faction in the party.[18] There was little of a symbolic or organizational break with the past: The party eventually changed its name to the Socialist Party of Albania (Partia Socialiste ë Shqipërisë, PSSH) during its Tenth Congress in June 1991, but it did not abandon Marxism-Leninism until 1996, did not replace its leadership, and instead gave prominent positions to hardliners.[19] The party retained its mass structures and a membership that numbered 150,000 (or

---

[14] Having entered an alliance with extremist and nationalist parties in 1992, it formalized this arrangement into a government coalition in January 1995. Pop-Elecheş, Grigore. "Separated at Birth or Separated by Birth? Communist Successor Parties in Romania and Hungary," *East European Politics and Societies*, Winter 1991: 117–47, p. 125.

[15] Pop-Elecheş 1991, p. 136.

[16] RFE/RL, 16 February 1990, p. 1.

[17] Biberaj, Elez, *Albania in Transition*. Boulder, CO: Westview Press, 1998, p. 100.

[18] Biberaj 1998, p. 282.

[19] Commission on Security and Cooperation in Europe, *Albania's Parliamentary Elections of 1997*, July 1997, p. 6.

about 5% of the population). No cohort of new, younger, and reform-minded leaders assumed power within the party.[20]

At no point did the party apologize for its past or commit itself to democratic values and economic reforms.[21] In fact, Fatos Nano and other party leaders strenuously objected to the creation of a multiparty system, and opposed political and economic reform.[22] Proparty transformation efforts were marginalized, and their chief promulgator was dismissed from the party in 1995.[23] Instead, the PSSH could rely on its continued populism and patronage to obtain support and to again win the 1997 elections.

In short, "regeneration" was in many ways a moot issue for these parties. None faced the same imperative or incentives to transform themselves as early and as decisively as their counterparts in the former Czechoslovakia, Poland, or Hungary. The limited nature of the regime collapse and of the new democratic competition meant they could hold on to power and win elections. They did not break with the past decisively, nor did they centralize, yet they could regain (or more precisely, retain) access to governance.

Nonetheless, the extent to which they were able to transform their organizations, program, electoral campaigns, and parliamentary efforts was a direct result of their elite skills and usable past. Mid-level communist elites determined the strategies of transformation, and their resources determined the scope and direction of change – hence the relatively greater Bulgarian regeneration (with its denunciation of the past and eventual program responsiveness), as compared to Albania or Romania.

What accounts for the difference between these two universes of communist successor parties? Fundamentally, the Bulgarian, Romanian, and Albanian parties retained control of the transition, and so did not face as sharp a critical juncture as their counterparts in the former Czechoslovakia, Poland, or Hungary did with the collapse of their communist regimes. They were not forced to exit from power, and so did not have to reconsider their organizations or appeals. Because they faced no reform consensus, they also did not have to formulate responsive programs or create new competitive dimensions beyond populist and nationalist appeals. Finally, because the competition was so weak, these parties did

[20] Biberaj 1998, p. 281.
[21] Ibid.
[22] Ibid., pp. 281–2.
[23] Ibid., p. 282.

not have to reinvent themselves or their campaigns. Ironically, the reason behind this initial divergence in transition outcomes partly lies within the communist parties themselves: The more stagnant and repressive they had been earlier, the less likely an opposition to mobilize before or during the transition, and the less likely the communist party to engage in policy reform or negotiation.

Three other parties were forced to exit from power, but did not regenerate fully. These were the East German Party of Democratic Socialism (Partei des Demokratischen Sozialismus, PDS), the Communist Party of the Russian Federation (Komunisticheskaya Partia Rossiskoy Federatsii, KPRF), and the South African National Party. These were the successors to the authoritarian Socialist Unity Party, the Communist Party of the Soviet Union, and the ruling National Party, respectively. The outcomes were similar to the Czech case, and illustrate similar mechanisms and causal factors, despite the distinct political contexts in which they functioned.

In East Germany, the communist Socialist Unity Party (Sozialistische Einheitspartei Deutschlands, SED) was forced out of power on 3 December 1989. Obsessed with West German "infiltration," the SED had earlier saturated society with an extensive network of party organizations and continual demands for ideological loyalty. It engaged in limited cycles of reform and repression after 1968, but it also advanced its elites from within, basing promotions on ideological loyalty.[24] Most reformists had left SED structures by the 1980s,[25] but a small group of reformists from the Academy of Sciences survived to become the new party leaders during the transition period.[26] However, they had even less experience in reform innovation than their Slovak counterparts. Thus, after 1989, they talked chiefly of the socialist nature of the party, and revitalizing it along Marxist and Gramscian lines.[27]

Given their limited political resources, these new elites were unable to transform the party fully in 1989–90. They eliminated the old leadership

---

[24] Interview with Dieter Segert, 7 July 1998, Berlin. It must be noted, however, that the "loyalty" demanded of the East German elites was far more of a bureaucratic loyalty to the perpetuation of the system and the party's organizational aims than it was an adherence to communist ideology itself.

[25] Interview with Dieter Segert, 7 July 1998, Berlin.

[26] As in Slovakia, the new elites established a temporary committee that took over the leadership. Land, Rainer, and Possekel, Ralf. "On the internal dynamics of the PDS: the Leninist Challenge and the Challenge to Leninism," *Constellations*, Vol. 2, No. 1, 1995: 51–61, p. 52.

[27] Interview with Gero Neugebauer, 23 July 1998, Berlin.

and changed the party's name at the February 1990 Extraordinary Congress,[28] but they retained the party organization and its hardline activists. The party retained its ideology.[29] In the name of party democracy, the leaders gave official recognition to party platforms (including the strongest, the Communist Platform) and attempted to increase the autonomy of local organizations.[30] Instead of streamlining, the party added several new advisory, administrative, and executive structures.[31]

The consequences were familiar from the Czech case – several reformers left in disgust over the party's perceived kowtowing to the orthodox platforms.[32] Elite reformists were continually challenged by the orthodox activists.[33] The party became dependent on the 130,000 party members for mobilization,[34] of whom 65% were pensioners, dominated by old party functionaries with strong antidemocratic attitudes.[35] These old functionaries of the East German communist regime remained highly influential in the party regional and local structures, where they continued to exert pressures on the party leadership.[36]

Even after Germany reunified in 1990, the PDS emphasized the communist tradition and its "unequivocal commitment to supplant the system."[37] As a result, it was excluded a priori from national governing coalitions.[38] On the other hand, the PDS consistently received more votes in the former East districts (Länder) than in the West: In 1990, the party received 11% in the East, compared to 0.3% in the West. In 1994, the party obtained 20% of the vote in the East, and in 1998 it received more than 19% in the East Länder. Among these voters, the PDS credibly

---

[28] Interview with Andre Brie, 31 July 1998, Berlin.
[29] Phillips, Ann. "Socialism with a New Face? The PDS in Search of Reform," *East European Politics and Societies*, Fall 1994: 495–530, p. 527.
[30] Interview with Andre Brie, 31 July 1998, Berlin.
[31] Phillips 1994, p. 507.
[32] Thompson, Wayne C. "The Party of Democratic Socialism in the New Germany," *Communist and Post-Communist Studies*, No. 4, 1996: 435–52, p. 444.
[33] Thompson 1996, p. 448.
[34] Thompson 1996, p. 436.
[35] Kleinfeld, Gerald. "The Return of the PDS," in Conradt, David, ed. *Germany's New Politics*, Providence, RI: Berghahn Books, 1995, p. 218.
[36] Interview with Dieter Segert, 7 July 1998, Berlin.
[37] Phillips 1994, p. 518.
[38] After 1994, the party rules in 175 municipalities and is represented in all five of the formerly East German Land parliaments. The SPD national party leadership denounced some Land-level coalitions formed after 1994, most notably with the Social Democrats.

represented East German identity and interests.[39] After all, 80% of the party's East German voters were disenchanted with the process and outcomes of reunification.[40]

However, this electoral success did not come about as a result of the party's mobilization efforts or program appeals. The party failed to respond to the growing identification of the PDS by the voters as a "East German" party until the elections of 1994. Until then, it focused attention on ecological issues, women's rights, and denouncing capitalism.[41] Its identification as a representative of East German interests was first made by its voters, and it took the PDS four years to realize why its constituency voted for it.[42] Insofar as it succeeded electorally, it did so in spite of the party's chosen strategy, and its role was limited to that of a "spoiler" party, able to take votes away from other parties at the margin and serve as an outlet for protest, but unable to establish a broad following of its own.

There was considerable reason to doubt that the PDS could have achieved electoral success, had Germany not reunified. After 1990, West German officials, academics, and bureaucrats "colonized" East German structures, throwing out of work tens of thousands of East German functionaries. Political parties were similarly imported from the West, and led by West German party representatives. The PDS was the only party that was not led or otherwise dominated by West Germans. Therefore, it was the only party that could credibly commit to representing East German interests exclusively.

A counterfactual scenario allows us to speculate on the fate of the PDS in an independent East Germany.[43] Had Germany not reunified, there would have been no West German "colonization" or the subsequent backlash against it. Several new parties were likely to have emerged from the Neue Forum mass movement and from historical parties, as they have done elsewhere in East Central Europe. *All* political parties in East Germany could claim they represented East Germans, and the PDS would be unable to get support on that basis.

[39] Betz, Hans-Georg, and Welsh, Helga. "The PDS in the New German Party System," *German Politics*, December 1995: 92–111, p. 100.

[40] Krisch 1996, p. 123.

[41] Krisch 1996, p. 113.

[42] Ziblatt, Daniel. "Putting Humpty-Dumpty Back Together Again: Communism's Collapse and the Reconstruction of the East German Ex-Communist Party," *German Politics and Society*, Spring 1998: 1–29.

[43] Fearon, James. "Counterfactuals and Hypothesis Testing in Political Science," *World Politics*, Vol. 43, No. 2, 1991: 169–95.

The Russian case was another one of limited transformation, as expected in a country that did not undergo a rapid or definitive transition to democracy.[44] It was a more ambiguous case of the formal collapse of the party on the one hand and the continued success of its former leaders on the other. After the attempted coup of August 1991, the Communist Party of the Soviet Union collapsed. Several national-level parties emerged to claim its mantle, and these eventually united in February 1993. While the party was delegalized again for two weeks in October 1993, local structures survived,[45] and the party continued to rely on its half a million members.[46]

Since it was not as discredited as its East Central European counterparts, the party gained relatively high popularity without either a break with the past or an organizational centralization. The party's leadership continued to be dominated by former party leaders, most notably Gennadii Zyuganov and Valentin Kuptsov. New elites ascended almost exclusively from a cohort that had engaged in little reform or negotiation.[47] Many were conservative communists. As party leaders admitted, the "best and the brightest" had left the party, and so "we value every communist."[48] As a result, the KPRF retained much of its extensive organizational structures and did not break with the past. As in East Germany, however, the party benefited from widespread discontent with post-1991 changes. It received 12.4% of the vote in 1993, 22% in 1996, and 24% in 1998. Zyuganov himself ran a close second to Boris Yeltsin in the 1996 presidential elections.

This support was less a confirmation of the party's policy proposals than a rejection of the post-1991 Russian order. The party's programs mixed nostalgia, an acceptance of the free market but with state regulation, and

[44] Two years elapsed between the coup of August 1991 and the parliamentary elections of 1993. Nor has there been a change of government "teams" – the same political groupings have remained in charge since 1991.

[45] Flikke, Geir. "Patriotic Left-Centrism: The Zigzags of the Communist Party of the Russian Federation," *Europe-Asia Studies*, March 1999: 275–98.

[46] Davidheiser, Evelyn. "Right and Left in the Hard Opposition," in Colton, Timothy, and Hough, Jerry, eds. *Growing Pains*. Washington, DC: Brookings Press, 1998: 177–209, p. 195.

[47] As Steven Solnick points out, numerous graduates of technical universities could have become the sort of mid-level elites recruited in Hungary, but they were never utilized. Solnick, Steven. *Stealing the State*. Cambridge, MA: Harvard University Press, 1998.

[48] FBIS, 13 May 1998. Interview with Gennadii Zyuganov by *Zaftra* editor Aleksandr Prokhanov.

both socialism and nationalism.[49] While the KPRF has railed against the "dictatorship" of then-President Yeltsin, it did not offer constructive policy proposals that reflected public priorities. Instead, it often simply obstructed policy proposals, and tended to rely on "condemning the system and its policies."[50] Its appeals often contradicted each other, not so surprising given the fact that many independent MPs ran under the party's label.

An even more distinct case was that of the South African National Party, which was unable to regenerate after the democratic transition (1993–4). Party leader F. W. De Klerk had begun the process of liberalization in 1989, when he assumed the country's presidency. His administration had freed Nelson Mandela and other opposition African National Congress (ANC) leaders, eliminated apartheid laws in 1991, and led the negotiations with the ANC that resulted in free elections with universal franchise in 1994.

For all these accomplishments, however, the party failed to regenerate after its exit from power in 1994. Without a set of mid-level elites who had the skills, ambition, and training to transform the party (most of the pragmatic and educated party officials had left in the mid-1980s[51]), the National Party did not break with the past or transform the organization. De Klerk insisted on retaining the party leadership, refused to change party leaders, and instead replaced departing elites with "old, white Nationalists."[52] Riven by factions and programmatic squabbles, the party left the Government of National Understanding (which it had formed with the ANC) in 1996.[53]

De Klerk finally resigned in August 1997, and Marthinus van Schalk-wyk became the new leader, over *three years* after the critical 1994 elec-

---

[49] Ishiyama, John. "The Sickle or the Rose: Previous Regime Types and the Evolution of the Ex-Communist Parties in Post-Communist Politics," *Comparative Political Studies*, June 1997: 299–300, p. 316.

[50] Sakwa, Richard. "Left or Right? CPRF and the Problem of Democratic Consolidation in Russia," *Journal of Communist Studies and Transition Politics*, January–June 1998: 128–58, p. 131.

[51] *Weekly Mail and Guardian*, 14 July 1995. This meant that while the representatives of non-government organizations (NGOs) and think tanks conducted the negotiations on behalf of the ANC, the National Party was already ill prepared to negotiate its, and South Africa's, future in 1994.

[52] *Weekly Mail and Guardian*, 22 December 1995.

[53] Southall, Roger. "The Centralisation and Fragmentation of South Africa's Dominant Party System," *African Affairs*, October 1998: 443–69.

tions. Van Schalkwyk had little legitimacy within the party.[54] Nonetheless, he changed the party name to the New National Party in 1997, introduced new symbols, and insisted on greater autonomy for local organizations (many of which had already collapsed by then).[55]

These belated efforts came to nought. As a departing National Party MP commented acidly, "the modernization drive of the National Party is too little, too late, and does not succeed in renewing the party from within."[56] The party's defense of the old order meant its commitment to democracy was not credible. Programmatic promises of security and education were belied by past state-sponsored torture and murders, and its denial of equal educational opportunities to its citizens prior to 1994. Its all-white candidate lists and its refusal to deal with its past meant it could not reach out to the black majority, while its white constituency grew increasingly impatient with the party's tired rhetoric and lack of transformation. Its support dropped precipitously: The party received 20% of the vote in 1994, but barely gained 6.9% in the 1999 elections. After losing a string of by-elections, the party began to hemorrhage MPs, and never developed parliamentary effectiveness.[57] Eventually, the party collapsed, and merged with the Democratic Party in June 2000.

The cases discussed above exhibit similar causal relationships to those found in the regeneration of the communist successor parties in East Central Europe. The practices of authoritarian regimes led to configurations of elite political resources, which in turn influenced organizational and programmatic choices. Without early and decisive action, new party elites were unable to consolidate their authority or to signal party transformation. In each case, the party's usable past determined which of its public appeals would be credible – hence the PDS's claims of East German representation, the KPRF's appeals to Soviet military glory, or the failure of the National Party's educational or security proposals. However,

---

[54] *Weekly Mail and Guardian*, 29 August 1997. He was quickly discovered to have been a paid agent of the security forces, which discredited him as much as the contempt of his fellow National Party MPs did. Schalkwyk was known as "Kortbroek," or "short pants," to his parliamentary colleagues.

[55] Herbst, Jeffrey. "Prospects for Elite-Driven Democracy in South Africa," *Political Science Quarterly*, Winter 1997/8: 595–615.

[56] Gerhard Koornhof, quoted in *Weekly Mail and Guardian*, 15 October 1998.

[57] The MPs departed despite a stipulation in the constitution that an MP loses his or her seat upon leaving the party. This proviso was the result of joint efforts by the ANC and the NP to retain their power and prevent the rise of the multiple schisms and parties that PR systems have produced elsewhere (including East Central Europe).

without elites with portable skills, and a history of trying to engage the society under the authoritarian regime, full party regeneration was unlikely.

Three implications emerge from these comparative cases. First, they show us that a non-transformed party can attain electoral success and access to governance – such parties still make claims, resonant with large portions of the electorate, that are theirs alone to make. They can gain considerable support as protest parties, from voters disappointed with the new system. Especially if they are not discredited, or if their opposition is weak, such parties do not have to change their appeals or strategies to do well in elections.

Second, the political environment, and the past record of state-society relations, determines what sort of appeals resonate with voters and other parties. For example, the appeals to competence and managerial expertise that served the Polish and Hungarian parties so well were successful thanks largely to the general consensus on reform. In other cases, regional concerns, antisystem protest, or populist appeals could prove far more attractive to the voters.

Third, these cases show that the less radical the break with the old regime, the less the *ancien regime* parties have to transform themselves. On the one hand, the East German and South African parties faced a regime break as radical as the main cases examined in this study – and their failure to regenerate led to their limited long-term access to governance.[58] On the other, the Bulgarian, Romanian, Albanian, and Russian parties gained electoral support and parliamentary effectiveness without a great deal of metamorphosis. Since they retained power, and did not face a strong opposition that could discredit them, they did not have to transform their organizations, and could continue to rely on old networks rather than on new programmatic appeals. The limited competition they faced meant that there was less need to centralize their organizations, while their retention of relatively high support meant there were few reasons to signal transformation.

---

[58] Thus, these additional cases further justify the focus on the parties' capacity to govern, rather than simply electoral support. (Herbert Kitschelt, for example, in his seminal study of social democratic adaptation, chose changes in the rate of relative electoral support as his dependent variable. Kitschelt 1994.) Popular support is one aspect of long-term access to governance, but it says far less about how responsive its programs may be to societal concerns, how legitimate the party is in the eyes of the broader electorate, or whether it can gain parliamentary acceptance and govern in parliamentary coalitions.

Thus, the Czech case may have appeared "overdetermined" at first – each aspect of its communist past and subsequent lack of political resources would seem enough to prevent its regeneration. However, the preceding comparisons show that while internal elite advancement, lack of policy reform, and failure to negotiate with the opposition each lessened the likelihood of successful regeneration, it was the combination of the three that was so devastating. Other parties had elite turnover, for example, without either reform or negotiation (the Bulgarian party) or had reformed somewhat during the communist era without either recruiting new elites or negotiating (as the East German party had done). As a result, they had some skills and usable pasts with which to sustain electoral support.

Theoretical Implications

These patterns have three implications for existing theories of organizational transformation, democratic regime transition, and party politics. First, established political organizations can survive external shocks and rebuild their reputations and support by taking advantage of the fluid institutional constraints that follow such a crisis. They can do so by converting skills and networks gained through past structures and practices, changing public expectations regarding the organization's future behavior. Such regeneration shows both the continuities we would expect in "marginal" change, and the radical turnaround in image and in function we see in more revolutionary situations. It is thus a "mid-level" shift, between the incremental change at the margins and the devastating critical junctures emphasized by historical institutionalist analyses.

As we have seen, changes in organizational *strategies* require transformations in organizational *tools* – the means by which parties and other organizations achieve their aims. Early and decisive action determines the scope and direction of this mid-level transformation. Sequencing, timing, and pacing played a crucial role. Consequently, strategies of party regeneration were most likely to succeed if the organizational transformation preceded other changes, if it was begun early and decisively, and if it was implemented rapidly. The key moments at which the elites exercised their agency and chose among the strategies available to them were the Extraordinary Congresses of 1989–90 – at these congresses, the transition to democracy both provided an impetus for party transformation and loosened the strictures on such change. The more the party organization decisively centralized at this point, the more the party elites could both consolidate their own power and implement transformative strategies during the transition period, setting the stage for subsequent regeneration. Conversely, gradual or belated efforts hindered elite consolidation and a credible commitment to transformation. Organizational continuity meant that actors bent on preserving their position and influence continued to sabotage elite reform proposals and subverted any reformist signals. Programs slid back into references to the glories of the past, campaigns sent inconsistent signals to the voters, and reformists were sabotaged.

Party trajectories tended to be highly contingent at the outset, but became increasingly fixed, as they solidified quickly. There were two parallel aspects to these path-dependent processes. First, organizational change was "reactive" – that is, a series of temporally ordered, causally related events, begun by an initial contingent event (the rise of skilled elites), with decisive causal impact on the outcome (party regeneration).[59] Each stage of party regeneration was made possible by the previous. Skilled and experienced elites streamlined and integrated the decision making within the party. Organizational centralization promoted responsive programs, effective campaigns, and parliamentary discipline. These in turn allowed the parties to seek successfully a broad electorate and gain access to governance.

On the other hand, a "self-reinforcing"[60] process characterized the *credibility* of these efforts, and the parties' attempts to rebuild their reputations. The more usable the party's past, the more credible the initial party change to the voters and to other parties. Such early transformation, in turn, made subsequent changes more feasible, and more credible as evidence of the party's new democratic commitments (belated change was more likely to be seen as opportunistic – an attempt to gather support by any means, rather than a sincere response to a regime crisis).

Thus, communist successor party regeneration demonstrates the processes and dynamics of mid-level change and emphasizes the relevance of timing and sequencing. Neither the processes nor the outcomes of organizational transformation are linear, but they are most dramatic and rapid at the outset, only to decelerate over time.

---

[59] Mahoney, James. "Path Dependence in Comparative-Historical Research," paper presented at the 1999 Annual Meeting of the American Political Science Association, Atlanta, 2–5 September 1999.

[60] Pierson 2000.

Theoretical Implications

A second theoretical implication speaks to the study of democratic transitions and new democratic systems. These continued to be influenced by the active participation of "old regime" actors, and this influence could prove unexpectedly supportive of new democracies. Studies of political transitions have often emphasized the elimination or cooptation of the old elites by the new democratic governments as a way to ensure democratic consolidation. This analysis instead argues that once they are forced to exit from power, authoritarian parties can be left alone to regenerate and prove themselves anew to the voters and to other political actors.

The collapse of one political regime and the transition to the next does not simply create a clean break with the past or a "window of opportunity" through which all actors pass with equal ease. Instead, authoritarian regimes had endowed some of the elite actors with political resources that were a considerable competitive advantage. As a result, even the most dramatic regime collapse will allow certain organizational and institutional continuities, may favor certain actors over others, and need not eliminate all the actors of the *ancien regime* for the new one to consolidate.

These authoritarian legacies can influence democratic developments in specific counterintuitive ways. As already noted, they were surprisingly helpful in creating democratic competitors. Moreover, these legacies also expanded the set of feasible strategic options and influence which ones would be implemented. Finally, legacies reinforced each other – for example, the more skilled the elites, the more they could take advantage of their usable past. The continuities neither determined the outcomes fully, nor were they simply eradicated by the new institutions that arose. Instead, they increased the likelihood of elites successfully "reading" the new environment and implementing strategies that promoted adaptive success.

Nor did the past matter indiscriminately. In disaggregating the "Leninist legacy," this study argued that only certain historical legacies can be argued to make a difference: those which are clear, sustained, and transmitted through personal or institutional mechanisms. These historical legacies exert their greatest influence in the chaos of the transition, reducing uncertainty as shortcuts for decisions and templates for actions.

Nor are all legacies equally long-lived – the legacies of the communist regime waned at different rates. Their "staying power" depended on how costly it was to rely on other sources of information and templates for behavior. Organizational, programmatic, and strategic choices then began to exert their own influence. While their usable past was the initial source of credibility and information, the successor parties' widely documented parliamentary and governmental record after 1989 would eventually supplant this past.

In contrast, individual skills were more likely to persist. They are more "expensive" to supplement or to change – in fact, education and experiences represent a considerable investment for the elites (and for other individuals) and cannot be readily abandoned or denounced. Moreover, the transition to democratic politics reinforced these skills, by calling on the elites to constantly use their existing know-how and expertise in making and implementing decisions. Historical legacies are thus far from linear and consistent in their effects; their influence varies across both categories and time.

The third theoretical implication addresses the literature on the sources of transformation of political parties. Elite actor orientations and strategies have been found to influence heavily regime change and policy shifts alike (Bunce 2000, Scharpf 2000), and this study allowed us to track both what role elites played in the transformation of political parties and how the elites' values and decisions translated into organizational strategies and institutional outcomes. Until now, after all, scholars have chiefly focused on the evolution of political parties in established democracies and stable institutional settings, and the factors that cause these transformations: changes in voter preferences, pressures from political competitors, and structural imperatives. However, this body of work has been less successful at accounting for how parties can react dramatically and to enormous systemic shocks such as the democratic transitions in East Central Europe.

Partly, this is because in new democracies we need to reverse these familiar causalities – the ruling parties of the old regime shaped political competition and electoral choice as much as the other parties and the electorates influenced the communist successor parties. First, party actors chose the very environments in which they would compete, since they influenced institutional choices in the new democracies, in areas as different as constitutional law, parliamentary systems, or market reforms.[61]

[61] Lijphart, Arend, and Waisman, Carlos. *Institutional Design in New Democracies: Eastern Europe and Latin America*. Boulder, CO: Westview Press, 1999. Elster, Offe, and Preuss, 1998. Hellman, Joel. "Winners Take All: The Politics of Partial Reform in Postcommist Transitions," *World Politics*, January 1998: 203–34.

Second, the communist parties had to exit from power in order for consolidated democracy to develop. If they did not leave power during the transition (as in Romania, Bulgaria, and much of the former Yugoslavia), the advantages they accrued in office prevented other political parties from competing freely. Democracy in those countries was neither fully realized, nor was it particularly stable. Third, if the communist successor parties began to regenerate, they effectively monopolized the Left. As a result, no significant social democratic alternatives arose where the successor parties could preempt their moderate leftist rhetoric. In contrast, where the communist parties failed to regenerate, other parties could take up the moderate left side of the political spectrum.

Instead of locating the causal factors exclusively in the political environment, then, the present analysis emphasized the role of elite agency and how elite decisions determined both organizational response and the shaping of political alternatives. It offered a distinct perspective on explaining party strategies in situations where the rules of the game changed overnight and success in the new political system demanded rapid and decisive transformation. As the critical link between the external shock and the parties' internal response, party elites determined both the scope and direction of the transformation as well as the credibility of such efforts. The lack of institutional constraints in the initial transition period meant that elite choices had considerable influence on future developments in several arenas.[62]

Thus, elite decisions, and especially the elites' initial organizational strategies, determined the parties' ability to make responsive appeals, effectively disseminate them, and maintain parliamentary cohesion. As a result, the member-voter trade off was not exogenous, but of the parties' own making. Similarly, the parties' ability to issue broad and responsive appeals successfully depended on earlier centralization of programs and campaigns. These relations were neither inherent in party organization nor an artefact of changing electoral preferences, but the result of earlier elite decisions.

As a final note, it is perhaps misleading to think of party regeneration as a stable outcome. Rather, it is a continuing process, often fraught with internal barriers, public distrust, and limitations of the elites themselves.

---

[62] Shain, Yossi, and Linz, Juan. *Between States*. Cambridge, UK: Cambridge University Press, 1995.

The nature of the public competition, sudden shifts in electoral loyalties, and economic or international shocks lead many political parties to reinvent themselves continually in an attempt to survive and succeed. Nonetheless, some parties have a considerably greater chance of succeeding at this game, by breaking off with a discredited past while making the most of the political resources it provides.

Appendix A

The Content Analysis of Programs

The party program database used in Chapter 3 consists of programmatic documents issued by the parties, and program declarations at party congresses. Several existing accounts of party stances have relied on the views of party supporters or the evaluations of experts to determine the parties' stances.[1] However, supporter views may differ considerably from the parties' stances. In fact, they cannot be assumed to correspond to either the party's official stances or its addressed constituency. Using supporter stances to measure party views also makes it impossible to determine whether the parties are responsive. Therefore, I emphasize content analysis of actual party programs and statements, as this method allows us to examine what the parties' actual messages were.

All programmatic documents available for each party after 1989 were coded in their entirety, translated by the author from the original language. Paragraphs in the party programs were the unit of analysis. This approach loses some reliability and accuracy, in comparison with coding sentences. It also biases the results toward the null hypothesis (that no change occurs in the party programs), since it may gloss over more minute changes within the program.[2] Nevertheless, coding the party programs by paragraph perhaps best reflects the intentions of their framers, since most of the party programs examined were divided into paragraphs, each with a specific

[1] Evans and Whitefield 1995. Kitschelt 1992. Huber, John, and Inglehart, Ronald. "Expert Interpretations of Party Space and Party Locations in 42 Societies," *Party Politics*, Vol. 1, No. 1, 1995: 73–111.

[2] Krippendorf, Klaus. *Content Analysis: An Introduction to its Methodology*. Beverly Hills, CA: Sage, 1980. See also Holsti, Ole. *Content Analysis for the Social Sciences and Humanities*. Reading, MA: Addison-Wesley, 1969. Pool, Ithiel de Sola. *Trends in Content Analysis*. Urbana, IL: University of Illinois Press, 1959. Rosengren, Erik Karl, ed. *Advances in Content Analysis*. Beverly Hills, CA: Sage, 1981.

policy statement or message. The paragraphs were coded both for content (within one of twenty categories) and for emphasis (on a scale of 1 to 4), where appropriate. If more than one firm statement was expressed within a paragraph, these ideas were also coded in an auxiliary column.

Documents Used

Czech Republic

I.89: "Dokumenty mimořadného sjezdu KSČ: akční program Komunistické Strany Československa" [Documents of the extraordinary congress of KSC: the action program of the KSC]. Prague: December 1989.

I.90: "Z uvodního slova Jiřího Machalika" [From the opening speech of Jiří Machalik, the Olomouc Congress]. *Naše Pravda*, 18 October 1990.

II.90: "Programové prohlášení KSČM" [Programmatic declaration of the KSČM]. Schvalené Dokumenty na ustavujicím sjezdu KSČM dně 31 brezna 1990. Prague: KSČM, 1990.

I.91: "Program Komunistické Strany Čech a Moravy." *Hálo Noviny*, 6 September 1991, pp. 5–6.

I.92: "Prohlášení Předsedy KSČM." *Naše Pravda*, 3 June 1992, p. 1.

III.92: "Program KSČM" Dokumenty II. Sjezdu KSČM, approved 13 December 1992.

I.93: "Program KSČM" Dokumenty III. Sjezdu KSČM, approved 13 December 1992 (same document as III.92).

II.93: "Žádnému diktátu nebudeme ustupovat." [We will not cede to any dictat]. *Naše Pravda*, 30 August 1993, pp. 3–4.

I.94: "Teze akčního programu Komunistické strany Čech a Moravy" [Theses of the Action Program of the KSČM]. *Hálo Noviny*, 6 June 1994.

I.95: "Nabízime alternativní čestu vývoje: Výstoupení předsedy ÚV KSČM Miroslava Grebrenička na IV. Sjezdu KSČM" [We will offer an alternative way of development: the speech of the chair of the Central Committee of the KSČM, Miroslav Grebreniček, at the IV Congress of the KSČM]. *Hálo Noviny*, 6 December 1995.

II.95: "Teze volebního programu KSČM: Za občanskŭ a socialní spravedl-nost" [Theses of the electoral program of the KSČM: for civic and social justice]. Dokumenty IV Sjezdu KSCM. Liberec: 2 December 1995.

I.98: "Volební program KSČM 1998" [Electoral program of the KSČM 1998]. Prague: KSČM, 1998.

Slovakia

I.90: "Kto sme a kam smerujeme?" [Who we are and where are we going?]. *Pravda*, 1 June 1990, p. 2.

II.90: "Deklarácia Komunistickej Strany Slovenska" [Declaration of the Communist party of Slovakia]. Dokumenty zjazdu KSS-Strany Demokrat-ickej Ľavice, Prešov, 20–21 Oktobra 1990. Bratislava: ÚV KSS-SDĽ, December 1990.

III.90: "Programová deklarácia Komunistickej Strany Československa" [Programmatic declaration of the Communist Party of Czechoslovakia]. 18 Zjazd KSČS, Praha, 3–4 November 1990.

I.91: "O čo sa usiluje Strana Demokratickej Ľavice" [What the SDĽ is working for]. Dokumenty Prvého Zjazdu SDĽ. Trenčín, 14–15 Decem-bra 1991.

II.91: "O čo sa usiluje Strana Demokratickej Ľavice" [What the SDĽ is working for]. *Príloha Nového Slova*, c. 19, 1991.

I.92: "Príležitosť schopným, istoty pracovitým: volebný program SDĽ" [To the able, their due, to the working, security: the electoral program of SDĽ]. *Pravda*, 15 May 1992, p. 9.

I.93: "Programový dokument: o čo sa usiluje SDĽ" [Programmatic doc-ument: what the SDL is working for]. Dokumenty druhého zjazdu SDĽ. Žilina, 22–3 May 1993.

II.93: "Ekonomický program SDĽ" [Economic program of the SDL]. Príloha SDĽ, *Nove Slovo*, 22 March 1993.

I.94: "Nádej Slovenska: volebný program Spoločnej Voľby" [The Hope of Slovakia: the electoral program of the Common Choice Coalition]. *Pravda*, 9 September 1994, p. 6.

I.95: "O čo sa usiluje SDĽ." Dokumenty Tretieho Zjazdu SDĽ, Poprad, 17–8 February 1995.

I.96: "Akčný program SDĽ" [Action Program of the SDĽ]. Dokumenty Štvrtého Zjazdu SDĽ, Nitra, 27–8 Aprila 1996.

II.96: "Politický program SDĽ" [Political Program of the SDĽ]. Dokumenty Štvrtého Zjazdu SDĽ, Nitra, 27–8 Aprila 1996.

Poland[3]

I.90: "Deklaracja Socjaldemokracji Rzeczpospolitej Polskiej." *Sprawy Bieżące*: Podstawowe Dokumenty Kongresu Założycielskiego Socjaldemokracji Rzeczpospolitej Polskiej [Declaration of the Social Democracy of the Republic of Poland. Current Events: Basic Documents of the Founding Congress of the Socialdemocracy of the Republic of Poland]. Warsaw, 4 February 1990.

II.90: "Stanowiska Kongresu SdRP." *Sprawy Bieżące*: Podstawowe Dokumenty Kongresu Założycielskiego Socjaldemokracji Rzeczpospolitej Polskiej [Stance of the SdRP Congress]. Warsaw, 4 February 1990.

III.90: "Do polskiej lewicy, do wszystkich ludzi postępu" [To the Polish Left, to all people of progress]. *Sprawy Bieżące*: Podstawowe Dokumenty Kongresu Założycielskiego Socjaldemokracji Rzeczpospolitej Polskiej. Warsaw, 4 February 1990.

IV.90: "Przemówienie Aleksandra Kwaśniewskiego na zakończenie obrad Kongresu" [The speech of Aleksander Kwaśniewski at the end of the Congress's deliberations]. *Sprawy Bieżące*: Podstawowe Dokumenty Kongresu Założycielskiego Socjaldemokracji Rzeczpospolitej Polskiej. Warsaw, 4 February 1990.

V.90: "Program społeczno-gospodarczy socjaldemokracjii RP" [The social-economic program of the SdRP]. *Trybuna Ludu*, 19 April 1990, p. 5.

I.91: "Polska postępu, prawa, i demokracji: Program społeczno-gospodarczy Socjaldemokracji Rzeczypospolitej Polskiej" [A Poland of progress, rule of law, and democracy: the social-economic program of the SdRP]. Warsaw, March 1991.

[3] Party meetings: Founding Congress, 28 January 1990; National Convention, 18 May 1991; II Congress, 20 March 1993; National Convention, 23 April 1994; III Congress, December 1996.

II.91: "Demokracja i sprawiedliwość: program społeczno-polityczny SdRP" [Democracy and justice: the socio-political program of the SdRP]. *Trybuna Ludu*, 12 June 1991, p. 32.

I.93: Untitled document, the result of a commission headed by Jerzy Wiatr in the fall of 1992, in charge of formulating new political program, as a result of the "change in the socio-political and economic situation after the parliamentary elections 1991 and the Second Convention of the SdRP in February 1992."

I.93: "Tak dalej być nie musi: program SLD" [It doesn't have to be this way: the program of the Democratic Left Alliance]. *Trybuna Ludu*, 7–16 August 1993.

II.93: "Socjaldemokratyczna alternatywa: Polska demokratyczna, sprawiedliwa, bezpieczna" [The Social Democratic alternative: a democratic, just, safe Poland]. *Biuletyn Wewnatrzpartyjny*, Nr. 6/93.

III.93: "Do polskich organizacji lewicowych!" [To the Polish Left organizations!] II Kongres SdRP, 20 March 1993.

I.97: "Program Socjaldemokracji Rzeczpospolitej Polskiej" [Program of the SdRP]. Warsaw: Verum, March 1997.

Coding Rules

1. Chosen constituency:
   a. All citizens
   b. Nation: ethnic or national groups mentioned (republics in Czechoslovakia)
   c. Class: workers, managers
   d. "losers of transition": specific mention of economic/political changes, and those who have seen their standard of life drop as a result
   e. sociodemographic groups: youth, women, elderly, union members
   f. minorities and minority groups
   g. valence groups: educators, researchers, etc.
   h. members
2. Evaluation of the past:
   a. very positive: no mention of past excesses or errors, emphasis on communist-era accomplishments

b. positive with reservations: mentions of excesses of Stalinist era, or other "mistakes," along with mentions of communist-era accomplishments

c. negative with reservations: mentions of some past accomplishments, but emphasis on past mistakes/mismanagement/corruption

d. very negative: no mention of past accomplishments, emphasis on errors and mistakes

e. no mention

3. Coalitions desired:
   a. with communist parties
   b. with the Left
   c. with democratic parties
   d. with government-making parties
   e. with unions

4. Democracy: competition, pluralism, citizen participation, individual rights, free press, free speech, and association
   a. favorable mentions of democracy, pluralism, party competition, participation of all citizens, democracy as a societal goal
   b. favorable, with reservations about democracy, etc.
   c. negative, with reservations: need to limit some of the above
   d. negative mentions of democracy, etc.
   e. no mention

5. Economy: in each issue area: 1. In favor of first option. 2. In favor of first with reservations. 3. In favor of second with reservations. 4. In favor of second option.
   a. Market (competition, incentives, invisible hand) versus planning (regulation, active role of state, control)
   b. Role of welfare state reduced (sacrifices, taxes as disincentives, new economy demands efficiency) versus welfare (full employment, pensions and benefits, taxes redistributive, full provision of health care, education, housing)
   c. Private property rights (restitution, privatization) versus state ownership (all forms of property to be respected, privatization as robbing society)
   d. Inequalities acceptable (meritocracy) versus egalitarianism (social justice demands equality)

6. Power centralization: strong central state, administrative reform, decentralization of power, local government empowerment, federalization, local self-determination
   a. very positive about the central state, its efficiency, and abilities
   b. positive about the central state, reservations in favor of local government
   c. positive about the local state, reservations about the central state
   d. very positive about the local state
   e. no mention

7. isolation versus internationalism: joining EU/NATO, openness to foreign investment, trade, cultural exchanges
   a. very favorable
   b. favorable with reservations
   c. neutrality
   d. negative with reservations
   e. very negative
   f. very negative with specifications: WTO, COMECON, as better, etc.
   g. no mention

8. secularization: doing away with clericalism, separation of church and state, "special role" of the Church, moral guidance of the Church, traditional respect for the Church, religious values versus secular or individual ones, abortion if mentioned as a church-state issue
   a. very secular
   b. secular with reservations: recognize the role of the Church in society
   c. clerical with reservations: some separation of church and state may be necessary
   d. very clerical

9. Nationalism: traditional/national way of life, traditional/national morals and values, identification of nation as priority, versus modernization, liberalization
   a. nation as ultimate value
   b. nation valued, with reservations: need for openness to the world and modernization
   c. cosmopolitan/modernizing with reservations: need to respect the nation
   d. have to drop outdated views/traditions regarding the nation

10. New Left concerns: in each case: 1. Main goal of party, 2. One goal of party, 3. Not a priority, 4. Not relevant.
    a. women's issues
    b. environment
    c. quality of life (in general)
    d. arts and leisure
    e. technical development/research
11. Expertise/managerial experience/skilled politicians and managers
    a. main party advantage
    b. one of party's advantages
    c. mentioned in passing
    d. defensive posture
12. National defense: need for more build-up of arms, to make the army more efficient: 1. Yes, 2. No.
13. Constitutional reform: need for a new constitution, content thereof marked
14. Party self-identification
    a. national communist tradition
    b. socialist tradition
    c. social democratic
    d. modern Left
    e. specific mentions of Socialist International
15. Relationship to past
    a. emphasis on continuity
    b. some new, but carry on old party traditions
    c. some continuity, but new party
    d. completely different party
16. Importance of members versus the electorate
    a. emphasis on members
    b. members slightly more than electorate
    c. electorate, others matter more
    d. members don't matter at all, electorate does
17. Evaluation of status quo
    a. very bad ("catastrophic," "tragic", etc.)
    b. bad
    c. good
    d. very good
18. Mentions of "autonomy"
    a. enterprise

The Content Analysis of Programs

     b. worker
     c. union
     d. institutions
     e. on societal level
19. Party self-characterization
     a. mass party, active in society outside of parliament
     b. internal democracy, discussion important
     c. electoral party
     d. programmatic party (i.e., organization does not matter, achieving goals does)
20. Party self-defense
     a. right to exist
     b. anti-decommunization

Appendix B

The Quantitative Analysis of Electorates

This appendix discusses the sources and methodology for the analyses in Chapters 3 and 4: the data, multinomial logit techniques, and the LERS machine learning algorithm. The data on public demands and priorities comes from the "Party Systems and Electoral Alignments in East Central Europe" database of public opinion surveys. Available in machine-readable data form, the database comprises public opinion polls in Poland, the Czech Republic, Slovakia, and Hungary regarding sociodemographics, evaluations of parties and the market transformation, and political identities. The project is supervised by Gábor Tóka of the Central European University and employed several polling agencies: CBOS in Poland, STEM in the Czech Republic and Slovakia, and Median in Hungary. The samples were representative of the adult population in each country. In Poland, clustered random sampling was used, with sample sizes of 149, 1,188, 1,468, 1,209, 1,162, 1,173, and 1,173. In Czech Republic and Slovakia, random clustered sampling was used in 1992, and quota sampling thereafter. The Czech sampling sizes were 815, 939, 1,117, 1,562, 1,515, 1,291, 1,569, 1,443, and 1,595. The Slovak samples were 712, 920, 871, 845, 757, 1,213, and 1,027. The Hungarian samples used clustered random sampling, and the sample size was 1,200 across the years, except for 1,196 in June 1995.

These population surveys were conducted annually in 1992–6 in the region. Since they started in 1992, we cannot trace the crucial transformations that took place in the party images in 1989–91, but can judge the evolution of their outcomes. Another limitation is that that respondents had to choose from among several categories rather than providing their own answers and priorities. Therefore, to supplement these findings, I used public opinion data gathered by several polling agencies in each country under consideration. While the methodologies differ in sampling techniques and questions, indirect comparisons are both feasible and fruitful.

First, respondents were asked how important the following issues were, and which parties were likely to achieve them: ensuring democracy, providing competent managers, maintaining political stability, decommunization, increasing the influence of the Church, strengthening patriotism, helping private enterprise, speeding up privatization, reducing unemployment, increasing pensions and benefits, and decreasing the economic burden. Second, I tested the effect of political opinions and sociodemographic variables, such as satisfaction with democracy, self-placements on left-right and liberal-conservative scales, age, residence, level of education (which also serves as a proxy for earnings potential), and church attendance on party support, using multinomial logit analysis (MNL).

MNL simultaneously estimates the models and outcomes for all the political parties. The dependent variable, "party support" (using the standard Michigan School question of "which party would you vote for if a vote were held today" question) is a categorical nominal variable. MNL allows us to compare simultaneously party choice, relative to one another, in comparison to the reference group – the party perceived by the communist successor party as its biggest rival. We cannot simply run as many individual logistic regressions as there are parties, since the outcomes are not independent of each other. Although MNL results present some difficulty in interpretation (since they represent the relative effect of each independent variable on the log/odds ratio of a given party in comparison to the reference category), one way to consider them is to think of the "coefficient" as the probability of supporting the party, relative to comparison category, given the level of the independent variable. The 95% confidence interval traces whether changes over time and comparisons among the parties can be attributed with reasonable certainty to underlying population parameters.

Finally, I combine the stances on political goals and an expanded set of sociodemographic factors (including perceived satisfaction with the new status quo, prior party membership, union membership, and occupation) to induce "rules" regarding party support using machine-learning techniques. The LERS (Learning from Examples using Rough Sets) system uses a machine learning algorithm to induce rules from the data set about the combinations of factors that lead to a "decision" (here, party support). The input data set is consistent if every pair of input examples (vectors of all attribute values) belong to the same concept (i.e., the same grouping of independent variables does not produce more than one outcome). The strength of a given rule is the measure of how well the rule has performed during "training" (the total number of examples correctly classified by the rule for a subset of the data). Results from the initial training subdata set are then validated using tenfold crossvalidation. Instead of using standard errors or confidence intervals, the "error rate" shows us the improvement over guessing the outcomes. The advantage of using rule induction is that the assumptions about the data, necessary for regression or logistic regression analyses, are relaxed. For example, not only are the results not skewed by any collinearity of the variables, but the rules also take account of the concurrence and possible interaction effects among the variables.

Rules for Party Support, Induced via the LERS Machine Learning Algorithm

Interpret figures in parentheses as follows:

- The first number is the count of variables in the rule.
- The second is the number of cases for which the rule works correctly (or the rule's "strength").
- The third figure is the number of cases that fit the rule.

The ratio of the third to the second number is the probability of the rule's validity. In each case, three strongest rules are represented.

Poland

1992: Inconsistency level: 0, error rate: 73.89% (error rate if guessing: 96.43%)
(4,8,8): believes reducing inequalities is very important & believes strengthening patriotism is very important & female & self-placement on Left-Right scale: 1
(3,8,8): believes abortion rights are very important & previously voted for the party & self-placement on Left-Right scale: 1

1993: Inconsistency level: 0, error rate: 71% (error rate if guessing: 96%)
(5,7,7): believes competent managers in charge are very important & believes abortion rights are very important & university education &

attends church a few times a year & believes decommunization is not desirable

(3,17,17): believes abortion rights are very important & previously voted for the party & self-placement on Left-Right scale: 1

(4,7,7): believes democracy and free speech are very important & believes strengthening patriotism is very important & self-placement on Left-Right scale: 1 & self-placement on Liberal-Conservative scale: 0

1994: Inconsistency level: 0, error rate: 63.77% (error rate if guessing: 96.43%)

(3,13,13): non-union member & previously voted for the party & self-placement on Left-Right scale: 2

(6,9,9): believes competent managers in charge are very important & not very satisfied with democracy & female & believes abortion rights are very important & believes ensuring political stability is very important & previously voted for the party

(5,7,7): non-communist party member & believes increasing pensions and benefits is very important & secondary education & self-placement on Left-Right scale: 1 & skilled, manual worker

1995: Inconsistency level: 0, error rate: 66.24% (error rate if guessing: 94.74%)

(3,17,17): non-communist party member & previously voted for the party & self-placement on Liberal-Conservative scale: 1

(4,7,7): non-union member & believes abortion rights are very important & communist party member & very interested in politics

(6,17,17): believes reducing unemployment is very important & believes competent managers in charge are very important & some interest in politics & believes abortion rights are very important & believes increasing the influence of the Church is undesirable & self-placement on Left-Right scale: 1

Czech Republic

1992: Inconsistency level: 0, error rate: 56.32% (error rate if guessing: ~96%)

(6,32,32): believes reducing the economic burden is very important & believes preserving friendly Czech-Slovak relations is very important & believes better health care and education are very important & believes the rapid separation of Czechoslovakia is undesirable & believes abortion rights are very important & previously voted for the party

(3,11,11): believes competent managers in charge are very important & previously voted for the party & believes reducing unjust inequalities is very important

(4,14,14): previously voted for the party & never attends church & believes preventing moral deterioration is very important & some interest in politics

1993: Inconsistency level: .18%, error rate: 56.49% (error rate if guessing: ~96%)

(3,14,14): member of apolitical union & previously voted for the party & not satisfied at all with democracy

(5,11,11): previously voted for the party & communist party member & believes preserving friendly Czech-Slovak relations is very important & believes decommunization is undesirable & not very satisfied with democracy

(5,10,10): previously voted for the party & female & state enterprise employee & retired & elementary education

1994: Inconsistency level: 0, error rate: 64.42% (error rate if guessing: ~96%)

(5,17,17): previously voted for the party & believes competent managers in charge are very important & believes increasing pensions and benefits is very important & non-union member & believes decommunization is undesirable

(5,10,10): communist party members & previously voted for the party & state enterprise employee & elementary education & believes decommunization is undesirable

(4,10,10): never attends church & previously voted for the party & believes reducing unemployment is very important & public sector employee

1995: Inconsistency level: 0, error rate: 60.88% (error rate if guessing: ~96%)

(3,15,15): never attends church & believes decommunization is undesirable & previously voted for the party

(4,14,14): communist party member & retired & non-union member & self-placement on Left-Right scale: 1

(4,14,14): non-union member & 61+ years old & communist party member & previously voted for the party

1996: Inconsistency level: 0, error rate: 64.13% (error rate if guessing: ~96%). Previous party vote was not asked in this poll, so it is not included in the analysis.

(4,17,17): communist party member & self-placement on Left-Right scale: 1 & believes ensuring political stability is very important & some interest in politics

(4,16,16): never attends church & communist party member & believes increasing pensions and benefits is very important & self-placement on Left-Right scale: 1

(3,13,13): female & believes protecting democracy and freedom of speech is important & self-placement on Left-Right scale: 1

(5,11,11): never attends church & not very satisfied with democracy & member of apolitical union & believes ensuring political stability is very important & believes decommunization is undesirable

Slovakia

1992: Inconsistency level: 0, error rate: 57.3% (error rate if guessing: ~96%)

(5,19,19): believes better health care and education are very important & believes preserving friendly Czech-Slovak relations is very important & believes environmental protection is very important & previously voted for the party & self-placement on Left-Right scale: 1

(4,12,12): believes environmental protection is very important & member of apolitical union & previously voted for the party & communist party member

(5,8,8): believes preventing moral deterioration is very important & believes defending human rights and individual freedoms is very important & believes the rapid separation of Czechoslovakia is undesirable & believes increasing the influence of the Church is undesirable & believes environmental protection is important

1993: Inconsistency level: 0, error rate: 61.42% (error rate if guessing: ~96%)

(5,15,15): male & believes competent managers in charge are very important & believes preserving friendly Czech-Slovak relations is very important & not very satisfied with democracy & self-placement on Left-Right scale: 2

(3,14,14): believes democracy and free speech are important & female & previously voted for the party

(4,13,13): believes increasing pensions and benefits is very important & believes strengthening patriotism is very important & previously voted for the party & male

1994: Inconsistency level: 0, error rate: 51.78% (error rate if guessing: ~96%)
(3,11,11): believes competent managers in charge are very important & previously voted for the party & self-placement on Left-Right scale: 2
(3,6,6): believes democracy and free speech are very important & university education & previously voted for the party

1995: Inconsistency level: 0, error rate: 57.3% (error rate if guessing: ~96%)
(2,22,22): previously voted for the party & 45–60 years old
(5,12,12): not very satisfied with democracy & believes reducing the economic burden is very important & previously voted for the party & believes increasing pensions and benefits is very important & is interested in politics
(5,12,12): not very satisfied with democracy & full-time employee & member of apolitical union & male & previously voted for the party

1996: Inconsistency level: 0, error rate: 59.10% (error rate if guessing: ~96%)
(4,13,13): non-union member & male & previously voted for the party & retired
(4,12,12): not very satisfied with democracy & believes protecting democracy and freedom of speech is & believes strengthening patriotism is important & previously voted for the party
(4,11,11): believes competent managers in charge are very important & 31–45 years old & is interested in politics & previously voted for the party

Hungary

1992: Inconsistency level: 0, error rate: 71.67% (error rate if guessing: ~96%)
(5,14,14): believes better health care and education are very important & believes reducing unjust inequalities is very important & believes reducing unemployment is very important & not satisfied at all with democracy & previously voted for the party

(5,10,10): believes reducing the economic burden is very important & believes reducing unjust inequalities is very important & full-time employee & communist party member & previously voted for the party
(3,8,8): believes it is very important to give the police proper means to fight crime & previously voted for the party & university education

1993: Inconsistency level: 0, error rate: 72.17% (error rate if guessing: ~96%)

(3,29,29): believes reducing the economic burden is very important & communist party member & previously voted for the party
(6,11,11): believes democracy and free speech are very important & believes increasing pensions and benefits is very important & non-union member & communist party member & male & very interested in politics
(4,8,8): believes competent managers in charge are very important & communist party member & very interested in politics & self-placement on Liberal-Conservative scale: 2

1994: Inconsistency level: 0, error rate: 77.67% (error rate if guessing: ~96%)

(4,7,7): believes helping private enterprises is important & believes reducing the economic burden is very important & non-union member & believes decommunization is undesirable
(5,7,7): believes competent managers in charge are very important & female & believes increasing the influence of the Church is undesirable & believes decommunization is undesirable & elementary education
(7,6,6): believes competent managers in charge are very important & believes reducing unemployment is very important & believes reducing the economic burden is very important & almost never attends church & communist party member & male & believes decommunization is undesirable

1995: Inconsistency level: 0, error rate: 70.65% (error rate if guessing: ~96%)

(4,13,13): believes competent managers in charge are very important & previously voted for the party & communist party member & higher administration/manager
(5,10,10): believes competent managers in charge are very important & previously voted for the party & female & lives in city with 2,000–19,999 inhabitants & incomplete elementary education

(6,8,8): previously voted for the party & non-communist party member & believes democracy and free speech are very important & full-time employee & 31–45 years old & believes increasing the influence of the Church is undesirable

Appendix C

Structures of Competition

Table C.1 presents two indices of the structures of competition and the relevant electoral institutions. First, the index of fractionalization measures the concentration of competitive strength among parties. The higher its value, the more dispersed the seats among parties in parliament. Second, the effective number of legislative parties measures the number of "relevant" parties in parliament necessary to form a coalition.

Table C.1. *Party fragmentation and electoral institutions.*

Nation/ year	Number of parties in elections	Number of elected parties	Index of fractioning[a]	Effective legislative parties[b]	Electoral system	Threshold (%)	District magnitude
Czech 1990	12	4	.55	2.2	PR	5%	8–32 (25 avg)
Czech 1992	20	6	.79	4.8	PR	5%	8–32 (25 avg)
Czech 1996	20	6	.76	4.1	PR	5%	8–32 (25 avg)
Czech 1998	18	5	.73	3.7	PR	5%	8–32 (25 avg)
Slovakia 1990	10	7	.80	5.0	PR	3%	12–50 (37.5 avg)
Slovakia 1992	23	5	.69	3.2	PR	5%	12–50 (37.5 avg)
Slovakia 1994	17	7	.77	4.4	PR	5%	12–50 (37.5 avg)
Slovakia 1998	17	6	.79	4.8	PR	5%	12–50 (37.5 avg)
Poland 1991	111	29	.90	10.2	PR	0%	7–17 (10.6 avg)
Poland 1993	35	6	.75	3.9	PR	5%	3–17 (7.3 avg)
Poland 1997	21	5	.67	3.0	PR	5%	3–17 (7.3 avg)
Hungary 1990	59	7	.71	3.5	Mixed SMD/PR	4%	4–28 (6 avg)
Hungary 1994	43	6	.65	2.8	Mixed SMD/PR	5%	4–28 (6 avg)
Hungary 1998	33	6	.74	3.8	Mixed SMD/PR	5%	4–28 (6 avg)

Notes: [a] As measured by $1 - \Sigma S_i^2$, where S_i is the seat share. The index measures the concentration of competitive strength among parties. A party system dominated by one party alone would have a fractioning index of 0, a two-party system with an even split of seats an index of .5, and so on. The higher the number, the more dispersed the seats, and the less strong any given party in the parliament. The average fractioning of a system under proportional representation is .70. See Rae, Douglas. *The Political Consequences of Electoral Laws.* New Haven, CT: Yale University Press, 1971, and esp. p. 98.
[b] As measured by $1/\Sigma S_i^2$, where S_i is the seat share of the *i*th party.

Note: Figures for Slovak and Czech elections in 1990 and in 1992 are for the National Councils in each country.
Source: Electoral commissions in each country, Rose, R., Munro, N., and Mackie, T. T. *Elections in Central and Eastern Europe,* http://www.strath.ac.uk/Departments/CSPP. Stanclik, Katarzyna. "Electoral Law and the Formation of Political Party Systems in the New East European Democracies," paper presented at the Annual Meeting of the American Political Science Association, Washington, DC, 28–31 August 1997, Parliamentary Documents Center, Parliamentary Indicators Series http://www.uncg.edu/psc/pdc/proportional.html.

Bibliography

Ágh, Attila. "Organizational Change in the Hungarian Socialist Party." Hungarian Electronic Library (gopher://gopher.mek.iif.hu:7070/00/porta/szint/tarsad/politika/hungpol/agh76.hun), 1994a.

"The Hungarian Party System and Party Theory in the Transition of Central Europe," *Journal of Theoretical Politics*, April 1994b: 217–38.

The Emergence of East Central European Parliaments: The First Steps. Budapest: Hungarian Centre of Democracy Studies, 1994c.

"Partial Consoliation of the East-Central European Parties," *Party Politics*, Vol. 1, No. 4, 1995a: 491–514.

ed. *The First Parliament: 1990–94*. Budapest: Hungarian Center for Democracy Foundation, 1995b.

"Defeat and Success as Promoters of Party Change," *Party Politics*, Vol. 3, No. 3, 1997a: 427–44.

"Parliaments as Policymaking Bodies in East Central Europe: The Case of Hungary," *International Political Science Review*, Vol. 18, No. 4, 1997b: 417–32.

"Parliamentary Committees in East Central Europe," in Longley, Lawrence, and Davidson, Roger, eds. *The New Roles of Parliamentary Committees*. Portland, OR: Frank Cass, 1998.

"Party Discipline in the Hungarian Parliament," in Bowler, Shaun, Farrell, David M., and Katz, Richard S., eds. *Party Discipline and Parliamentary Government*. Columbus, OH: Ohio State Press, 1999.

"Party Formation Process and the 1998 Elections in Hungary: Defeat as Promoter of Change for the HSP," *East European Politics and Societies*, Winter 2000: 288–315.

Ágh, Attila, and Kurtán, Sandor, eds. *The First Parliament*. Budapest: Centre for Democracy Studies, 1995.

Aldrich, Howard. *Organizations and Environments*. Englewood Cliffs, NJ: Prentice Hall, 1979.

Aldrich, John. "A Downsian Spatial Model with Party Activism," *American Political Science Review*, 1983: 947–90.

Anderson, Christopher. "The Dynamics of Public Support for Coalition Governments," *Comparative Political Studies*, October 1995: 350–83.

Andorka, Rudolf. "Regime Transitions in Hungary in the 20th Century," *Governance*, July 1993: 358–71.

Appel, Hilary. "The Ideological Determinants of Liberal Economic Reform: The Case of Privatization," *World Politics*, July 2000: 520–49.

Arato, Andrew. "Constitution and Continuity in the East European Transitions. Part I: Continuity and its Crisis," *Constellations*, January 1994: 92–112.

"Two Lectures on the Electoral Victory of the Hungarian Socialists," *Constellations*, January 1995, pp. 75–80.

Arthur, Brian. *Increasing Returns and Path Dependence in Economy*. Ann Arbor MI: University of Michigan Press, 1994.

Ash, Timothy Garton. *The Uses of Adversity*. New York: Vintage, 1990.

Barany, Zoltan. "Socialist-Liberal Government Stumbles Through Its First Year," *Transition*, 28 July 1995: 64–9.

Barany, Zoltan, and Volgyes, Ivan, ed. *The Legacies of Communism in Eastern Europe*. Baltimore, MD: Johns Hopkins Press, 1995.

Bartlett, David L. "Democracy, Institutional Change, and Stabilisation Policy in Hungary," *Europe-Asia Studies*, No. 1, 1996: 47–83.

Bauman, Zygmunt. "Living Without an Alternative," *Political Quarterly*, January–March 1991: 35–44.

Berend, T. Ivan. "Alternatives of Transformation: Choices and Determinants – East-Central Europe in the 1990s," in Crawford, Beverly, ed. *Markets, States, and Democracy*. Boulder, CO: Westview Press, 1995: 130–49.

Central and Eastern Europe, 1944–1993: Detour from the Periphery to the Periphery. New York: Cambridge University Press, 1996.

Bermeo, Nancy. "Democracy and the Lessons of Dictatorship," *Comprative Politics*, July 1992: 463–76.

Bernhard, Michael. "Institutional Choice after Communism: A Critique of Theory-Building in an Empirical Wasteland," *East European Politics and Societies*, Summer 2000: 316–47.

Betz, Hans-Georg, and Welsh, Helga. "The PDS in the New German Party System," *German Politics*, December 1995: 92–111.

Biberaj, Elez. *Albania in Transition*. Boulder, CO: Westview Press, 1998.

Bielasiak, Jack. "Substance and Process in the Development of Party Systems in East Central Europe," *Communist and Post-Communist Studies*, Vol. 30, No. 1, 1997: 23–44.

Blahož, Josef. "Political Parties in the Czech and Slovak Federal Republics: First Steps Toward the Rebirth of Democracy," in Kay Lawson, ed. *How Political Parties Work: Perspectives from Within*. London: Praeger, 1994: 229–48.

Blahož, Josef, Brokl, Lubomír, and Mansfeldová, Zdenka. "Czech Political Parties and Cleavages after 1989," in Lawson, Kay, Römmele, Andrea, and Georgi Karasimeonov, eds. *Cleavages, Parties, and Voters*. Westport, CT: Praeger, 1999.

Błażyca, George. "The Politics of the Economic Transformation," in White, Stephen, Batt, Judy, and Lewis, Paul, eds. *Developments in Central and East European Politics 2*. Durham, NC: Duke University Press, 1998.

Bibliography

Błażyca, George, and Rapacki, Ryszard. "Continuity and Change in Polish Economic Policy: The Impact of the 1993 Election," *Europe-Asia Studies*, No. 1, 1996: 85–100.

Blyth, Mark. "From Ideas and Institutions to Ideas and Interests: Beyond the Usual Suspects?" Paper presented at the Eleventh Conference of Europeanists, Baltimore, MD, 26–8 February 1998.

Bowler, Shaun, Farrell, David M., and Katz, Richard S. *Party Discipline and Parliamentary Government*. Columbus, OH: Ohio State Press, 1999.

Bozóki, András. "Hungary's Road to Systemic Change: The Opposition Roundtable," in Kiraly, Bela, ed. *Lawful Revolution in Hungary, 1989–94*. Boulder, CO: Social Science Monographs, distrib. by New York: Columbia University Press, 1995.

Brokl, Lubomír, and Mansfeldová, Zdenka. "Political Parties and Their Programs," *East Europe 2000: The Czech Republic Background Studies*. Prague: Institute of Sociology, Academy of Sciences of the Czech Republic, May 1993.

Brown, J. F. *Eastern Europe and Communist Rule*. Durham, NC: Duke University Press, 1988.

The Establishment of Communist Regimes in Eastern Europe, 1944–1949. Boulder, CO: Westview Press, 1997.

Brumberg, Abraham, ed. *Poland: Genesis of a Revolution*. New York: Random House, 1983.

Brus, Włodzimierz. "Economy and Politics: the Fatal Link" in Brumberg, Abraham, ed. *Poland: Genesis of a Revolution*. New York: Random House, 1983: 26–41.

Bruszt, László. "Transformative Politics: Social Costs and Social Peace in East Central Europe," *East European Politics and Societies*, Winter 1992: 54–72.

Bruszt, László, and Stark, David. "Remaking the Political Field in Hungary," *Journal of International Affairs*, Summer 1991: 201–45.

Budge, Ian, and Farlie, Dennis J. *Explaining and Predicting Elections*. London: Allen & Unwin, 1983.

Budge, Ian, and Keman, Hans. *Parties and Democracy: Coalition Formation and Government Functioning in Twenty States*. Oxford, UK: Oxford University Press, 1990.

Budge, Ian, and Laver, Michael. "The Policy Basis of Government Coalitions: A Comparative Investigation," *British Journal of Poltiical Science*, October 1993.

Budge, Ian, Robertson, David, and Hearl, Derek, eds. *Ideology, Strategy, and Party Change: Spatial Analyses of Post-War Election Programmes in 19 Democracies*. Cambridge, UK: Cambridge University Press, 1987.

Bukowski, Charles, and Cichock, Mark, eds. *Prospects for Change in Socialist Systems*. New York: Praeger, 1987.

Bunce, Valerie. "The Return of the Left and the Future of Democracy in Central and Eastern Europe," paper presented at the Tenth International Conference of Europeanists, Chicago, 14–6 March 1996.

Subversive Institutions. Cambridge, UK: Cambridge University Press, 1999.

"The Political Economy of Post-Socialism," *Slavic Review*, Winter 1999: 756–93.

"Comparative Democratization: Big and Bounded Generalizations," *Comparative Political Studies*, Vol. 33, No. 6/7, August/September 2000: 703–34.

Bunce, Valerie, and Csanadi, Maria. "Uncertainty in Transition: Post-Communists in Hungary," *East European Politics and Societies*, Spring 1993: 240–73.

Bútorová, Zora. "The Citizen as Respondent and a Voter: Reflection on Election Polling," in Szomolányi, Sonia, and Mesežnikov, Grigorij, eds. *Slovakia: Parliamentary Elections 1994*. Bratislava: Slovak Political Science Association and Friedrich Ebert Foundation, 1995.

CBOS, *Społeczna Ocena Działalności Instytucji Politycznych*. Komunikat z Badań, October 1990. Warsaw, Poland.

Preferencje wyborcze w czerwcu 1993. Komunikat z Badań, June 1993. Warsaw, Poland.

Wyborcy zwycięskich partii. Komunikat z Badań, December 1993. Warsaw, Poland.

Elektoraty partii politycznych rok po wyborach. Komunikat z Badań, October 1994. Warsaw, Poland.

Instytucje publiczne w opinii społecznej. Komunikat z Badań, November 1994. Warsaw, Poland.

Wybory Parlamentarne–potencjalne elektoraty Komunikat z Badań, June 1995, Warsaw, Poland.

Centrum pre Socialnu analizu. *Slovensko pred vol'bami*. April 1992, Bratislava, Slovakia.

Česky Statistický Úřád, *Volby do Poslanecké Sněmovny Parlamentu České Republiky 1996*, Praha, June 1996.

Česky Statistický Úřád, *Volby do ČNR 5 a 6 června 1992*, Praha, June 1992.

Chirot, Daniel, ed. *The Crisis of Leninism and the Decline of the Left: The Revolutions of 1989*. Seattle, WA: University of Washington Press.

Ciganek, František, ed. *Kronika Demokratického Parlamentu 1989–1992*. Prague: Cesty, 1992.

Cline, Mary. "The Demographics of Party Support in Poland," *RFE/RL Research Report*, 10 September 1993.

Collier, David, and Mahon, James. "Conceptual 'Stretching' Revisited: Adopting Categories in Comparative Analysis," *American Political Science Review*, December 1993: 845–55.

Collier, Ruth Berins, and Collier, David. *Shaping the Political Arena*. Princeton, NJ: Princeton University Press, 1991.

Colton, Timothy, and Hough, Jerry, eds. *Growing Pains*. Washington, DC: Brookings Press, 1998.

Comisso, Ellen. "Where Have We Been and Where Are We Going," in W. Crotty, ed. *Political Science: Looking to the Future*. Evanston, IL: NW University Press, 1991: 77–122.

"Legacies of the Past or New Institutions?" *Comparative Political Studies*, Vol. 28, No. 2, July 1995: 200–38.

Commission on Security and Cooperation in Europe. *Albania's Parliamentary Elections of 1997*, July 1997.

Conradt, David, ed. *Germany's New Politics*, Providence, RI: Berghahn Books, 1995.

Conway, Margaret. "Political Parties and Political Mobilization," *American Review of Politics*, Winter 1993: 549–63.

Cotta, Maurizio. "Building Party System After the Dictatorship: The East European Cases in a Comparative Perspective," in Pridham, Geoffrey, and Vanhanen, Tatu, eds. *Democratization in Eastern Europe: Domestic and International Perspectives*. London: Routledge, 1994.

Cox, Gary W. "Electoral Equilibrium Under Alternative Voting Institutions," *American Journal of Political Science*, February 1987: 82–108.

Making Votes Count. Cambridge, UK: Cambridge University Press, 1997.

Crawford, Beverly, ed. *Markets, States, and Democracy*. Boulder, CO: Westview Press, 1995.

Crawford, Beverly, and Lijphart, Arend. "Explaining Political and Economic Post-Communist Eastern Europe," *Comparative Political Studies*, Vol. 28, July 1995: 171–99.

Liberalization and Leninist Legacies: Comparative Perspectives on Democratic Transitions. Berkeley, CA: University of California Press, 1997.

Cziria, Ludovit. "The Czech and Slovak Republics" in Thirkell, John, Scase, Richard, and Vickerstaff, Sarah, ed.. *Labor Relations and Political Change in Eastern Europe: A Comparative Perspective*. Ithaca, NY: Cornell University Press, 1995: 61–80.

Dahrendorf, Ralf. *Society and Democracy in Germany*. New York: W.W. Norton and Co., 1967.

Daalder, Hans, and Mair, Peter, eds. *Western European Party Systems*. London: Sage Publications, 1983.

Dalton, Russell J., ed. *Germans Divided: The 1994 Bundestag Elections and the Evolution of the German Party System*. Oxford, UK: Berg, 1996.

Davidheiser, Evelyn. "Right and Left in the Hard Opposition," in Colton, Timothy, and Hough, Jerry, eds. *Growing Pains*. Washington, DC: Brookings Press, 1998: 177–209.

Dawisha, Karen. *Eastern Europe, Gorbachev, and Reform*. Cambridge, UK: Cambridge University Press, 1988.

Dehnel-Sznyc, Małgorzata, and Stachura, Jadwiga. *Gry Polityczne: Orientacje Na Dziś*. Warsaw: Volumen, 1991.

Dennett, Daniel. *Elbow Room: The Varieties of Free Will Worth Wanting*. Cambridge, MA: MIT Press, 1993.

DiPalma, Giuseppe. "Legitimation from the Top to Civil Society," *World Politics*, Spring 1991.

Dixit, Avinash, and Nalebuff, Barry. *Thinking Strategically*. New York: W.W. Norton and Company, 1991.

Dodd, Lawrence. *Coalitions in Parliamentary Government*. Princeton, NJ: Princeton University Press, 1976.

Dogan, Mattei. *Pathways to Power*. Boulder, CO: Westview Press, 1989.

Döring, Herbert, ed. *Parliaments and Majority Rule in Western Europe*. Frankfurt: Campus Verlag, 1995.

Downs, Anthony. *An Economic Theory of Democracy*. New York: Harper and Brothers, 1957.

Inside Bureaucracy. Prospect Heights, IL: Waveland Press, 1994.

Duverger, Maurice. *Political Parties*. London: Methuen, 1954.

Dvořaková, Vladimira, and Gerloch, Aleš, eds. *Krystalizace struktury politckých stran v České republice po roce 1989*. Prague: Czech Political Science Association, 1996.

Easton, David. *Systems Analysis of Political Life*. New York: John Wiley & Sons, 1965.

Edinger, Lewis. "Post-Totalitarian Leadership: Elites in the German Federal Republic," *American Political Science Review*, Vol. 54, March 1960: 58–82.

Ekiert, Grzegorz. "Democratization Processes in East Central Europe: Theoretical Reconsiderations," *British Journal of Political Science*, July 1991: 285–313.

"Peculiarities of Post-Communist Politics: The Case of Poland," *Studies in Comparative Communism*, December 1992: 341–61.

The State Against Society: Political Crises and Their Aftermath in East Central Europe. Princeton, NJ: Princeton University Press, 1996.

Ekiert, Grzegorz, and Kubik, Jan. "Collective Protest in Post-Communist Poland: A Research Report," *Communist and Post-Communist Studies*, June 1998: 91–117.

"Contentious Politics in New Democracies: East Germany, Hungary, Poland, and Slovakia, 1989–1993," *World Politics* July 1998: 547–581.

Eldersveld, Samuel. *Political Parties. A Behavioral Analysis*. Chicago: Rand McNally, 1964.

Elster, Jon. *Nuts and Bolts for the Social Sciences*. Cambridge, UK: Cambridge University Press, 1989.

Political Psychology. Cambridge, UK: Cambridge University Press, 1993.

Ulysses and the Sirens. Cambridge, UK: Cambridge University Press, 1979/1996.

Elster, Jon, Offe, Klaus, and Presuss, Ulrich Klaus. *Institutional Design in Post-Communist Societies: Rebuilding the Ship at Sea*. Cambridge, UK: Cambridge University Press, 1998.

Epstein, Leon. *Political Parties in Western Democracies*. New York: Praeger, 1967.

Eulau, Heinz, and Czudnowski, Moshe, eds. *Elite Recruitment in Democratic Polities*. New York: Sage Publications, 1976.

Evans, Geoffrey, and Whitefield, Stephen. "Identifying the Bases of Party Competition in Eastern Europe," *British Journal of Political Science*, October 1993: 521–48.

"Economic Ideology and Political Success: Communist-Successor Parties in the Czech Republic, Slovakia and Hungary Compared," *Party Politics*. October 1995: 565–78.

Fearon, James. "Counterfactuals and Hypothesis Testing in Political Science," *World Politics*, Vol. 43, No. 2, 1991: 169–95.

Federalní Shromaždeni VI. Volební Obdobi. Prague: 1990.

Federalní Shromaždeni VII. Volební Obdobi. Prague: 1992.

Fish, Steven. "The Determinants of Economic Reform in the Post-Communist World," *East European Politics and Societies*, Spring 1998: 31–77.

Flikke, Geir. "Patriotic Left-Centrism: The Zigzags of the Communist Party of the Russian Federation," *Europe-Asia Studies*, March 1999: 275–98.

Bibliography

FOCUS. "Aktualne Problemy Slovenska" [Current Problems of Slovakia]. 1993–6. Bratislava, Slovakia.

Franklin, Mark, and Mackie, Thomas. "Familiarity and Inertia in the Formation of Governing Coalitions in Parliamentary Democracies," *British Journal of Political Science*, July 1983: 275–98.

Gabal, Ivan, ed. *The 1990 Election to the Czechoslovakian Federal Assembly*. Berlin: Sigma, 1996.

Gallagher, Michael, Laver, Michael, and Mair, Peter. *Representative Government in Western Europe*. New York: McGraw-Hill, 1992.

Gati, Charles. *The Politics of Modernization in Eastern Europe: Testing the Soviet Model*. New York: Praeger 1974.

Gebethner, Stanisław. *Wybory Parlamentarne 1991 i 1993 a Polska Scena Polityczna*. Warsaw: Wydawnictwo Sejmowe, 1995.

Geddes, Barbara. "A Comparative Perspective on the Leninist Legacy in Eastern Europe," *Comparative Political Studies*, Vol. 28, No. 2, July 1995: 239–74.

Gillespie, Richard. *The Spanish Socialist Party: A History of Factionalism*. Oxford, UK: Clarendon Press, 1989.

Gillespie, Richard, Waller, Michael, and Nieto, Lourdes Lopez, eds. *Factional Politics and Democratisation*. London: Frank Cass, 1995.

Gombar, Csabá, et al., eds. *Question Marks: The Hungarian Government 1994–5*. Budapest: Korridor 1995.

Balance: The Hungarian Government 1990–1994. Budapest: Korridor, 1994.

Gross, Jan. "The Social Consequences of War: Preliminaries to the Study of Imposition of Communist Regimes in East Central Europe," *East European Politics and Societies*, Vol. 3, No. 2, Spring 1989: 198–214.

"Poland: From Civil Society to Political Nation," in Banac, Ivo, ed. *Eastern Europe in Revolution*. Ithaca, NY: Cornell University Press, 1992: p. 62.

Grzybowski, Leszek. *Milczenie Ideologów*. Warszawa: Krajowa Agencja Wydawnicza, 1985.

"Jaka Partia?" Warsaw: Książka i Wiedza, February 1989.

Grzymała-Busse, Anna. "Determining the Public Image and Support of Political Parties in East Central Europe, 1992–6," paper presented at the American Political Science Association Annual Meeting, 3–7 September 1998, Boston, MA.

"Reform Efforts in the Czech and Slovak Communist Parties and Their Successors, 1988–1993," *East European Politics and Societies*, Fall 1998: 442–71.

Grzymała-Busse, Jerzy. "Rule induction system LERS" *Bulletin of Intornational Rough Set Society* 2, 1998: 18–20.

Gunther, Richard, Sani, Giacomo, and Shabad, Goldie. *Spain After Franco: The Making of a Competitive Party System*. Berkeley, CA: University of California Press, 1988.

Haggard, Stephan, and Kauffman, Robert. *The Political Economy of Democratic Transitions*. Princeton, NJ: Princeton University Press, 1995.

Hahn, Werner. *Democracy in a Communist Party*. New York: Columbia University Press, 1987.

Hall, Peter A. "Policy Paradigms, Social Learning, and the State," *Comparative Politics*, April 1993: 275–96.

Hall, Peter, and Taylor, Rosemary. "Political Science and the Three New Institutionalisms," *Political Studies*, December 1996: 936–57.

Hanley, Eric. "Cadre Capitalism in Hungary and Poland: Property Accumulation Among Communist-Era Elites," *East European Politics and Societies*, Winter 2000: 143–78.

Hanson, Stephen. "The Leninist Legacy and Institutional Change," *Comparative Political Studies*, July 1995: 306–14.

Hanzel, Vladimír. *Zrychlený Těp Dějín*. Prague: OK Centrum, 1991.

Haraszti, Miklós. "Animal Farm Scenarios: The Comeback of the Former Communists and Why It Is No Reason to Worry," *Constellations*, January 1995: 81–93.

Harmel, Robert, and Janda, Kenneth. *Parties and Their Environments: Limits to Reform?* New York: Longman, 1982.

"An Integrated Theory of Party Goals and Party Change," *Journal of Theoretical Politics* 6, 1994: 259–87.

Harmel, Robert, Heo, Uk, Tan, Alexander, and Janda, Kenneth. "Performance, Leadership, Factions, and Party Change: An Empirical Analysis," *West European Politics*, January 1995: 1–33.

Harrop, Martin, and Miller, William L. *Elections and Voters: A Comparative Introduction*. London: MacMillan, 1987.

Hausner, Jerzy. "Organizacje interesu i stosunki przemysłowe w krajach postsocjalistycznych." *Studia Polityczne*, XLIII, 1994: 10–26.

Havel, Václav. *Open Letters*. New York: Vintage Books, 1992.

Held, Joseph. *Democracy and Right-Wing Politics in Eastern Europe in the 1990s*. Boulder, CO: Westview Press, East European Monographs, 1993.

Held, Joseph, ed. *The Columbia History of Eastern Europe in the Twentieth Century*. New York: Columbia University Press, 1992.

Hellman, Stephen. *Organization and Ideology in Four Italian Communist Federations*. PhD. dissertation, Yale University, 1973.

Italian Communism in Transition. New York: Oxford University Press, 1988.

Herbst, Jeffrey. "Prospects for Elite-Driven Democracy in South Africa," *Political Science Quarterly*, Winter 1997/8: 595–615.

Higley, John, Pakulski, Jan, and Wesolowski, Wlodzimierz, eds. *Postcommunist Elites and Democracy in Eastern Europe*. Basingstoke, UK: MacMillan Press, 1998.

Hinich, Melvin, and Munger, Michael. *Ideology and the Theory of Political Choice*. Ann Arbor, MI: University of Michigan Press, 1994.

Historická Statistická Ročenka ČSSR. Praha: Alfa, 1985.

Hoensch, Jorg K. *A History of Modern Hungary 1867–1986*. London: Longman Publishing, 1988.

Hoffstetter, Richard C. "The Amateur Politician: A Problem in Construct Validation," *Midwestern Journal of Political Science* 15, 1971: 31–56.

Holmes, Leslie. *Politics in the Communist World*. Oxford, UK: Clarendon Press, 1986.

Holsti, Ole. *Content Analysis for the Social Sciences and Humanities*. Reading, MA: Addison-Wesley 1969.

Huber, John, and Inglehart, Ronald. "Expert Interpretations of Party Space and Party Locations in 42 Societies," *Party Politics*, Vol. 1, No. 1, 1995: 73–111.

Hughes, Stephen. "Living with the Past: Trade Unionism in Hungary Since Political Pluralism," *Industrial Relations Journal*, Winter 1992: 293–303.

Huntington, Samuel. *Political Order in Changing Societies*. New Haven, CT: Yale University Press, 1968.

Illonszki, Gabriela. "Institutionalisation and Professionalisation in the First Parliament," in Ágh, Attila, and Kurtán, Sandor, eds. *The First Parliament*. Budapest: Centre for Democracy Studies, 1995.

Inglehart, Ronald. *The Silent Revolution: Changing Values and Political Styles Among Western Publics*. Princeton, NJ: Princeton University Press, 1977.

Ishiyama, John T. "Communist Parties in Transition: Structures, Leaders, and Process of Democratization in Eastern Europe," *Comparative Politics*, Vol. 27, January 1995: 147–66.

"The Sickle or the Rose: Previous Regime Types and the Evolution of the Ex-Communist Parties in Post-Communist Politics," *Comparative Political Studies*, June 1997: 299–300.

"Transitional Electoral Systems in Post-Communist Eastern Europe," *Political Science Quarterly*, Vol. 112, No. 1, 1997: 95–115.

Iversen, Torben. "The Logics of Electoral Politics: Spatial, Directional, and Mobilizational Effects," *Comparative Political Studies*, July 1994: 155–89.

Jakeš, Miloš. *Dva Roky Generalním Tajemnikem*. Praha: Dokumenty, 1996.

Jancar, Barbara Wolfe. *Czechoslovakia and the Absolute Monopoly of Power*. New York: Praeger, 1971.

Janos, Andrew. "Continuity and Change in Eastern Europe: Strategies of Post-Communist Politics," *East European Politics and Societies*, Winter 1994: 1–31.

Jasiewicz, Krzysztof. "Polish Politics on the Eve of the 1993 Elections," *Communist and Post-Communist Studies*, December 1993a: 387–411.

"Structures of Representation," in White, Stephen, Batt, Judy, and Lewis, Paul, eds. *Developments in East European Politics*, London: McMillan, 1993b.

Jehlička, Petr, Kostelecký, Tomaš, Sýkora, Ludek. "Czechoslovak Parliamentary Elections 1990: Old Patterns, New Trends, and Lots of Surprises," in O'Loughlin, John, and van der Wusten, Herman, eds. *The New Political Geography of Eastern Europe*. London: Belhaven, 1993: 235–53.

Jones Luong, Pauline. *Institutional Change and Political Continuity in Post-Soviet Central Asia: Power, Perceptions, and Pacts*. Cambridge, UK: Cambridge University Press, forthcoming.

Jowitt, Ken. *New World Disorder*. Berkeley, CA: University of California Press, 1992.

Kancelaria Sejmu. *Sejm Rzeczpospolitej Polskiej: Informacja o Działaności Sejmu*. I Kadencja. Warsaw, October 1993.

Kancelaria Sejmu. *Sejm Rzeczpospolitej Polskiej: Informacja o Działaności Sejmu*. II Kadencja. Warsaw, January 1997.

Kaplan, Karel. *Utvařeni generalní linie výstavby socialismu v Československu; od února do IX sjezdu KSČ*. Praha: Academia, 1966.

Political Persecution in Czechoslovakia. Research project "Crises in Soviet-Type Systems," No. 3. Köln: Index, 1983.

The Communist Party in Power: A Profile of Party Politics in Czechoslovakia. Boulder, CO: Westview Press, 1987.

Aparát ÚV KSČ v letech 1948–68. Prague: Sešity Ústavu Pro Soudobé Dějiny, Sv. 10, 1993.

Sociální souvislosti krizí komunistického režimu v letech 1953–1957 a 1968–1975 (The Social underpinnings of the crises of the communist regime in 1953–7 and in 1968–75). Prague: Sešity Ústavu Pro Soudobé Dějiny, 1993.

"Kappa." *Partia Stanu Wojennego*. Warsaw: Samizdat, 1984. Available at the National Library, Warsaw.

Karasimeonov, Georgi. "Bulgaria's New Party System," in Pridham, Geoffrey, and Lewis, Paul G., eds. *Stabilising Fragile Democracies: Comparing New Party Systems in Southern and Eastern Europe*. London: Routledge, 1996.

Katz, Richard. *A Theory of Parties and Electoral Systems*. Baltimore, MD: Johns Hopkins University Press, 1980.

Katz, Richard, and Mair, Peter, eds. *How Parties Organize: Change and Adaptation in Party Organizations in Western Democracies*. London: Sage Publications, 1994.

Kavan, Jan. "Parties for Everyone," *East European Reporter*, Spring/Summer 1991: 44–51.

Keri, László. "Decision-Making of the Government from the Point of View of Organizational Sociology," in Gombar, Csabá et al., eds. *Balance: The Hungarian Government 1990–1994*. Budapest: Korridor, 1994.

Kimball, L. "Nostalgia Wins the Day in Poland," *New Statesman and Society*, 1 November 1993, pp. 20–1.

King, Anthony, ed. *New Labour Triumphs: Britain at the Polls*. Chatham, NJ: Chatham House Publishers, 1998.

Kingdon, John. *Agendas, Alternatives, and Public Choices*. Glenview, IL: Scott, Foresman, and Company, 1984.

Király, Béla, ed. *Lawful Revolution in Hungary, 1989–1994*. Boulder, CO: Social Science Monographs, distributed by Columbia University Press, 1995.

Kirchheimer, Otto. "The Transformation of the Western European Party System," in LaPalombara, Joseph, and Weiner, Myron. *Political Parties and Political Development*. Princeton, NJ: Princeton University Press, 1966: 177–200.

Kis, János. *Politics in Hungary: For a Democratic Alternative*. Boulder, CO: Social Science Monographs, distributed by Columbia University Press, 1989.

"Between Reform and Revolution," *Constellations*, 3, 1995: 399–421.

Interview with János Kis, *Constellations*, January 1995: 12–20.

Kitschelt, Herbert. "The Law of Curvilinear Disparity Revisited," *Political Studies*, 1989a: 400–21.

The Logics of Party Formation. Ithaca, NY: Cornell University Press, 1989b.

"The Formation of Party Systems in East Central Europe," *Politics and Society*, March 1992: 7–50.

The Transformation of European Social Democracy. Cambridge, UK: Cambridge University Press, 1994.

"Formation of Party Cleavages in Post-Communist Democracies," *Party Politics* October 1995a: 447–72.

"Party Systems in East Central Europe: Consolidation or Fluidity?" *Studies in Public Policy*, No. 241 (Glasgow: University of Strathclyde), 1995b.

"Accounting for Outcomes of Post-Communist Regime Change. Causal Depth or Shallowness in Rival Explanations," paper presented at the 1999 Annual Meeting of the American Political Science Association, Atlanta, 1–5 September 1999.

Kitschelt, Herbert. Mansfeldová, Zdenka, Markowski, Radosław, and Tóka, Gábor. *Post-Communist Party Systems*. Cambridge, UK: Cambridge University Press, 1999.

Kleinfeld, Gerald. "The Return of the PDS," in Conradt, David, ed. *Germany's New Politics*. Providence, RI: Berghahn Books, 1995.

Klingemann, Hans-Dieter, Hofferbert, Richard, and Budge, Ian. *Parties, Policy, and Democracy*. Boulder, CO: Westview Press, 1994.

Kochański, Aleksander, ed. *Protokoły posiedzeń Biura Politycznego KC PPR 1944–45*. Warsaw: ISP PAN, 1992.

Kolarska-Bobińska, Lena. "Social Interests, Egalitarian Attitudes, and the Change of Economic Order," *Social Research*, Vol. 55 No. 1–2, Spring/Summer 1988: 111–38.

Konrad, Györgyi, and Szelenyi, Iván. *Intellectuals on the Road to Class Power*. New York: Harcourt Brace Jovanovich, 1979.

Koole, Ruud. "Cadre, Catch-all, or Cartel? A comment on the notion of the Cartel Party," *Party Politics*, No. 4 1996: 507–23.

Kopecký, Petr. "Developing Party Organizations in East-Central Europe," *Party Politics*, 1995, No. 4: 515–34.

"Parties in the Czech Parliament: From Transformative Towards Arena Type of Legislature," in Lewis, Paul G., ed. *Party Structure and Organization in East-Central Europe*. Cheltenham, UK: Edward Elgar, 1996.

Korboński, Andrzej. "Poland: 1918–1990," in Held, Joseph, ed. *The Columbia History of Eastern Europe in the Twentieth Century*. New York: Columbia University Press, 1992: 229–76.

Kornai, János. "The Hungarian Reform Process: Visions, Hopes, and Reality," in Nee, Victor, and Stark, David, eds. *Remaking the Economic Institutions of Socialism*. Stanford, CA: Stanford University Press, 1989: 32–94.

Körösényi, András. "Revival of the Past or New Beginning?" *Political Quarterly*, January–March 1991: 52–74.

"Stable or Fragile Democracy? Political Cleavages and Party System in Hungary," *Government and Opposition*, Winter 1993: 87–104.

"The Reasons for the Defeat of the Right," Windsor Klub Occasional Paper No. 1, July 1994.

Kostelecký, Tomaš. "Results of the 1990 Election in a Regional Perspective," in Gabal, Iván, ed. *The 1990 Election to the Czechoslovakian Federal Assembly*. Berlin: Editions Sigma, 1996.

Kovács, András. "Two Lectures on the Electoral Victory of the Hungarian Socialists," *Constellations*, January 1995, pp. 72–5.

"Did the Losers Really Win? An Analysis of Electoral Behavior in Hungary in 1994," *Social Research* No. 2, 1996: 511–29.

Kovács, Zoltán. "The Geography of Hungarian Parliamentary Elections 1990," in O'Loughlin, John, and van der Wusten, Herman, eds. *The New Political Geography of Eastern Europe*. London and New York: Belhaven Press, 1993.

Kovrig, Bennett. *Communism in Hungary*. Stanford, CA: Hoover Institution Press, 1979.

Krause, Kevin Deegan. "System politických stran v Česke republice, demokracie a volby roku 1996" (The Czech Political Party System, Democracy, and the 1996 Elections.), *Sociologický Časopis* (Czech Journal of Sociology), Fall 1996: 423–38.

Krippendorf, Klaus. *Content Analysis: An Introduction to Its Methodology*. Beverly Hills, CA: Sage, 1980.

Krisch, Henry. "The Party of Democratic Socialism: Left and East," in Dalton, Russell J., ed. *Germans Divided: The 1994 Bundestag Elections and the Evolution of the German Party System*. Oxford, UK: Berg, 1996: 109–31.

Krivý, Vladimír. "The Parliamentary Elections 1994: The Profile of Supporters of the Political Parties, the Profile of Regions," in Szomolányi, Soňa, and Mesežnikov, Grigorij, eds. *Slovakia: Parliamentary Elections 1994*. Bratislava: Slovak Political Science Association and Friedrich Ebert Foundation, 1995.

Kukorelli, István. "The Birth, Testing and Results of the 1989 Hungarian Electoral Law," *Soviet Studies*, No. 1, 1991: 137–56.

Kurski, Jacek. *Lewy Czerwcowy*. Warsaw: Editions Spotkania, 1993.

Kusín, Vladimír, ed. *The Czechoslovak Reform Movement 1968*. Santa Barbara, CA: Clio Press, 1973.

Kusín, Vladimír. *The Intellectual Origins of the Prague Spring*. Cambridge, UK: Cambridge University Press, 1971.
Political Grouping in the Czechoslovak Reform Movement. New York, Columbia University Press, 1972.

Land, Rainer, and Possekel, Ralf. "On the Internal Dynamics of the PDS: the Leninist Challenge and the Challenge to Leninism," *Constellations*, Vol. 2, No. 1, 1995: 51–61.

LaPalombara, Joseph, and Weiner, Myron, eds. *Political Parties and Political Development*. Princeton, NJ: Princeton University Press, 1972 (1966).

Laver, Michael J., and Budge, Ian, eds. *Party Policy and Government Coalitions*. New York: St. Martin's Press, 1992.

Laver, Michael, and Schofield, Norman. *Multiparty Government: The Politics of Coalition in Europe*. Oxford, UK: Oxford University Press, 1990.

Laver, Michael, and Shepsle, Kenneth. *Making and Breaking Governments: Cabinets and Legislatures in Parliamentary Democracies*. Cambridge, UK: Cambridge University Press, 1996.

Lawson, Kay. *The Comparative Study of Political Parties*. New York: St. Martin's Press, 1976.
"Renewing Party Scholarship: Lessons from Abroad," *American Review of Politics*, Winter 1993: 577–92.
How Political Parties Work: Perspectives from Within. Westport, CT: Praeger, 1994.

Lawson, Kay, and Merkl, Peter, eds. *When Parties Fail: Emerging Alternative Organizations*. Princeton, NJ: Princeton University Press, 1988.

Lawson, Kay, Römmele, Andrea, and Georgi Karasimeonov, eds. *Cleavages, Parties, and Voters: Studies from Bulgaria, the Czech Republic, Hungary, Poland, and Romania*. Westport, CT: Praeger, 1999.

Lazar, Marc. "Communist Parties and Trade Unions: Crisis of a Relationship," in Waller, Michael, Courtois, Stephanie, and Lazar, Marc, eds. *Comrades and Brothers: Communism and Trade Unions in Europe*. London: Frank Cass, 1991.

Leff, Carol Skalnik. *National Conflict in Czechoslovakia: The Making and Remaking of a State*. Princeton, NJ: Princeton University Press, 1988.

Lelinska, Krystyna. "Sejm I kadencji w Świadomości posłów, in Wesołowski, Włodzimierz, and Panków, Irena, eds. *Świat elity politycznej*. Warsaw: IFiSPAN, 1995.

Lengyel, László. "The Mousetrap," in Gombar, Csabé, et al., eds. *Question Marks: The Hungarian Government 1994–5*. Budapest: Korridor, 1995.

Lewis, Paul, ed. *Party Strucure and Organisation in East-Central Europe*, Cheltenham, UK: Edward Elgar, 1996.

Lewis, Paul. *Political Authority and Party Secretaries in Poland 1975–1986*. Cambridge, UK: Cambridge University Press, 1989.

"Political Institutionalisation and Party Development in Post-Communist Poland," *Europe-Asia Studies*, No. 5, 1994: 779–99.

Lewis, Paul, and Gortat, Radzislawa. "Models of Party Development and Questions of State Dependendence in Poland," *Party Politics*, No. 4, 1995: 599–608.

Lijphart, Arend. *Democracies*. New Haven, CT: Yale University Press, 1984.

"The Political Consequences of Electoral Laws, 1945–85," APSR, Vol. 84, No. 2, June 1990: 481–96.

Lijphart, Arend, and Grofman, Bernhard. *Choosing and Electoral System: Issues and Alternatives*. New York: Praeger, 1984.

Lijphart, Arend, and Waisman, Carlos. *Institutional Design in New Democracies: Eastern Europe and Latin America*. Boulder, CO: Westview Press, 1999.

Lipset, Seymour, and Rokkan, Stein, eds. *Party Systems and Voter Alignments: Cross-National Perspectives*. New York: The Free Press, 1967.

Lipset, Seymour Martin. "No Third Way: A Comparative Perspective on the Left," in Daniel Chirot, ed. *The Crisis of Leninism and the Decline of the Left: the Revolutions of 1989*. Seattle: University of Washington Press, 1991.

Lomax, Bill. "Impediments to Democratization in East-Central Europe," in Gordon Wightman, ed. *Party Formation in East Central Europe*. Aldershot, UK: Edward Elgar, 1995, p. 121.

Longley, Lawrence, and Davidson, Roger. *The New Roles of Parliamentary Committees*. Portland, OR: Frank Cass, 1998.

Luebbert, Gregory. *Liberalism, Fascism, or Social Democracy*. New York: Oxford University Press, 1991.

Magyar Gallup Intezet. *Party Popularity Polls*, 1993–1996. Budapest, Hungary.

Mahoney, James. "Nominal, Ordinal, and Narrative Appraisal in Macrocausal Analysis," *American Journal of Sociology*, January 1999: 1154–96.

"Path Dependence in Comparative-Historical Research," paper presented at the 1999 Annual Meeting of the American Political Science Association, Atlanta, 2–5 September 1999.

Mahr, Alison, and Nagle, John. "Resurrection of the Successor Parties and Democratization in East-Central Europe," *Communist and Post-Communist Studies*. No. 4, 1995: 393–409.

Mair, Peter, ed. *The West European Party System*. Oxford, UK: Oxford University Press, 1990.

Malová, Darina. "The Institutionalisation of Parliamentary Parties and Political Representation in Slovakia," paper presented for the Third Annual Conference on the Individual Versus the State, CEU, Budapest, 16–17 June 1995.

Malová, Darina, and Šivaková, Dana. "The National Council of the Slovak Republic: Between Democratic Transition and National State-Building," in Olson, David, and Norton, Philip, eds. *The New Parliaments of Central and Eastern Europe*. Portland, OR: Frank Cass, 1996.

Mansfeldová, Zdenka. "The First Czech Parliament in the View of the Members of Parliament," paper prepared for the International Conference on "The New Democratic Parliaments," Ljubljana, Slovenia, 24–6 June 1996.

Marada, Radim. "Who's Right in Czech Politics?" *Constellations*, January 1995: 62–71.

March, James, and Olsen, Johan. *Rediscovering Institutions*. New York: Free Press, 1989.

Markowski, Radosław. "Political Competition and Ideological Dimensions in East Central Europe," Glasgow: Center for the Study of Politics, No. 257, 1995.

"Political Parties and Ideological Spaces in East Central Europe," *Communist and Post-Communist Studies*, No. 3, 1997: 221–54.

Márkus, György. "Cleavages and Parties in Hungary After 1989," in Lawson, Kay, Römmele, Andrea, and Karasimeonov, Georgi, eds. *Cleavages, Parties, and Voters*. Westport, CT: Praeger, 1999.

Marody, Mira. "Three Stages of Party System Emergence in Poland," *Communist and Post-Communist Studies*, No. 2, 1995: 263–70.

Marquand, David. "After Socialism," *Political Studies*, 1993: 43–56.

Marx, Karl. *The Eighteenth Brumaire of Louis Bonaparte*. New York: International Publishers, 1963.

Mason, David. "Membership of the Polish United Workers' Party," *Polish Review*, No. 3–4, 1982: 138–53.

"The Polish Party in Crisis, 1980–1982," *Slavic Review*, Spring 1984: 30–45.

"Poland," in White, Stephen, Batt, Judy, and Lewis, Paul, eds. *Developments in East European Politics*. Durham, NC: Duke University Press, 1993.

Mateju, Petr. "In Search of Explanations for Recent Left-Turns in Post Communist Countries," *International Review of Comparative Public Policy*, Fall 1995.

Mateju, Petr, and Vlachová, Klara. "The Crystallization of Political Attitudes and Political Spectrum in the Czech Republic," working papers of the research project "Social Trends," Institute of Sociology, Academy of Sciences of the Czech Republic, No. 9, 1997.

May, John D. "Opinion Structures of Political Parties: The Special Law of Curvilinear Disparity," *Political Studies* 21, 1973: 135–51.

Mayhew, David. *Congress: The Electoral Connection*. New Haven, CT: Yale University Press, 1974.

McAdam, Doug, McCarthy, John D., and Zald, Mayer. *Comparative Perspectives on Social Movements*. Cambridge, UK: Cambridge University Press, 1996.

McFalls, Laurence. "Political Culture, Partisan Strategies, and the PDS," *German Politics and Society*, Spring 1995: 50–61.

Media and Opinion Research Surveys, Radio Free Europe/Radio Liberty, Inc. Spring 1994 Surveys: the Czech Republic, Slovakia, Poland, Ukraine.

Michels, Robert. *Political Parties*. New York: Free Press, (1911) 1962.

Michnik, Adam, interview with. *Constellations*, January 1995: 4–11.

Millar, James, and Sharon Wolchik, eds. *The Social Legacy of Communism*. Washington, DC: Woodnow Wilson Center Press, 1994.

Millard, Frances. "The Polish Parliamentary Elections of October 1991," *Soviet Studies*, No. 5, 1992: 837–55.

"The Shaping of the Polish Party System, 1989–93," *East European Politics and Societies*, Fall 1994a: 467–94.

"The Polish Parliamentary Election of September, 1993," *Communist and Post-Communist Studies*, No. 3, 1994b.

Miller, William L., White, Stephen, and Heywood, Paul. *Values and Political Change in Postcommunist Europe*. New York: St. Martin's Press, 1998.

Modzelewski, Karol. "Where Did Solidarity Go?" *Uncaptive Minds*, Winter–Spring 1994: 63–72.

Molnar, Miklós. *From Béla Kun to János Kádár*. New York: St. Martin's Press, 1990.

Moraski, Bryon, and Loewenberg, Gerhard. "The Effect of Legal Thresholds on the Revival of Former Communist Parties in East-Central Europe," paper presented at the Annual Meeting of the American Political Science Association, Washington, DC, 28–31 August, 1997.

Morlang, Diana. "Socialists Building Capitalism: Electoral Laws and Party Discipline in Hungary," paper presented at the Annual Meeting of the American Political Science Association, Boston, MA, 3–7 September 1998.

Mosca, Gaetano. *The Ruling Class*. Westport, CT: Greenwood Press, 1980.

Moser, Robert. "Electoral Systems and the Number of Parties in Postcommunist States," *World Politics* 51 (2), 1999: 359–84.

Narodná Rada Slovenskej Republiky. *I. Volebné obdobie*. Bratislava: NRSR, 1996.

Nelson, Daniel, and White, Stephen, eds. *Communist Legislatures in Comparative Perspective*. New York: SUNY Press, 1982.

North, Douglass. *Institutions, Institutional Change, and Economic Performance*. Cambridge, UK: Cambridge University Press, 1990.

OBOP. *Pożądane i niepożądane cechy kandydatów na posłów*, August 1991. Warsaw, Poland.

Społeczne wizerunki partii politycznych, December 1996. Warsaw, Poland.

Wizerunki partii politycznych, 21–4 September 1996. Warsaw, Poland.

319

Offe, Claus. "Capitalism by Democatic Design? Democratic Theory Facing the Triple Transition in East Central Europe," *Social Research*, Winter 1991: 865–902.

O'Loughlin, John, and van der Wusten, Herman, eds. *The New Political Geography of Eastern Europe*. London: Belhaven, 1993.

Olson, David M. "Dissolution of the State: Political Parties and the 1992 Election in Czechoslovakia," *Communist and Post-Communist Studies*, September 1993: 301–13.

    "The New Parliaments of New Democracies: The Experience of the Federal Assembly for the Czech and Slovak Federal Republic," in Ágh, Attila, ed. *First Steps*, Budapest: Hungarian Centre for Democracy Studies, 1994a, p. 40.

    "The Sundered State: Federalism and Parliament in Czechoslovakia," in Thomas Remington, ed. *Parliaments in Transition*. Boulder, CO: Westview Press, 1994b, p. 104.

    "Paradoxes of Institutional Development: The New Democratic Parliaments of East Central Europe," *International Political Science Review*, Vol. 18, No. 4, 1997: 401–16.

Olson, David, and Crowther, William. "Committees in New and Established Democratic Parliaments: Indicators of Institutionalization," paper presented at Midwest Political Science Association, Chicago, IL, April 22–6, 1998.

Olson, David, and Norton, Philip, eds. *The New Parliaments of Central and Eastern Europe*. Portland, OR: Frank Cass, 1996.

Oltay, Edith. "The Return of the Former Communists," *Transition*, 30 January 1995.

O'Neil, Patrick. "Revolution from Within: Institutional Analysis, Transitions from Authoritarianisms, and the Case of Hungary," *World Politics*, July 1996: 579–603.

Ordeshook, Peter, and Shvetsova, Olga. "Ethnic Heterogeneity, District Magnitude, and the Number of Parties," *American Journal of Political Science*, February 1994: 100–23.

Orenstein, Mitchell. *Out of the Red: Economic Reform in Poland and in Czechoslovakia* Ph.D. Dissertation, Yale University, 1997.

    "A Genealogy of Communist Successor Parties in East-Central Europe and the Determinants of Their Success," *East European Politics and Societies*, Fall 1998: 472–99.

Otáhal, Milan. *Opozice, Moc, Společnost: 1969/1989*. Praha: Maxdorf/ÚSD AV ČR, 1994.

Palczak, Andrzej. *Procesy Stalinizacji w Polsce w latach 1947–56*. Zabrze: Wydawnictwo APEX, 1996.

Panebianco, Angelo. *Political Parties: Organization and Power*. Cambridge, UK: Cambridge University Press, 1988.

Państwowa Komisja Wyborcza. "Wybory do Sejmu Rzeczpospolitej," 1991 and 1993 volumes. Warsaw: PKW, 1991 and 1993.

    "Wyniki Wyborów," *Monitor Polski*. MP#64, poz. 620 (1997).

Bibliography

Pareto, Vilfredo. *The Rise and Fall of the Elites*. Totowa, NJ: Bedminster Press, 1968.

Pasti, Vladimir. *The Challenges of Transition: Romania in Transition*. Boulder, CO: East European Monographs, 1997.

Pataki, Judith. "Hungary: Trade Unions Slow to Change," *Report on Eastern Europe*, 29 March 1991.

"Trade Unions' Role in Victory of Former Communists in Hungary," *RFE/RL Reports*, 1 July 1994.

"Former Communist Trade Union Strengthens Its Positions," *Report on Eastern Europe*, 5 July 1991.

Perry, Duncan. "The Bulgarian Socialist Party Congress: Conservatism Preserved," *RFE Report on Eastern Europe*, 26 October 1990: 4–9.

Perzkowski, Stanisław, ed. *Tajne dokumenty Biura Politycznego I Sekretariatu KC: Ostatni Rok Władzy, 1988–9*. London: Aneks, 1994.

Phillips, Ann. "Socialism with a New Face? The PDS in Search of Reform," *East European Politics and Societies*, Fall 1994: 495–530.

Pierson, Paul. "When Effect Becomes Cause: Policy Feedback and Political Change," *World Politics*, July 1993: 595–628.

"Increasing Returns, Path Dependence, and the Study of Politics," *American Political Science Review*, June 2000: 251–67.

Politologický Kabinet SAV. *Slovenská Spoločnost v krizových rokoch 1967–1970*. Zbornik studii III. Bratislava: SAV 1992.

Pomian, Grażyna, ed. *Protokoły tzw. Komisji Grabskiego*. Warsaw: Międzyzakładowa Struktura "Solidarności," 1987.

Pool, Ithiel de Sola. *Trends in Content Analysis*. Urbana, IL: University of Illinois Press, 1959.

Pop-Elecheş, Grigore. "Separated at Birth or Separated by Birth? Communist Successor Parties in Romania and Hungary," *East European Politics and Societies*, Winter 1991: 117–47.

Poslanecká Sněmovna. *Parlament České Republiky. 1. Volebni obdobi*. Prague: Poslanecká Sněmovna, 1994.

Poslanecká Sněmovna. *Parlament České Republiky. 2. Volebni obdobi*. Prague: Poslanecká Sněmovna, 1996.

Powell, Walter, and DiMaggio, Paul, eds. *The New Institutionalism in Organisational Analysis*. Chicago: University of Chicago Press, 1991.

Powers, Denise V., and Cox, James. "Echoes from the Past: The Relationship Between Satisfaction with Economic Reforms and Voting Behavior in Poland," *American Political Science Review*, September 1997: 617–33.

Pridham, Geoffrey, and Lewis, Paul G., eds. *Stabilising Fragile Democracies: Comparing New Party Systems in Southern and Eastern Europe*. London: Routledge, 1996.

Pridham, Geoffrey, and Vanhanen, Tatu. *Democratization in Eastern Europe: Domestic and International Perspectives*. London: Routledge, 1994.

Przeworski, Adam. *Democracy and the Market*. Cambridge, UK: Cambridge University Press, 1992.

Przeworski, Adam, and Sprague, John. *Paper Stones: A History of Electoral Socialism*. Chicago: University of Chicago Press, 1986.

Putnam, Robert. *The Beliefs of Politicians*. New Haven, CT: Yale University Press, 1973.

The Comparative Study of Political Elites. Englewood Cliffs, NJ: Prentice Hall, 1976.

Pyszczek, Grzegorz. "Tematy kampanii wyborczej 1993 roku," in Wesołowski, Włodzimierz and Panków, Irena, eds. *Świat elity politycznej*. Warsaw: Wydawnictwo IfiS PAN, 1995.

Racz, Barnabas. "Political Pluralisation in Hungary: The 1990 Elections," *Soviet Studies*, No. 1, 1991: 107–36.

"The Socialist-Left Opposition in Hungary," *Europe-Asia Studies*, No. 4, 1993: 647–70.

Rae, Douglas W. *The Political Consequences of Electoral Laws*. New Haven, CT: Yale University Press, 1971.

Raeff, Marc. "The People, the Intelligentsia, and Russian Political Culture," *Political Studies*, 1993: 93–106.

Rakowski, Mieczysław. *Jak to sie stało*. Warsaw: BGW, 1991.

Zanim Stanę Przed Trybunałem. Warsaw: BGW, 1993.

Reisch, Alfred. "Hungarian Socialist Party Looks Ahead," *RFE/RL Research Report*, 10 July 1992.

Remington, Thomas, ed. *Parliaments in Transition*. Boulder, CO: Westview Press, 1994.

Renner, Hans. *A History of Czechoslovakia Since 1945*. London: Routledge, 1989.

Renner, Hans. *Dějiny Československa po roku 1945*. Bratislava: SAP, 1993.

Riker, William H. *The Art of Political Manipulation*. New Haven, CT: Yale University Press, 1986.

Agenda Formation, Ann Arbor, MI: University of Michigan Press, 1993.

Robertson, David. *A Theory of Party Competition*. London: John Wiley & Sons, 1976.

Rocznik Statystyczny. Warsaw: Główny Urząd Statystyczny, 1948–1991.

Rose, Richard. *Do Parties Make a Difference?* London: Chatham House, 1984.

Rosengren, Erik Karl, ed. *Advances in Content Analysis*. Beverly Hills, CA: Sage, 1981.

Rothschild, Joseph. *Communist Eastern Europe*. New York: Walker, 1964.

Return to Diversity: A Political History of East Central Europe Since World War II. New York: Oxford University Press, 1989.

Saalfeld, Thomas. "Rational Choice Theory in Legislative Studies: Models of Politics Without Romanticism," *Journal of Legislative Studies*, No. 1, 1995: 32–64.

Sakwa, Richard. "Left or Right? CPRF and the Problem of Democratic Consolidation in Russia," *Journal of Communist Studies and Transition Politics*, January–June 1998: 128–58.

Sartori, Giovanni. "Concept Misformation in Comparative Politics," *American Political Science Review*, December 1970: 1033–53.

Parties and Party Systems. Cambridge, UK: Cambridge University Press, 1976.

Scharpf, Fritz. "Institutions in Comparative Policy Research," *Comparative Political Studies*, Vol. 33, No. 6/7, August/September 2000: 762–90.

Bibliography

Schelling, Thomas. *The Strategy of Conflict.* Cambridge, MA: Harvard University Press, 1960.

Schlesinger, Joseph. "On the Theory of Party Organization," *Journal of Politics,* May 1984: 369–400.

Schmitter, Philippe C. "Intermediaries in the Consolidation of Neo-Democracies: The Role of Parties, Associations and Movements," working paper No. 130, Barcelona: Institut de Ciencies Politiques Syocials, 1997.

Schöpflin, George. *Politics in Eastern Europe, 1945–1992.* Oxford: Blackwell, 1993.

Schumpeter, Joseph. *Imperialism and Social Classes.* New York: Meridian Books, 1960.

Scott, Richard W. *Organizations: Rational, Natural, and Open Systems.* Englewood Cliffs, NJ: Prentice Hall, 1992.

Sejm Rzeczpospolitej Polskiej: Informator(2). I Kadencja. Warsaw: Wydawnictwo Sejmowe, 1992.

Sejm Rzeczpospolitej Polskiej: Informator. II Kadencja. Warsaw: Wydawnictwo Sejmowe, 1993.

Sewell, William H, Jr. "A Theory of Structure: Duality, Agency, Transformation," *American Journal of Sociology,* July 1992: 1–29.

Shain, Yossi, and Linz, Juan. *Between States.* Cambridge, UK: Cambridge University Press, 1995.

Shefter, Martin. *Political Parties and the State: The American Experience.* Princeton, NJ: Princeton University Press, 1994.

Shopov, Vladimir. "How the Voters Respond in Bulgaria," in Lawson, Kay, Römmele, Andrea, and Karasimeonov, Georgi, eds. *Cleavages, Parties, and Voters.* Westport, CT: Praeger, 1999.

Šik, Ota. *The Communist power system.* New York: Praeger, 1976/1981.

Sikorski, Radek. "How We Lost Poland," *Foreign Affairs,* September/October 1996.

Simečka, Milan. *The Restoration of Order: The Normalization of Czechoslovakia 1969–1976.* Lonon: Verso, 1984.

Sjöblom, Gunnar. *Party Strategies in a Multiparty System.* Lund: Berlingska Boktryckeriet, 1968.

"Political Change and Political Accountability," in Daalder, Hans, and Mair, Peter, eds. *Western European Party Systems.* London: Sage Publications, 1983: 370–403.

Skilling, H. Gordon. *Communism, National and International: Eastern Europe After Stalin.* Toronto: University of Toronto Press, 1964.

Czechoslovakia's Interrupted Revolution. Princeton, NJ: Princeton University Press, 1976.

"Stalinism and Czechoslovak Political Culture," in Tucker, Robert, ed. *Stalinism.* New York: W.W. Norton, 1977.

Slovak Statistical Office, *Nazory,* 4.1991–12.1994, Bratislava.

Sokorski, Włodzimierz. *Udana Klęska.* Warsaw: Savimpress, 1990.

Solnick, Steven. *Stealing the State.* Cambridge, MA: Harvard University Press, 1998.

Southall, Roger. "The Centralisation and Fragmentation of South Africa's Dominant Party System," *African Affairs*, October 1998: 443–69.

Staar, Richard Felix. *The Communist Regimes in Eastern Europe: An Introduction.* Stanford, CA: Hoover Institution on War, Revolution, and Peace, 1988.

Stanclik, Katarzyna. "Electoral Law and the Formation of Political Party Systems in the New East European Democracies," paper presented at the Annual Meeting of the American Political Science Association, Washington, DC, 28–31 August 1997.

Staniszkis, Jadwiga. *The Dynamics of Breakthrough in Central Europe.* Berkeley, CA: University of California Press, 1992.

Statistická Ročenka ČSSR. Praha: Federalní Statistický Uřad, 1948–1990.

Štatistický Úrad Slovenskej Republiky. *Vol'by do Narodnej Rady Slovenskej Republiky konane 30.9 a 1.10.1994.* Bratislava, 1994.

Štatistický Úrad Slovenskej Republiky. *Vol'by 1994.* Bratislava, 1994.

Steinmo, Sven, Thelen, Kathleen, and Longstreth, Frank, eds. *Structuring Politics: Historical Institutionalism in Comparative Analysis.* Cambridge, UK: Cambridge University Press, 1992.

Šťepan, Miroslav. *Zpoved vězne samětové revoluce.* Praha: grafit, 1991.

Stokes, Gale. *And the Walls Came Tumbling Down.* New York: Oxford University Press, 1993.

Strom, Kaare. "A Behavioral Theory of Competitive Political Parties," *American Journal of Political Science*, May 1990: 565–98.

Strom, Kaare, Budge, Ian, and Laver, Michael J. "Constraints on Cabinet Formation in Parliamentary Democracies," *American Journal of Political Science*, May 1994: 303–35.

Suda, Zdenek. *Zealots and Rebels: A History of the Communist Party of Czechoslovakia.* Stanford, CA: Hoover Institution Press, 1980.

Suk, Pavel. *Kronos Listopad a Prosinec 1989*, Rukopis připravovaný do výdani. Prague: ÚSD, 1996.

Suleiman, Ezra. *Elites in French Society* Princeton, NJ: Princeton University Press, 1978.

Sułek, Antoni. "The Polish United Worker's Party: From Mobilisation to Non-Representation," *Soviet Studies*, July 1990: 499–511.

Szajkowski, Bogdan. *Political Parties of Eastern Europe, Russia, and the Successor States.* Harlow, Essex, UK: Longman, 1994.

Szalai. Erzsébet. "The Metamorphosis of the Elites," in Király, Béla, ed. Lawful Revolution in Hungary, 1989–94. Boulder, CO: Social Science Monographs, distributed by Columbia University Press, 1995.

Szarvas, László. "Parties and Party-Factions in the Hungarian Parliament," Budapest Papers on Democratic Transition, No. 34, Hungarian Electronic Library, 1992.

"Personnel and Structural Changes in the First Hungarian Parliament," in Ágh, Attila, and Kurtán, Sándor, eds. *The First Parliament: 1990–1994.* Budapest: Hungarian Centre for Democracy Studies, 1995.

Szczerbak, Aleks. "Interests and Values: Polish Parties and Their Electorates," *Europe-Asia Studies*, Vol. 51, No. 8, 1999: 1401–32.

Bibliography

Szelenyi, Iván, Fodor, Eva, and Hanley, Eric. "Left Turn in Post Communist Politics: Bringing Class Back in?" *EEPS*, Winter 1997: 190–224.

Szelenyi, Iván. *Socialist Entrepreneurs*. Madison, WI: University of Wisconsin Press, 1988.

Szelenyi, Szonja, Szelenyi, Iván, and Poster, Winifred. "Interests and Symbols in Post-Communist Political Culture: The Case of Hungary," *American Sociological Review*, June 1996: 466–77.

Szilagyi, Zsofia. "Communication Breakdown Between the Government and the Public," *Transition*, 22 March 1996: 41–3.

Szomolányi, Soňa, and Mesežnikov, Grigorij, eds. *The Slovak Path of Transition – To Democracy?* Bratislava: Slovak Political Science Association, 1994.

Slovakia: Parliamentary Elections 1994. Bratislava: Slovak Political Science Association and Friedrich Ebert Foundation, 1995.

Taagepera, Rein, and Shugart, Matthew. *Seats and Votes: The Effects and Determinants of Electoral Systems*. New Haven, CT: Yale University Press, 1989.

Tamás, Bernard. "Spatial Distance or Historical Division: When Does the Public Reject a Party's Ideological Shift?" paper presented at the Annual Meeting of the American Political Science Association, Washington, DC, 31 August–3 September 2000.

Party Competence: The Struggle for Political Survival in Post-Communist Hungary. Book manuscript, 2000.

Tamás, Gaspar Miklos. "The Legacy of Dissent: Irony, Ambiguity, Duplicity," *Uncaptive Minds*, Summer 1994: 19–34.

Tarrow, Sidney. *Power in Movement*. Cambridge, UK: Cambridge University Press, 1994.

Tarrow, Sidney, and Smith, V. Lamonte. "Crisis Recruitment and the Political Involvement of Local Elites: Some Evidence from Italy and France," in Eulau, Heinz, and Czudnowski, Moshe, eds. *Elite Recruitment in Democratic Polities*. New York: Sage Publications, 1976.

Thelen, Kathleen. "Historical Institutionalism in Comparative Politics," *Annual Review of Political Science*, 1999: 369–404.

Thirkell, John, Scase, Richard, and Vickerstaff, Sarah. *Labor Relations and Political Change in Eastern Europe: A Comparative Perspective*. Ithaca, NY: Cornell University Press, 1995.

Thompson, Wayne. "The Party of Democratic Socialism in the New Germany," *Communist and Post-Communist Studies*, No. 4, 1996: 435–52.

Tilly, Charles. *Big Structures, Large Processes, Huge Comparisons*. New York: Russell Sage, 1984, p. 14.

Tóka, Gábor. "Electoral Choices in East-Central Europe," in Pridham, Geoffrey, and Lewis, Paul G. eds. *Stabilising Fragile Democracies: Comparing New Party Systems in Southern and Eastern Europe*. London: Routledge, 1996.

"Political Parties and Democratic Consolidation in East Central Europe." Glasgow: Center for the Study of Politics, 1997.

"Party Appeals and Voter Loyalty in New Democracies," *Political Studies*, 1998: 589–610.

Tóka, Gábor, ed. *The 1990 Election to the Hungarian National Assembly.* Berlin: Sigma, 1995.

Tökés, Rudolf. *Hungary's Negotiated Revolution.* Cambridge, UK: Cambridge University Press, 1996.

Tökés, Rudolf, ed. *Opposition in Eastern Europe.* Baltimore, MD: Johns Hopkins Press, 1979.

Triška, Jan F. *Political Development in Eastern Europe.* New York: Praeger, 1977.

Troxel, Luan. "Socialist Persistence in the Bulgarian Elections of 1990–1991," *East European Quarterly,* January 1993: 407–30.

Tsebelis, George. *Nested Games.* Berkeley, CA: University of California Press, 1990.

Tucker, Robert, ed. *Stalinism.* New York: W.W. Norton, 1977.

Tworzecki, Hubert, *Parties and Politics in Post 1989 Poland.* Boulder, CO: Westview, 1996.

Ulč, Otto. *Politics in Czechoslovakia.* San Francisco: W. H. Freeman and Co., 1974.

"Legislative Politics in Czechoslovakia" in Nelson, Daniel, and White, Stephen, eds. *Communist Legislatures in Comparative Perspective.* New York: SUNY Press, 1982.

Urban, Jan. "The Communists are Playing Dead," *Uncaptive Minds,* Summer 1991: 99–100. Original appeared in 2 March 1991, *Lidove Noviny.*

Vachudová, Milada Anna. "Divisions in the Czech Communist Party," *RFE/RL Report,* 17 September 1993: 28–33.

Vachudová, Milada Anna, and Snyder, Timothy. "Are Transitions Transitory? Two Types of Political Change in Eastern Europe Since 1989," *Eastern European Politics and Societies,* Winter 1997: 1–35.

Vass, László. "Changes in Hungary's Governmental System," in Ágh, Attila, ed. *The First Steps.* Hungarian Centre for Democracy Studies, 1994.

Vlachová, Klara. "Volby 1996 – vice sila zvyku něž nové rozhodnuti" [Elections 1996 – more power of habit than a new decision], Lidové Noviny, 3 August 1996.

Von Beyme, Klaus. *Political Parties in Western Democracies.* Aldershot, UK: Gower, 1985.

"Regime Transition and Recruitment of Elites in Eastern Europe," *Governance,* July 1993: 409–25.

Wade, Larry, Lavelle, Peter, and Groth, Alexander. "Searching for Voting Patterns in Post-Communist Poland's Sejm Elections," *Communist and Post-Communist Studies,* December 1995: 411–25.

Waller, Michael. "Adaptation of the Former Communist Parties of East Central Europe," *Party Politics,* October 1995a: 473–90.

"Starting Up Problems: Communists, Social Democrats, and Greens," in Wightman, Gordon, ed. *Party Formation in East-Central Europe.* Aldershot, UK: Edward Elgar, 1995b.

"Party Inheritances and Party Identities," in Pridham, Geoffrey, and Lewis, Paul G., eds. *Stabilising Fragile Democracies: Comparing New Party Systems in Southern and Eastern Europe.* London: Routledge, 1996.

Waller, Michael, Coppieters, Bruno, and Deschouwer, Kris, eds. *Social Democracy in a Post-Communist Europe.* London: Frank Cass, 1994.

Waltz, Kenneth. *Foreign Policy and Democratic Politics*. New Haven, CT: Yale University Press, 1967.

Ware, Alan. *The Logic of Party Democracy*. London: MacMillan, 1979.

Warwick, Paul. *Government Survival in Parliamentary Democracies*. Cambridge, UK: Cambridge University Press, 1994.

Wasilewski, Jacek. "The Patterns of Bureaucratic Elite Recruitment in Poland in the 1970s and 1980s," *Soviet Studies*, No. 4, 1990: 743–57.

Wasilewski, Jacek, ed. *Konsolidacja Elit Politycznych w Polsce 1991–1993*. Warsaw: IFiSPAN, 1994.

Ważniewski, Władysław. *Walka polityczna w kierownictwie PPR i PZPR 1944–64*. Torun: Adam Marszalek, 1991.

Wesołowski, Włodzimierz, and Panków, Irena, eds. *Świat Elity politycznej*. Warsaw: IFiSPAN, 1995.

de Weydenthal, Jan. *The Communists of Poland*. Stanford, CA: Hoover Institution Press, 1986.

White, Stephen. "Economic Performance and Communist Legitimacy," *World Politics*, April 1986: 462–82.

White, Stephen, Batt, Judy, and Lewis, Paul, eds. *Developments in East European Politics*. London: MacMillan, 1993.

Developments in Central and East European Politics 2. Durham, NC: Duke University Press, 1998.

White, Stephen, Gardener, John, and Schopflin, George. *Communist Political Systems*. New York: St. Martin's Press, 1982.

White, Stephen, and Nelson, Daniel, eds. *Communist Legislatures in Comparative Perspective*. New York: SUNY Press, 1982.

Whitefield, Stephen, ed. *The New Institutional Architecture of Eastern Europe*. London: McMillan, 1993.

Wiatr, Jerzy. *Krótki Sejm*. Warsaw: BGW, 1993.

"From Communist Party to 'The Socialist-Democracy of the Polish Republic'," in Kay Lawson, ed. *How Political Parties Work: Perspectives from Within*. Westport, CT: Praeger, 1994.

"Poland's Three Parliaments in the Era of Transition, 1989–1995," *International Political Science Review*, No. 4, 1997: 443–50.

Wightman, Gordon, ed. *Party Formation in East-Central Europe*. Aldershot, UK: Edward Elgar, 1995.

Wightman, Gordon, and Brown, Archie. "Changes in the Level of Membership and Social Composition of the Communist Party of Czechoslovakia, 1945–73," *Soviet Studies*, July 1975: 396–417.

Wilk, Ewa. "Ordynacka rządzi Polską," *Polityka*, 23 December 1995: 20–6.

Wilson, Frank. "The Sources of Party Change: The Social Democratic Parties of Britain, France, Germany, and Spain," in Kay Lawson, ed. *How Political Parties Work*. London: Praeger, 1994: 263–83.

Wilson, James Q. *The Amateur Democrat*. Chicago: Chicago University Press, 1966.

Wolchik, Sharon. "Economic Performance and Political Change in Czechoslovakia," in Bukowski, Charles, and Cichock, Mark, eds. *Prospects for Change in Socialist Systems*. New York: Praeger, 1987.

Czechoslovakia in Transition. London: Pinter 1991.
"The Repluralization of Politics in Czechoslovakia," *Communist and Post-Communist Studies*, December 1993: 412–31.
"The Politics of Ethnicity in Post-Communist Czechoslovakia," *East European Politics and Societies*, Winter 1994: 153–88.
Wong, Raymond Sin-Kwok. "The Social Composition of the Czechoslovak and Hungarian Communist Parties in the 1980s," *Social Forces*, September 1996: 61–90.
Wyman, Matthew, White, Stephen, Miller, Bill, and Heywood, Paul. "The Place of 'Party' in Post-Communist Europe," *Party Politics*, No. 4, 1995: 535–48.
Žiak, Miloš. *Slovensko: Od komunizmu kam?* Bratislava: Archa, 1996.
Ziblatt, Daniel. "Putting Humpty-Dumpty Back Together Again: Communism's Collapse and the Reconstruction of the East German Ex-Communist Party," *German Politics and Society*, Spring 1998: 1–29.
Zielonka, Jan. "New Institutions in the Old Bloc," *Journal of Democracy*, Winter 1994: 87–104.
Zinoviev, Aleksandr. *Homo Sovieticus*. London: Victor Gollancz, 1985.
Zubek, Voytek. "Poland's Party Self-Destructs," *Orbis*, Vol. 34, Spring 1990: 179–94.
"The Rise and Fall of Rule by Poland's Best and Brightest," *Soviet Studies*, No. 4, 1992: 579–608.
"The Fragmentation of Poland's Political Party System," *Communist and Post-Communist Studies*, March 1993: 47–71.
"The Reassertion of the Left in Post-Communist Poland," *Europe-Asia Studies*, No. 5, 1994: 801–37.
"Phoenix out of the Ashes: The Rise to Power of Poland's Post-Communist SdRP," *Communist and Post-Communist Studies*, No. 3, 1995: 275–303.

Party Publications (Arranged Chronologically by Party)

KSČS

"Informace o stavů členské zakladny a zakladních organizaci, klubů v KSČS k 30.6.1990" (Information about the status of the membership and the basic organizations and clubs in the Czechoslovak Communist Party until 30 June 1990). ÚV KSČM, Praha: 1990.
Dokumenty 18. Sjezdu KSČS, Praha, 3–4.11.1990. Praha: ÚV KSČS, 1990.

KSČM

"Dokumenty mimořadného sjezdu KSČ: akční program Komunistické Strany Československa" [Documents of the extraordinary congress of KSČ: the action program of the KSČ]. Prague: December 1989.
Dokumenty Ustavujícího Sjezdu KSČM (Documents of the Founding Congress of KSČM), 31 March 1990. Prague: 1990.

Bibliography

Schvalene Dokumenty na ustavujiíim sjezdu KSČM dn 31 brezna 1990 (The documents passed at the Founding Congress of the KSČM). Prague: KSČM, 1990.

Teze Zprávy ÚV KSČM o Činnosti Ustavujicího sjezdu KSČM do 1. Sjezdu KSČM (Theses of the Central Committee Report about the functioning of the party from the Founding Congress to the First Congress). ÚV KSČM, Prague: 1992.

Dokumenty II Sjezdu KSČM. Praha: KSČM, 1993.

Dokumenty III Sjezdu KSČM. Praha: KSČM, 1993.

KSČM v Parlamentu ČR. Prague: Klub poslanců KSČM, 1995.

Klub levicových sociologů a psychologů, "Zaverečna Zpráva ze sociologického výzkumu levicové smyslejících občanů Česke Republiky," čislo 13–1995 (The Closing Report of the Sociological Research on Left-Thinking Citizens of the Czech Republic), Prepared for the forty-second meeting of the VV ÚV KSČM, 15 September 1995.

Klub levicových sociologů a psychologů, "Zaverečna Zpráva ze sociologického výzkumu levicové smyslejících občanů Česke Republiky." Prague: KSČM, čislo 14–1995 (November 1995).

"Zpráva ÚV KSČM IV. Sjezdu KSČM o činnosti Strany v obdobi po III. Sjezdu (červen 1993-prosinec 1995)" (Report of the Central Committee of the KSČM to the IV Congress KSČM about the party's activity in the period after the III Congress (June 1993–December 1995), *Haló Noviny* (supplement), 18 December 1995.

"Volební program KSČM 1998" (The Electoral Program of the KSČM 1998). Praha: KSČM, 1998.

KSS-SDĽ

Zjazd KSS, konany v dnoch 20–21.1990 v Prešove. I–II čast. Bratislava: ÚV KSS-SDĽ, December 1990.

Politika Komunistickej Strany Slovenska v obodobi prechodu k spoločnosti s trhovou ekonomikou. Prešov: 1990.

Dokumenty Zjazdu KSS-SDĽ Prešov, 20–21 Oktobra 1990. Bratislava: UV KSS-SDĽ, 1990.

SDĽ

Dokumenty Prvého Zjazdu SDĽ. Trenčín, 14–15 Decembra 1991.

Dokumenty Druhého zjazdu SDĽ. Zilina, 22–3 May 1993.

Dokumenty Tretieho Zjazdu SDĽ. Poprad, 17–18.2.1995.

Dokumenty Štvrtého Zjazdu SDĽ. Nitra 27–8 Aprila 1996.

PZPR

Partia w przemianach, przemiany w parti. X Plenum PZPR, 20–21.12.1988 (The party during changes, changes in the party. The Tenth Plenum of the PZPR). Warsaw: PZPR, 1989.

SdRP

Sprawy Bieżące: Podstawowe Dokumenty Kongresu Założycielskiego Socjaldemokracji Rzeczpospolitej Polskiej [Declaration of the Social Democracy of the Republic of Poland. Current Events: Basic Documents of the Founding Congress of the Socialdemocracy of the Republic of Poland]. Warsaw, 4 February 1990.

SdRP. *Dokumenty Programowe 1990–1991.* May 1990.

"Polska postępu, prawa, i demokracji: Program społeczno-gospodarczy Socjaldemokracji Rzeczypospolitej Polskiej" [A Poland of progress, rule of law, and democracy: the social-economic program of the SdRP]. Warsaw, March 1991.

"Socjaldemokratyczna alternatywa: Polska demokratyczna, sprawiedliwa, bezpieczna" [The Social Democratic alternative: a democratic, just, safe Poland]. *Biuletyn Wewnątrzpartyjny,* Nr. 6/93.

Biuletyn II Kongresu SdRP. 20–1 March 1993.

Sojusz Lewicy Demokratycznej. *Dwa Lata Pracy Parlamentarnej (19.9.1993–19.9.1995).* Warsaw: SLD Parliamentary Club, 1995.

Sojusz Lewicy Demokratycznej. *Nasz Program dla Polski: Trzy lata Pracy Parlamentarnej SLD.* Warsaw: SLD Parliamentary Club, 1996.

"Program Socjaldemokracji Rzeczpospolitej Polskiej" [Program of the SdRP]. Warsaw: Verum, March 1997.

SLD. "Zasady postępowania Klubu Parlamentarnego SLD w Przyszłej Kadencji Sejmu," (Rules of behavior of the SLD Parliamentary Club in the Future Parliament). Warsaw, June 1997.

Archival Sources

Archiwum Akt Nowych, Warsaw (formerly Archiwum Zakładu Historii Partii):
119: Komitet Akcji Jednolitego Frontu
158: KPP
237: KC PZPR: VI CKKP, VIII Wydział Organizacyjny
248: Centralne Biuro Komunistów: Polskie przedstawicielstwo KC PPR w Moskwie
295: KC PPR
325: Spuścizna Jakuba Bermana
Státní Ústřední Archiv, Prague:
Fond 02/1: Předsednictvo ÚV KSČ
Fond 02/4 Sekretariat ÚV KSČ
Státní Archiv, Bratislava:
Fond ÚV KSS Predsednictvo
Fond ÚV KSS Politbyro

Bibliography

Open Society Archives, Budapest:
Hungary Files: Local, Party Life, Congress, Personnel Changes, Politburo, Recruitment.
Poland Files: 114.21 Congresses, 114.201 History, 114.202 Apparatus, 114.28 Membership, 114.4 SdRP, 114.55 Party Influence, 114.6 Discipline, 114.62 Fractions.
Radio Free Europe Situation Reports.

Newspapers and News Services

Poland

PAP (Polish Press Agency holdings, Warsaw)
Gazeta Wyborcza (1989–)
Nowe Drogi (1947–89)
Polityka (1957–)
Przedświt (1988–)
Rzeczpospolita (1990–)
Sztandar Młodych (1962–)
Trybuna Ludu (1948–90)
Trybuna (1990–)
Tygodnik Solidarność (1981–)
Wprost (1992–)
Życie Partii (1949–89)
Życie Warszawy (1944–)

Slovakia

TASR (Slovak Press Agency holdings, Bratislava)
Narodna Obroda (1990–)
Nové Slovo (1990–)
Právda (1991–)
Sme (1995–)

Czech Republic

Haló Noviny, Prague (1990–)
Hospodarské Noviny (1990–)
Lidové Noviny (1948–)
Mlada Fronta Dnes (1990–)
Naše Pravda (1990–)
Právo (1990–)

Rudé Pravo (1990–)
Život Strany (1954–89)

Hungary

MTI (Hungarian Press Agency holdings, Budapest)
Partelet (1956–89)

Index

Abortion: 162, 168–9, 253
Activists:
  orthodox:
    KSČM: 84–5, 87–8, 136, 140–1,
      145–7, 189, 273
    MSzP: 109, 115, 217
    SDĽ: 159
    SdRP: 102
  reformist:
    KSČM: 83–4
    MSzP: 109–10
    SDĽ: 93, 96
    SdRP: 101, 103
Adamec, Ladislav: 59–60, 91, 140,
  238
Age, as a determinant of electoral
  support: 190, 193, 202, 210
Akcja Wyborcza Solidarność (AWS):
  214–5, 255–6
Alliance of Free Democrats: see
  Szabad Demokraták Szövetsége
  (SzDSz)
All–Polish Alliance of Trade Unions:
  see OPZZ
Antall, József: 223
Apparat, communist party: 4, 44, 118,
  256
Association for the Republic –
  Republican Party of the Czech
  Republic: see Sdruženi Pro
  Republiku–Republikanská
  Strana Česka

Association of Slovak Workers: see
  Združenie Robotníkov
  Slovenska (ZRS)

Balcerowicz Plan: 164
Balgarska Socialisticheska Partija
  (BSP): 267–8
Békesi, László: 261
Bielecki, Jan Krzysztof: 170, 181fn
Blue Coalition: see Modrá Koalícia
Bokros, Lajos: 261–2
Brucan, Silviu: 269
Bulgarian Socialist Party: see
  Balgarska Socialisticheska
  Partija (BSP)

Case selection: 15–7
Catch-all parties: 75, 77, 112
Ceauşescu, Nikolai: 269
Centralization: see Organizational
  transformation, and Institutions
Centrist parties: 104, 170, 211, 249,
  251, 255
Česká Strana Sociálne Demokratická
  (ČSSD): 24, 186–7, 194–7,
  238–43
Christian Democratic Movement: see
  Krest'ansko-demokratické
  Hnutie (KDH)
Christian Democratic Party: see
  Kereszténydemokrata Néppárt
  (KDNP)

Christian-National Alliance: see
    Zjednoczenie Chrześcijańsko-
    Narodowe (ZChN)
Cimoszewicz, Włodzimierz: 207,
    256
Civic Democratic Alliance: see
    Občanská Demokratická
    Aliance
Civic Democratic Party: see Občanská
    Demokratická Strana (ODS)
Civic Forum: 82
Coalitions/Alliances: 83, 214, 222,
    227–84, see also Parliamentary
    acceptance
Common Choice Coalition: see
    Spoločná Vol'ba
Communist parties: 5–6, 26–30,
    69–71, 264–5, see also
    individual listings
  Czechoslovak:
    economic and political reform:
      34–6
    negotiation with society: 39–41
    organization: 31–3
    policies of advancement: 37–9
    reformist movements: 34, 38–9
    takeover of power: 30–1
  Hungarian:
    economic and political reform:
      51–3
    negotiation with society: 56–8
    organization: 51–2
    policies of advancement: 53–6
    reformist movements: 56, 62,
      109–10
    takeover of power: 50–1
  Polish:
    economic and political reform:
      44–5
    negotiation with society: 49–50
    organization: 42–3
    policies of advancement: 45–9
    reformist movements: 48–9, 62,
      99–101, 106
    takeover of power: 41–4
  Slovak: 35–8

Communist Party of Bohemia and
    Moravia: see Komunistická
    Strana Čech a Moravy
    (KSČM)
Communist Party of Czechoslovakia:
    see Komunistická Strana
    Československa (KSČ)
Communist Party of the Russian
    Federation: see
    Komunisticheskaya Partia
    Rossiskoy Federatsii (KPRF)
Communist regimes: 69–71
  collapse: 20, 58, 82–122
  rise: 26–8, 30–1, 41–2, 50–1
Communist successors, definition: 14
Competence, managerial, as campaign
    issue: 137–8, 149–50, 159–60,
    169–71
Competition, political party:
  dimensions of: 126–7, 131, 139
  electoral: 17, 23–4, 60, 62, 75–6,
    100, 108, 175–226
  internal, within parties: 81, 102, 115
Confederation for an Independent
    Poland: see Konfederacja
    Polski Niepodległej (KPN)
Confederation of Hungarian Trade
    Unions: see Magyar
    Szakszervezetek Országos
    Szövetsége (MSzOSz)
Congresses, party:
  KSČM: 47, 82–92
  MSzP: 107–14
  SDL': 198, 248
  SdRP: 99–107, 256–7
Constituencies, political party:
  characteristics: 87, 117, 132–4,
    141–3, 178–9, 183–7
  development: 112, 139, 141–4,
    154–5, 162, 175, 178–9, 191–5,
    200–2, 208–12, 218–22
Content analysis: 18, 132, 155, 169,
    285–93, see also Programs
Czech Social Democratic Party: see
    Česká Strana Sociálne
    Demokratická (ČSSD)

De Klerk, F. W: 276
Democracy, transitions to: 1–7, 11–2,
    58–65, 72, 281–2
  Czech Republic: 82–4
  Hungary: 107–9
  Poland: 99–104
  Slovakia: 92–3
Democratic centralism, 73
Democratic Forum of Communists:
    see Demokratické Forum
    Komunistů (DFK)
Democratic Left: see Demokratická
    Levice (DL)
Democratic Left Alliance: see Sojusz
    Lewicy Demokratycznej
    (SLD)
Democratic Party: see Demokratická
    Strana (DS)
Democratic Party of Labor: see
    Demokratická Strana Prace
    (DSP)
Democratic Union (Poland): see Unia
    Demokratyczna (UD)
Democratic Union (Slovakia): see
    Demokratická Únia (DU)
Demokratická Levice (DL): 88, 190,
    242
Demokratická Strana (DS): 204fn
Demokratická Strana Prace (DSP):
    88
Demokratická Únia (DU): 181fn,
    203–4, 246fn
Demokratické Forum Komunistů
    (DFK): 83, 91
Dienstbier, Jiří: 239
Divides and cleavages, popular: 215
  economic: 3–4, 177–9, 183
  electoral: 135–9, 266
  non-standard vs. democratic: 151–2,
    159–60, 197–8, 232–3
  regime: 9, 44, 49–50, 58, 218–9,
    228–9, 231–4, 238, 240, 244–5,
    248–9, 251, 258, 264

Economic well-being, as a
    determinant of electoral

support: 3–4, 178, 185–6, 192,
    196, 210–1
Elections:
  Czech Republic: 195–7
  Hungary: 222–4
  Poland: 62, 99–100, 212–5
  Slovakia: 203–4
Electoral Action Solidarity: see Akcja
    Wyborcza Solidarność (AWS)
Electoral campaigns: 176–7, 188–91,
    198–9, 205–6, 215–6, 225–6
  slogans: 188, 198–9, 206, 215
  strategies: 176–7
Electoral parties: 71, 75, 86, 207
Electoral results: 102, 177–226
Electorates: see Constituencies,
    political party
Elites:
  advancement: 5–6, 10, 28–9, 37–9,
    45–9, 53–6
  mid-level: 14, 29, 45–8, 54–5, 62, 81
  recruitment patterns: 5–6, 10, 28–9,
    42, 101–2, 177
  resources: 5, 9, 19, 25–6, 76–7,
    82–122, 265–6, see also Past,
    usable
  skills: 6, 13, 23–4, 28, 76–7, 121,
    131, 150, 194, 265–6, 281–2,
    see also Portable skills
  turnover: 28, 32, 44, 54–5, 71–3,
    120, 235–6
Extraordinary Congresses: 59, 62, 81,
    90, 93, 113, 163
  KSČM: 81, 83–5, 98
  MSzP: 110
  SDĽ: 97–8, 257
  SdRP: 102–7, 161, 163, 256–7

Fiatal Demokraták Szövetsége (Fidesz):
    216fn, 222, 224–6, 260
Fiszbach, Tadeusz: 106
Fogaš, Lubomír: 245
Freedom Union: see Unia Wolności
    (UW)
Frontul Salvarii Nationale (FSN):
    269–70

Ftačnik, Milan: 61, 93
Független Kisgazdapárt (FKGP): 51,
   223–4, 260

Gorbachev, Mikhail: 40, 100
Gottwald, Klement: 40
Governments, democratic:
   Czech: 138–9, 196–7
   Hungarian: 181–3, 222–3, 260–2
   Polish: 170–1, 181, 250
   Slovak: 150–2
Grebreniček, Miroslav: 117, 141
Green Party: see Strana Zelených na
   Slovensku (SZS)
Grosz, Karoly: 108

Havel, Václav: 151, 239
Heresthetics: 126–7, 164, 170–1, 176,
   194
Hnutie za Demokratické Slovensko
   (HZDS): 151–2, 154fn, 157–9,
   197–204, 244–9, 245fn, 246fn,
   247fn, 248fn, 249fn
Horn, Gyula: 64, 120, 173, 217, 219,
   260–1, 263
Hoxha, Enver: 270
Hungarian Communist Party: see
   Magyar Komuniszta Párt
   (MKP)
Hungarian Democratic Forum: see
   Magyar Demokrata Fórum
   (MDF)
Hungarian Life and Justice Party: see
   Magyar Igazság és Élet Pártja
   (MIEP)
Hungarian Socialist Party: see Magyar
   Szocialista Párt (MSzP)
Hungarian Socialist Workers' Party:
   see Magyar Szocialista Munkás
   párt (MSzMP)
Husák, Gustav: 38

Iliescu, Ion: 269–70
Independent Smallholders' Party: see
   Független Kisgazdapárt
   (FKGP)

Institutions:
   electoral: 12, 76, 108–9, 175ff,
      228–35, 245, 258, 266, 303–4
   endogeneity of: 12–3, 282–3
   mechanisms of reproduction and
      change: 11, 67–8, 80, 120–1,
      134, 244, 267
   sequencing, of transformation: 80–2,
      114–5, 120–1
   timing, of transformation: 8, 80–1,
      114–5, 117, 131, 266–9, 279
   transformation of: 10–1, 279–81
Iwiński, Tadeusz: 252

Jakeš, Miloš: 35, 38, 40, 83, 243
Jaruzelski, General Wojciech: 48
Jaśkiewicz, Leszek: 63, 103
July 8 Movement: 101

Kádár, János: 53–4, 114fn
Kanis, Pavol: 61, 93, 96, 245–8
Kavan, Jan: 24
Kereszténydemokrata Néppárt
   (KDNP): 222
Klaus, Václav: 138, 143, 145, 188, 196,
   238
Komárek, Valtr: 24
Komunisticheskaya Partia Rossiskoy
   Federatsii, (KPRF): 272, 275–
   8
Komunisticka Strana Čech a Moravy
   (KSČM): 2, 16, 83–92, 95–6,
   117–9, 138–50, 188–96, 230–3,
   238–44
   break with past: 89–90
   coalitions: 191
   electoral campaigns: 188–91
   electoral results: 190–7
   members: 140, 146–7
   organizational transformation: 84–9
   parliamentary effectiveness: 138–44
   popular perceptions: 191–5
   programs: 136, 138, 141–50
Komunistická Strana Československa
   (KSČ): 30–9, 30fn, 51, 58,
   90

Index

Konfederacja Polski Niepodległej
  (KPN): 251
Kongres Liberalno-Demokratyczny
  (KLD): 253
Kovač, Michael: 204
Kovacs, László: 120
Krest'ansko-demokratické Hnutie
  (KDH): 152, 204, 204fn
Kuptsov, Valentin: 275
Kwaśniewski, Aleksander: 63, 102–5,
  107, 111, 118, 166–7, 210–1,
  218, 253, 258

L'avirovanie: 156, see also Strana
  Demokratickej L'avici,
  Programs
Labor Union: see Unia Pracy (UP)
Left Bloc Party: see Strana Levý Blok
  (SLB)
Legacies, communist: 5, 10–2, 15,
  20–6, 58–9, 65–8, 76, 80,
  121–2, 234–5, 264–5,
  281–2
"Lessons of the Crisis Development"
  ("Poučeni z Krizového Vývoje
  ve Strane a Společnosti"): 35,
  84, 97
Liberal-Democratic Congress: see
  Kongres Liberalno-
  Demokratyczny (KLD)
Local party organizations:
  communist: 77–80, 94
  successor: 189, 199, 205, 216
  workplace: 11, 83, 86, 98, 109, 114,
    184, 207
L'uptak, Jan: 97

Machine learning methods: 187–8,
  296–302
Magvaši, Peter: 245
Magyar Demokrata Fórum (MDF):
  108, 216, 218, 222–4, 260
Magyar Igazság és Élet Pártja (MIEP):
  82fn
Magyar Komuniszta Párt (MKP):
  50–1

Magyar Szakszervezetek Országos
  Szövetsége (MSzOSz): 113,
  261–2
Magyar Szocialista Munkáspárt: 50–6,
  110, 221
Magyar Szocialista Párt (MSzP): 3, 16,
  65, 77, 107–14, 171–3, 215–24,
  259–62
  break with past: 113–4
  electoral campaigns: 215–7
  electoral results: 222–4
  organizational transformation:
    111–3
  parliamentary effectiveness: 259–63
  popular perceptions: 218–22
  programs: 138, 172–3
Mandela, Nelson: 276
Mass parties: 71, 75fn, 77
Mazowiecki, Tadeusz: 181fn, 250,
  253fn
Mečiar, Vladimir: 151, 197, 203,
  244
Mecl, Jozef: 116
Members, party:
  communist: 31–3, 42–3, 51–2
  numbers: 74, 85–7, 96, 103–4,
    112–3
  orthodoxy of: 87–8, 96, 101, 112,
    115
  roles of: 119, 130–1, 140, 146–7,
    153, 189–90, 199, 206
Miller, Leszek: 118–9, 252
Milošević, Slobodan: 179
Mladenov, Petûr: 267
Modrá Koalícia: 203–4
Mohorita, Vasil: 59, 91
Movement for a Democratic Slovakia:
  see Hnutie za Demokratické
  Slovensko (HZDS)
Movement of People of Labor: see
  Ruch Ludzi Pracy (RLP)
Multinomial logit: 187–8, 295
Munkáspárt (MP): 114

Nagy, Sándor: 261
Nałęcz, Tomasz: 103, 106

Name, party transformations of: 90–1,
    98–9, 105–6, 114
  KSČM: 90–1, 139
  MSzP: 114
  SDL': 98–9
  SdRP: 105–7
Nano, Fatos: 271
National Salvation Front: see Frontul
    Salvarii Nationale (FSN)
Németh, Miklós: 64, 108, 110, 217,
    262
New Economic Mechanism (NEM):
    49, 56–7
Newspapers and media, party-owned:
    34, 86, 98, 269–70
Nyers, Rezsô: 64, 110, 217

Občanská Demokratická Alliance
    (ODA): 193, 239fn
Občanská Demokratická Strana
    (ODS): 148, 188, 193–4, 194fn,
    195fn, 197, 238, 239fn
Obzina, Jaromír: 88
Oleksy, Józef: 119, 171, 214
Olszewski, Jan: 170, 181fn, 214
Opinion platforms: 104
  KSČM: 86, 88, 189
  MSzP: 113, 116, 119
  SDL': 97
  SdRP: 101, 104
OPZZ (Ogólnopolskie Porozumienie
    Związków Zawodowych):
    104–5, 207
Organizational transformation, party:
    see also Institutions
  as basis for electoral strategies:
    176–7, 180–1, 199
  as basis for parliamentary
    effectiveness: 205, 236–7
  as basis for programmatic change:
    130–1, 137–8, 150, 171–3
  centralization: 7, 69, 73–7, 84–8,
    94–105, 111–3, 121–2, 131–2,
    140–1, 265
  literature on: 12–3, 279–81
  pacing: 8, 80–2, 114–20, 266–9

  reinforcing other changes: 121–2
  sequencing: 8, 80
  streamlining: 8, 73–4, 81, 103,
    130–2, 172, 177, 197
  timing: 8, 80, 131, 265
  vertical integration: 8, 73–4, 84,
    111, 130, 177, 197
Ortman, Jaroslav: 116

Parliamentary:
  acceptance: 7, 14, 227–34, 238–41,
    244–8, 250–5, 259–62
  activity: 182, 241
  clubs: 228, 230–6, 241–4, 258–9,
    263
  cohesiveness: 14, 234–7, 241–4,
    248–9, 256–8, 262–3
  committees: 227, 230, 232, 240–1,
    245–7, 252, 258–9
  effectiveness: 6, 227–65, 278
Parliaments: 227ff
Partei des Demokratischen
    Sozialismus (PDS): 272–4, 277
Partia Socialiste ë Shqipërisë (PSSH):
    270–1
Partidul Democraţiei Sociale din
    România (PDSR): 270–1
Party of the Democratic Left: see
    Strana Demokratické Levice
    (SDL)
Party of Democratic Socialism: see
    Partei des Demokratischen
    Sozialismus (PDS)
Party of Social Democracy in
    Romania: see Partidul
    Democraţiei Sociale din
    România (PDSR)
Past:
  break with: 6, 71, 77, 79–80, 89–90,
    265
  usable: 5, 7–10, 26, 63–5, 77–9, 240,
    258, 265–6, 280
Patronage: 124–5
Pawlak, Waldemar: 181fn, 251, 255
Perceptions, popular:
  KSČM: 191–5

MSzP: 218–22
SDL': 200–3
SdRP: 208–12
Petô, Ivan: 224
Plenum, 10th (PZPR): 48, 99
Plevza, Viliam: 38, 93
Polish Beer Lovers' Party: see
    Polska Partia Przyjaciół Piwa
    (PPP)
Polish Peasants' Party: see Polskie
    Stronnictwo Ludowe (PSL)
Polish Social Democratic Union:
    see Polska Unia
    Socjaldemokratyczna (PUS)
Polish Socialist Party: see Polska
    Partia Socjalistyczna (PPS)
Polish United Workers' Party: see
    Polska Zjednoczona Partia
    Robotnicza (PZPR)
Polska Partia Przyjaciół Piwa (PPP):
    251fn
Polska Partia Socjalistyczna (PPS):
    100fn
Polska Unia Socjaldemokratyczna
    (PUS): 106, 106fn, 118
Polska Zjednoczona Partia Robotnicza
    (PZPR): 42–5, 99–100, 102–6,
    207fn, 250
Polskie Stronnictwo Ludowe (PSL): 3,
    125, 214, 253–5
Popular support:
    bases of: 182–8, 249, see also
        Perceptions, popular
    levels: 14
    KSČM: 195–7
    MSzP: 222–4
    SDL': 203–4
    SdRP: 208–12
Portable skills, elite: 5, 17, 23, 26, 29,
    76–7, 265–6
Pozsgay, Imre: 56, 114, 217
Principal-agent problem, 257
Programs: see also Heresthetics
    content analysis of: 18, 132, 155,
        169, 285–93
    core beliefs: 126, 167

development of: 104, 123–9,
    138–44, 150–7, 160–4, 171–3
responsiveness of: 14, 123, 125–6,
    131–3, 179–81
role of: 127–9, 151–2, 162–3
stances:
    abortion: 162, 168–9, 253
    competence: 137–8, 149–50,
        159–60, 169–71, 278
    economic policy: 134–6, 145–8,
        157–8, 164–7
    nationalism: 136–7, 148, 158–9,
        167–9, 268, 270–1, 276
    secularism: 136–7, 148, 158–9,
        167–9
Prostějov congress: 85
Public Against Violence: 82, 153

Rakowski, Mieczysław: 48, 101, 161
Recruitment, elite: see Elites,
    recruitment patterns
Referenda:
    national: 92, 268
    within parties: 90–1, 99, 106, 109,
        115
Regeneration, definition: 14
Reputations, party: 7–8
Round Tables: see Democracy,
    transitions to
Ruch Ludzi Pracy (RLP): 207

Samosprava: 149–50
Schalkwyk, Marthinus: 276–7
Schmögnerová, Brigita: 61, 93
Sdruženi Pro Republiku-
    Republikanská Strana Česka
    (SPR-RSČ): 193
Siemiątkowski, Zbigniew: 103
Sierakowska, Izabela: 252
Šik, Ota: 34
Široký, Jan: 93
Skills, elite: see Elites, skills, and
    Communist parties
Slovak Democratic Coalition: see
    Slovenská Demokratická
    Koalícia (SDK)

Slovak National Party: see Slovenská
Narodná Strana (SNS)
Slovak Party of the Democratic Left:
see Strana Demokratickej
Ľavici, SDL'
Slovenská Demokratická Koalícia
(SDK): 204, 247–8, 247fn
Slovenská Narodná Strana (SNS): 152,
159, 247
Social Democracy of the Republic of
Poland: see Socjaldemokracja
Rzeczpospolitej Polskiej (SdRP)
Social Democratic Party: see
Sociálnodemokratická strana
Slovenska (SDSS)
Socialist Party of Albania: see Partia
Socialiste ë Shqipërisë (PSSH)
Socialist Union of Polish Students: see
Socjalistyczny Związek
Studentów Polskich (SZSP)
Socialist Unity Party of Germany: see
Sozialistische Einheitspartei
Deutschlands (SED)
Sociálnodemokratická strana Slovenska
(SDSS): 246
Socjaldemokracja Rzeczpospolitej
Polskiej (SdRP): 160–70,
205–14, 233–4, 249–58
break with past: 105–7
coalitions: 253–5
electoral campaigns: 205–8
electoral results: 167, 212–5
organizational transformation:
101–5
parliamentary effectiveness: 250–8
popular perceptions: 200–3, 208–12
programs: 135, 138, 161–9
Socjalistyczny Związek Studentów
Polskich (SZSP): 45–6, 63,
64fn
Sojusz Lewicy Demokratycznej (SLD):
104–5, 119, 206–7, 213–4,
250–8
Solidarity: 100–3, 214, 233, 250–3
Sozialistische Einheitspartei
Deutschlands (SED): 272

Splinter parties: 97, 221, 241–2, 243f,
270
KSČM:
orthodox: 88
reform: 83, 88, 116
MSzP:
orthodox: 114
reform: 110
SDL':
orthodox: 97, 199
reform: 199
SdRP:
orthodox: 106
reform: 106, 207
Spoločna Voľba: 246
"Spontaneous privatization": 101
Šťěpan, Miroslav: 83, 88–9
Strana Demokratické Levice (SDL):
116, 206–7
Strana Demokratickej Ľavici, (SDL'):
2–3, 150–9, 197–204, 231–3,
245–8
break with past: 97–9
coalitions: 203–4
electoral campaigns: 198–9
electoral results: 155, 203–4
members: 153
organizational transformation: 94–7
parliamentary effectiveness: 244–9
popular perceptions: 200–2, 208–12
programs: 135–6, 138, 152–60
Strana Levý Blok (SLB): 116, 116fn
Strana Zelených na Slovensku (SZS):
92fn, 199, 204fn
Suchocka, Hanna: 170, 181fn, 257
Svoboda, Jiří: 60, 90–2, 97, 115
Symbols, party transformation of:
78–80, 97–9, 105–7, 113–4, 140
Szabad Demokraták Szövetsége
(SzDSz): 3, 108, 221, 260–1
Szmajdziński, Jerzy: 63, 119
Szűrös, Mátyás: 217

Törgyan, József: 223
Trade unions: 45, 55, 73, 84–6, 99,
104–5, 113, 178, 183–5, 207–8,

217–8, 261–2, see also OPZZ and MSzOSz

Unia Demokratyczna (UD): 176, 203, 251, 251fn, 253
Unia Pracy (UP): 253
Unia Wolności (UW): 104, 208–11, 253
Union of Polish Communists "Proletariat": see Związek Komunistów Polskich "Proletariat" (ZKP)
United Peasants Party: see Zjednoczone Stronnictwo Ludowe (ZSL)
Urbanek, Karel: 59, 83

Vote maximization: 75, 96, 127, 138, 176

Wałęsa, Lech: 160fn, 170
Weiss, Peter: 61, 93–8, 102, 111, 118, 152
Workers' Party: see Munkáspárt, (MP)

Yeltsin, Boris: 275–6

Združenie Robotníkov Slovenska (ZRS): 97, 97fn, 152, 199, 247
Zhivkov, Todor: 267–8
Zjednoczenie Chrześcijańsko-Narodowe (ZChN): 251
Zjednoczone Stronnictwo Ludowe: 42–3
Związek Komunistów Polskich "Proletariat": 107fn, 207fn
Zyuganov, Gennadii: 275

Continued from page iii

Torben Iversen, Jonas Pontusson, David Soskice, eds., *Unions, Employers, and Central Banks: Macroeconomic Coordination and Institutional Change in Social Market Economies*

Thomas Janoski and Alexander M. Hicks, eds., *The Comparative Political Economy of the Welfare State*

Robert O. Keohane and Helen B. Milner, eds., *Internationalization and Domestic Politics*

Herbert Kitschelt, *The Transformation of European Social Democracy*

Herbert Kitschelt, Peter Lange, Gary Marks, and John D. Stephens, eds., *Continuity and Change in Contemporary Capitalism*

Herbert Kitschelt, Zdenka Mansfeldova, Radek Markowski, and Gabor Toka, *Post-Communist Party Systems*

David Knoke, Franz Urban Pappi, Jeffrey Broadbent, and Yutaka Tsujinaka, eds., *Comparing Policy Networks*

Allan Kornberg and Harold D. Clarke, *Citizens and Community: Political Support in a Representative Democracy*

David D. Laitin, *Language Repertories and State Construction in Africa*

Mark Irving Lichbach and Alan S. Zuckerman, eds., *Comparative Politics: Rationality, Culture, and Structure*

Doug McAdam, John McCarthy, and Mayer Zald, eds., *Comparative Perspectives on Social Movements*

Scott Mainwaring and Matthew Soberg Shugart, eds., *Presidentialism and Democracy in Latin America*

Anthony W. Marx, *Making Race, Making Nations: A Comparison of South Africa, the United States and Brazil*

Joel S. Migdal, Atul Kohli, and Vivienne Shue, eds., *State Power and Social Forces: Domination and Transformation in the Third World*

Wolfgang C. Muller and Kaare Strom, *Policy, Office, or Votes?*

Tom Notermans, *Money, Markets, and the State: Social Democratic Economic Policies Since 1918*

Paul Pierson, *Dismantling the Welfare State?: Reagan, Thatcher and the Politics of Retrenchment*

Marino Regini, *Uncertain Boundaries: The Social and Political Construction of European Economies*

Yossi Shain and Juan Linz, eds., *Interim Governments and Democratic Transitions*

Theda Skocpol, *Social Revolutions in the Modern World*

David Stark and László Bruszt, *Postsocialist Pathways: Transforming Politics and Property in East Central Europe*

Sven Steinmo, Kathleen Thelan, and Frank Longstreth, eds., *Structuring Politics: Historical Institutionalism in Comparative Analysis*

Sidney Tarrow, *Power in Movement: Social Movements and Contentious Politics*

Ashutosh Varshney, *Democracy, Development, and the Countryside*

Elisabeth Jean Wood, *Forging Democracy from Below: Insurgent Transitions in South Africa and El Salvador*